Peer-Assisted Learning

Edited by

Keith Topping
University of Dundee, Scotland

Stewart Ehly
The University of Iowa

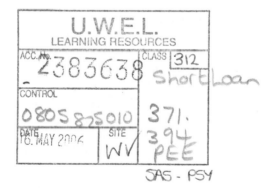
 LEA

LAWRENCE ERLBAUM ASSOCIATES, PUBLISHERS
1998   Mahwah, New Jersey   London

Lawrence Erlbaum Associates, Inc., Publishers
10 Industrial Avenue
Mahwah, NJ 07430

Cover design by Kathryn Houghtaling Lacey

Library of Congress Cataloging-in-Publication Data

Peer-assisted learning / edited by Keith Topping, Stewart Ehly.
      p. cm.
    Includes bibliographical references and indexes.
    ISBN 0-8058-2501-0 (cloth : alk. paper). -- ISBN 0-8058-2502-9 (pbk. : alk. paper)
      1. Peer-group tutoring of students. I. Topping, Keith J. II. Ehly, Stewart W., 1949– .
LB1031.5.P44   1998
371.39'4--dc21

                    98-20777
                    CIP

Printed in the United States of America
10 9 8 7 6 5 4 3 2 1

Contents

Foreword

Herbert J. Walberg
University of Illinois at Chicago

The editors of this book, Keith Topping and Stewart Ehly, have brought together much of the best educational research on peer-assisted learning—fellow students helping and supporting one another's efforts. The research is not only rigorous but relevant to educational practice. It provides strong, robust findings, and it shows how new methods can be put into practice.

This book, moreover, is timely: Educators are deluged by a huge amount of opinion and advocacy. Much of it is poorly conceived, ill-written, and biased. Little is based on the findings of rigorous inquiry. For this reason, education has not made the fact-based productivity strides enjoyed by other professions and industries. This book, because it is authoritative, well written, and practical, can be a great help in enhancing educational effectiveness and efficiency. We live in an age that demands more from schools and other educative institutions. Far less important for our lives are agriculture, mining, and even manufacturing. Ours is the *Age of Information*—in which knowledge, skills, and technology have become larger determinants of individual and national prosperity and the quality of life. Productive methods can enable schools to make larger contributions to human welfare.

EVIDENCE

A particularly strong point of this book is its explicit basis in published scientific evidence. Earlier reviews of research (Bloom, 1984; Walberg, 1984) highlighted the substantial effects of predecessors of peer-assisted learning (PAL). Bloom held that effective means of instruction might raise the typical student's achievement to that of highly accomplished learners. Estimates suggested that the best instructional methods of the early 1980s such as mastery learning and cooperative learning might get students about halfway to Bloom's criterion. As these methods are extended and carefully employed as we approach the year 2000, they might even attain it.

The contributors to this volume show how these early methods and their creative elaborations can be widely and effectively implemented. The efforts and results are highly encouraging. As shown here, imaginative applications can produce good results in a wide variety of settings. PAL yields gains, not only in knowledge, but in positive attitudes toward the subject matter and intended behavioral skills. Importantly, in this era of financial pressures on schools, PAL incurs little additional cost. It need not, for example, require any special equipment.

Although external support is helpful, especially initially, it is possible for some teachers merely to study and develop PAL on their own—greatly facilitated by this book. They can then institute one or more of the strategies represented here. Better yet, they may employ the principles and examples to create new versions in line with their own views and circumstances.

ADVANTAGES

PAL appears to work well for several reasons. It complements didactic or direct teaching and independent study, either of which, if unremitting, can be deadening. PAL also provides rapid feedback: Working alone or during teacher presentations, learners can carry forward and even practice mistakes. In a small group or pairs, however, they need not wait; they can quickly compare and correct their understandings. Peers, by definition, are close to each other in age, ability, status, ethnicity, and other characteristics. They are approachable and have insights into learning difficulties that even the most skilled teachers may lack. Indeed, masters of the subject matter may have the greatest difficulty in seeing the novices' obstacles.

Peer assistance, moreover, seems especially appropriate for the new world of changing occupations and vocations. When accurate execution of instructions is paramount, it is hard to beat machines and computers. For this reason, good jobs and recreation increasingly depend on value added to activity by individual initiative and social entrepreneurship. They call for independent preparation and critical thinking, combined with responsible teamwork to ensure both individual and group success—main features of PAL. Thus, PAL yields not only greater learning but transferable skills necessary for participation in economic and civic life. These are only a few advantages of PAL. In the introductory chapter, the editors describe many more that are elaborated and exemplified in the rest of the book.

THEORY

PAL can be traced to Socrates, Plato, Aristotle, and their colleagues. Reclining over food and wine in small groups, Socrates and colleagues questioned one another's ideas. Aristotle discussed all matters while strolling in the Lyceum of ancient Athens. Although the Greeks argued variously that knowledge must be drawn out or poured in, they exemplified the combination that only a dialog or small group can enact. As the editors set forth in the introductory chapter, psychologists of this century, for example Piaget, Vygotsky, and Rogoff, have carried classic ideas forward. Their followers have stimulated practitioners and have been stimulated by them. Some have worked directly in classrooms and have had to revise their contentions and methods. This is progress.

The editors and authors can now set forth central theoretical principles of PAL. They can also describe many variations and examples that have been practically implemented in a variety of settings. They are unlike academics who ask if programs working well in practice could possibly work in theory. As exemplified here, mutual enrichment of theory and practice seems better. Readers will find the great number and variety of examples of enormous help in considering what particularities of PAL they find most appealing. The editors' introduction, moreover, provides an elegant theoretical map or typology of major variants of PAL that should help in further development and implementation.

COMPREHENSIVENESS

This book provides both variety and comprehensiveness. In the editors' introductory chapter, the typology shows how the variants of PAL can be grouped logically or categorized. It enables us to imagine how the classifications and principles might be extended to, say, distance learning and the Internet. Representing a number of countries, the chapter authors show how the variants have worked in diverse educational and social settings. Such international representation provides a selection of research and programs that are mutually reinforcing.

THE WAY AHEAD

This foreword can end no better than does the editors' introduction. Their self-referential advice is to read this book about PAL with a pal—then act. Wise words.

REFERENCES

Bloom, B. S. (1984). The search for methods of group instruction as effective as one-to-one tutoring. *Educational Leadership, 41*(8), 4–17.

Walberg, H. J. (1984). Improving the productivity of America's schools. *Educational Leadership, 41*(8), 19–30.

Preface

FOCUS AND OBJECTIVE OF THE BOOK

This book seeks to help ensure children and young people learn more effectively. It blends descriptions of good practice with research findings on effectiveness. It aims to be accessible and useful to educators and other practitioners and also of interest to the research community.

This book is about peers consciously assisting others to learn and in so doing, learning themselves. Peer tutoring is the most obvious example, where tutor and tutee are clear about their respective and separate roles and goals. However, peer-assisted learning (PAL) also encompasses peer education and counseling, and peer modeling, monitoring, and assessment.

PAL is presented as a dynamic, robust, effective, and flexible approach to teaching and learning, which can be used opportunistically in a host of different settings. The book seeks to achieve the following.

- Review and bring together some strategies that will already be familiar to many readers.
- Show how these have been extended by innovators.
- Introduce some more recent related developments.
- Review the evidence for effectiveness.
- Enable the reader to see the family likenesses and develop an integrated and reflective view of the whole area.
- Give the reader sufficient organizational detail to prompt thoughts about innovation in their own practice.

For many readers, the general notion of peer tutoring is already familiar. However, reciprocal tutoring, classwide tutoring, paired learning methods and the deployment of students with special needs as tutors may be relatively unfamiliar. Thus, the average reader's understanding of peer tutoring is likely to be deepened and extended by the book. The establishment of the broader concept of PAL, with extension to perhaps even less familiar areas such as peer modeling, monitoring and assessment, and peer education and counseling, should enable readers to see many new possibilities and make new connections to help develop their existing practices.

AUDIENCE

This book should be of interest and use to teachers and those who employ, train, support, consult with, and evaluate teachers. Contributors seek accessibility for well-informed and well-motivated teachers. Many chapters aim to help them to replicate these cost-effective procedures in their own school environment.

Most contributors were asked to review the best of current thinking and practice in their area, indicate how to replicate this, and show that it works. Inevitably, a few chapters cover such a wide span that they fall short of some of these aims, but suggestions for further detailed reading and associated practical resources are plentiful.

The book should also be of interest to those who have a more academic and/or research interest in the field, including education and psychology departments in universities and colleges. In addition, community educators might be interested in the implications for action beyond the school, as might employers and others interested in postschool entry and training.

Although many of the contributors are from North America, others are from Europe and Australia, and worldwide applicability is intended. Vocabulary that is specific to the educational systems of particular countries is explained in a later section of this preface.

OVERVIEW OF CONTENT

This book deals with procedures that can be applied to all areas of the curriculum in schools. They can be used with tutors and tutees of all levels of ability, including the gifted and slow or disabled learners.

The focus here is on *learning*: acquiring and consolidating new information, concepts, and skills. Peer interventions to change problem *behavior* are referred to only tangentially. The social and affective benefits of PAL are also emphasized, particularly relevant to bridging divides between ages, genders, races, abilities, and so on.

The text is informed throughout by the view that PAL can and should be (a) a group of learning strategies complementary to professional teaching but definitely not surrogate professional teaching; (b) structured to ensure gains for all participants in one or more domains; (c) available to all on an equal opportunity basis, because all have something to give; and (d) carefully organized and monitored by professional teachers with an extended conception of their role. PAL capitalizes on the unique qualities and richness of peer interaction and empowers students democratically to take more responsibility for their own learning.

THE STRUCTURE OF THE BOOK

The foreword and this preface lead into the introduction (chap. 1), which sets out the overall framework and context for the book, the content of which is drawn together at the end in the summary and conclusions (chap. 17) and an afterword. Between these are the five major parts of the book. Part I develops the introductory material, and Part V discusses embedding and extending PAL within and beyond schools. Between these are the substantive core of the book: Part II (on peer tutoring), Part III (on peer facilitation and education), and Part IV (on peer feedback). References accompany each chapter. A list of relevant practical resources is provided in an appendix, together with biographical information about the contributors and an index for the book. More detail of the structure follows here.

The introduction (chap. 1) maps the territory of PAL. A typology and definitions of methods are outlined, discriminating one approach from another and from related methods not covered in the book. Some of the major theoretical and research underpinnings of PAL are reviewed. Linkage with current educational, political, and financial issues is made.

Part I (chap. 2–4) considers the basis and benefits of PAL. Part I discusses relevant theory and fundamental research in educational, developmental, and social psychology. Advantages and disadvantages of PAL are also reviewed and key components and mechanisms for robust and successful organization of the methods are outlined.

Part II (chap. 5–9) covers various aspects of peer tutoring. Included are specific structured methods for peer tutoring of literacy, classwide peer tutoring, and reciprocal peer tutoring, before discussing the involvement of those with learning and behavior problems as both peer tutors and tutees.

Part III (chap. 10–12) explores the perhaps more challenging methods of peer facilitation and education, including peer modeling, peer education programs (especially in health), and peer counseling, often found to be as effective as counseling from trained professionals.

Part IV (chap. 13–14) investigates perhaps the most underused methods in the book: forms of peer feedback including peer monitoring and peer assessment.

Part V further develops the theme of the book, reflecting on the need to embed and extend PAL within organizations, to give multiple developmental opportunities so that the experience of tutoring can become a normal lifelong expectation.

The book ends with summary and conclusions, resource guide, biographical information, and index.

HOW TO USE THE BOOK

Readers are strongly recommended to read this preface and the introduction (chap. 1) in some detail first (with the possible exception of the theoretical section in chap. 1).

After that, teachers might wish to explore chapters in the core (Parts II, III, and IV) and perhaps look into the resources appendix. Those with an academic inclination might wish to read the theoretical section in chap. 1 and items in Part I sooner. Part V on embedding and extending PAL will be clearer if read after much of the rest of the book. The summary and conclusions chapter could be read at any time after the introduction, but might well benefit from rereading.

INTERNATIONAL VOCABULARY

Different countries organize their educational systems differently and use different vocabulary to describe them. Two kinds of confusion can arise: where different words are used for the same thing, and where the same words are used for different things. Some of the most common differences in vocabulary are discussed next.

Students and Pupils

In North America, learners in all kinds of schools, colleges, and universities are often called *students*. In the United Kingdom, the term *students* is used only for learners in colleges and universities, whereas learners in schools are termed *pupils* or *schoolchildren*.

Grade

In North America, grades are developmental levels of competence in school, roughly corresponding to chronological years, but often with the implication that children must meet the minimum level of competence for one grade before being allowed to proceed to the next. This is also the case in parts of South America. Most of the rest of the world groups children simply in chronological years, and all children progress with advancing age, except in small (often rural) schools, which may have children from several years in one class. North American Grade 1 (5- to 6-year olds) roughly equates to English Year 1 (but in England there is an unlabeled year of school before that) and to Scottish Primary 2, and so on.

Types of Schools

In North America, *elementary schools* are for children from 5 to 11 years of age. They are called *primary schools* in the United Kingdom, and other things elsewhere in the world. Schools for children from 11 to 18 are called *high schools* in North America, *secondary schools* in the United Kingdom, and other things elsewhere in the world. In some parts of both North America and the United Kingdom, *middle schools* are found, enrolling children from about 9 to 10 years through 12 to 13 years.

Special Needs

Children with unusual or exceptional difficulties or needs in learning or coping with the school environment are termed children with *special educational needs* in the United Kingdom. In North America, the vernacular expression *special ed. students* is sometimes heard, but is now often unacceptable to the students and their families. North America has an elaborate quasi-medical typology for labeling different kinds of difficulty in children (*DSM-IV*), but in the United Kingdom, legislation largely prohibits such labeling and mandates a more specific and pragmatic focus on the special educational needs of the individual in relation to their current context.

Children from a minority background, in relation to the dominant local population, are sometimes so identified in both continents, with the nature of the minority specified (ethnic minority, religious minority, cultural minority, etc.). Children whose first language at home is not English are sometimes identified as having English as a second or additional language needs in both continents.

In relation to this, the standard, usual materials, arrangements, and so forth are often called *regular* in North America and *ordinary* or *normal* in the United Kingdom. Educational programs that require the removal of children (usually in a small group or singly) from the main classroom are often called *pull-out* programs in North America, and *withdrawal* in the United Kingdom.

THE DISTINCTIVE CONTRIBUTION OF THIS BOOK

This is the first book to cover the whole range of PAL methods, distinct from the umbrella term of *cooperative learning*. It is the first text to draw together in accessible and consistent form, a wide range of related user-friendly and cost-effective PAL methods. The editors and contributors wish all readers well in their future development of these methods.

1

Introduction to Peer-Assisted Learning

Keith Topping
University of Dundee
Stewart Ehly
University of Iowa

Building on the foundation of the preface, this introduction seeks to map the territory of peer-assisted learning (PAL) and give the reader a framework within which to relate and understand the component parts of the field. Definitions and a typology are offered, distinguishing one approach from another and from related methods not covered in the book. Linkage with current educational, political, and financial issues is made. Some of the major theoretical and research underpinnings of PAL are discussed and summarized. A brief review of the contributed chapters then leads into the main part of the book.

WHAT IS PAL?

Learning is to acquire knowledge and/or skill by study, experience, or teaching. To assist is to aid, help, promote, support, or succor. A peer is an equal in standing or rank, a matched companion (Onions, 1978).

It follows that PAL is the acquisition of knowledge and skill through active helping and supporting among status equals or matched companions. PAL is people from similar social groupings, who are not professional teachers, helping each other to learn and by so doing, learning themselves.

As becomes evident here, this simple definition has many and powerful ramifications. Some PAL methods are more suited to the acquisition of knowledge, whereas others are more suited to the development of skills. In some PAL methods, peer helpers are more intensively and consciously

1

active in the helping role than in other methods. In some applications of PAL, the definition of *peer* might seem somewhat stretched, as when university students tutor young school children. However, a peer always remains very different from a salaried, and ultimately controlling, professional teacher.

Archaic perceptions of PAL considered the peer helper as a surrogate teacher, in a linear model of the transmission of knowledge, from teacher to peer helper to tutee. Traditionally, there was an assumption that peer helpers should be among the best students (i.e., those who were most like the professional teachers). However, the differential in levels of ability and interest in such a situation could prove understimulating for the helper, who was unlikely to gain cognitively from the interactions. Later, it was realized that the peer helping interaction was qualitatively different from that between a professional teacher and a child or young person, and involved different advantages and disadvantages.

Recently, there has been more interest in deploying helpers whose capabilities are nearer to those of the helped, so that both members of the pair find some cognitive challenge in their joint activities. The helper is intended to be learning by teaching and is also a more proximate and credible model under these circumstances. Thus, PAL projects now almost always target gains for both helpers and helped; double added value.

WHY IS PAL IMPORTANT?

Raising Standards

The education system is frequently criticized for failing to raise standards in literacy, numeracy, and science and is often blamed for apparent declines. Additionally, there is criticism for failing to promote the development of vocationally relevant transferable skills in high schools. The quality and cost-effectiveness of teaching and learning methods and resources has never before been so closely scrutinized.

The occasional clarion calls of "back to basics" are paradoxical. Didactic curriculum delivery, coupled with crude and brief summative assessment methods, are known to promote a surface approach to learning—the kind of learning of which machines are now capable—rather than a deep or intelligent approach.

Government attempts to be seen to be doing something about it too frequently result only in increased administration and bureaucracy, reducing the time, energy, motivation, and other resources available for teaching.

Such initiatives are frequently set in the context of reductions in levels of resourcing at the grass roots.

Cost-Effectiveness

The dual requirement to improve teaching quality while doing more with less has recently increased interest in PAL. Just as it is unwise to assume that more teaching resources automatically yield better results, it also would be unwise to seize upon PAL as a universal, undifferentiated, and instant panacea.

Undoubtedly however, PAL is important because it is effective and cost-effective. In the case of peer tutoring, a recent review identified 28 previous reviews and meta-analyses of evaluation research (Topping, 1992). Sharpley and Sharpley (1981) and Cohen, Kulik, and Kulik (1982) found strong evidence of cognitive gains for tutees and tutors and some evidence for improved attitudes and self-image (which are, of course, more difficult to measure). They also found that training improved outcomes, structured procedures improved outcomes, and that same-age tutoring was as effective as cross-age tutoring.

Bloom (1984) reported a series of studies comparing the outcomes of different educational methods. The average student exposed to one-on-one tutoring scored about two standard deviations above the average student receiving conventional classroom instruction. Bloom's description of the search for other methods as effective as tutoring as the "two-sigma problem" subsequently became famous. He also pointed out that his results demonstrated that *most* children have the potential to achieve to high levels.

The Information Age

For the new millennium, competence in information technology will be crucial, yet, computers alone are not a panacea. Levin, Glass, and Meister (1987) conducted a cost-effectiveness analysis of four different interventions to improve reading and mathematics: computer-assisted learning, reduction of class size, lengthening the school day, and cross-age peer tutoring. The best method—peer tutoring—was four times more cost-effective than the least.

However, consider the benefits of PAL in an information technology environment. The most computer literate person in a classroom is only rarely the teacher. Transmission of information technology skills through the peer group is already happening. Teachers can channel and organize this powerful force.

Social Benefits

For the future, in a competitive world, children need to be able to compete. To survive, they also need to be able to cooperate, because in a world full of individualists, all time would be unproductively spent in futile competition. Johnson and Johnson (1983) compared the effects of competitive, cooperative, and individualistic learning experiences on schoolchildren. Cooperation resulted in greater positive feelings between children and higher self-esteem and empathy.

Many of us live in divided, fragmented, frightened societies, in which caring is no longer seen as fashionable. The breakdown of the traditional family has left many young people increasingly socially isolated and relying ever more on the peer group. Arguably, humans are social animals, deriving a good deal of their identity, satisfaction, and well-being from positive social relationships. PAL is a vehicle for engineering positive contact between groups who would otherwise remain alienated—contact across the divides of age, gender, ethnic origin, social class, and so on.

Politically, peer tutoring delegates the management of learning to the learners in a democratic way, seeks to empower students rather than de-skill them by dependency on imitation of a master culture, and might reduce student dissatisfaction and unrest.

Affective Benefits

Of course, education is not just about *knowledge* (what I need to know) and *skill* (what I need to be able to do). It is also about *motivation* (how much I want to be able to know and do) and *confidence* (my belief that I am able to know and do). Even if the assistance and support given by a peer helper is of a lesser quality than that from a professional teacher, what it lacks in quality it might compensate for in quantity and immediacy. But perhaps more importantly, if PAL can help develop motivation and confidence, its impact could be profound.

PAL, like other forms of service learning, has been described as "humanly rewarding" (Goodlad, 1979). Tutors can learn to be nurturing toward their tutees, and in so doing, develop a sense of pride and responsibility. Partners can learn to feel good about each other, and about themselves as well. PAL has been and will become even more important for all of these reasons: educational, economic, political, social, and affective. These are large claims. To evaluate them, first we need to consider just what is meant by PAL and move toward some definitions.

DEFINITIONS BY INCLUSION

Teachers might not, of course, agree about whether their efforts target gains in knowledge or skill—or what proportion of which. A definition of training is that it is to drill and instruct in, or for, some particular art, profession, occupation or practice. The targeted outcomes are very particular; training is clearly skill oriented. (Note, however, the secondary definition from horticulture—"to manage so as to cause to grow in some desired direction"!)

Education, by contrast, is seen as a "process of nourishing, rearing, bringing up ... culture or development of powers, formation of character." These are clearly attitudinal and behavioral correlates of a very generalized nature, reflecting the origin of the word education from "educe": to bring out, to elicit, to develop. In fact, you do not always get *just* or *only* what you targeted, so philosophical debate is almost certainly pointless until you have actually tried out some of the PAL methods defined next.

Peer Tutoring

Peer tutoring, the most widely known PAL method, often targets skill gains. However, much wider (educational) gains often accrue as serendipitous side effects.

Peer tutoring is characterized by specific role-taking: at any point someone has the job of tutor, whereas the other (or the others) is in role as tutee(s). It has high focus on curriculum content. Projects usually also outline quite specific procedures for interaction, in which the participants are likely to have training that is specific or generic, or both. In addition, their interaction may be further scaffolded by the provision of structured materials, among which a greater or lesser degree of student choice may be available.

Confusion between *tutoring* and *mentoring* is evident in the literature, not least because of the differences in language use between different workers in different countries. In the United States, the terms are sometimes used as if synonymous, but in this book, a sharp distinction is made between them. Indeed, *tutoring* is discussed a great deal, whereas *mentoring* is considered only in chap. 16, and the working definition of mentoring for this book is found in the definition by exclusion section.

Peer Modeling

There are elements of modeling in peer tutoring, but in chap. 10, peer modeling by itself is discussed. Demonstration has long been acknowledged as a powerful aid to learning of all kinds, but it can involve much more than just showing how to do something.

Peer modeling is the provision of a competent exemplar of desirable learning behavior by a member or members of a group with the intention that others in the group will imitate it. Peer modeling is likely to be associated with stronger identification between intended imitator and model than modeling on professional adults—the teacher is super competent and too distant a mastery model. Peer modeling might also be more concrete than that from the teacher, and more related to the imitator's everyday life. This may yield earlier, albeit perhaps mechanistic, success—the teacher can develop understanding of abstract principles once motivation and self-belief is engaged.

Peer modeling can have strong social and attitudinal effects. Peers can model enthusiasm and cooperation. They can show that something is possible, even for peers who had no belief in their capability. Peer models are competent but not necessarily perfect—peers can also model problem solving, including modeling of coping and self-correction. It follows that peer modeling is likely to be associated with better attributions of success to effort. There might also be gains in self-image for the model. Imitation is the sincerest form of flattery—a very powerful kind of feedback, whether intended or not.

Observing others gives the observer time and space to perceive the elements of competent performance with a clarity that might not be evident to the performer themselves (the latter being preoccupied with the business of actually performing). This is reflected in the parallel meanings of the word *model*: a three-dimensional representation of a structure showing the proportions and arrangements of parts, a pattern for building. Observing how others do things heightens awareness of how you do things, through comparison and contrast. Modeling on and by peers can thus lead to greater metacognitive awareness, and thereby more self-regulation.

Peer Education

We noted earlier that *education* means to bring out, to develop—to empower through knowledge, to help others develop their own conscious value system and make informed choices—even if they are different from ours.

Peer education usually involves the offering of sensitive information from credible peers who are seen to identify with and understand the life circumstances of the recipients. This is coupled with opportunities to discuss the material in an informal group peer setting, hopefully likely to maximize disclosure of resistance, misconception, and ignorance. This tends to lead to exploration of different social and emotional responses to the material, affecting self-perceptions, group identification and attitudes—and possibly subsequent behavior.

Informal peer education has always occurred all the time, of course—whom among us cannot remember the misinformation about human sexual behavior that we acquired during break times at school? Peer education programs seek to capitalize on this naturally occurring and inevitable phenomenon, while improving the reliability of the information in circulation and giving all children an equal opportunity to participate.

A brief definition of *peer education* would look something like: "peers offering credible and reliable information about sensitive life issues and the opportunity to discuss this in an informal peer group setting." Chapter 11 discusses this area in detail, reviewing gains for peer educators and those educated.

Peer Counseling

Professional counselors might not be able to agree on a definition of counseling, but peer counseling (see chap. 12) can have no exotic or esoteric pretensions. We propose this definition of *peer counseling*: people from similar groupings who are not professional teachers or line managers who help clarify general life problems and identify solutions by listening, feeding back, summarizing and being positive and supportive. As with other forms of PAL, this might occur on a one-on-one basis or in groups.

Students in difficulty can be very reluctant to approach a professional counselor. Disclosure to a peer counselor might be more likely, not least because of higher perceived empathy. However, peer counselors must be protected from getting in too deep. Simple problems may be handled by the peer counselor, but perhaps more importantly, they can encourage the other to seek an appropriate person for help.

Peer Monitoring

Peer monitoring (chap. 13) is about peers keeping an eye on whether their partners are going through appropriate and effective processes and procedures of learning. These latter could also be termed *study behaviors,* but this seems a little grandiose for younger children, for whom simple indicators such as time engaged with task, time on-task, or just time in seat are more relevant.

Of course, some of these children will be quite aware that they spend very little time on task, and this might be a deliberate strategy or a conscious goal. For such children, peer monitoring alone is unlikely to have a profound impact. However, many other children are unaware of the true size of the amount (often very large) of time spent off-task, and credible feedback about this is itself effective in producing greater effort toward self-improvement in the monitored child.

This is also true of other, more complex, learning behaviors, such as managing time and work load, doing appropriate reading, meeting deadlines, and so on. Of course, teachers do not have enough time to monitor all children in need closely enough, so peer monitoring might prove the only practical, feasible option. As with other PAL methods, there are metacognitive implications. Feedback from peer monitoring enables the learner to better self-regulate their actions toward the desired goal. Also, practice in checking for off-task behavior in others tends to sensitize the child to their own off-task behaviors. A brief definition of *peer monitoring* could thus be: Peers observing and checking the process learning behaviors of others in the group with respect to appropriateness and effectiveness.

Peer Assessment

Assessment is the determination of the amount, level, value, or worth of something. Chapter 14 considers arrangements for peers to consider the level, value, or worth of the work of others in the group. In practice, this is often written work, although there are other possibilities.

The feedback from peer assessment is intended to be formative—enabling the learner to improve performance. Peer assessment is not costly in teacher time and is in ready supply. Thus, it can be given when a learning product or output is in the development stage, rather than at the end (when it is too late). It can be given more frequently and immediately than teacher assessment.

Again, there are strong metacognitive implications for all participants. Like other PAL methods, peer assessment is reflexive, and focuses the peer assessor's own mind on what actually constitutes good work in the area. A clearer view of what you have to do to be right is likely to improve assessed performance, especially when the criteria for assessment have been discussed or even negotiated with all participants. Peer assessment can thus be a vehicle for improved self-assessment. Interestingly, in higher education, self-assessment has traditionally been more common than peer assessment. A brief definition of *peer assessment* could thus be: peers formatively and qualitatively evaluating the products or outcomes of learning of others in the group.

DEFINITION BY EXCLUSION

Cooperative Learning

The generic term *cooperative learning* (CL) can be and is applied to any form of working together in schools. The term has been subject to much corruption. In the United Kingdom, for instance, some teachers have been found to assert that they "do cooperative learning" because they sit children in small groups around tables in the classroom—when inspection often reveals that the children are actually working individually, not together. This looseness of nomenclature is doubtless aggravating to the proponents of specific, structured, well-researched methods for CL (e.g., Slavin, 1990), for whom CL is about "structuring positive interdependence."

CL should at least involve small groups in which students have to jointly organize their time and resources to work toward some specific goal. For instance, the whole task might be divided into specialist areas in which one group member becomes expert, and then everyone's new knowledge and skills are jigsawed back together to achieve the joint goal. Many other arrangements are possible.

It could be argued that all PAL methods are a form of working together and thus come under the general umbrella of CL. However, this is of no advantage. The differentiation of cooperative from *collaborative* learning is also a difficult question, and many people use the terms synonymously. Damon and Phelps (1989) proposed that collaborative learning is characterized by highly mutual working and a single joint task (i.e., no division of labor). At least in the United States, CL usually implies a degree of process regulation by the teacher, which collaborative learning need not.

Peer Mentoring

Mentoring is an encouraging and supportive one-on-one relationship with a more experienced worker (who is not a line manager) in a joint area of interest. It is characterized by positive role modeling, promoting raised aspirations, positive reinforcement, open-ended counseling, and joint problem solving. It is often cross-age, always fixed-role (although the mentor might gain something also), quite often cross institution, and often targeted on disadvantaged groups. It should not be confused with peer tutoring.

A TYPOLOGY OF PEER-ASSISTED LEARNING

Methods of PAL can vary on at least 13 organizational dimensions:

- Curriculum content
- Contact constellations
- Within or between institutions
- Within or across year groups
- Same- or across-ability matching
- Fixed or reciprocal roles
- Timing
- Location
- Characteristics of helpers
- Characteristics of helped
- Objectives
- Voluntary or compulsory
- Reinforcement

These methods are explored in more detail here.

1. Curriculum Content: Knowledge or skills or combination to be covered. The scope of PAL is very wide, and projects are reported in the literature in virtually every imaginable subject.

2. Contact Constellation: Some projects operate with one helper working with a group of peers, but the size of group can vary from 2 to 30 or more. Sometimes two or more helpers take a group together. More intensive is PAL in pairs (dyads)—there is less opportunity to drift into token participation in a pair (see chap. 5).

3. Within or Between Institutions: Although most PAL takes place within the same institution, it can also take place between different institutions, as when young people from a high school tutor in their neighborhood elementary (primary) school, or university students help in regular schools (see chap. 16).

4. Year of Study: Helpers and helped may be from the same or different years of study.

5. Ability: Although many projects operate on a cross-ability basis (even if they are same-year), there is increasing interest in same-ability PAL. Here, the helper might have superior mastery of only a very small portion of the curriculum, or all might be of equal ability but working toward a shared, deeper, and hopefully correct understanding. Certainly, clear operational

structures are necessary to avoid the pooling of ignorance. Indeed, *meta-ignorance* can be a problem–the helper does not know that they do not know the correct facts.

   6. Role Continuity: Especially in same-ability projects, roles need not be permanent. Structured switching of roles at strategic moments (reciprocal PAL) can have the advantage of involving greater novelty and a wider boost to self-esteem, in that all participants get to be helpers (see chap. 7).

   7. Time: PAL might be scheduled in regular class contact time, outside of this, or in a combination of both, depending on the extent to which it is substitutional or supplementary for regular teaching.

   8. Place: Correspondingly, PAL can vary enormously in location of operation.

   9. Helper Characteristics: The traditional assumption was that helpers should be the *best* students (i.e., those most like the professional teachers). However, very large differentials in ability can prove understimulating for the helper, and other large differences can inhibit modeling. If helpers are those who are merely average (or even less), all partners should find some challenge in their joint activities. Although the gain of the helped might not be so great, the aggregate gain of both combined may be greater. Many projects have deployed those with learning and behavior difficulties as helpers, to the benefit of the helpers themselves (see chaps. 8 and 9).

   10. Characteristics of the Helped: Projects may be for all or a targeted subgroup (e.g., the especially able or gifted, those with disabilities, those considered at risk of underachievement, failure or dropout, or those from ethnic, religious, and other minorities; see chaps. 8 and 9).

   11. Objectives: Projects may target intellectual (cognitive) gains, formal academic achievement, affective and attitudinal gains, social and emotional gains, self-image and self-concept gains, or any combination. Organizational objectives might include reducing dropout or increasing access.

   12. Voluntary or Compulsory: Some projects require participation, whereas in others, helpers self-select. This can have marked effects on the quality of what ensues.

   13. Reinforcement: Some projects involve extrinsic reinforcement for the helpers (and sometimes also the helped), whereas others rely on intrinsic motivation. Beyond simple social praise, extrinsic reward can take the form of certification, course credit, or more tangible reinforcement such as money. Extrinsic reward is much more common in North America than elsewhere, and this has led to some debate about possible excess in this regard. Reassuringly, the research evidence suggests that providing extrinsic reinforcement does not damage intrinsic reinforcement (Cameron & Pierce, 1994). However, its availability can have effects on recruitment in voluntary projects, which might be good or bad.

THEORETICAL UNDERPINNINGS:
WHY AND HOW DOES PAL WORK?

This chapter has already presented some comments on how PAL creates its effects. This is explored in more detail now and in chaps. 2, 3, and 4.

Piaget

A neo-Piagetian interpretation of individual development through the cognitive conflict and challenge inherent in many forms of PAL between equals with different points of view was offered by Doise and Mugny (1984). *Equilibration* (the reconciliation of cognitive conflict) seems especially relevant to verbal ideas or concepts of some abstraction.

Vygotsky

However, PAL can also be understood through the social interactionist (or sociocultural) view of cognitive development, which can be traced back at least as far as Vygotsky. He saw the key mechanism as supported (or scaffolded) exploration through social and cognitive interaction with a more experienced peer, in relation to a task of a level of difficulty within the tutee's *zone of proximal development* (Vygotsky, 1978). This might relate to concepts, information, skills, or some combination of these—learning through the challenge of application perhaps.

Rogoff

These themes were further developed by Rogoff (1990) and her associates under the label of *apprenticeship in thinking*, involving "bridging procedures" to transfer responsibility from master to apprentice. Ellis and Rogoff (1982) showed young peer tutors often used more nonverbal demonstrations and linked instruction to specific items, whereas adults typically used more verbal instruction and related information to be learned to other material. They also made the point that peers use the same language and have had the same or similar problems—they can model coping (also see Collins, Brown, & Newman, 1989; Hogan & Tudge, in press; Radziszewska & Rogoff, 1988; Tudge & Rogoff, 1989).

Learning By Teaching

Peer tutoring (in particular) is often promoted on the grounds that, for the tutors, it is "learning by teaching." This view is expanded in the old saying, "to teach is to learn twice," a view shared by many professional teachers.

Simply preparing to be a peer helper has been proposed to enhance cognitive processing in the helper—by increasing attention to and motivation for the task, and necessitating review of existing knowledge and skills. Consequently, existing knowledge is transformed by reorganization, involving new associations and a new integration. The act of helping itself involves further cognitive challenge, particularly with respect to simplification, clarification and exemplification.

An excellent study by Annis (1983) compared three groups of students: One that merely read the material to be studied, one that read the material in the expectation of having to teach it to a peer, and a third that read the material with the expectation of teaching it to a peer and then actually carried this out. Allocation to conditions was random. A 48-item test of both specific and general competence was the outcome measure. The *read-only* group gained less than the *read-to-teach* group, which in turn gained less than the *read-and-teach* group. The tutors gained more than the tutees. Similarly, Benware and Deci (1984) found their learn-to-teach group performed better than a learn-only group on higher order conceptual understanding, and perceived their experience as more active and interesting.

Theoretical Cognitive Advantages

Many other advantages have been claimed for peer tutoring and related forms of PAL (e.g., Greenwood, Carta, & Kamps, 1990). Pedagogical advantages include active and participative learning, the incorporation of potent and proximal modeling and demonstration, immediate feedback, swift prompting, lowered anxiety with correspondingly higher self-disclosure, and greater student ownership of the learning process.

The student–teacher ratio is much reduced (although perhaps also the quality of teaching) and engaged time on-task increased. Opportunities to respond are high, opportunities to make errors and be corrected are high, and opportunities for the helper to give social reinforcement are high. Social reinforcement from peers is qualitatively different from that from teachers, and might be equally or more effective if only on account of its novelty value. Practice consolidates a skill, promotes fluency, and minimizes forgetting. The more you do it, the better you get and the more you want to do it. However, it is important that the practice is positive (i.e., successful). PAL provides an excellent vehicle for supported positive practice.

In addition to immediate cognitive gains, improved retention, greater metacognitive awareness and better application of knowledge and skills to new situations have been claimed. Motivational and attitudinal gains could include greater commitment, improved self-esteem, self-confidence, and greater empathy with others. Much of this links with work on self-efficacy and motivated learning, leading to the self-regulation of learning and performance (see chap. 10). Attributional feedback is important here—perhaps PAL can go some way toward combating the dependency culture associated with superficial learning.

Many of the writers on the cognitive processes involved in PAL over the years have emphasized the value of explaining and questioning by the partners (e.g., Bargh & Schul, 1980; Durling & Schick, 1976; Foot, Shute, Morgan, & Barron, 1990; Forman, 1994; Gartner, Kohler, & Riessman, 1971; Webb, 1982). This has developed into a field of inquiry with a cumbersome name.

Cognitive Co-Constructionism

Beyond the Piagetian view of cognitive conflict between equals and the Vygotskian view of scaffolded cross-ability interaction lies a compromise, which might be termed the *cognitive co-constructionist* view. The tutoring interaction is perceived as mutual cognitive elaboration, the interaction increasing the levels of active processing of information in all partners (O'Donnell & King, in press; O'Donnell & O'Kelly, 1994).

Analysis of tutoring interactions often highlights frequently occurring behaviors: Helper asking initiating question, partner(s) giving preliminary answer, helper giving feedback on answer, then prompting or scaffolding to develop or elaborate the preliminary answer, leading to iterative cycles of question ➡ answer ➡ feedback ➡ prompting, with the helper concurrently seeking to assess partner comprehension (Graesser, Pearson, & Magliano, 1995).

A more elaborate analytical framework was used by Van Lehn, Chi, Baggett, and Murray (1995). Helper behaviors included giving reviews, summaries, reminders, analogies, prompts, didactic explanations, advice on which steps to take, corrective feedback, hints, encouragement, asking questions, diagnosing misconceived knowledge; and assessing missing knowledge and deviations from the ideal. Behaviors of the helped included giving answers, asking questions, thinking, writing, and exhibiting confusion.

The Quality of Questioning.   Chi, Bassok, Lewis, Reimann, and Glaser (1989) emphasized the importance of self-questioning and self-explanations. Graesser et al. (1995) reported that helpers' initial questions tended to be orienting macroquestions, later moving to a microlevel of detail. At the latter, questioning could remain driven by the helper's conception of what his or her partner(s) must learn (and perhaps how they must learn it), but could equally open windows onto cognitions that permitted diagnosis of misconceived knowledge, or indeed an alternative way of knowing the same truth.

The quality and purpose of helper questioning can thus be of great significance in determining the direction, depth, ethos, and consequently value of the interaction. Some helpers prove more capable than others of asking intelligent questions that are adaptive to their peers. Others might be capable, but unwilling, given their conception of tutoring—that training would seek to modify.

Types of Feedback. Giving feedback is subcategorized into corrective feedback, reinforcing feedback, didactic explanations, and suggestive feedback by Chi (1996). One of the frequently cited advantages of PAL is the availability of immediate corrective feedback in the event of error, ensuring higher rates of productive time on-task. However, merely supplying the correct factual fragment does not ensure that the recipient can integrate this independently into a valid, semantic whole, and might result in superficial, rote learning of disconnected information.

Confirmatory or corroborative feedback is equally important because although the tutee is correct, he or she might not know that he or she is correct. However, by the same token, immediate simplistic confirmatory feedback might result in the tutee knowing from external reference that some factual fragment was correct, but not knowing why it was correct or what its significance was. Where helper feedback takes the form of long didactic explanations, there is little evidence of resultant learning. This is of course also true of lectures delivered by professional teachers.

Suggestive feedback, by contrast, is more open-ended, and perhaps more likely to occur when the tutee's response is only partially rather than wholly incorrect. It might include more nonverbal components, rather than an excess of verbalization, and may amount to little more than alerting the partner to the problematic issue. A further specific content-related question could constitute a more strongly suggestive form of feedback, because it signals incompleteness or other inadequacy in the tutee's previous response, as well as gently guiding him or her toward a potentially more productive line of thought. Suggestive feedback seems intrinsically more likely to lead into iterative cycles than other kinds of feedback.

Scaffolding and Prompting.   Chi (1996) proposed discriminating scaffolding from prompting (in her definition, the latter would include only simple elucidative verbalizations such as "go on," "tell me some more," "what comes next?" or "how do you mean?"). Thus, the helper prompts for tutee self-construction, but scaffolds for co-construction. A typology of scaffolding would include describing the problem to orient the tutee to the significant feature, comparing the current problem or concept to a previous one, suggesting a specific goal, questioning the tutee in relation to the helper's goal for the session, completing (or clozing or splicing in) the tutee's reasoning sequence, and initiating a reasoning sequence and asking the tutee to complete it. Chi noted that although scaffolding is possible (although by no means inevitable) in a high quality PAL setting, it is rare in the regular classroom, where teachers typically dwell only briefly on each student and tend to excessive use of closed questions.

Diagnosing Misconception.   Helpers often have difficulty gauging whether their partner(s) have really understood. Often those helped are themselves unsure of whether they really understand (metaignorance), but might be reluctant to admit otherwise, for fear of seeming unintelligent or unappreciative of the efforts of their helper. Or they may be grossly overly or underconfident in this respect. Thus, the habit of many helpers of merely asking the helped if they (now) understand is often futile (Glenberg, Wilkinson, & Epstein, 1982). Without intelligent and adaptive questioning from helpers to facilitate diagnosis of misconceived knowledge, correct factual fragments might remain embedded in misconception like sapphires in clay. It seems that although peer helpers are often quite good at noticing gaps in tutee knowledge, especially according to some predetermined template of what constitutes the received wisdom, they are less good at diagnosing misconceptions (Graesser et al., 1995).

Explaining.   Despite the doubtful value of long, didactic lectures and the immediate purely factual answer, the giving of explanations by both helper and helped is clearly an important part of the tutoring process, which might promote cognitive reconstruction in all partners (Webb, 1989). The construction of an explanation elicited by another amounts to explaining the same to oneself, but perhaps with greater rigor and clarity (Chi, 1996). Overt verbalization to another goes beyond internal thinking, and requires further cognitive transformation (Yager, Johnson, & Johnson, 1985). Questioning and eliciting explanations may likewise come from either helper or helped. There is evidence that expert tutors prompt tutees for self-explanations and virtually never provide answers to problems (Lepper, Woolverton, Mumme, & Gurtner, 1993). The deeper and more frequent the questions and explanations from either party, the richer the interaction is likely to be, and the more it will tend toward joint construction of deeper understanding. This may be the key to the value added through the interaction itself (King, 1994; Perret-Clermont, Perret, & Bell, 1991).

Implications. If this is so, there are practical implications for the organization of tutoring. It is possible that a Piagetian cognitive conflict between equals will lead merely to the pooling of ignorance, a very high error rate, and frustration. On the other hand, the Vygotskian apprenticeship model might prove too rigid if the tutor had an overly fixed notion of the knowledge to be transmitted, too little appreciation of the starting point of the tutee, and too little stimulation from the developmentally distant questioning of their much less capable partner. Merrill, Reiser, Merrill, and Landes (1995) commented on the need for tutors to avoid leading their tutees too strongly, terming the appropriate (and effective) point of balance as *guided learning by doing*. Tutorial partnerships incorporating a moderate differential in ability might efficiently facilitate the balanced collaborative construction of knowledge through many productive reciprocal iterations of question, explanation, and feedback.

In any case, PAL does not create effects by purely cognitive means. Juel (1996) listed the interactive qualities of her cross-age, cross-ability dyads who were most successful in terms of test gains. These were (a) affection and bonding, (b) verbal and nonverbal reinforcement, (c) many scaffolded experiences, and (d) much explicit cognitive and affective modeling by tutors.

Relevant variables in influencing the outcomes of tutoring seem likely to include initial tutor and tutee characteristics, the physical and social environment, the nature of task specified, the equipment (hardware) and materials (software) provided, the behaviors prescribed for tutor and tutee, the actual behaviors of tutor and tutee, and the interactions between all of these. Different factors and interactions of factors are likely to operate to different degrees in different situations. This may be true of any teaching–learning situation. It is possible to construct from the literature a summary list of factors that might operate in any given situation.

Summary: Why and How Does PAL Work?

Cognitively, PAL might work by increasing the following, for helpers, helped, or both:

Attention
Time on-task, engagement
Immediacy, timeliness of tutor intervention
Individualization of learning
Accountability, responsibility
Goal specification
Preparation and planning
Review and rehearsal
Simplification, clarification
Reorganization, cognitive restructuring
New associations and integrations
Exemplification and analogizing, elaboration
Explaining—In vernacular language (linguistic congruence)
Active listening
Questioning—Intelligently and adaptively
Predicting and estimating
Modulation of information processing—Preventing
    overload
Reminding
Prompting—Stepwise if needed
Modeling–Demonstration—Proximate–Credible—Can be
    stepwise
Positive practice
Responding opportunities
Error opportunities
Error identification and analysis (high vs. low-level errors)
Self-correction opportunities
Feedback opportunities—Confirmatory, suggestive, corrective
Feedback—Evaluative (giving and receiving)
Reinforcement—Verbal/nonverbal/other
Problem identification, definition, and solving
Self-disclosure and thus assessment of understanding
Requesting help (for task completion, not dependency)
Diagnosis and remediation of misconception
Identification of gaps and engineering closure
Revising, reconstructing, redrafting
Summarizing
Fluency—Speed of response
Retention of understanding

Post hoc reflection
Generalization to new situations
Self-assessment
Metacognitive self-awareness
Understanding how others learn
Self-regulation and self-organization

Affectively, PAL might work by increasing the following for helpers, helped, or both:

Variety–Interest
Activity–Interactivity
Peer ownership of/Commitment to learning
Encouragement/Motivation
Identification and bonding (possibly mutual)
Modeling—of enthusiasm,coping
Self-confidence–Self-belief–Self-efficacy (+ possibly
    lower anxiety)
Self-attribution for success (and external attribution for failure)
Sense of self-control
Self-esteem
Aspirations
Empathy with others
Equality of opportunity and inclusivity

Of course, the editors themselves were not clear about all this until they had to sit down and explain it here to the reader. A brief review of the contributed chapters now leads readers to the main body of this book.

A BRIEF TOUR OF THE BOOK AND ITS PEOPLE

Between the foreword and afterword, the book has five main parts. Part I develops themes in this introduction, and Part V discusses embedding and extending PAL within and beyond schools. Between these are the substantive core of the book: Part II on peer tutoring, Part III on peer facilitation and education, and Part IV on peer feedback. The core content is drawn together at the end in the summary and conclusions (chap. 17). A list of relevant practical resources is appended.

Part I, "The Basis and Benefits of Peer-Assisted Learning," seeks to enable improvement in the application of known procedures and the design of new procedures, as well as enabling better prediction of outcomes. Chapter 2 by Foot and Howe (Scotland) further considers theory and fundamental research in educational, developmental, and social psychology that illuminates the impact of PAL. In chap. 3, Maheady (United States) reviews the advantages and disadvantages that PAL can have in relation to teacher mediated instruction. In chap. 4, Chapman (Australia) considers key organizational components and mechanisms in PAL that are associated with successful outcomes.

Part II considers both long-standing and newer developments in effective peer tutoring. Chapter 5 by Topping (Scotland) reviews specific methods for paired peer tutoring of reading, spelling, and writing that have been extensively applied and evaluated. Then, in chap. 6, Arreaga-Mayer, Terry, and Greenwood from the Juniper Gardens Children's Project (United States) show how whole classes can be involved in peer tutoring, with organizational and ecological advantages.

In chap. 7, Fantuzzo and Ginsburg-Block (United States) discuss reciprocal peer tutoring. This is methodologically important as it focuses attention on the structure and quality of interaction in the pair as the main vehicle for improved learning and is affectively and ethically important in that everyone gets to be a tutor.

Developing the theme that all students have something to give and can themselves benefit by giving, Maher and his coauthors (United States) consider in chap. 8 programs that deploy disruptive students as tutors. Scruggs and Mastropieri (United States) then review the deployment of students with other kinds of special educational needs as both tutees and tutors in chap. 9. These chapters demonstrate that peer tutoring is a robust method that can be used with apparently unpromising populations to good effect.

Under the general heading of "Peer Facilitation and Education," Part III first considers peer modeling. Schunk (United States) sets his chap. 10 on this topic in the context of motivation, self-efficacy, and self-managed and independent learning. In many challenging areas peers have proved more effective than teachers in promoting deeper understanding in students about vital life issues: health, HIV and AIDS, drugs, sex, smoking, alcohol, driving, violence prevention, and so on. Mathie and Ford (England), chap. 11, have conducted a number of action research studies in peer health education and focus on these here. Ehly and Vazquez (United States), in chap. 12, review peer counseling, which has been found in many studies to be as effective as counseling from trained professionals.

Part IV explores the yet more innovative area of structured peer feedback. In chap. 13, Henington and Skinner (United States) discuss peer monitoring and the impact of this kind of process checking on study behaviors on learning outcomes. Subsequently, in chap. 14, O'Donnell (United States) considers how peer assessment of the quality of the final products of learning can concentrate the mind of assessor and assessed, and permit more immediate feedback than an overworked teacher could offer.

Part V considers embedding and extending PAL, because too many approaches in education come and go, according to changes in fashion rather than their effectiveness. Gartner's seminal work in the United States with Riessman on peer tutoring dates back many years; current work particularly addresses developmental and chronological progression in tutoring experience and systemic expansion and embedding across the school (chap. 15).

Then, chap. 16 summarizes the use of PAL beyond school. Hill (Scotland), Gay (England), and Topping (Scotland) consider evidence on college students tutoring regular school students, peer tutoring within further and higher education establishments, and mentoring within and between universities and the professional and industrial workplace. Given multiple developmental opportunities, tutoring can become a normal lifelong expectation, and the experience of being a tutee is the best preparation for becoming a tutor.

The final chapter offers a summary and conclusions that seek to draw together the enormously rich and varied field that is PAL, and seek to give some pointers to the next wave of expansion and development.

The best way to really use this book effectively is to read it, discuss it with a peer, then make an innovative action plan collaboratively with a peer.

REFERENCES

Annis, L. F. (1983). The processes and effects of peer tutoring. *Human Learning, 2*(1), 39–47.
Bargh, J. A., & Schul, Y. (1980). On the cognitive benefits of teaching. *Journal of Educational Psychology, 72*(5), 593–604.
Benware, C. A., & Deci, E. L. (1984). Quality of learning with an active versus passive motivational set. *American Educational Research Journal, 21*(4), 755–765.
Bloom, B. S. (1984). The search for methods of group instruction as effective as one-to-one tutoring. *Educational Leadership, 41*(8), 4–17.
Cameron, J., & Pierce, D. (1994). Reinforcement, reward and intrinsic motivation: A meta-analysis. *Review of Educational Research, 64*(3), 363–423.
Chi, M. T. H. (1996). Constructing self-explanations and scaffolded explanations in tutoring. *Applied Cognitive Psychology, 10,* 33–49.
Chi, M. T. H., Bassok, M., Lewis, M. W., Reimann, P., & Glaser, R. (1989). Self-explanations: How students study and use examples in learning to solve problems. *Cognitive Science, 13,* 145–182.
Cohen, P. A., Kulik, J. A., & Kulik, C. C. (1982). Educational outcomes of tutoring: A meta-analysis of findings. *American Educational Research Journal, 19*(2), 237–248.
Collins, A., Brown, J. S., & Newman, S. E. (1989). Cognitive apprenticeship: Teaching the crafts of reading, writing and mathematics. In L. B. Resnick (Ed.), *Knowing, learning and instruction* 435–439. Hillsdale, NJ: Lawrence Erlbaum Associates.

Damon, W., & Phelps, E. (1989). Critical distinctions among three approaches to peer education. *International Journal of Educational Research, 58*(2), 9–19.

Doise, W., & Mugny, G. (1984). *The social development of the intellect.* Oxford: Pergamon Press.

Durling, R., & Schick, C. (1976). Concept attainment by pairs and individuals as a function of vocalization. *Journal of Educational Psychology, 68*(1), 83–91.

Ellis, S., & Rogoff, B. (1982). The strategies and efficacy of child versus adult teachers. *Child Development, 53,* 730–735.

Foot, H. C., Shute, R. H., Morgan, M. J., & Barron, A. (1990). Theoretical issues in peer tutoring. In H. C. Foot, M. J. Morgan, & R. H. Shute (Eds.), *Children helping children* (pp. 65–92). London & New York: Wiley.

Forman, E. (1994). Peer collaboration as situated activity: Examples from research on scientific problem solving. In H. C. Foot, C. J. Howe, A. Anderson, A. K. Tolmie, & D. A. Warden (Eds.), *Group and interactive learning* (pp. 3–8). Southampton & Boston: Computational Mechanics.

Gartner, S., Kohler, M., & Riessman, F. (1971). *Children teach children: Learning by teaching.* New York: Harper & Row.

Glenberg, A. M., Wilkinson, A. C., & Epstein, W. (1982). The illusion of knowing: Failure in the self-assessment of comprehension. *Memory and Cognition, 10,* 597–602.

Goodlad, S. (1979). *Learning by teaching: An introduction to tutoring.* London: Community Service Volunteers.

Graesser, A. C., Pearson, N. K., & Magliano, J. P. (1995). Collaborative dialogue patterns in naturalistic one-to-one tutoring. *Applied Cognitive Psychology, 9,* 495–522.

Greenwood, C. R., Carta, J. J., & Kamps, D. (1990). Teacher-mediated versus peer-mediated instruction: A review of educational advantages and disadvantages. In H. C. Foot, M. J. Morgan, & R. H. Shute (Eds.), *Children helping children* (pp. 177–206). London & New York: Wiley.

Hartman, H. J. (1990). Factors affecting the tutoring process. *Journal of Educational Development, 14*(2), 2–6.

Hogan, D. M., & Tudge, J. R. H. (in press). Implications of Vygotskian theory for peer learning. In A. M. O'Donnell & A. King (Eds.), *Cognitive perspectives on peer learning.* Mahwah, NJ: Lawrence Erlbaum Associates.

Johnson, R. T., & Johnson, D. W. (1983). Effects of co-operative, competitive and individualistic learning experiences on social development. *Exceptional Children, 49*(4), 323–329.

Juel, C. (1996). What makes literacy tutoring effective? *Reading Research Quarterly, 31*(3), 268–289.

King, A. (1994). Guiding knowledge construction in the classroom: Effects of teaching children how to question and how to explain. *American Educational Research Journal, 31,* 338–368.

Lepper, M. R., Woolverton, M., Mumme, D. L., & Gurtner, J. L. (1993). Motivational techniques of expert human tutors: Lessons for the design of computer-based tutors. In S. P. Lajoie, & S. Derry (Eds.), *Computers as Cognitive Tools* (pp. 67–89). Hillsdale, NJ: Lawrence Erlbaum Associates.

Levin, H. M., Glass, G. V., & Meister, G. R. (1987). A cost-effectiveness analysis of computer-assisted instruction. *Evaluation Review, 11*(1), 50–72.

Merrill, D. C., Reiser, B. J., Merrill, S. K., & Landes, S. (1995). Tutoring: Guided learning by doing. *Cognition and Instruction, 13*(3), 315–372.

O'Donnell, A. M., & King, A. (Eds.) (in press). *Cognitive perspectives on peer learning.* Mahwah, NJ: Lawrence Erlbaum Associates.

O'Donnell, A. M., & O'Kelly, J. (1994). Learning from peers: Beyond the rhetoric of positive results. *Educational Psychology Review, 6,* 321–349.

Onions, C. T. (Ed.) (1978). *The shorter Oxford English dictionary on historical principles.* Oxford: Clarendon.

Perret-Clermont, A. N., Perret, J. F., & Bell, N. (1991). The social construction of meaning and cognitive activity in elementary school children. In L. B. Resnick, J. M. Levine, & S. D. Teasley (Eds.), *Perspectives on socially shared cognition* (pp. 41–62). Washington, DC: American Psychological Association.

Radziszewska, B., & Rogoff, B. (1988). Influence of adult and peer collaborators on children's planning skills. *Developmental Psychology, 24,* 840–848.

Rogoff, B. (1990). *Apprenticeship in thinking: Cognitive development in social context.* Oxford & New York: Oxford University Press.

Schunk, D. H. (1987). Self-efficacy and motivated learning. In N. Hastings & J. Schwieso (Eds.), *New directions in educational psychology: Behavior and motivation in the classroom* (pp. 233–252). London & New York: Falmer Press.

Schunk, D. H., & Zimmermann, B. J. (Eds.). (1994). *Self-regulation of learning and performance.* Hillsdale, NJ: Lawrence Erlbaum Associates.

Sharpley, A. M., & Sharpley, C. F. (1981). Peer tutoring: A review of the literature. *Collected Original Resources in Education, 5*(3), 7–C11.

Slavin, R. E. (1990). *Co-operative learning: Theory, research and practice.* Englewood Cliffs, NJ: Prentice Hall.

Sternberg, R. J. (1985). *Beyond I.Q.* Cambridge & New York: Cambridge University Press.

Topping, K. J. (1992). Co-operative learning and peer tutoring: An overview. *The Psychologist, 5,* 151–161.

Tudge, J. R. H., & Rogoff, B. (1989). Peer influences on cognitive development: Piagetian and Vygotskian perspectives. In M. Bornstein, & J. Bruner (Eds.), *Interaction in human development* (pp. 17–40). Hillsdale, NJ: Lawrence Erlbaum Associates.

Van Lehn, K. A., Chi, M. T. H., Baggett, W., & Murray, R. C. (1995). *Progress report: Towards a theory learning during tutoring.* Pittsburgh, PA: Learning Research and Development Center, University of Pittsburgh.

Vygotsky, L. S. (1978). *Mind in society: The development of higher psychological processes.* Cambridge, MA: MIT Press.

Webb, N. M. (1982). Peer interaction and learning in co-operative small groups. *Journal of Educational Psychology, 5*(74), 642–655.

Webb, N. M. (1989). Peer interaction and learning in small groups. *International Journal of Educational Research, 13,* 13–40.

Yager, S., Johnson, D. W., & Johnson, R. T. (1985). Oral discussions, group-to-individual transfer and achievement in cooperative learning groups. *Journal of Educational Psychology, 77,* 60–66.

I

The Basis and Benefits
of Peer-Assisted Learning

2

The Psychoeducational Basis of Peer-Assisted Learning

Hugh Foot
Christine Howe
University of Strathclyde

The educational success of peer-assisted instructional methods is founded
on their capacity for eliciting and combining many elements that are crucial
to the learning process. Not the least of these elements is that students are
likely to be much more active and involved in their own learning: They
work together and learn in pairs or small groups in such a way that their
motivation and attention are greater, their capacity to contribute, question,
and receive feedback is greater and their own learning achievements are
more visible to them.

Different specific peer-based techniques, of course, emphasize different
elements and objectives. Some techniques of small-group learning stress
engagement in the task, exploration of ideas and information, reconstruction and reorganization of information and reflection on what has been
achieved (e.g., Reid, Forrestal, & Cook, 1989). Others stress personal
responsibility for learning, accountability, and positive role interdependence (e.g., Johnson & Johnson, 1991). Others again stress the individualized
and tailored guidance that can be offered for facilitating understanding and
concept acquisition, and for problem-solving and rule-based educational
tasks (e.g., Rogoff, 1990). In essence, these elements of successful learning
strategies through peer interaction stem from two fundamental psychoedu-
cationally based approaches: collaborative learning and peer tutoring.

This chapter outlines what is meant by collaborative learning and peer
tutoring, and focuses on what recent research has had to say about their
effectiveness. The conclusion is drawn that the two traditions are comple-

mentary rather than in any sense contradictory. Taken together, the processes they describe and seek to explain underpin virtually all the PAL techniques currently in educational practice. However, it is equally important to realize that each tradition has spawned a different set of generic techniques, and it is the processes and variables involved in each set that are now to be addressed. Collaborative learning techniques are based on the use of reciprocal relationships; peer tutoring approaches have stressed the complementarity of roles in the learning relationship.

COLLABORATIVE LEARNING

Current psychological research into collaborative learning is itself informed by two previously autonomous strands. The first strand stems ultimately from the theorizing of Piaget (1932), but was developed into an empirical program by Piaget's colleagues Doise and Mugny (1984). A consistent theme within Piaget's theory is that learning depends on *equilibration*, a process involving the reconciliation of conflict between prior and newly experienced beliefs. As such, equilibration implies that students should be provided with beliefs that differ from their existing ones, but which, by virtue of not being too advanced, can be related to these. Thus, there is a clear implication that collaboration between students ought to be productive, so long as beliefs differ and tasks are structured to draw differences out. Piaget noted the implication himself, but did not research it directly.

However, in the late 1970s and early 1980s, Doise and Mugny conducted studies into what they called *sociocognitive conflict*, and these studies were all attempts to bring evidence to bear on Piaget's claims. The majority of Doise and Mugny's studies were centered on Piaget's classic tasks, conservation and spatial transformation (i.e., the famous *three mountains* task) being particular favorites, and hence were somewhat removed from classroom practice. Nevertheless, they set an agenda that led to research in other contexts, starting with social topics such as morality and legality (Berkowitz, Gibbs, & Broughton, 1980; Kruger, 1992; Roy & Howe, 1990) and moving in recent years to standard curriculum subjects including literacy, mathematics, and science (e.g., Howe, Tolmie, & Mackenzie, 1995; Pontecorvo, Paoletti, & Orsolini, 1989; Webb, 1989).

The second strand informing psychological research into collaborative learning stems from work, conducted initially in the United States, into *cooperative learning* (CL). Cooperative learning is probably best characterized in terms of the following defining features:

1. Students work in teams toward the attainment of some superordinate goal.
2. Labor is divided between team members, such that each individual takes responsibility for a different subgoal.
3. Individual contributions are pooled into a composite product to ensure that the goal is reached.

Within that framework, CL programs differ over the extent to which the individual work is undertaken entirely independently, as opposed to being monitored by other team members.

At one extreme, there is the approach taken by Sharan (1984) in which team members work almost completely on their own, preparing reports for the subsequent pooling; at the other, there are programs like Cohen's (1986) that encourage collective planning and team feedback at all stages of the work. Nevertheless, even at its most interactive, CL is inevitably less collaborative than the Piagetian initiatives, and this for Damon and Phelps (1988) was a major point of contrast. They characterize CL as being low to moderate in *mutuality* and the Piagetian work as being high, a distinction which leads them to write as if CL is the poor relation. Nevertheless, even if this is justified as regards immediate impact on learning, it is worth noting that CL mimics more closely the practices that operate in the world of work. Thus, it may provide experiences of considerable longer term value.

When discussing the two strands of work, Damon and Phelps referred to the Piagetian approach as *peer collaboration*, and thus seemed to differentiate collaborative from learning CL. However, their treatment of the strands as points on a dimension serves to obscure any hard-and-fast distinctions and to highlight events during mutual engagement as the important ones to study. Thus, Damon and Phelps' paper may have been a significant factor in the recent tendency to focus on engagement, and to borrow freely from both the Piagetian and the cooperative traditions. The researchers involved in this seeming eclecticism frequently subsume their activities under the term *collaborative learning*, and indeed a key seminar held in Oxford during 1993 and synthesizing the two traditions (see Hoyles & Forman, 1995, for selected papers) was entitled "Collaborative Learning: What Can Children Learn Together—Specific Skills or General Concepts?" Evidence amassed at the seminar pointed to a conclusion that Damon and Phelps seem to have anticipated, that collaborative contexts may be more appropriate for general concepts than specific skills.

Although students can learn skills from other students, tutorial contexts where one student imparts information to another may be more effective for these forms of knowledge than genuine learning together. However, although collaboration between students can be effective when it comes to conceptual learning, effectiveness is not guaranteed. Thus, it is possible to think of collaborations as more or less successful, raising two major issues: (a) characteristics of successful collaborations, and (b) conditions under which they will most likely occur. These issues are reviewed next.

Characteristics of Successful Collaborations

Superficially, it might seem as if collaborations that are successful with regard to the learning of concepts would require that students jointly construct the target concepts while they are working together. For example, joint construction of *density* might seem to be required for successful collaboration over object flotation, and joint construction of *profit* might seem to be required for successful collaboration over economic transaction. In reality, this is unlikely to be the case.

Howe and colleagues (e.g., Howe, Rodgers, & Tolmie, 1990; Howe, Tolmie, & Rodgers, 1992; Tolmie, Howe, Mackenzie, & Greer, 1993) conducted studies where 8- to 12-year-old children worked in foursomes toward the joint interpretation of physical events. These explanations were coded for approximation to concepts in the relevant formal physics (flotation or motion in all cases). Group participants were individually pretested on the relevant physics prior to the group tasks and individually posttested a few weeks afterward. Positive pretest to posttest change provided unmistakable evidence that the children had learned from their collaborative experiences, but this learning cannot have been contingent on joint construction.

First, joint construction was rare, despite the task instructions that stressed it, with group participants frequently asserting their own views in opposition to their partners. Second, concepts that were jointly constructed within the groups were no better on average than concepts that were individually asserted. Third, concepts generated within the groups, whether joint or individual, were often worse than concepts expressed during the pretests, let alone during the posttests. Fourth, there was little relation between within-group concepts and pretest to posttest change.

Faced with these results, Howe and colleagues concluded that whether the target concept is constructed during collaboration is beside the point. Indeed, their results suggested that it did not matter what was constructed during collaboration, for the bulk of the learning was taking place afterward.

In one study, the children were posttested immediately after the group tasks as well as a few weeks later: Immediate posttest performance was indistinguishable from pretest, whereas later posttest performance was markedly better. In another study, there were again two posttests, but this time one was 4 weeks after the group tasks, whereas the other was 11 weeks after. Change from the pretest to the 4-week posttest was positive, but it was far exceeded by change from the 4-week posttest to the 11-week.

However, even though the learning was postcollaborative, other evidence obtained by Howe and colleagues showed that it was still in direct response to the group interaction, and not the product of subsequent research. This led them to construe group interaction as a catalyst toward private reflection and subsequent consolidation, an interpretation that relates to the Piagetian notion of equilibration but is perhaps more specific. However, if group interaction is important and yet not via joint constructions, what features are actually significant and what therefore should teachers be trying to promote? The Howe data point to a form of dialogue that was first highlighted by Berkowitz and Gibbs (1983), and that was referred to by these authors as *operational transacts*.

Operational transacts take reasoning that is expressed in dialogue and transform it in some way; for example with "I think the bottle will float because it's glass" followed by "But it's got water in and that will make it sink." The transformation can involve a justification for disagreement as in the example, but it can also involve a clarification or an elaboration. Operational transacts can lead to joint constructions but this will not necessarily happen: in the example given, the dialogue can progress regardless of whether the merits and demerits of glass and water inside are debated and resolved. Interestingly, operational transacts are consistent with the Piagetian approach in that the debating of differences or sociocognitive conflict should definitely engender them. However, because operational transacts can occur through clarification and elaboration as well as disagreement, they should also be supported by the pooling, feedback, and co-construction emphasized in CL.

Thus, the vitality of the two traditions over a decade or more might reflect their mutual fostering of an essentially similar dialogue function. Certainly, the Howe research and the work of Berkowitz and Gibbs (1983) suggest that operational transacts, no matter what form they take, are central to ensuring that collaborative experiences produce conceptual growth, and there is further evidence to make the same point. Kruger's (1992, 1993) work on moral reasoning and Roy and Howe's (1990) on legal constructs are two specific examples. All in all, it seems legitimate given the research that currently exists to answer the first of the two questions raised previously by saying that successful collaboration can be characterized in terms of transactive dialogue.

Conditions for Successful Collaboration

Considering the conditions under which successful collaboration is most likely to occur, and translating this into the conditions that foster operational transacts, there is an obvious steer toward the Piagetian emphasis on conceptual difference, and the research of Howe and colleagues provides empirical evidence that this is correct. Some of the studies with 8- to 12-year-olds cited previously (i.e., Howe, Rodgers, & Tolmie, 1990; Howe, Tolmie, & Rodgers, 1992) compared groups where all members started with differing conceptions with groups where all members were conceptually similar. Subsequent studies by Howe, Tolmie, and Mackenzie (1995) and Howe, Tolmie, Anderson, and Mackenzie (1992) did this with respectively 12- to 15-year-olds and undergraduates. In all cases, pretest to posttest gain was greater under conditions of conceptual difference.

Given conceptual difference, it did not matter whether some group members were more advanced than others, or whether (as with individuals who believe that glass and water inside are relevant to flotation) group members differed, despite having understanding at much the same level. Thus, although the emphasis on difference provides some warrant for mixed-ability teaching, at least when the task is conceptual, it also goes beyond this. This can be contrasted with peer tutoring, where any ability combination can be successful and where the only requirement is that tutors should be more expert than learners in the task to be tutored. Nevertheless, although the Howe research endorses conceptual differences, one study (Howe, Tolmie, Anderson, & Mackenzie, 1992) suggests that the differences must lie within a broader framework of shared vocabulary and perspective. This may be why studies by Azmitia and Montgomery (1993), Nelson and Aboud (1985), and Newcomb and Brady (1982) showed that collaborations between friends are characterizable by some or all of more expressed differences, more operational transacts, and more conceptual gain than collaborations between mere acquaintances.

The implication is thus that to foster operational transacts, and thereafter conceptual growth, students should be grouped in accordance with both cognitive (conceptual difference) and social (friendship) considerations.

However, it would be wrong to pretend that collaborations between friends who differ conceptually will invariably result in learning. There is no doubt that the nature of the collaborative task exerts considerable influence on the form of dialogue, and hence on its outcome. Unfortunately, there is presently little systematic research into how this occurs. Rather, investigators typically experiment with tasks as part of their pilot work, and opt for the single version that inexplicably seems to work best.

However, a few exceptions were reported by Howe, Tolmie, Greer and Mackenzie (1995) in relation to heat transfer and Tolmie, Howe, Mackenzie, and Greer (1993) in relation to object flotation. Their message is that task features operate in an extremely subtle fashion. Some features, for example controlled versus unsystematic experimentation, were counterproductive in isolation but essential in combination with other features. Other features, such as the formulation of summary rules, were counterproductive in some forms but valuable in others. For instance, it proved very useful to get students to write down the things that are important for heating and cooling/floating and sinking. However, a multiple-choice exercise where students had to choose between statements of the form "X is important for heating and cooling/floating and sinking" and "X does not matter" was worse than nothing. There were suggestions that the latter exercise brought on premature closure that undermined the postgroup reflection. It is, of course, currently unclear how generalizable these results are beyond the domain of physics. Nevertheless, they suggest that more attention must be paid to task than has previously been the case, and this is certainly an area for further research.

PEER TUTORING

Research into peer tutoring is founded firmly on the theorizing of Vygotsky (1962, 1978) who, like Piaget, saw interaction as the key by which learning proceeds. Children are introduced to new patterns of thought and new understandings by engaging in dialogue with others and "internalizing the very communicative procedures that the child experiences when interacting with a peer" (Damon, 1984, p. 334). Learning is thus the outcome of joint cognitive activity becoming internalized and enabling a restructuring of the child's independent cognitive functioning.

Unlike Piaget's emphasis on symmetrical, reciprocal relationships, however, Vygotsky emphasized complementary relationships in which one of the interactants is more knowledgeable and expert than the other and thus able to instruct, guide and encourage his or her partner. Complementary or asymmetrical interactions define the exchanges that Vygotsky saw as occurring within the *zone of proximal development* and stretching the learner to the leading edge of their comprehension. This expert-novice model accepts parent-child, teacher-pupil, and peer interactions all as potentially powerful relationships for intellectual change, as long as the more expert is guiding the less expert. This model of guided learning lies at the heart of peer tutoring, which is a procedure in which children teach tasks (normally academic tasks) to other children, and usually on a one-on-one basis. Most research has focused on tutor-tutee pairings and considered the impact of such tutoring on both participants in the relationship.

It is difficult to challenge Tabacek, McLaughlin, and Howard's (1994) assertion that "peer tutoring has become one of the most soundly documented procedures of our time for facilitating academic and social gains for children" (p. 62). Reviews of the literature on both research and educational practice since the 1960s have implicitly or explicitly confirmed the conclusion that peer tutoring has positive social and cognitive benefits for at least some of the participants (e.g., Gartner, Kohler, & Riessman, 1971; Topping, 1988). Although a few studies may have shown little or no benefits to any of the participants, not one has produced outcomes suggesting a detrimental effect. This is not to imply that peer tutoring is necessarily superior to adult tutoring. Where direct comparisons between adult and child tutors have been made (Schmidt, Arend, van der Kokx, & Boon, 1995; Shute, Foot, & Morgan, 1992), adult tutors sometimes do better. However, as teachers, they do not have time for sustained one-on-one intervention. Educational advocacy is that peer tutoring should never be viewed as a means of replacing the classroom teacher. Rather, it is a means of reinforcing teaching instruction of already partially acquired skills (Tabacek et al., 1994).

Perhaps we should not be too surprised. As indicated, peer tutoring is nearly always offered as direct, face-to-face teaching on a one-on-one basis, and assumes, in accordance with Rogoff's (1986) principle of guided participation, that the tutor has some, albeit sometimes limited, extra knowledge or expertise that the tutee does not possess. Faced with a structured and mutually recognized tutoring situation, what tutor is going to blunder ahead, giving instruction without any realization of the impact that their instruction is having on the tutee? The impressive feature, as will be illustrated shortly, is that even children with mild, and sometimes severe, learning difficulties can gain some benefit as tutors, as well as tutees.

This does, of course, only describe the minimal situation, and much research and theory, especially since the late 1980s, has been aimed at refining and optimizing the tutoring relationship and has sought to extend its useful applications for different tasks, for different populations, and for different contexts.

Building on Vygotsky's theoretical platform, let us therefore review a few of the concepts and variables that are, in large measure, held to be important for shaping the beneficial effects for tutor and for tutee: the social interactional context for learning; the cognitive restructuring that takes place through tutoring; and individual differences.

The Social Interactional Context for Learning

As Glynn (1994) argued, simple behavioral strategies have been used effectively to maintain students' attention in the classroom and to reduce disruptive and off-task behaviors. In a one-on-one teaching relationship, the manipulation of such strategies is relatively easy because each participant in the interaction holds the focused attention of the other, and each one's responses are uniquely contingent on those of the other. Thus, for example, the "pause, prompt, and praise" strategies of Wheldall and Glynn (1988) have been effectively used in reading projects. Other programs involve the specification and display of a few positively stated classroom rules. Researchers (Merrett & Wheldall, 1988, Wheldall & Merrett, 1985) have developed behavioral skills packages for in-service training of primary and secondary schools teachers that operate effectively as whole-school approaches to discipline, and in which an entire school staff can be trained.

However, a behavioral interactionist perspective does not imply the simple application of a set of classroom rules. It is premised on "the social interactional relationships and on reciprocally reinforcing events between learners and teachers which occur in naturally occurring learning contexts" (Glynn, 1994, p. 28). This implies a wider knowledge of human development and communication. The mere implementation of a peer tutoring system acknowledges that learning contexts should provide children with (a) opportunities to initiate learning interactions, (b) performance feedback that is responsive rather than purely corrective, and (c) opportunities for reciprocal gains in skill between learners and teachers. Tutoring effectiveness is substantially related to tutors' actual behavior and how they actually teach. Successful tutoring of a set of rules or procedures can never be a purely mechanical exercise. It necessarily involves skills and sensitivities relating to (a) motivating the tutee, (b) imparting certain principles under-lying the task, and (c) delivering the actual instruction (Foot & Kleinberg, 1993). The importance of adequate tutor training and monitoring is widely recognized (Greer & Polirstock, 1982; LaPlante & Zane, 1994).

The interactive nature of peer tutoring is likely, therefore, to encourage natural language generation, social management skills, and the estab-lishment of friendships, which are fundamental to the development of effective communication.

Cognitive Restructuring

Cognitive benefits of peer tutoring are widely reported (e.g., Annis, 1983; Rekrut, 1994), but probably least well understood. As already outlined for collaborative learning, the very process of generating dialogue, of having one's beliefs and ideas challenged, and of achieving equilibration, is nec-essary for provoking cognitive change. These processes are inevitably integral to the tutoring and learning process, especially when one child is trying to make another understand, thus requiring the use of argument and persuasion. What has only become clear more recently is that the learning and cognitive changes that occur are not necessarily the immediate product of joint constructions and sudden realizations (although these may be elements in some learning), but a more drawn-out process of gradual cognitive change, which depends on postinteractive reflection. Because our knowledge and belief systems are so intertwined, any new insight or piece of knowledge may take time seeping through to be integrated and reconciled with other parts of the knowledge system to which it is related.

Although this may appear a difficult process to research, it is consistent with evidence relating to the training of slow-reading tutors (Houghton & Glynn, 1993). These researchers have shown that slow-reading children can be successfully taught to master one separate component of a tutoring strategy at a time—allowing time for each component to sink in—whereas they may not be able to cope with learning a total tutoring package. As they pointed out, this training approach might lead to the inclusion of children in peer tutoring programs as tutors who were previously excluded on the basis of their inability to learn a total tutoring program in one hit. The implication is clearly that, once triggered, cognitive restructuring is by no means an instantaneous process. Indeed it has to be suitably protracted to be successful, and the difference between normal children and those with learning difficulties might be purely a matter of degree.

Cognitive restructuring considerations are, of course, equally applicable to adult, cross-age, and peer tutors and focus purely on the ingredients of new knowledge that stimulate the reorganization of thinking. The advantage of using students who are peers rather than nonpeers in this process is that there is greater congruence between their cognitive structures (Collier, 1980). This cognitive congruence renders tutors who are specifically peers better able to understand the difficulties encountered by their tutees and equips them to respond in a more adequate manner. These arguments echo the sentiments of Allen (1976) and Bruner (1985) that peers speak the same language and, therefore, find it easier to engage in effective dialogue.

Individual Differences

Accepting the potential benefits to both tutor and tutee in the tutoring relationship, much of the recent research has been devoted to the structuring and composition of PAL in pairs and groups in terms of ability, age, and gender.

Ability.   Riggio, Whatley, and Neale (1994) suggested that high ability students might benefit more from peer tutoring than low ability students, and "the pairing of two low ability students in a peer tutoring paradigm might lead to lesser cognitive gains" (p. 530). However, research by Wiegmann, Dansereau and Patterson (1992) showed that high ability students in CL pairs benefited most from playing the student role, whereas low ability students benefited most from playing the teaching role.

The structuring of student pairs in reciprocal peer tutoring (RPT) is potentially problematic regarding ability because in this paradigm, by definition, students alternately play the role of tutor and tutee. Riggio and his colleagues examined specifically whether university students of high, medium, and low academic ability would benefit to the same extent from engaging in RPT learning strategies. They systematically varied the composition of the pairings through four conditions (low–low, low–high, medium–medium, and high–high) and found that cognitive gains achieved through RPT were relatively unaffected by academic ability level. This makes sense, they argued, because the strength of the technique stems from requiring each student to play the tutor role, and therefore to prepare and teach instructional materials to their partner—processes that are crucial to making cognitive gains. These results suggest that for RPT, at least the composition of pairs need not worry the classroom teacher too much, as any ability combination is likely to achieve some success. For this reason, many would argue that RPT is more robust, consistent, and equitable in its treatment of students than more traditional forms of peer tutoring in which not all students have the opportunity to prepare for and practice the tutor role. In other PAL paradigms, however, the same might not be true. We have already seen previously that ability mix may be more important for collaborative learning.

The question of ability, of course, becomes particularly salient in discussion of the applications of PAL techniques for students with mild and severe learning disability, and there is an increasing body of literature here (Byrd, 1990). Mathes and Fuchs (1994) reviewed the literature on the efficacy of peer tutoring in reading for students with mild disability and concluded that, regardless of setting, students with mild disabilities who participated in peer-tutored reading interventions "made greater reading achievement gains than control students who experienced typical teacher-directed reading instruction without researcher direction" (p. 76). However, peer tutoring was no more effective than one-on-one teacher-led tutoring or teacher-led small-group instruction. Students with disabilities gained most by being paired with normal reading peers or when being allowed to act in the role of tutor (RPT) for some of the time.

More generally, Byrd (1990) reviewed the research on peer tutoring for special education and students with learning difficulties (LD). He reported various advantages for the peer tutoring technique: support for the integration of LD children into mainstream school settings, improved self-esteem and academic achievement, an aid in classroom management, and a reinforcing system for learning. Integrating LD children into normal classroom environments often requires adaptation in the manner in which instruction is delivered (Wolery, Werts, Snyder, & Caldwell, 1994), and the introduction of PAL techniques is an obvious way of ensuring that exceptional learners do not make excessive demands on the teacher's time (Salend, 1990).

In relation to severe learning disabilities, there is also a growing literature that peer tutoring can be effective, largely through the individualized instruction and attention that such students receive (Kamps, Locke, Delquadri, & Hall, 1989). There is often a double challenge here insofar as the student may show aberrant behavior problems as well as acute motivational and learning disability. More longitudinal and case study peer tutoring approaches have shown that compliance to requests can be improved and aberrant behaviors and negative statements can be reduced (Martella, Marchand-Martella, Young, & MacFarlane, 1995).

Age.   Age is of relatively little psychoeducational concern for PAL techniques, as they can be applied successfully at almost any age level. Tabacek et al. (1994) argued that preschool children can play an active role in their own education and cite evidence that PAL increases their active participation and opportunities to respond. Peer tutoring assists young children in developing their cognitive and language skills and their social skills. These investigators showed specifically that even preschool children with disabilities (language and cognitive disabilities and attention deficit hyperactivity disorder) can engage successfully in RPT in order to teach their partners preacademic concepts such as color, shape, and number identifications. Those who learn the tutoring skills most quickly are likely to produce the quickest learning in their tutees. At the other end of the educational spectrum there are increasing applications of PAL techniques in the higher education sector, mainly of the field-study type. There are, for example, long-standing successful applications in the United Kingdom of PAL techniques, as in the British Petroleum (BP) student mentoring and tutoring project and the student tutoring program of the Community Service Volunteers learning together scheme.

Gender.   For most classroom group activities, including computer-based work, teachers may prefer mixed-gender groups: Most collaborative groups are a mix of boys and girls. However, many peer tutoring activities tend typically to involve same gender pairings, perhaps for pragmatic reasons or on the implicit assumption that the students prefer this because of the way they interact in the classroom. Topping and Whiteley (1993) reviewed the relatively sparse literature on gender differences, drawing attention to some of the contradictory findings about the relative efficacy of boys and girls as tutors. One result that does appear to be fairly robust, reflected in their own study of paired reading involving 372 children across seven schools, is that male–male tutoring combinations performed generally well, both from the tutors' and tutees' perspectives. Mixed-gender combinations were better for tutors than for tutees. Girl–girl combinations were better for the tutees than for the tutors. As Topping and Whiteley stated, "the supposition that same-sex pairings are more effective than mixed-sex pairings is clearly a gross over-simplification" (p. 65).

CONCLUSIONS

We have focused on collaborative learning and peer tutoring as the main two generic forms of PAL, and we have endeavored to show that they complement rather than contradict each other. As indicated at the outset, they are essentially the most clearly differentiated, both in theory and in application. Most of the specific techniques covered in subsequent chapters are variations of these themes either in method (e.g., reciprocal peer tutoring) or in practice (e.g., peer counseling). It would not be correct, however, to assume that the manner in which a PAL technique is designed and deployed assigns it automatically and uniquely to the collaborative or tutoring category. The distinction between collaborative learning and peer tutoring and techniques can be sometimes blurred, because the processes that children or students engage in at the point of dialogue can vary substantially. The participants are, at the end of the day, free to choose the interactive mode that suits their needs of the moment. On any given issue, one child may actually have superior knowledge to another; on another given issue that child may actually be equally naive. The children's conversation is likely to slide backward and forward between, on the one hand, an equally contributive but uninformed joint search for a solution to a problem and, on the other hand, a one-sided, assertive homily by one of the interactants.

Such, of course, is the richness of natural conversation. The strength of PAL techniques lies in the very fact that interactants may draw on whatever resource they can pool and share, as and when they need it, no matter from which model of effective communication it derives. This may somewhat ease the anxiety of the classroom teacher confronted with a large array of specific PAL techniques and not quite sure which technique to select for his or her own purposes. As McNeil (1994) argued, teachers act as instructional managers, and they may need to restructure how the partnerships operate to maximize the learning process in any given subject area.

However, such fluctuations in process within an interaction should not obscure the general principle that, at the level of task, it is very likely that different techniques are, generally speaking, suited for different purposes. As mentioned earlier, considerably more research needs to be undertaken to establish the best fit between educational task and appropriate technique. For noncurriculum purposes (e.g., use of PAL for peer counseling, peer education, and peer monitoring) then, the techniques described later in this book may, in a sense, self-evidently meet the requirements for which they are designed. However, it is not necessarily so obvious, when dealing with day-to-day curriculum subjects in the classroom, how best to structure the students' peer-assisted experience. There is some evidence (Damon & Phelps, 1988) that a collaborative learning approach is most suitable for problem-solving tasks and those that involve the manipulation of ideas and understanding of concepts. Our own work (e.g., Howe et al., 1992; Howe, Tolmie, Greer, & Mackenzie, 1995) on the learning of concepts in physics would clearly support this view. By contrast, tasks involving the learning of rules and application of principles, designed more to elaborate the child's repertoire of skills, may be more suited to tutoring approaches (Damon, 1984).

Whatever the optimal choice of PAL technique may be for a particular learning activity, there are a number of clear practical conclusions that can be drawn from the research:

1. Children need preparation and practice if group work is likely to pay dividends, so immediate success should not be expected. In the case of peer tutoring, tutors need some training.
2. The structuring of work groups or tutoring pairs by ability and gender is not a crucial concern and may only have a marginal impact.
3. Successful learning outcomes are correlated with rich interaction; therefore, learners need to be encouraged to talk, deliver instructions, and exchange information and ideas.
4. Interactions need to be managed to ensure that dialogue takes as many forms as possible: This may involve the pooling of information, agreements, questioning, clarification and elaboration, and giving feedback; it may also involve conflict and argument, disagreements, challenging, and defending. Probably a mix of these interaction types is desirable for maximum benefit. Conflict and argument should, however, be focused on issues and problems, and not be personal and destructive.
5. Learners need time and encouragement to reflect on their interactive experience. Much of the cognitive work that stimulates learning comes after the interaction has concluded.

Teachers themselves need to become increasingly involved in designing and implementing PAL techniques. Their enthusiasm for successfully deploying such techniques in the classroom crucially depends on our ability to produce and refine creative learning models.

REFERENCES

Allen, V. L. (1976). *Children as teachers: Theory and research on tutoring.* New York: Academic Press.
Annis, L. F. (1983). The processes and effects of peer tutoring. *Human Learning, 2,* 39–47.

Azmitia, M., & Montgomery, R. (1993). Friendship, transactive dialogues, and the development of scientific reasoning. *Social Development, 2,* 202–221.

Berkowitz, M. W., & Gibbs, J. C. (1983). Measuring the developmental features of moral discussion. *Merrill-Palmer Quarterly, 29,* 399–410.

Berkowitz, M. W., Gibbs, J. C., & Broughton, J. M. (1980). The relation of moral judgment stage disparity to developmental effects of peer dialogues. *Merrill-Palmer Quarterly, 26,* 341–357.

Bruner, J. (1985). Vygotsky: A historical and conceptual perspective. In J. V. Wertsch (Ed.), *Culture, communication and cognition: Vygotskian perspectives.* Cambridge, England: Cambridge University Press.

Byrd, D. E. (1990). Peer tutoring with the learning disabled: A critical review. *Journal of Educational Research, 84,* 115–118.

Cohen, E. G. (1986). *Designing groupwork: Strategies for the heterogeneous classroom.* New York: Teachers College Press.

Collier, G. K. (1980). Peer group learning in higher education: The development of higher order skills. *Studies in Higher Education, 5,* 55–62.

Damon, W. (1984). Peer education: The untapped potential. *Journal of Applied Developmental Psychology, 5,* 331–343.

Damon, W., & Phelps, E. (1988, April). *Three approaches to learning and their educational uses.* Paper presented at American Educational Research Association conference, New Orleans, LA.

Doise, W., & Mugny, G. (1984). *The social development of the intellect.* Oxford: Pergamon.

Foot, H., & Kleinberg, S. (1993). Training children as peer tutors. *Topic (NFER-Nelson), 10*(2), 1–6.

Gartner, A., Kohler, M. C., & Riessman, F. (1971). *Children teach children: Learning by teaching.* New York: Harper & Row.

Glynn, T. (1994). Behavioral intervention strategies in education: Implications for training educational professionals. *Behavior Change, 11,* 27–37.

Greer, R. D., & Polirstock, S. R. (1982). Collateral gains and short-term maintenance in reading and on-task by inner-city adolescents as a function of their use of social reinforcement while tutoring. *Journal of Applied Behavior Analysis, 15,* 123–129.

Houghton, S., & Glynn, T. (1993). Peer tutoring of below average secondary school readers using Pause, Prompt and Praise: The successive introduction of tutoring components. *Behavior Change, 10,* 75–85.

Howe, C. J., Rodgers, C., & Tolmie, A. (1990). Physics in the primary school: Peer interaction and the understanding of floating and sinking. *European Journal of Psychology of Education, V,* 459–475.

Howe, C. J., Tolmie, A., Anderson, A., & Mackenzie, M. (1992). Conceptual knowledge in physics: The role of group interaction in computer-supported teaching. *Learning and Instruction, 2,* 161–183.

Howe, C. J., Tolmie, A., Greer, K., & Mackenzie, M. (1995). Peer collaboration and conceptual growth in physics: Task influences on children's understanding of heating and cooling. *Cognition and Instruction, 13,* 483–503.

Howe, C. J., Tolmie, A., & Mackenzie, M. (1995). Collaborative learning in physics: Some implications for computer design. In C. O'Malley (Ed.), *Computer-supported collaborative learning* (pp. 365–397). Berlin: Springer-Verlag.

Howe, C. J., Tolmie, A., & Rodgers, C. (1992). The acquisition of conceptual knowledge in science by primary school children: Group interaction and the understanding of motion down an inclined plane. *British Journal of Developmental Psychology, 10,* 113–130.

Hoyles, C., & Forman, E. A. (Eds.). (1995). *Processes and products of collaborative problem solving: Some interdisciplinary perspectives.* Mahwah, NJ: Lawrence Erlbaum Associates.

Johnson, D. W., & Johnson, R. (1991). *Learning together and alone: Cooperation, competition and individualization* (3rd ed.). Englewood Cliffs, NJ: Prentice-Hall.

Kamps, D., Locke, P., Delquadri, J., & Hall, R. V. (1989). Increasing academic skills of students with autism using fifth grade peers as tutors. *Education and Treatment of Children, 12,* 38–51.

Kruger, A. C. (1992). The effect of peer and adult-child transactive discussions on moral reasoning. *Merrill-Palmer Quarterly, 38,* 191–211.

Kruger, A. C. (1993). Peer collaboration: Conflict, cooperation or both? *Social Development, 2,* 165–182.

LaPlante, L., & Zane, N. (1994). Partner learning systems. In J. S. Thousand, R. A. Villa, & A. I. Nevin (Eds.), *Creativity and collaborative learning* (pp. 261–273). Baltimore: Paul H. Brookes.

McNeil, M. (1994). Creating powerful partnerships through partner learning. In J. S. Thousand, R. A. Villa, & A. I. Nevin (Eds.). *Creativity and collaborative learning* (pp. 243–259). Baltimore: Paul H. Brookes.

Martella, R. C., Marchand-Martella, N. E., Young, K. R., & MacFarlane, C. A. (1995). Determining the collateral effects of peer tutor training on a student with severe disabilities. *Behavior Modification, 19,* 170–191.

Mathes, P. G., & Fuchs, L. S. (1994). The efficacy of peer tutoring in reading for students with mild disabilities: A best-evidence synthesis. *School Psychology Review, 23,* 59–80.

Merrett, F., & Wheldall, K. (1988). *The behavioural approach to teaching with secondary aged children (BATSAC) training package.* Birmingham: Positive Products.

Nelson, J., & Aboud, F. (1985). The resolution of social conflict between friends. *Child Development, 56,* 1009–1017.

Newcomb, A. F., & Brady, J. E. (1982). Mutuality in boys' friendship relations. *Child Development, 53,* 393–395.

Piaget, J. (1932). *The moral judgment of the child.* London: Routledge & Kegan Paul.

Pontecorvo, C., Paoletti, G., & Orsolini, M. (1989). Use of the computer and social interaction in a language curriculum. *Golem, 5,* 12–14.

Reid, J., Forrestal, P., & Cook, J. (1989). *Small group learning in the classroom.* Scarborough, Australia: Chalkface Press; Portsmouth, NH: Heinemann.

Rekrut, M. D. (1994). Teaching to learn: Strategy utilization through peer tutoring. *High School Journal, 77,* 304–314.

Riggio, R. E., Whatley, M. A., & Neale, P. (1994). Effects of student academic ability on cognitive gains using reciprocal peer tutoring. *Journal of Social Behavior and Personality, 9,* 529–542.

Rogoff, B. (1986). Adult assistance of children's learning. In T. E. Raphael (Ed.), *Contexts of school based literacy.* New York: Random House.

Rogoff, B. (1990). *Apprenticeship in thinking: Cognitive development in social contexts.* New York: Oxford University Press.

Roy, A. W. N., & Howe, C. J. (1990). Effects of cognitive conflict, socio-cognitive conflict and imitation on children's socio-legal thinking. *European Journal of Social Psychology, 20,* 241–252.

Salend, S. (1990). *Effective mainstreaming.* New York: Macmillan.

Schmidt, H., Arend, A., van der Kokx, I., & Boon, L. (1995). Peer versus staff tutoring in problem based learning. *Instructional Science, 22,* 279–285.

Sharan, S. (1984). *Cooperative learning.* Hillsdale, NJ: Lawrence Erlbaum Associates.

Shute, R. H., Foot, H. C., & Morgan, M. J. (1992). The sensitivity of children and adults as tutors. *Educational Studies, 18,* 21–36.

Tabacek, D. A., McLaughlin, T. F., & Howard, V. F. (1994). Teaching preschool children with disabilities tutoring skills: Effects on preacademic behaviors. *Child and Family Behavior Therapy, 16,* 43–63.

Tolmie, A., Howe, C. J., Mackenzie, M., & Greer, K. (1993). Task design as an influence on dialogue and learning: Primary school group work with object flotation. *Social Development, 2,* 183–201.

Topping, K. (1988). *The peer tutoring handbook: Promoting co-operative learning.* London: Croom Helm.

Topping, K., & Whiteley, M. (1993). Sex differences in the effectiveness of peer tutoring. *School Psychology International, 14,* 57–67.

Vygotsky, L. S. (1962). *Thought and language.* Cambridge, MA: MIT Press.

Vygotsky, L. S. (1978). *Mind in society.* Cambridge, MA: Harvard University Press.

Webb, N. (1989). Peer interaction and learning in small groups. *International Journal of Educational Research, 13,* 21–39.

Wheldall, K., & Glynn, T. (1988). Contingencies in contexts: A behavioral interactionist perspective in education. *Educational Psychology, 8,* 5–19.

Wheldall, K., & Merrett, F. (1985). *The behavioural approach to teaching package for use in primary and middle schools (BATPAC).* Birmingham: Positive Products.

Wiegmann, D. A., Dansereau, D. F., & Patterson, M. E. (1992). Cooperative learning: Effects of role-playing and ability on performance. *Journal of Experimental Education, 60,* 109–116.

Wolery, M., Werts, M. G., Snyder, E. D., & Caldwell, N. K. (1994). Efficacy of constant time delay implemented by peer tutors in general education classrooms. *Journal of Behavioral Education, 4,* 415–436.

Advantages and Disadvantages of Peer-Assisted Learning Strategies

Larry Maheady
State University of New York, College at Fredonia

Teaching is more difficult in the 1990s than in the past, and most educators predict that it will become even more challenging in years to come. Exponential increases within the school curriculum, spectacular changes in student demographic characteristics (Hodgkinson, 1991), and dwindling instructional resources make it extremely difficult for even the most responsive teachers to provide a high quality education for all children in their classrooms (Miller, Barbetta, & Heron, 1994). For most teachers, there simply is not enough time in the day to meet all of their students' instructional and emotional needs. Ironically, whereas teachers have searched for more effective strategies to cope with these escalating instructional demands, many may have overlooked one potentially powerful educational resource immediately at their disposal: the children seated in front of them. Children can serve as powerful instructional resources for one another, and the systematic use of peers as teaching assistants offers a viable instructional option for meeting many of the daily educational challenges that will confront teachers in the future.

This chapter focuses specifically on the advantages and disadvantages of peer-assisted learning (PAL) approaches. Here, PAL refers to a set of alternative teaching arrangements in which students serve as instructional assistants for classmates and/or other children (Maheady, Harper, & Mallette, 1991). Peer teaching roles can be either direct or indirect in nature and can focus on fellow students' academic and/or social behavior (Kalfus, 1984). Two general PAL approaches, cooperative learning (CL) and peer tutoring, have emerged as particularly appealing instructional alternatives for 21st-century classrooms (e.g., Delquadri, Greenwood, Whorton, Carta, & Hall, 1986; Johnson & Johnson, 1989; Slavin, 1990a). In this chapter, I first describe the major advantages associated with using such PAL approaches at three distinct, but interrelated levels — the child, teacher, and system. This is followed by a description of some potential disadvantages that may accrue from the use of peer teaching arrangements. Such concerns may be conceptual, procedural, or organizational in nature, and each lends itself to differing levels of intervention. The pros and cons associated with the use of PAL approaches are summarized in tabular fashion, and an action checklist is provided to guide implementation efforts.

Before proceeding, however, a few caveats are in order. First, the literature review is intended to be illustrative rather than exhaustive. Primary focus is on peer teaching approaches that have been used with school-aged populations of students enrolled in general, remedial, and special education classrooms. Moreover, these peer teaching applications concentrate mainly on basic academic skill development (i.e., reading, spelling, math), as well as the acquisition, retention, and application of factual knowledge in content area courses (e.g., social studies, science, health, foreign languages, and English).

Many other similarly effective peer teaching approaches are available for those interested in working on higher order cognitive development (e.g., Davidson, 1994; Palincsar & Brown, 1984), and/or using these procedures with more severely challenged youngsters at either the preschool (Odom, McConnell, & McEvoy, 1992) or young adult (Gaylord-Ross & Haring, 1987) levels. Second, comments are directed primarily to those peer teaching procedures with which I have had the most direct contact and experience. As such, classwide peer tutoring (CWPT) programs are described, as well as some selected types of CL arrangements (i.e., simple structures, jigsaw, and group investigation). Third, the discussion of advantages and disadvantages is a mixture of both research and practice. Databased reviews are supplemented with anecdotal reports and daily observations of pupils working in small learning groups at both the elementary and secondary levels. Finally, the analysis of the relative advantages and disadvantages of PAL must be tempered somewhat by the fact that very few direct comparisons have been made in the literature between peer teaching and other comparable instructional approaches such as teacher-led and/or student-regulated instruction (Greenwood, Terry, Delquadri, Elliott, & Arreaga-Mayer, 1995). Instead, most empirical studies have compared total instructional systems in which the mediator (i.e., peer vs. teacher) plus other components of instructional practice (e.g., the sequencing of the curriculum, error correction, and reinforcement) have been contrasted simultaneously. Therefore, it is difficult to identify clearly the specific contribution of just peer or teacher roles in most empirical investigations (Greenwood et al., 1995).

ADVANTAGES OF PAL APPROACHES

Two distinct and rather extensive lines of empirical research (i.e., CL and peer tutoring) speak to the relative advantages of PAL over other forms of instructional intervention. The first, CL, provides a large database consisting of more than 600 empirical studies and at least 6 comprehensive literature reviews (Johnson & Johnson, 1989; Johnson, Johnson, & Maruyama, 1983; Johnson, Maruyama, Johnson, Nelson, & Skon, 1981; Newmann & Thompson, 1987; Slavin, 1983, 1990a). The general consensus across all reviews is that CL can, and usually does, produce positive student outcomes in three primary domains: academic achievement, interpersonal attraction, and personal–social development. The second research line, peer tutoring, is equally as extensive and provides additional support for the instructional superiority of PAL strategies (e.g., Bennett, 1986; Bloom, 1984; Cohen, Kulik, & Kulik, 1982). Following is a brief summary of the purported advantages from each research domain, and a comprehensive listing and discussion of the collective advantages associated with their use is included.

Educational Advantages Associated with the Use of CL Approaches

Interestingly, most CL research has not focused primarily on the advantages of using peer-assisted over teacher-led or student-regulated instructional methods. Instead, the majority of empirical studies in this literature compared the effects of three distinct teaching–learning conditions: cooperative versus competitive versus individualistic goal and reward structures. (It is generally assumed that classroom teachers are the primary mediators of instruction within their own classrooms, and that they utilize either competitive, cooperative, or individualistic goal and reward structures.) The effects of these three, varied instructional conditions were compared on a plethora of student outcome measures at all school-age levels, in almost every curriculum area, and with substantially diverse populations of pupils from many different countries (see e.g., Johnson & Johnson, 1994; Qin,

Johnson, & Johnson, 1995; Slavin, 1990a). As noted earlier, this extensive database indicates that CL typically produces higher levels of academic achievement, improved interpersonal relationships among students, and greater personal and social development than either competitive or individualistic instructional conditions.

Regarding academic achievement, Johnson and Johnson (1994) noted more specifically that the use of CL "resulted in more higher level reasoning, more frequent generation of new ideas and solutions (i.e., process gain), and greater transfer of what is learned within one situation to another (i.e., group-to-individual transfer) than did competitive or individualistic learning" (p. 38). In the interpersonal domain, Johnson and Johnson (1994), among others, noted that the use of CL also promotes constructive relationships and positive attitudes among heterogeneous groups of students, an important and long-standing goal of most, if not all, school systems. Students reportedly like one another better, are more accepting of individual differences (e.g., cultural, racial, linguistic, and exceptionality based), and increase their frequencies of positive social interactions both within and outside of the classroom when they are engaged in CL arrangements. Finally, Slavin (1990a), as well as Johnson and Johnson (1994), noted that the use of CL typically has a powerful impact on students' personal and social development. They reported, for example, that students' self-esteem and feelings of self-worth are enhanced greatly through their involvement in CL, as opposed to competitive and individualistic, learning conditions. Slavin (1990a) noted further that it is somewhat surprising that a relatively brief exposure to CL (e.g., a few weeks or months in one or two classes) could fundamentally change a student's self-esteem. On the other hand, he observed that, "two of the most important components of students' self-esteem are the feeling that they are well liked by their peers and the feeling that they are doing well academically" (p. 44). Because CL has been shown to affect both domains consistently and positively, it may not be so surprising to find that students feel much better about themselves as individuals.

EDUCATIONAL ADVANTAGES ASSOCIATED WITH PEER TUTORING PROGRAMS

Generally, the peer tutoring literature has mirrored the powerful effects that children can exert on the academic and interpersonal development of their classmates and/or other students. Bloom (1984) noted, for example, that one-on-one tutoring by a fully skilled peer was more effective than both conventional (i.e., teachers' lecturing) and mastery learning (i.e., student-regulated) methods of teaching. Across several replications of academic content and student age levels, Bloom (1984) reported that peer tutoring programs produced effect sizes on the order of 2 standard deviations above the mean of the control group (i.e., students receiving conventional lecture-based instruction), compared with 1.3 standard deviations for mastery learning. (Effect sizes larger than .25 of 1 standard deviation were described as educationally significant.) Slavin (1990b) concluded similarly that, "one-to-one tutoring is the most effective form of instruction known" (p. 44). It should be noted as well that peer tutoring programs have demonstrated their significant academic benefits when utilized on a same-age (Cohen et al., 1982), cross-age (Osguthorpe & Scruggs, 1986), and classwide (Fuchs, Fuchs, Mathes, & Simmons, 1997; Greenwood, Carta, & Maheady, 1991) basis. Equally impressive is the fact that many empirical investigations have documented that mutual benefits accrue from the systematic use of peer tutoring programs. That is, children who serve as tutors often make academic gains comparable to those who receive tutorial assistance (e.g., Chiang, Thorpe, & Darch, 1980; Miller et al., 1994).

An emerging body of evidence suggests that social and interpersonal benefits may also result from the use of peer tutoring programs. For example, students engaged in peer tutoring reportedly increased their frequencies of positive social interactions (Franca, Kerr, Reitz, & Lambert, 1990; Maheady & Sainato, 1985), reduced their levels of inappropriate behavior (Folio & Norman, 1981), significantly decreased truancy and tardiness rates (Lazerson, Foster, Brown, & Hummel, 1988), and shown improved self-concepts and attitudes toward school, as well as enhanced racial relations (Jenkins & Jenkins, 1981). Other studies have found that students involved in a CWPT program consistently reported that others liked them more, thought they were smarter, and were more friendly to them in nontutoring settings (e.g., Maheady, Harper, Mallette, & Winstanley, 1991; Maheady, Sacca, & Harper, 1988). There is also some evidence to suggest that peer tutoring may be a cost-effective instructional intervention. Levin, Glass, and Meister (1984) noted, for example, that tutoring programs produced the greatest gain in achievement per dollar spent than three well-known reform strategies: reduced class size, computer-assisted instruction, and a longer school day.

Finally, Greenwood and his colleagues (1995) identified at least seven additional advantages to PAL over more traditional educational approaches. They noted that, in general, peer teaching programs (a) create more favorable pupil–teacher ratios, (b) increase pupils' time on-task, (c) offer students more opportunities to respond, (d) increase the opportunity for and immediacy of error corrections, (e) enhance student motivation, (f) increase students' opportunities for receiving individualized help and encouragement, and (g) provide a functional context for students to learn to work collaboratively with others toward a common instructional goal. Miller et al. (1994) and Fuchs et al. (1997) argued as well that PAL approaches provided on a classwide basis may serve as useful vehicles for individualizing instruction on a whole group basis, and simultaneously accommodating more cultural, linguistic, and instructional diversity within a common setting (e.g., general education classroom).

COLLECTIVE ADVANTAGES TO THE USE OF PAL

To synthesize and illuminate the potential advantages of using PAL strategies, a tabular presentation of benefits at the student, teacher, and system levels is offered in Table 3.1.

As seen in Table 3.1, PAL offers students, teachers, and school systems some distinct advantages over more conventional forms of teacher-led instruction. At the student level, children are provided with a set of instructional experiences that may simultaneously improve their academic achievement and interpersonal relationships, increase their feelings of self-worth, and create a more positive learning environment. Perhaps the greatest advantage for children, however, is that peer teaching methods seem to make learning more fun and exciting. After observing students of all ages working collaboratively with partners or in small teams over the years, it remains amazing how energized they become with the process and subject matter. They discuss, debate, question, clarify, and quiz one another in their attempts to learn and share newly acquired knowledge and skills. This stands in stark contrast to their behavior and engagement levels during teacher-led and independent seatwork activities. To a large extent, peer teaching arrangements allow students to engage in many of the behaviors they so much enjoy (e.g., talking with peers, playing instructional games, and receiving recognition for their academic efforts).

PAL also provides classroom teachers with a number of advantages over more conventional instructional approaches. First, these programs offer teachers a variety of ways to individualize instruction without imposing a constant demand on their time (e.g., Ehly & Larson, 1980; Miller et al., 1994). Similarly, PAL strategies provide teachers with additional ways to plan, deliver, and evaluate their instruction. At the very least, peer teaching procedures should expand most teachers' instructional repertoires, an im-

TABLE 3.1
**Purported Advantages of PAL Over Traditional Teacher-Led Instructional Approaches Across
Student, Teacher, and System Levels**

Teaching Factor–Educational Outcome

Student Level

Higher academic achievement

- standardized achievement tests
- curriculum-specific measures
- higher levels of cognitive reasoning
- more frequent generation of new ideas and solutions
- greater transfer of learning across time and settings

Improved interpersonal relationships

- increased liking among students
- more acceptance of individual differences (i.e., racial, cultural, linguistic and exceptionality-based groups)
- more frequent positive social interactions within and outside of school

Enhanced personal and social development

- more positive self-concepts and feelings of self-worth
- more favorable attitudes toward school, learning, and specific academic disciplines

More positive learning environment

- more favorable pupil–teacher ratios
- increased amounts of active student engagement
- more frequent opportunities to respond
- more frequent and immediate feedback on academic performance (i.e. both corrective and positive feedback)
- increased opportunities for assistance and support

Motivation

- preferred teaching arrangement over teacher-led or student-regulated options
- more fun and increased opportunities to socialize with peers

Teacher Level

Instructional

- procedures for individualizing instruction without constant demands on teacher time
- techniques for expanding one's instructional repertoire
- strategies designed to accommodate diverse learning groups
- approaches for facilitating academic integration of students from special and remedial education settings (e.g., inclusion and mainstreaming)
- increased opportunities to observe and monitor individual student performance

Classroom management

- strategies for teaching new, socially appropriate classroom behavior
- procedures for reducing inappropriate academic and interpersonal behavior

Training and implementation requirements

- initially high effort for "start up," low to moderate maintenance efforts
- relatively explicit and non-time consuming training requirements
- low to moderate curriculum adaptations required

- strategies can be utilized in multiple curriculum areas
- relatively cost effective

System Level
- comprehensive set of strategies for enhancing student achievement
- collection of interventions for facilitating inclusion, improving general classroom discipline, and preventing academic failure
- procedures for enhancing faculty's instructional capacity
- vehicle for promoting educational reforms (e.g., inclusion, merger of special and general education programs)
- cost effective instructional interventions

portant professional development outcome in and of itself. What is particularly intriguing about peer teaching options is that they appear to be unusually effective with heterogeneous learning groups (Fuchs et al., 1997) and can be used to affect academic and behavioral change simultaneously. As such, they may serve as effective strategies for the following:

1. Facilitating mainstreaming and inclusion of children with special learning needs into general education classrooms (e.g., Bell, Young, Blair, & Nelson, 1990; Kamps, Barbetta, Leonard, & Delquadri, 1994).
2. Enhancing racial relations within schools (e.g., Oakes, 1995).
3. Accommodating the increasing range of diversity found in typical classroom settings (e.g., Jenkins, Jewell, Leceister, Jenkins, & Troutner, 1990).
4. Improving student discipline in a proactive and positive manner (Greenwood, Carta, & Hall, 1988).

Third, PAL provides teachers with more opportunities to observe, evaluate, and provide feedback to their students' regarding their academic and interpersonal performance. In contrast to traditional stand-and-deliver instructional approaches, classroom teachers can move readily among their students, listen and watch as they work, and offer support and direction for their instructional efforts. Finally, peer teaching methods may provide classroom teachers with a set of efficient and socially acceptable instructional options. Experience suggests, for example, that most peer teaching strategies can be implemented in a feasible manner (i.e., no excessive demands on teacher time and effort), and that pupils generally prefer such approaches over both teacher-led and student-led instructional methods.

When applied systematically, PAL can also offer school systems some distinct educational advantages. First, any school system should function more effectively if a greater proportion of its teachers are using more powerful academic interventions. PAL strategies provide school systems with validated sets of instructional practices that can be applied to remediate existing learning difficulties, and perhaps more importantly, to prevent future academic and behavioral failure (e.g., Delquadri & Elliot, 1990; Greenwood et al., 1988). Moreover, if school systems can infuse PAL principles and practices into their ongoing professional development activities (e.g., collaborative professional development, peer coaching, and mentoring), then one might reasonably expect exponential increases in professionals' instructional competence.

Second, the systematic implementation of PAL approaches may assist school systems in their ongoing educational reform efforts. It was noted earlier, for example, that peer teaching strategies may be particularly useful in facilitating mainstreaming and inclusionary practices, enhancing ethnic and racial relationships, and improving student discipline. All three issues are at the forefront of debate within general and special education reform. The latter outcome, enhanced student discipline, is particularly significant given the escalating nature of aggression and violence in our schools. Schools must utilize proactive, instructive, and positive types of interventions if they are to substantially improve discipline within our schools (Rhode, Jenson, & Reavis, 1992). It is argued that PAL approaches are particularly well suited vehicles for delivering such services. Finally, peer teaching approaches may be especially appealing at the system level in terms of their cost effectiveness. At a time when school systems are hard-pressed to find the necessary fiscal resources to deliver high quality instruction to all children, peer teaching methods offer a cost-efficient, yet effective, service delivery option.

DISADVANTAGES OF PAL APPROACHES

Given the rather extensive list of advantages associated with the use of peer teaching methods, one might inadvertently assume that there are no drawbacks to their use. Here, six specific concerns that have been raised about PAL are discussed and some possible areas for intervention are offered. Specific concerns and/or potential disadvantages are outlined in Table 3.2.

Ironically, many disadvantages inherent in the use of PAL strategies may stem largely from attempts to use them systematically. For example, Greenwood et al. (1995) argued persuasively that the most effective peer teaching methods are those that systematically train students in their teaching roles and then monitor the ongoing accuracy and effectiveness of their implementation. Unfortunately, systematic peer training and ongoing evaluation and monitoring require additional time, a demand not present in teacher-led instruction. Unless teachers are prepared for these additional time demands,

TABLE 3.2
Purported Disadvantages of PAL Strategies Compared to Teacher-Led Instruction

Teaching Factor/Educational Outcome	Mediator	
	Teacher	Peer
Peer training requirements	Few	Many
Quality control requirement	Few	Many
Content coverage	Good	Variable
Curriculum adaptations	Few	Variable
Ethical concerns	Few	Increased
Theoretical concerns about appropriateness and effectiveness	Few	Increased

they may not persist in their efforts to implement peer teaching programs. Specific start-up costs are most noticeable and include additional planning time, material development demands, initial teacher and pupil training, ongoing consultation with other users, and monitoring of program effects. Teachers should be informed in advance that most additional time demands will be present during start-up time, and that the overall advantages to the use of these methods will generally outweigh the initial costs (Greenwood et al., 1995; Miller et al., 1994). Other suggestions would be to help teachers develop all necessary materials for initial implementation prior to peer training activities, and assisting teachers in their initial attempts to use selected strategies.

Maintaining quality control of peer teaching procedures may also present some distinct challenges for classroom teachers. For example, teachers must move about the classroom and observe peer teaching interactions, collect ongoing measures of students' academic performance (e.g., oral reading rates, weekly quiz scores), and review pupil work products (e.g., written work, daily point earning) in order to ensure high quality implementation. These activities are essential to the success of PAL, yet may not be as prevalent during teacher-led instruction. The literature is quite clear in noting, however, that many peer teaching procedures fail because of poor student and/or teacher implementation. If teachers fail to monitor student use of instructional procedures, then critical procedural components may be omitted, incorrect student responding may go undetected, classroom disruptions may occur, and student cheating may arise (Maheady et al., 1991). Once more, teachers must be prepared for the additional time demands required to maintain accuracy in the use of peer teaching methods. Special procedures can also be developed for reducing time demands on teachers by enlisting student assistance in ongoing data collection, using random selection of student products for ongoing monitoring, and establishing reinforcement contingencies for high levels of implementation accuracy.

A third potential disadvantage associated with the use of PAL has to do with the amount of content coverage possible during teacher-led versus peer teaching methods. Interestingly, the literature has been relatively silent on this issue, an issue that holds rather high interest among many teachers and school administrators. At a very basic level, some practitioners have argued that peer teaching methods slow down the pace at which new content can be introduced and covered. Given the excessive demands placed on many teachers to cover all the material within prespecified time periods, this concern takes on added importance. Experience suggests that some teachers have more difficulty with instructional pacing during peer teaching activities (i.e., mostly because peer learning, not teacher presentation, will dictate the instructional pace). However, what may be lost in breadth of coverage can certainly be offset by depth and mastery of new student learning.

Perhaps by focusing student learning on mastery of critical curricular concepts and principles (i.e., big ideas) as opposed to isolated facts, many pacing concerns can be reconciled. In any event, the impact of PAL on content coverage appears to be a viable domain for future empirical inquiry. A fourth related disadvantage has to do with required adaptations to curricular materials. The only commercially available curricula designed for use within a PAL approach appears to be those contained in student team learning programs (Slavin, 1990a). Here, teachers have both materials and procedures necessary to begin using peer teaching on a daily basis. Most other programs, however, require teachers to adapt their classroom objectives and materials somewhat in order to fit a peer teaching format. It should be noted, however, that this is not often a difficult task because most peer teaching methods are highly adaptable to existing objectives and materials (Fuchs et al., 1997; Greenwood et al., 1995). Yet, the additional demands associated with using a peer-led rather than teacher-led format must be recognized and addressed in a proactive manner.

The use of PAL strategies also raises three areas of ethical concern not necessarily present during conventional teacher-led instruction. These include accountability, peer competence, and informed consent (Greenwood et al., 1995). Regarding accountability, procedures must be developed and implemented to ensure that all students (e.g., tutors as well as tutees) benefit from peer teaching methods, and that no one is affected negatively. Highly skilled students, for example, should not be short changed by frequent tutoring assignments (with lower level materials) that reduce their opportunity to learn more challenging content. Similarly, lower skilled learners should not be stigmatized by always being a tutee or lower ability learner in a peer teaching program. Regarding peer teaching competence, one must ensure that tutors are trained properly to carry out their instructional roles effectively and efficiently. Failure to prepare peers adequately may place them at risk in terms of receiving negative reactions or overt rejections from their classmates (as well as classmates' parents and administrators).

Finally, it is recommended that informed consent be obtained prior to involving students in ongoing peer teaching programs. Participants and their parents must be told exactly what will be required of them, as well as the possible effects that their assistance may have on their relationship with other students. For example, some have suggested that lower skilled students in CL groups may receive undue peer pressure to improve their academic performance in order to enhance overall team scores, or that high ability students may reduce their contributions if they perceive that others are not pulling their weight (Cosden & Haring, 1992). Furthermore, it is important that pupils have the opportunity to decide not to participate if they find it difficult or aversive. Indeed, the prospect of forcing students to work cooperatively does not conure up favorable impressions in most educators' minds.

A sixth potential disadvantage to the use of PAL appears to stem from some generalized misperceptions about the role or function of such instructional activities. For example, some educators and parents have argued that students do not come to school to be teachers, and that undue reliance on peer teaching methods will somehow impede their children's opportunities to make sufficient progress on more relevant curricular activities. Others have suggested that peer teaching methods may not even be effective for certain special student populations (e.g., learning disabled, gifted and talented, and the physically impaired; e.g., Cosden & Haring, 1992; Lloyd, Crawley, Kohler, & Strain, 1988; Tateyama-Sniezek, 1990). Obviously, any type of instructional intervention is open to misapplication (e.g., assigning students to peer teams with inappropriate academic objectives, failing to prepare students adequately, omitting critical procedural components outlined by developers), and there is a distinct need for additional research on the impact of peer teaching methods on children with special learning needs. However, the assumption that children are not learning while they are engaged in peer teaching activities is simply erroneous. Educators, of all people, should recognize the powerful impact that teaching others has had on their own learning.

POTENTIAL APPLICATIONS OF PAL

If one is convinced that the use of PAL is an acceptable set of instructional options, then the next step is to address a set of questions that revolve around how to implement these procedures in an effective and efficient manner: Which peer teaching methods should be used? When, where, and for how long should a particular approach be used? How should a peer teaching program be set up, implemented, and evaluated? What should be done, if and when, problems do arise? In this final section, these implementation concerns are addressed and some general recommendations are offered for facilitating one's use of such procedure. A 20-item action checklist has been included in Table 3.3 to guide educators' implementation efforts in this regard.

SELECTING PAL APPROACHES

Educators have a number of instructional options to select from in both the peer tutoring and CL literatures. Only a few of these alternatives were discussed in this particular chapter. Perhaps the best rule of thumb is to select a peer teaching approach that is consistent with one's existing instructional goals and objectives. For example, if the goal is to develop student fluency in basic academic skills (e.g., oral reading fluency, math computational skills, and/or spelling), then the Juniper Gardens CWPT program (Delquadri et al., 1986), cross-age (Osguthorpe & Scruggs, 1986), and/or same-age (Cohen et al., 1982) tutoring formats would be most appropriate.

Similarly, if the goal is to find a comprehensive peer teaching approach in the area of reading that combines elements of oral reading fluency and student comprehension (i.e., Grades 1-6), then the Peabody CWPT may be quite suitable (Fuchs & Fuchs, 1992–1993). If, on the other hand, one were interested in teaching students to reach consensus on controversial issues, settle disputes in a nonaggressive manner, discuss thoughts, feelings, and/or values, and share content-related information in an equitable manner, then the learning together (Johnson & Johnson, 1989) or information-sharing strategies within Kagan's (1992) structural approach to CL would be most relevant. The important point is that one select strategies that match their instructional goals and objectives.

TABLE 3.3
Action Checklist for Using PAL Strategies

Practitioner Concerns	Yes	No	NA
Selection Criteria			
1. Is the PAL strategy consistent with existing instructional goals and objectives?	____	____	____
2. Does the PAL strategy have empirical evidence to support its effectiveness?	____	____	____
3. Is the PAL strategy feasible to implement under existing classroom conditions?	____	____	____
4. Is PAL something that you and your students will enjoy doing?	____	____	____
Logistical Concerns			
5. When will PAL be used:			
(a) on an ongoing basis as routine part of instruction?	____	____	____
(b) on an "as-needed" basis?	____	____	____
6. Will PAL be used in place of an existing instructional activity?	____	____	____
Implementation Requirements			
7. Have you obtained informed consent for students to participate in PAL strategies?	____	____	____
8. Have you developed procedures to ensure that all students benefit from a PAL program?	____	____	____
9. Have you developed alternative activities for pupils who do not wish to participate?	____	____	____
10. Have you identified and developed instructional materials to be used with PAL?	____	____	____
11. Have you developed a strategy for selecting students and/or assigning them to groups?	____	____	____
12. Have you scheduled time to conduct PAL?	____	____	____
13. Have you scheduled PAL training time?	____	____	____
14. Have you developed training procedures and rationale for using a PAL program?	____	____	____
15. Have you developed strategies to monitor students' performance during PAL?	____	____	____
16. Have you developed strategies to evaluate the effectiveness of PAL?	____	____	____
Problem Solving			
17. Have you developed procedures to minimize student noise levels?	____	____	____
18. Have you developed strategies to deal with student complaints and bickering?	____	____	____
19. Have you develop procedures for recognizing pupils for following PAL procedures?	____	____	____
20. Have you developed strategies to minimize student cheating or point inflation?	____	____	____

cont.

Additional concerns or questions about using PAL:

_____

_____

_____

_____

Additional criteria to use in selecting PAL strategies should include documented effectiveness, procedural efficiency, and social acceptability. Because all peer teaching methods are not equally effective, practitioners must select those methods that have the most empirical support. Similarly, teachers should choose those procedures that are feasible to implement under existing instructional conditions. Material development demands, student training requirements, and ease of daily implementation should be taken into consideration when deciding which approach to use. Finally, teachers should select methods that they and their students will enjoy. If students and teachers do not like selected procedures, it is highly unlikely they will continue to use them. In assessing satisfaction, teachers should consider the general level of agreement with particular program goals, the acceptability of recommended procedures, and their satisfaction with specific outcomes (i.e., academic and interpersonal) produced by that method.

Logistical Considerations

After having identified a particular peer teaching approach, teachers must decide when, to what extent, and for how long the specific procedures should be used. Obviously, when to use PAL should be determined on an individual basis. Some educators may prefer to use peer teaching methods quite often as part of their regular teaching repertoire, whereas others may be more comfortable with their use on an as-needed basis. Certainly, PAL should not be viewed as *the* solution to all the academic and behavioral problems teachers face. Rather, it is a set of instructional options among a variety of teacher-led, student-regulated, and technology-assisted alternatives. The proper balance of instructional practices must be determined to a large extent by the existing needs and interests of individual teachers. Generally, PAL seems to be most appropriate as a set of alternative practice activities that can be used instead of independent seatwork. These procedures are designed to supplant existing instructional arrangements rather than being added on to the litany of things teachers already do. Moreover, it seems reasonable to use many of these peer teaching methods following initial teacher-led instruction. It is not clear empirically or ethically that peers should be involved in the initial instruction of new curricular content.

Determining how much PAL to use and for how long to continue using these approaches are equally important logistical questions. Again, the final decision should be made on an individual basis. Johnson and Johnson (1989) suggested, for example, that their CL approach should be used up to 60% of the school day (Edwards & Stout, 1989–1990). Kagan (1992) recommended using his simple structures approach whenever teachers want their students to work cooperatively rather than competitively or individually. Greenwood et al. (1995) advocated the use of CWPT for 90 minutes per day, 5 days per week at the elementary level, whereas Fuchs and Fuchs (1992–1993) recommend the use of their reading tutoring program for 30 minutes per day, three times each week.

Personal experience suggests that students rarely get tired or bored with peer teaching arrangements. Interestingly, when asked why they did not get tired of a CWPT program that was in effect the entire school year, one secondary student responded, "What's the alternative, working by ourselves or listening to the teacher; and we've been doing that stuff for years." It is thus recommended to use a healthy variety of teacher-led, peer-assisted, student-regulated, and technology-augmented approaches throughout the school year. Ultimately, however, student responsiveness to peer teaching procedures should dictate the frequency with which such approaches are utilized.

Implementation Requirements

Although a considerable amount has been written about the characteristics and effects of using PAL, very little attention has been directed toward ongoing implementation requirements. As noted earlier, using PAL correctly will require additional time and effort, at least initially. One might conceptualize these implementation requirements in terms of three, distinct instructional phases: preparation, actual implementation, and evaluation.

Preparation. Preparation requirements include the development of appropriate instructional materials, the training of teachers and students to use the approach, and the scheduling of activities to fit the existing regularities in the classroom. The amount of preparation time will vary as a function of the complexity of the method selected, how often it will be implemented, and how much existing material can be used. Generally, most peer teaching procedures can be adapted readily to existing curricular materials. In one study examining the implementation requirements associated with using the Juniper Gardens' CWPT program, Maheady et al. (1991) found that teachers perceived planning demands to be comparable to conventional teaching routines. More recently, Fuchs et al. (1997) noted that classroom teachers did not perceive additional time demands associated with the use of their classwide reading tutoring program.

Actual Implementation.   Regarding actual implementation, teachers must consider the amount of time it will take to use PAL on a daily basis. Initial implementation requirements will include minimally (a) a verbal explanation of teaching procedures and their rationale, (b) modeling demonstrations using individuals and the entire class, and (c) role playing with corrective feedback. Once students have been trained, daily implementation requirements will include material distribution and collection, monitoring of student interactions (i.e., moving throughout the classroom), and evaluation of pupil performance (i.e., random monitoring of work products). If daily point earning and tracking is required within the peer teaching program (e.g., CWPT), then these may place additional time demands on ongoing use of the system. Again, the amount of time required to use a particular peer teaching method will vary depending on the complexity of the system, the difficulty level of instructional materials, and the teacher's fluency in carrying out the selected approach. Maheady et al. (1991) reported that, on average, it took about 2 hours for each of eight elementary teachers to use Juniper Gardens CWPT with at least 90% accuracy and no consultant assistance in their own classrooms.

Evaluation.   To ensure that PAL is working, teachers must monitor their students' performance on an ongoing basis. Program evaluation, therefore, is an integral part of the implementation requirements. There does not appear a need for an elaborate evaluation design or process. Rather, teachers can collect ongoing data on naturally occurring student outcomes. For example, as teachers move routinely through the classroom, they can observe the frequency and nature of student interactions. If pupils are off-task, engaged in disruptions or disputes, or are simply refusing to work collaboratively, then some form of intervention is warranted. If, on the other hand, all students are actively engaged in academically relevant behaviors, the teacher can recognize positively the importance of their hard work. By the same token, teachers can randomly select two to three student work products daily to assess the quantity and quality of work being completed.

The collection of naturally occurring, curriculum-specific measures (e.g., weekly quizzes, Friday spelling test scores, and/or oral reading fluency and comprehension rates) on an ongoing basis should also provide sufficient information for teachers, pupils, parents, and administrators to evaluate the effectiveness of peer teaching methods. These data can even be plotted on simple line graphs and contrasted with student performance under teacher-led instruction to assess the comparative effects of these different instructional arrangements. Obviously, poor student performance on ongoing curriculum-specific measures should prompt teachers to intervene immediately. Quite often, careful observations of students during PAL sessions will provide insights into possible remedial strategies.

Problem Solving

Like any other innovative instructional practice, one may encounter problems when implementing PAL strategies. Three common problems encountered include increased noise levels, student complaints about tutoring partners or teammates, and student cheating and point inflation.

Noise Levels. Without question, noise levels within classrooms using peer teaching increase. Part of this noise is simply the result of students being actively engaged in instructional interactions (e.g., reading to one another, questioning partners, providing explanations to teammates' questions), whereas another part may result from student excitement about using these procedures. Increased noise levels can be problematic for those who teach in open space classrooms or settings separated by plastic dividers. The following may aid in controlling noise levels: develop three simple rules (e.g., speak only during the tutoring session, speak only to your partner(s), and use your inside voices), provide reinforcement (e.g., praise, bonus points) for those who comply with rules, and administer a reductive consequence (e.g., time out from reinforcement) for those who fail to comply.

Student Complaints. Student complaints about partners and teammates appear to be more common than many proponents of PAL have inferred. Few classrooms appear to exist in which everyone is perfectly satisfied with their partners and teammates, at least initially. Student complaints are understandable to some extent because peer teaching methods strive to place children in heterogeneous groupings. However, complaints cannot be accepted as legitimate reasons for not working with others. From personal research, student complaining was used as an opportunity to teach pupils (i.e., complainers in particular) that this is an unacceptable social response. Complaints are generally ignored, yet cooperative work is publicly recognized. Occasionally, bonus points (i.e., given in close proximity to complainers) are used to reinforce those who are working cooperatively. Over time, students learn that complaining and bickering does not work, and they typically settle into cooperative working relationships.

Student Cheating.   One final problem that may arise involves student cheating during peer teaching sessions. Quite often, this involves giving answers to teammates, overlooking errors they have made, and/or inflating point totals earned during peer teaching sessions. Frequent random movement throughout the classroom while students work in their teams, ongoing recognition for use of appropriate instructional strategies, and occasional random checking of pupils' work products is usually sufficient to minimize such difficulties.

SUMMARY AND CONCLUSIONS

Most educational experts agree that teaching in tomorrow's schools will be excessively demanding. As such, teachers must be prepared to use classroom-based interventions that can meet effectively the needs of heterogeneous learning groups, and yet be applied in a feasible and socially acceptable manner. It is argued that PAL provides educators with one such set of instructional options. Advantages associated with the use of peer teaching methods were outlined at the child, teacher, and system levels, and potential drawbacks were reviewed. Finally, readers were provided with a 20-item action checklist designed to guide their intervention efforts when they decide to use PAL in their own classrooms.

REFERENCES

Bell, K., Young, K. R., Blair, M., & Nelson, R. (1990). Facilitating mainstreaming of students with behavioral disorders using classwide peer tutoring. *School Psychology Review, 19,* 564–573.
Bennett, W. J. (1986). *Tutoring. What works: Research about teaching and learning. Washington, DC: U.S. Department of Education.*
Bloom, B. S. (1984). The 2 sigma problem: The search for methods of group instruction as effective as one-to-one tutoring. *Educational Researcher, 13,* 4–16.
Chiang, B., Thorpe, W. W., & Darch, C. B. (1980). Effects of cross-age tutoring on word recognition performance of learning disabled students. *Learning Disability Quarterly, 3,* 11–19.

Cohen, P. A., Kulik, J. A., & Kulik, C. L. (1982). Educational outcomes of tutoring. *American Educational Research Journal, 19*, 237–248.

Cosden, M. A., & Haring, T. G. (1992). Cooperative learning in the classroom: Contingencies, group interactions, and students with special needs. *Journal of Behavioral Education, 2*, 53–71.

Davidson, N. (1994). Cooperative and collaborative learning: An integrative perspective. In J. S. Thousand, R. A. Villa, & A. I. Nevin (Eds.), *Creativity and collaborative learning: A practical guide to empowering student and teachers* (pp. 13–30). Baltimore, MD: Paul H. Brookes.

Delquadri, J. C., & Elliot, M. (1990). The effects of the administrative component on the large scale implementation of classwide peer tutoring. In C. R. Greenwood (Chair), *Large scale dissemination of peer mediated intervention procedures: Issues, procedures, and results.* Symposium presented at the 16th Annual Convention of the Association for Behavior Analysis, Nashville, TN.

Delquadri, J. C., Greenwood, C. R., Whorton, D., Carta, J. J., & Hall, R. V. (1986). Classwide peer tutoring. *Exceptional Children, 52*, 535–542.

Edwards, C., & Stout, J. (1989–1990). Cooperative learning: The first year. *Educational Leadership, 47*(4), 38–41.

Ehly, S. W., & Larsen, S. C. (1980). *Peer tutoring for individualized instruction.* Boston: Allyn & Bacon.

Folio, M. R., & Norman, A. (1981). Toward more success in mainstreaming: A peer teacher approach to physical education. *Teaching Exceptional Children, 13*, 110–114.

Franca, V. M., Kerr, M. M., Reitz, A. L., & Lambert, D. (1990). Peer tutoring among behaviorally disordered students: Academic and social benefits to tutor and tutee. *Education and Treatment of Children, 13*, 109–128.

Fuchs, D., & Fuchs, L. S. (1992–1993). *Peabody classwide peer tutoring: Reading methods.* Nashville, TN: Department of Special Education, Peabody College, Vanderbilt University.

Fuchs, D., Fuchs, L. S., Mathes, P. G., & Simmons, D. C. (1997). Peer-assisted learning strategies: Making classrooms more responsive to diversity. *American Educational Research Journal, 34*, 174–206.

Gaylord-Ross, R., & Haring, T. (1987). Social interaction research for adolescents with severe handicaps. *Behavioral Disorders, 12*, 264–275.

Greenwood, C. R., Carta, J. J., & Hall, R. V. (1988). The use of peer tutoring strategies in classroom management and educational instruction. *School Psychology Review, 17*, 258–275.

Greenwood, C. R., Carta, J. J., & Maheady, L. (1991). Peer tutoring programs in the regular education classroom. In G. Stoner, M. R. Shinn, & H. Walker (Eds.), *Interventions for achievement and behavior problems* (pp. 179–200). Washington, DC: National Association of School Psychologists.

Greenwood, C. R., Terry, B., Delquadri, J., Elliott, M., & Arreaga-Mayer, C. (1995). *ClassWide Peer Tutoring (CWPT): Effective teaching and research review.* Kansas City, KS: Juniper Gardens Children's Project, University of Kansas.

Hodgkinson, H. (1991). Reform versus reality. *Phi Delta Kappan, 73*, 9–15.

Jenkins, J. R., & Jenkins, L. M. (1981). *Cross-age and peer tutoring: Help for children with learning problems.* Reston, VA: Council for Exceptional Children.

Jenkins, J. R., Jewell, M., Leceister, N., Jenkins, L., & Troutner, N. (1990). *Development of a school building model for educating handicapped and at risk students in general education classrooms.* Paper presented at the annual meeting of the American Educational Research Association, Boston.

Johnson, D. W., & Johnson, R. T. (1989). *Cooperation and competition: Theory and research.* Edina, MN: Interaction Book Co.

Johnson, R. T., & Johnson, D. W. (1994). An overview of cooperative learning. In J. S. Thousand, R. A. Villa, & A. I. Nevin (Eds.), *Creativity and collaborative learning: A practical guide to empowering student and teachers* (pp. 31–44). Baltimore, MD: Paul H. Brookes.

Johnson, D. W., Johnson, R. T., & Maruyama, G. (1983). Interdependence and interpersonal attraction among heterogeneous and homogeneous individuals: A theoretical formulation and a meta-analysis of the research. *Review of Educational Research, 53*, 5–54.

Johnson, D. W., Maruyama, G., Johnson, R. T., Nelson, D., & Skon, L. (1981). Effects of cooperative, competitive, and individualistic goal structures on achievement: A meta-analysis. *Psychological Bulletin, 89*, 47–62.

Kagan, S. (1992). *Cooperative learning* (9th ed.). San Juan Capistrano, CA: Resources for Teachers, Inc.

Kalfus, G. R. (1984). Peer-mediated instruction: A critical review. *Child Development and Family Behavior Therapy, 6*, 17–43.

Kamps, D. M., Barbetta, P. M., Leonard, B. R., & Delquadri, J. (1994). Classwide peer tutoring: An integration strategy to improve and promote peer interactions among students with autism and general education peers. Special section: Behavior analysis in school psychology. *Journal of Applied Behavior Analysis, 27,* 49–61.

Lazerson, D. B., Foster, H. L., Brown, S. I., & Hummel, J. W. (1988). The effectiveness of cross-age tutoring with truant junior high students with learning disabilities. *Journal of Learning Disabilities, 21,* 253–255.

Levin, H., Glass, G., & Meister, G. (1984). *Cost effectiveness of four educational interventions* (Report No. 84-A11). Stanford, CA: Institute for Research in Educational Finance and Governance, Stanford University.

Lloyd, J., Crawley, E. P., Kohler, F., & Strain, P. S. (1988). Redefining the applied research agenda: Cooperative learning, prereferral, teacher consultation, and peer-mediated intervention. *Journal of Learning Disabilities, 21,* 43–52.

Maheady, L., Harper, G. F., & Mallette, B. (1991). Peer-mediated instruction: A review of potential applications for special education. *Reading, Writing, and Learning Disabilities International, 7*(2), 75–103.

Maheady, L., Harper, G. F., Mallette, B., & Winstanley, N. (1991). Implementation requirements associated with the use of a classwide peer tutoring system. *Education and Treatment of Children, 14*(3), 177–198.

Maheady, L., Sacca, M. K., & Harper, G. F. (1988). Classwide peer tutoring with mildly handicapped high school students. *Exceptional Children, 55,* 52–59.

Maheady, L., & Sainato, D. M. (1985). The effects of peer tutoring upon the social status and social interaction patterns of high and low status elementary students. *Education and Treatment of Children, 8,* 51–65.

Miller, A. D., Barbetta, P. M., & Heron, T. E. (1994). START tutoring: Designing, training, implementing, adapting, and evaluating tutoring programs for school and home settings. In R. Gardner III, D. M. Sainato, J. O. Cooper, T. E. Heron, W. L. Heward, J. Eshleman, & T. A. Grossi (Eds.), *Behavior analysis in education: Focus on measurably superior instruction* (pp. 265–282).

Newmann, F. H., & Thompson, J. (1987). *Effects of cooperative learning on achievement in secondary schools: A summary of research.* Madison, WI: University of Wisconsin, National Center on Effective Secondary Schools.

Oakes, J. (1995). Tracking, diversity, and educational equity: What's new in the research? Revision of paper prepared for the Common Destiny Alliance Consensus Panel meeting, August, 1994. In Fuchs, D., Fuchs, L. S., Mathes, P. G., & Simmons, D. C. (in press). Peer-assisted learning strategies: Making classrooms more responsive to diversity. *American Educational Research Journal.* Belmont, CA: Brooks/Cole.

Odom, S. L., McConnell, S. R., & McEvoy, M. A. (1992). Peer-related social competence and its significance for young children with disabilities. In S. L. Odom, S. R. McConnell, & M. A. McEvoy, (Eds.), *Social competence of young children with disabilities* (pp. 3–35). Baltimore, MD: Paul H. Brookes.

Osguthorpe, R. T., & Scruggs, T. E. (1986). Special education students as tutors: A review and analysis. *Remedial and Special Education, 7*(4), 15–26.

Palincsar, A. M., & Brown, A. L. (1984). Reciprocal teaching of comprehension-fostering and comprehension-monitoring activities. *Cognition and Instruction, 1,* 117–175.

Qin, Z., Johnson, D. W., & Johnson, R. T. (1995). Cooperative versus competitive efforts and problem solving. *Review of Educational Research, 65,* 129–143.

Rhode, G., Jenson, W. R., & Reavis, H. K. (1992). *The tough kid book: Practical classroom management strategies.* Longmont, CO: Sopris West, Inc.

Slavin, R. E. (1983). When does cooperative learning increase student achievement? *Psychological Bulletin, 94,* 429–445.

Slavin, R. E. (1990a). *Cooperative learning: Theory, research, and practice.* Englewood Cliffs, NJ: Prentice-Hall.

Slavin, R. E. (1990b). General education under the Regular Education Initiative: How must it change? *Remedial and Special Education, 11,* 40–50.

Tateyama-Sniezek, K. (1990). Cooperative learning: Does it improve the academic achievement of students with handicaps? *Exceptional Children, 56,* 426–437.

4

Key Considerations in the Design and Implementation of Effective Peer-Assisted Learning Programs

Elaine S. Chapman
University of Sydney, Australia

The peer-assisted learning (PAL) approaches described in this book have been found to produce positive cognitive, social, and affective outcomes over a broad range of target populations (e.g., academically handicapped, socially disadvantaged, regular education students) and settings (e.g., special and regular classes). In general, PAL coordinators will achieve the best results by implementing these procedures as they are described in the ensuing chapters and other published evaluations. However, in order to meet the needs of specific target students or contextual constraints (e.g. on time or resources), it is sometimes necessary to adapt or extend specific components of a selected approach.

As PAL procedures often include a number of potentially active treatment variables, discriminating between optional (i.e., safely alterable) and critical procedural components can be difficult. Failure to do so can lead to unsystematic adaptations, reduced program effects and, ultimately, loss of community or administrative support for use of the approach. To guide practitioners in tailoring PAL procedures to their own circumstances, this chapter highlights design and implementation factors that have been demonstrated empirically to moderate (i.e., alter the direction or magnitude of) PAL program effects.

PEER TUTORING

Of the PAL strategies described in this book, peer tutoring is the most widely researched and disseminated. Support for the use of peer tutoring to improve student learning outcomes derives from a number of diverse sources (e.g., Allen, 1976; Bargh & Schul, 1980; Cohen, 1986; Vygotsky, 1978; and see chaps. 2 and 3, this volume). On the whole, the research suggests that effective tutoring procedures are those in which carefully matched students are trained, supervised, and motivated to engage in high-quality interactions on suitably challenging academic tasks.

Participant Selection, Matching, and Role Assignment

Although research on the relationship between social composition factors and tutoring outcomes has generally produced inconsistent results (e.g., Sharpley & Sharpley, 1981), there is some evidence to suggest that low achievers make greater learning gains in mixed-ability pairs (Tudge & Rogoff, 1989). For example, Jones and Carter (1994) found that low-achieving fifth-graders who collaborated with other low-achievers exhibited more off-task behaviors and used less effective problem-solving strategies than those who worked with higher achieving classmates. However, as noted by Tudge and Rogoff (1989), the asymmetry in competence should not be so great that it precludes the development of mutual understanding between partners. Furthermore, findings reported by Tudge (1992) suggest that the moderating effects found for ability composition in these studies may be qualified by the level of confidence exhibited by higher ability members. In this study, low-achieving students who worked with students who were higher achieving but uncertain of their reasoning strategies gained no more than those who collaborated with other low-achievers.

The findings of early studies that compared tutoring outcomes for tutors and tutees also suggest that students who act as both agents and recipients of peer tutoring will make greater learning gains than those who participate in fixed recipient roles (e.g., Rosen, Powell, Schubot, & Rollins, 1978). Bargh and Schul (1980) proposed that although tutoring would facilitate content-specific gains for both tutors and tutees (i.e., increased understanding and retention of the specific subject matter taught), tutors could also make generalized gains by enacting the processes of cognitive reorganization and self-regulation involved in the teaching process. Advantages for alternating role procedures have also been found for tutoring programs that involve handicapped students. A number of studies have demonstrated that handicapped students can effectively act as tutors for their handicapped and in some cases non-handicapped peers (Durrer & McLaughlin, 1995; Osguthorpe & Scruggs, 1986; see chap. 9), and results of a recent meta-analysis (Mathes & Fuchs, 1991) confirmed that these students learn more in alternating, rather than fixed tutee roles.

Program Content and Structure

Research by Greenwood, Terry, Arrega-Mayer, and Finney (1992; and see chap. 6, this volume) demonstrated the use of suitably challenging tasks to be a key determinant of student learning gains in classwide peer tutoring (CWPT). Their design of such tasks relied heavily on task-analyzed curriculum materials and frequent tests of content mastery. As an alternative to designing their own tasks, which may impose prohibitive demands on time and resources, teachers could consider adapting published materials that are typically used in more traditional teaching formats. For example, the scripted lessons developed by Engelmann, Becker, Carnine, and Gersten (1988) provide an excellent basis for developing suitable tutoring tasks. In one recent study, Harper, Mallette, Maheady, and Brennan (1993) effectively combined the use of classwide student tutoring teams and direct instruction mathematics protocols to improve second-graders' use of strategies to solve math word problems. Direct instruction programs can be used to provide daily instruction over a full school year in most basic skill domains (e.g., reading, arithmetic, and language), as well as in a number of more advanced subject areas (see Kinder & Carnine, 1991).

Training

Participant training is a key element of effective tutoring programs. Trained tutors are found consistently to use more effective teaching strategies than untrained tutors, including those required to promote tutees' active engagement and independent problem-solving skills (e.g., Fuchs, Fuchs, Bentz, Phillips, & Hamlett, 1994). Tutor training procedures generally use a combination of direct instruction, modeling, and supervised practice activities (e.g., role plays) to teach behaviors such as giving clear instructions, using prompting and positive reinforcement to facilitate concept acquisition, providing effective feedback, and systematic error correction (e.g., Parson & Heward, 1979). Studies that have illustrated positive associations between providing/receiving explanations and learning in cooperative groups (e.g., Webb, 1992) also suggest that tutors be trained to provide timely, elaborated explanations in response to tutee questions. More tailored protocols are also available for use in specific subject areas, such as the Paired Reading and Cued Spelling procedures described in chap. 5.

Tutees should be trained to exhibit effective learning behaviors such as attending to instructions, responding to questions, and applying feedback appropriately (Enright & Axelrod, 1995). Seeking clarification when needed (see Newman & Goldin, 1990) and requesting help that will promote independent problem solving (i.e., instrumental help-seeking behavior; Nelson-LeGall & Glor-Scheib, 1985) are also trainable skills that may enhance tutee learning gains.

Reinforcement

Use of an appropriate reinforcement system can facilitate transfer and maintenance of trained skills to the tutoring context. Group reinforcement contingencies in which two or more students receive reinforcers based on their collective, rather than individual, achievements, have been found to promote student learning and cooperative behaviors in many dyadic learning situations (see Fantuzzo, King, & Heller, 1992; Piggott & Heggie, 1986). Although some contributors to the peer learning literature (e.g., Kohn, 1993) claim that using extrinsic reinforcers reduces students' intrinsic motivation levels, a recent meta-analysis (Cameron & Pierce, 1994) provided no support for this proposition. Group reinforcement contingencies are integral components of the CWPT and reciprocal peer tutoring (RPT) procedures outlined in chaps. 6 and 7.

Monitoring and Supervision

Frequent monitoring of tutor–tutee behaviors and other aspects of program implementation should be conducted to maintain procedural integrity and enhance the durability of tutoring outcomes. Lapses in treatment strength (e.g., reduced scheduling of tutoring sessions) and integrity (e.g., reduced levels of trial pacing and deterioration in tutors' error correction accuracy) have been directly linked to declines in student achievement during CWPT (Greenwood et al., 1992). Such lapses may signal the need for retraining or reinforcement contingencies that specifically target adherence to program procedures. Frequent assessments of student achievement should help ensure that the effects of such deviations are readily detected. Curriculum-based assessment procedures (Fuchs & Fuchs, 1986) may also be used to provide regular formative evaluations of tutoring outcomes (see Phillips, Fuchs, & Fuchs, 1994). In well-established programs, teachers may wish to consider involving peers in the administration of curriculum-based assessment probes.

PEER MODELING

Peer modeling procedures, in which students are trained to exhibit specific behavioral sequences that prompt similar behaviors and related thoughts and attitudes in their peers, are currently used to produce changes in students' academic and social behaviors in both regular and special education settings (Perry & Furukawa, 1986). Interpretations of modeling effects typically draw on the tenets of Bandura's social learning theory (e.g., Bandura, 1986), which depict social modeling as a two-stage observational learning process. In the acquisition phase, observers attend to key components of modeled acts and form symbolic representations of these in memory. In the performance phase, observers initiate actions from their stored symbolic representations. These processes are hypothesized to be subject to four subprocesses: attention and retention, which primarily affect the acquisition of new behaviors, and production and motivation, which determine whether acquired responses are subsequently performed.

Participant Selection: Observer Attributes

This formulation suggests that modeling will be moderated by two kinds of factors: those intrinsic to the observer (i.e., observer attributes) and those extrinsic to the observer (i.e., characteristics of the model or the modeled act). Intrinsic factors such as perceptual capabilities (e.g., ability to identify important features of modeled acts) and cognitive level (i.e., ability to comprehend the meaning of modeled responses) will be most influential in the acquisition of new behaviors. Whether acquired responses are subsequently performed depends on such factors as the observer's physical capabilities (i.e., ability to perform components of modeled responses) and perceived self-efficacy (i.e., beliefs in their ability to implement actions necessary to reproduce these responses). As factors intrinsic to observers are generally less alterable than extrinsic factors, information about observer characteristics typically guide decisions about model selection and choice of modeling presentation procedures.

Participant Selection: Model Characteristics

Model–observer similarity (e.g., in age or gender) and perceived model competence have both been found to moderate modeling effects. Although the findings of studies that have examined effects for model–observer similarity have not been entirely consistent, perceived similarity factors may be most influential when observers use these to form conclusions about the appropriateness of the modeled responses, task-related self-efficacy, or probable consequences of imitating the model's behaviors (see Schunk, 1987; chap. 10, this volume). Thus, perceived similarity of characteristics such as gender and age may be important in the modeling of behaviors that are typically judged by appropriateness criteria (e.g., conversational skills), but not for behaviors that will be judged by other standards (e.g., cognitive problem solving). For the latter class of behaviors, research clearly suggests that competent models are more likely to be imitated than incompetent models (Schunk, 1987). Conversely, however, as observers may use perceived similarity of model competence to make task-related self-efficacy judgments (Schunk, Hanson, & Cox, 1987), models perceived as similar to observers in their general potential to acquire new responses may facilitate performance by enhancing observers' perceived self-efficacy.

Program Content and Structure: Presentation Characteristics

Taking both factors into account, the most effective models may be those who are not generally more competent than their target observers, but who become competent at performing modeled responses over time. This proposition is supported by research that indicates a superiority for coping models of performance (who demonstrate increasing levels of competence at performing target responses with persistent effort) over mastery models (who demonstrate faultless performance from the outset) for increasing task-related self-efficacy and inducing modeling effects (Schunk, 1987). Schunk noted that the use of coping models may be particularly important with target students who have a history of learning failures. These students may also benefit from the use of incentives or instructions to highlight key features of the model's responses, progressive introduction of component skills required to perform target responses, and immediate, repeated practice at using newly acquired behavioral repertoires (see Bandura, 1986).

Reinforcement

Vicarious and direct reinforcement (i.e., consequences to the model or the target student) may be used to facilitate the acquisition of modeled behaviors (e.g., to maintain observers' attention and highlight important components of a target response) and their subsequent performance (e.g., to inform observers of modeled behaviors that are likely to be reinforced and to maintain use of these behaviors once performed). However, as noted by

Hallenbeck and Kauffman (1995), vicarious reinforcement does not always produce effects in the desired direction. In some cases, target children may interpret reinforcement to others as a form of implicit punishment. As students' interpretations of reinforcement to others may depend on their beliefs in their ability to reproduce the model's reinforced behaviors (i.e., self-efficacy judgments) and their outcome expectations, use of procedures that enhance self-efficacy (e.g., coping models) and establish clear expectations that modeled responses will be recognized and reinforced, may mitigate against such negative effects. These considerations may be particularly important for students who have limited histories of receiving reinforcement for appropriate behavior (e.g., behaviorally disordered students).

Monitoring and Supervision, Maintenance and Generalization

For most skills, appropriate prompt-fading procedures and direct reinforcement to promote independent use of acquired behaviors in appropriate contexts will be required to enhance durability and generalization of modeling effects. The constant and progressive time-delay procedures used by Doyle, Gast, Wolery, Ault, and Farmer (1990) and Venn and Wolery (1992), for example, have been found to be effective and easily implemented in peer modeling interventions. Direct consequences to target students will also determine whether modeled behaviors will be maintained over time. Several texts describe appropriate procedures for manipulating reinforcement schedules to facilitate maintenance of newly acquired skills (e.g., Wolery, Bailey, & Sugai, 1988). In addition, reinforcers should be routinely assessed for effectiveness, particularly in interventions with behaviorally disordered children, who may be unresponsive to consequences that typically reinforce non-handicapped students. Procedures for determining reinforcer preferences are also described by Wolery et al. (1988).

PEER EDUCATION

Peer education programs use positive peer influence strategies to promote awareness of, and appropriate attitudes to, developmentally relevant social issues. Peer educators have often been used in the area of health education (e.g., Perry, Klepp, Halper, Hawkins, & Murray, 1986), and, more recently, in prevention programs for drug and alcohol abuse (e.g., Klepp, Halper, & Perry, 1986) and HIV/AIDS transmission (Baldwin, 1995). Although a number of studies have found peer education to be more effective than teacher-based alternatives (Tobler, 1986), these results have not been obtained in all cases (see Klepp, Halper, & Perry, 1986). To date, however, no systematic research into the factors that moderate program efficacy has been reported. The potential moderators identified in this section draw from research on social modeling processes (e.g., Schunk, 1987) and are based on an interpretation of peer education as a social learning process in which students model arguments and behaviors that mitigate against the effects of detrimental social influences.

Participant Selection and Matching

Teacher and principal nominations are commonly used to select peer educators (Tindall, 1989). However, because the efficacy of peer educators will rely largely on social influence factors, sociometric assessments of potential peer educators should be a key source of information in selection decisions. For example, in a study by Klepp et al. (1986), peer leader elections (in which target students nominated other students that they liked, admired, and would like to be like) were used to select peer educators. Given that rating scales tend to be more comprehensive and reliable than nomination measures (e.g., Asher, Singleton, Tinsley, & Hymel, 1979), variations of this procedure based on sociometric rating scales are recommended here. The use of multiple educators from diverse subgroups of the target population (e.g., from both high- and low-status cliques) should also be considered to increase the likelihood that all target students will perceive themselves to be similar to at least one of the peer educators (see Schunk, 1987). This, in turn, will establish the social appropriateness of the attitudes and behaviors modeled for cliques with divergent social norms. Population subgroups may be determined by a number of means, such as analyzing response clusters on sociometric rating scales.

Training

A number of training manuals for peer educators have been published over the past decade. For example, the CHAMPS (Children Are Making Progress in School) peer leadership manuals (e.g., Vallenari & Epps, 1991) provide information on a range of staff preparation, student training, and program implementation issues, and include a number of useful suggestions about projects, resources, and evaluation procedures that may be used in specific content areas. To date, however, the effects of such training packages on peer educators and program recipients have not been systematically evaluated. Thus, in selecting or designing an appropriate training procedure, coordinators should evaluate the skills covered in a range of different manuals, and ensure that the procedure they choose prepares students for all of the duties implied by the educator role (e.g., acting as positive role models, teaching relevant social skills, delivering instruction in relevant subject areas). For example, in a study by Perry et al. (1986), peer educators reported feeling unprepared to deal with the social interaction problems they encountered in discussion groups (e.g., keeping groups quiet and getting everyone to participate). Thus, at a minimum, training programs should teach skills required to effectively facilitate small-group discussions.

Evaluation

Although evaluation requirements will vary with the content and structure of the education program, impact assessments should generally include both process measures (e.g., assessments by peer educators of training adequacy) and quantitative indices of effects on peer agents and target students (e.g., rating scales that measure attitudes towards smoking or drug abuse). Peer educators should also be trained to maintain their own session records (e.g., descriptive recordings of recipients' verbal reactions to specific program components). Klepp et al. (1986) further emphasized the need for adult supervision of program implementation, recommending that teachers remain informed of and review curriculum content with educators immediately prior to each program session.

PEER COUNSELING

Peer counseling programs, in which trained students deliver interpersonal helping services to other students under supervision (Varenhorst, 1984), represent a relatively new but increasingly popular application of PAL principles in school settings. The rapid proliferation of these programs across Canada and the United States over the past two decades has been marked by the appearance of a number of associated professional journals (e.g., the *Peer Facilitator Quarterly*), and the founding of organizing bodies such as the U.S. National Peer Helpers Association. Although these networks have done much to establish minimal implementation standards and communication channels among peer counseling coordinators, research on the efficacy of these procedures with school populations remains scarce. In particular, few efforts have been made to systematically identify factors that moderate intervention outcomes for both agents and recipients of peer counseling services. Published manuals in the area, however, generally suggest intuitively important factors in the selection, training, and supervision of peer counselors as potential outcome moderators (Guttman, 1987).

Participant Selection and Matching

The outcomes of a survey by Carr (1988) indicated that although coordinators tend to use similar tools to identify candidates for peer counselor training (the most common of which are self-selection, trainer–coordinator interviews, and teacher nominations), they differ widely in their views about the criterion attributes these should be used to assess. Training manuals identify a broad range of personal characteristics that may enhance peer counselor effectiveness, such as receptivity to developing self-awareness (Carr, 1981), tolerance for divergent value systems (Tindall, 1989), and social leadership potential (Guttman, 1985).

In general, however, because involving all parties who will participate in the program may facilitate long-term community support (Foster & Tindall, 1993), selection decisions should be based on information from at least four sources: potential recipients (e.g., asking students to nominate peers they would be willing to discuss problems with); potential peer counselors (e.g., asking candidates to assess their own motivation and suitability to act as peer counselors); school staff who will be directly or indirectly involved in program implementation (e.g., recommendations from teachers and school principals); and program coordinators (e.g., data collected in structured interviews). Use of a two-stage (i.e., pretraining and posttraining) selection procedure (Giddan & Austin, 1982) should also be considered to ensure that students recruited through this process are able to acquire the requisite skills emphasized in the chosen training approach.

Training

Most published training manuals (e.g., Carr & Saunders, 1979; Myrick & Sorenson, 1992; Tindall, 1989) focus on teaching effective communication skills (e.g., active listening, questioning, and summarizing skills) and self-awareness (e.g., self-assessment of personal assertiveness or problem-solving skills), through a combination of direct instruction and experiential learning activities (De Rosenroll, 1988). However, because many programs are based on a combination of components selected on intuitive grounds, some may be insufficiently integrative to achieve generality of effects across diverse student populations, or may include components that are mutually compromising in their effects (Messer, 1989).

Thus, in selecting a training approach, coordinators should familiarize themselves with a range of procedures and analyze their content for empirical validity and internal consistency. (Are the individual components supported by available empirical evidence? Do any of the components conflict in a way that could attenuate the efficacy of the overall training package?) If empirical evaluations of the composite package have been conducted, the proximal similarity (e.g., similarity in age or grade level) of intended peer agents/recipients to evaluation participants should be considered. Approaches with a self-help focus and a balanced emphasis on feelings, thoughts, and actions in all areas of student functioning (e.g., school and family relationships; Nelson-Jones, 1985), may also be more appropriate for peer-based interventions than less comprehensive or more counselor-directed approaches (i.e., those that rely more on the counselor to initiate steps in the change process).

Monitoring, Supervision, and Evaluation

Evaluations of program outcomes should include the results of both formative and summative impact assessments. Monitoring and supervision sessions should be conducted frequently (e.g., once per week), and focus on developing peer agents' self-monitoring skills. A number of tools may be used to assess adherence to program procedures, including behavior rating scales (which assess counselor performance on coordinator-specified criteria) and experiential learning records (in which counselors record their own experiences and observations during training and supervision sessions). Most published manuals also include their own inventories for assessing performance of specific requisite behaviors (e.g., Tindall, 1989). The use of group, as well as individual, supervision sessions will promote the development of peer support and independent problem-solving skills, as well as providing an appropriate forum for discussing special issues topics (e.g., responding to suicide threats; Gougeon, 1989). Summative evaluations should include results on quantitative measures of agent–recipient outcomes, such as standardized self-report inventories (e.g., the Children's Depression Inventory), ratings of target symptoms by significant others (e.g., the Children's Behavior Checklist), and direct indices of behavior change (e.g., numbers of disciplinary referrals received over specified time intervals).

PEER MONITORING

Procedures that involve training students to systematically record information about their peers' behavior have been found to produce positive effects in a range of outcome areas (Fowler, 1986). In addition to producing comparable short-term effects to those obtained in teacher-implemented programs, peers may be able to provide continuous monitoring of target behaviors across a broader range of settings than teachers (Smith & Fowler, 1984), thus enhancing the durability and generality of obtained treatment effects. Although most applications of peer monitoring focus on reducing deviant or negative student behaviors (e.g., Dougherty, Fowler, & Paine, 1985), this section addresses those designed to enhance academic self-regu-latory skills (e.g., staying on-task; Schunk, 1995). Effects of such programs are likely to vary with the kinds of behaviors that are selected for monitor-ing, the suitability of observational procedures and recording materials used, and training/supervision factors.

Program Structure and Content: Target Behaviors

In general, procedures that target behaviors or events that are easy to observe and record are mastered and implemented more readily by peer monitors. For this reason, simple behaviors or events are generally preferred to more complex alternatives, even when the latter measures are likely to be more strongly associated with student learning gains. For example, time on-task is often chosen over alternative time measures that predict academic achievement more reliably, such as academic learning time (Fisher et al., 1981), because it is relatively easy for peers to monitor. In addition, some studies have demonstrated that exclusive monitoring of self-regulatory skills may produce increases in these behaviors without having clear collateral effects on academic performance (e.g., Kohler, Schwartz, Cross, & Fowler, 1989; Stern, Fowler, & Kohler, 1988). As such, when learning gains are a primary intervention goal, self-regulatory and achievement behaviors should be monitored concurrently.

Program Structure and Content: Peer Monitoring Procedures

Monitoring tasks assigned to peer agents should also be clearly defined and well-structured to ensure that they will be able to fulfill their roles inde-pendently of teacher assistance and prompting. For example, operational definitions of target behaviors must be clearly explained and supported with numerous positive and negative examples that are relevant to the context in which they will be used. The observational system selected should also be relatively easy for agents to master. Momentary time sampling and event recording procedures are commonly used because they are applicable to a broad range of target behaviors and readily mastered by peer monitors. Behavioral checklists (e.g., Stern et al., 1988) may also be used to improve monitors' consistency and accuracy in using these procedures.

Training

Before implementing monitoring procedures within the target context, peers should be trained to mastery in relevant observation techniques and in the use of program materials to record their observations. The recommendations made by Fowler (1986) suggest that effective training procedures should include an explanation of rules governing the behavior to be monitored, practice of the monitoring strategy and desired target responses by monitors and target students, contingent feedback on monitored behaviors and on peer agents' use of requisite monitoring skills, gradual reduction of teacher prompts and feedback during practice, transfer of the monitoring procedure to appropriate classroom activities, and supervision of peer monitors and target students to ensure that the procedure works as intended. In a study by Stern et al. (1988), a six-component procedure that incorporated these features was effectively used to train fifth- and sixth-graders to monitor their peers' on-task and off-task and disruptive behaviors.

Monitoring, Supervision, Maintenance, and Generalization

Use of appropriate prompt-fading procedures facilitates transfer of trained monitoring behaviors to the target setting (Smith & Fowler, 1984). In addition, strategies to maintain compliance to specified monitoring protocols (e.g., intermittent supervision and reinforcement of correct monitoring behaviors) will be essential to maintain effects in long-term interventions (i.e., those that extend over a number of weeks or months). Finally, as the roles of peer monitor and target student are likely to produce similar effects on student behavior (e.g., Kohler et al., 1989), having participants exchange roles regularly may mitigate against stigmatization of target students in prolonged implementations.

PEER ASSESSMENT

Activities in which students assess and provide feedback on the quality of their peers' work have recently been recognized as a means to promote students' self-evaluation and learning management skills (e.g., Oldfield & MacAlpine, 1995). Although the use of these procedures has been more frequent in university-level classrooms, peer-implemented curriculum-based measurement (CBM) and peer response groups in writing are found increasingly within elementary and secondary schools. In CBM, peers are generally trained to apply teacher-developed criteria to assess the quality of their peers' work (e.g., McCurdy & Shapiro, 1992). In peer response groups, students often participate in both the development and the application of the assessment criteria (DiPardo & Freedman, 1988).

Program Structure and Content: Assessment Methods and Criteria

When students are involved in assessing divergent learning products (e.g., creative writing essays), explicit guidelines for developing and applying appropriate assessment criteria should be provided. For example, some teachers advocate the use of editing sheets to structure interactions in peer response groups (e.g., Lamberg, 1980). Carefully designed guidelines or question protocols are likely to improve the quality of interaction in response groups and dyads by prompting elaborated explanations and providing students with an appropriate language to convey their thoughts (Ross & Cousins, 1995).

For example, in the guided cooperative questioning procedures described by King (1991), students develop their own questions about specific topics from generic question *stems* that are designed to promote elaborative cognitive processing (e.g., integrating new concepts with relevant previous knowledge). These strategies were found to produce greater learning gains than encouraging students to generate their own questions without guidance (King, 1991) and could easily be adapted for use with peer response groups and dyads. Teachers may also choose to vary the level of structure imposed, according to the developmental level and experience of the students involved. For example, inexperienced students could initially be provided with a list of specific criteria to apply in assessing one another's work (e.g., uses tense appropriately) but subsequently encouraged to generate their own specific criteria from lists of general subheadings (e.g., essay style).

Training

Training, monitoring, and task structure requirements vary with different kinds of peer assessment tasks. For example, when students are involved in assessing convergent problem-solving or response skills (i.e., for which there is only one correct answer) such as oral reading accuracy, program success will be determined largely by the quality of the training and monitoring procedures used. The six-part training procedure used by Stern et al. (1988) could be adapted readily to train students in the use of specific assessment protocols.

Training should seek to ensure that peer feedback is descriptive, specific, and nonjudgmental, and that students assimilate the problem-solving strategies modeled in peer assessment tasks (see Webb, 1992). Regardless of whether students work in pairs or in groups, training should target all component skills required for effective involvement in all stages of the assessment process. For example, active participation in peer response groups requires the use of skills in expressive writing, developing/applying assessment criteria to written work, and contributing effectively to group discussions. Group discussion rules (e.g., requiring comments from each group member on all work assessed) and group reinforcement contingencies (e.g., reinforcement to all group members based on how well members chosen at random apply feedback to their own work) will also ensure that students are motivated to participate actively in response sessions, to provide high-quality feedback to other group members, and to effectively apply the feedback provided to them.

Monitoring, Supervision, and Maintenance

Monitoring and retraining may also be necessary to maintain procedural integrity. For example, deterioration in the use of prescribed error correction procedures are commonly reported in long-term CWPT evaluations (e.g., Harper et al., 1993), and have been directly linked with declines in student learning outcomes (e.g., Greenwood et al., 1992). In such cases, the use of an appropriate reinforcement system to maintain students' error correction accuracy should be considered.

GENERAL CONCLUSIONS

As indicated, the effects of each of the PAL approaches described in this book are likely to be moderated by a number of design and implementation factors. Factors common to all methods include the appropriate selection and matching of peer participants, choice of program content and structure, efficacy of training methods used, and the use of suitable monitoring and supervision procedures. As the independent contributions of these factors to intervention effects may be difficult to determine, effective programs should be designed to take all of these factors into account. Given that not all moderating factors can be accurately identified at the planning stage, however, practitioners must also be prepared to initiate their own action research on the relationship between procedural variations and program effects, and to review and modify their methods in response to these data.

As this approach relies on clear communication among all program staff and participants, coordinators need to enlist the support of these parties prior to implementation (e.g., by distributing proposals that outline program rationale, goals, and objectives, basic procedures, and expected outcomes), establish clear lines of responsibility among contributors (e.g., teachers, principals, peer agents), establish formal communication channels between these parties (e.g., regular program maintenance meetings), and provide regular feedback based on formative and summative evaluation results. As community and administrative support may depend on the perceived success of initial implementation attempts, new projects should generally be modest in scope. For example, coordinators may choose to try out new PAL procedures with small groups of students before attempting larger scale projects. In summary, PAL coordinators can do much to enhance their chances of success through careful planning and implementation. This, in turn, will help to ensure that the benefits of PAL procedures are sustained through their continued use and dissemination in applied settings.

REFERENCES

Allen, V. L. (1976). *Children as teachers: Theory and research.* New York: Academic Press.

Asher, S. R., Singleton, L. C., Tinsley, B. R., & Hymel, S. (1979). A reliable sociometric measure for preschool children. *Developmental Psychology, 15,* 443–444.

Baldwin, J. (1995). Using peer education approaches in HIV/AIDS programmes for youth: A review of the literature. *Peer Facilitator Quarterly,12*(3), 34–37.

Bandura, A. (1986). *Social foundations of thought and action: A social cognitive theory.* Englewood Cliffs, NJ: Prentice-Hall.

Bargh, J. A., & Schul, Y. (1980). On the cognitive benefits of teaching. *Journal of Educational Psychology, 72,* 593–604.

Cameron, J., & Pierce, W. D. (1994). Reinforcement, reward, and intrinsic motivation: A meta-analysis. *Review of Educational Research, 64*(3), 363–423.

Carr, R. A. (1981). *Theory and practice of peer counselling* (Monograph). Ottawa, Canada: Employment and Immigration Commission.

Carr, R. A. (1988). Selecting peer counsellors. *Peer Counsellor, 5,* 1.

Carr, R. A., & Saunders, G. (1979). *Peer counselling starter kit.* Victoria, B.C.: University of Victoria.

Cohen, J. (1986). Theoretical considerations of peer tutoring. *Psychology in the Schools, 23,* 175–186.

De Rosenroll, D. A. (1988, June). *Peer counselling: Implementation and programme maintenance issues.* Paper presented at the annual meeting of the National Peer Helpers Association Conference, Fort Collins, CO. (ED 298 361)

DiPardo, A., & Freedman, S. W. (1988). Peer response groups in the writing classroom: Theoretic foundations and new directions. *Review of Educational Research, 58*(2), 119–149.

Dougherty, B. S., Fowler, S. A., & Paine, S. C. (1985). The use of peer monitors to reduce negative interaction during recess. *Journal of Applied Behavior Analysis, 18,* 141–153.

Doyle, P. M., Gast, D. L., Wolery, M., Ault, M. J., & Farmer, J. A., (1990). Use of constant time delay in small group instruction: A study of observational and incidental learning. *The Journal of Special Education, 23*(4), 369–385.

Durrer, B., & McLaughlin, T. F. (1995). The use of peer tutoring interventions involving students with behaviour disorders. *B.C. Journal of Special Education, 19*(1), 20–27.

Engelmann, S., Becker, W. C., Carnine, D., & Gersten, R. (1988). The Direct Instruction follow through model: Design and outcomes. *Education and Treatment of Children, 11*(4), 303–317.

Enright, S. M., & Axelrod, S. (1995). Peer tutoring: applied behavior analysis working in the classroom. *School Psychology Quarterly, 10*(1), 29–40.

Fantuzzo, J. W., King, J. A., & Heller, L. R. (1992). Effects of reciprocal peer tutoring in mathematics and school adjustment: A component analysis. *Journal of Educational Psychology, 84,* 331–339.

Fisher, C. W. , Berliner, D. L., Filby, N. N., Marliave, R., Cahen, L. S., & Dishaw, M. M. (1981). Teaching behaviors, academic learning time, and student achievement: An overview. *The Journal of Classroom Interaction, 17*(1), 2–15.

Foster, E. S., & Tindall, J. A. (1993, February). *The principal's role in establishing a peer helping programme.* Paper presented at the 77th Annual Meeting of the National Association of Secondary School Principals, Las Vegas, NV. (ED 357 497)

Fowler, S. A. (1986). Peer-monitoring and self-monitoring: Alternatives to traditional teacher management. *Exceptional Children, 52,* 573–581.

Fuchs, L. S., & Fuchs, D. (1986). Effects of systematic formative evaluation on student achievement. *Exceptional Children, 53,* 199–208.

Fuchs, L. S., Fuchs, D., Bentz, J., Phillips, N. B., & Hamlett, C. L. (1994). The nature of student interactions during peer tutoring with and without prior training and experience. *American Educational Research Journal, 31*(1), 75–103.

Giddan, N. S., & Austin, M. J. (1982). Introduction: College peer counselling and self-help perspectives. In N. S. Giddan and M. J. Austin (Eds.), *Peer counselling and self-help groups on campus* (pp. 155–160). Springfield, IL: Charles C. Thomas.

Gougeon, C. (1989). Guidelines for special issues training sessions in secondary school peer counselling programmes. *Canadian Journal of Counselling, 23*(1), 120–126.

Greenwood, C. R., Terry, B., Arrega-Mayer, C., & Finney, R. (1992). The classwide peer tutoring programme: Implementation factors moderating students' achievement. *Journal of Applied Behavior Analysis, 25,* 101–116.

Guttman, M. A. (1985). A peer counselling model: Social outreach. *Canadian Counsellor, 19,* 135–143.

Guttman, M. A. (1987). Verbal interactions of peer-led group counselling. *Canadian Journal of Counselling, 21(1),* 49–58.

Hallenbeck, B. A., & Kauffman, J. M. (1995). How does observational learning affect the behaviour of students with emotional or behavioural disorders? A review of the research. *The Journal of Special Education, 29*(1), 45–71.

Harper, G. F., Mallette, B., Maheady, L., & Brennan, G. (1993). Classwide student tutoring teams and Direct Instruction as a combined instructional programme to teach generalisable strategies for mathematics word problems. *Education and Treatment of Children, 16*(2), 115–134.

Jones, M. G., & Carter, G. (1994). Verbal and non-verbal behaviour of ability-grouped dyads. *Journal of Research in Science Teaching, 31*(6), 603–619.

Kinder, D., & Carnine, D. (1991). Direct Instruction: What it is and what it is becoming. *Journal of Behavioural Education, 1*(2), 193–213.

King, A. (1991). Effects of training and strategic questioning on children's problem-solving performance. *Journal of Educational Psychology, 83,* 307–317.

Klepp, K., Halper, A., & Perry, C. L. (1986). The efficacy of peer leaders in drug abuse prevention. *Journal of School Health, 56*(9), 407–411.

Kohler, F. W., Schwartz, I. A., Cross, J. A., & Fowler, S. A. (1989). The effects of two alternating peer intervention roles on independent work skills. *Education and Treatment of Children, 12*(3), 205–218.

Kohn, A. (1993). *Punished by Rewards.* Boston: Houghton-Mifflin.

Lamberg, W. (1980). Self-provided and peer-provided feedback. *College Composition and Communication, 31,* 63–69.

Mathes, P. G., & Fuchs, L. S. (1991). *The efficacy of peer tutoring in reading for students with disabilities: A best-evidence synthesis.* Nashville, TN: Vanderbilt University Press. (ED 344 352)

Messer, S. B. (1989). Integration and eclecticism in counselling and psychotherapy: Cautionary notes. *British Journal of Guidance and Counselling, 17*(3), 274–285.

McCurdy, B. L., & Shapiro, E. S. (1992). A comparison of teacher, peer, and self-monitoring with curriculum-based measurement in reading among students with learning disabilities. *The Journal of Special Education, 26*(2), 162–180.

Myrick, R. D., & Sorenson, D. L. (1992). *Helping skills for middle school students.* Minneapolis, MN: Educational Media Corporation.

Nelson-Jones, R. (1985). Eclecticism, integration and comprehensiveness in counselling theory and practice. *British Journal of Guidance and Counselling, 13*(2), 129–138.

Nelson-LeGall, S., & Glor-Scheib, S. (1985). Help-seeking in elementary classrooms: An observational study. *Contemporary Educational Psychology, 10,* 58–71.

Newman, R. S., & Goldin, L. (1990). Children's reluctance to seek help with schoolwork. *Journal of*

Educational Psychology, 82, 92–100.

Oldfield, K. A., & MacAlpine, M. K. (1995). Peer and self-assessment at tertiary level—an experiential report. *Assessment and Evaluation in Higher Education, 20*(1), 125–132.

Osguthorpe, R. T., & Scruggs, T. E. (1986). Special education students as tutors: A review and analysis. *Remedial and Special Education, 7*(4), 15–26.

Parson, L. R., & Heward, W. L. (1979). Training peers to tutor: Evaluation of a tutor training package for primary learning disabled students. *Journal of Applied Behavior Analysis, 12,* 309–310.

Perry, M., & Furukawa, M. (1986). Modelling methods. In F. Kanfer and A. Goldstein (Eds.), *Helping people change: A textbook of methods* (3rd ed., pp. 66–110). New York: Pergamon.

Perry, C. L., Klepp, K., Halper, A., Hawkins, K. G., & Murray, D. M. (1986). A process evaluation study of peer leaders in health education. *Journal of School Health, 56*(2), 62–67.

Phillips, N. B., Fuchs, L. S., & Fuchs, D. (1994). Effects of classwide curriculum-based measurement and peer tutoring: A collaborative researcher-practitioner interview study. *Journal of Learning Disabilities, 27*(7), 420–434.

Piggott, H. E., & Heggie, D. L. (1986). Interpreting the conflicting results of individual versus group contingencies in classrooms: The targeted behaviour as a mediating variable. *Child and Family Behaviour Therapy, 7*(4), 1–15.

Rosen, S., Powell, E. R., Schubot, D. B., & Rollins, P. (1978). Peer-tutoring outcomes as influenced by the equity and type of role assignment. *Journal of Educational Psychology, 69,* 244–252.

Ross, J. A., & Cousins, J. B. (1995). Giving and receiving explanations in cooperative groups. *The Alberta Journal of Educational Research, 41*(1), 103–121.

Schunk, D. H. (1987). Peer models and children's behavioural change. *Review of Educational Research, 57*(2), 149–174.

Schunk, D. H. (1995, March). *Social origins of self-regulatory competence: The role of observational learning through peer modelling.* Paper presented at the 61st Biennial Meeting of the Society for Research in Child Development, Indianapolis. (ED 381 275)

Schunk, D. H., Hanson, A. R., & Cox, P. D. (1987). Peer model attributes and children's achievement behaviours. *Journal of Educational Psychology, 79,* 54–61.

Sharpley, A. M., & Sharpley, C. F. (1981). Peer tutoring: A review of the literature. *Collected Original Resources in Education, 5*(3), 7–C11.

Smith, L. K. C., & Fowler, S. A. (1984). Positive peer pressure: The effects of peer monitoring on children's disruptive behaviour. *Journal of Applied Behavior Analysis, 17,* 213–227.

Stern, G. W., Fowler, S. A., & Kohler, F. W. (1988). A comparison of two intervention roles: Peer monitor and point earner. *Journal of Applied Behavior Analysis, 21,* 103–109.

Tindall, J. A. (1989). Peer counselling: An in-depth look at training peer helpers (3rd ed.).Muncie, IN: Accelerated Development.

Tobler, N. (1986). Meta-analysis of 1433 adolescent drug prevention programes: Quantitative outcome results of program participants compared to a control or comparison group. *Journal of Drug Issues, 16,* 537–567.

Tudge, J. (1992). Processes and consequences of peer collaboration: A Vygotskian analysis. *Child Development, 63,* 1364–1379.

Tudge, J., & Rogoff, B. (1989). Peer influences on cognitive development: Piagetian and Vygotskian perspectives. In M. H. Bornstein & J. S. Bruner (Eds.), *Interaction in Human Development* (pp. 17–40). Hillsdale, NJ: Lawrence Erlbaum Associates.

Vallenari, A. C., & Epps, P. H. (1991). *CHAMPS: Peer leadership programe training manual.* Scottsdale, AZ: CHAMPS Peer Leadership, Inc.

Varenhorst, B. B. (1984). Peer counselling: Past promises, current status, and future directions. In S. D. Brown & R. W. Lent (Eds.), *Handbook of counselling psychology* (pp. 716–750). New York: Wiley.

Venn, M. L., & Wolery, M. (1992, December). *Using progressive time delay in arts/crafts activities to teach peer imitation to preschoolers with disabilities.* Paper presented at the Annual International Conference of the Council for Exceptional Children, Washington, DC. (ED 352 792)

Vygotsky, L. S. (1978). *Mind in society.* Cambridge, MA: Harvard University Press.

Webb, N. M. (1992). Testing a theoretical model of student interaction and learning in small groups. In R. Hertz-Lazarowitz & N. Miller, *Interaction in cooperative groups: The theoretical anatomy of group learning* (pp. 102–119). New York: Cambridge University Press.

Wolery, M., Bailey, D. B., & Sugai, G. M. (1988). *Effective teaching: Principles and procedures of applied behavior analysis with exceptional students.* Needham, MA: Allyn & Bacon.

II

PEER TUTORING

Paired Learning in Literacy

Keith Topping
University of Dundee

Reviews of research on peer tutoring consistently find that structured methods of tutoring are associated with better measured outcomes (e.g., Cohen, Kulik, & Kulik, 1982; Sharpley & Sharpley, 1981). However, *structured methods* can be a synonym for mindless drill and practice, leading only to short-term rote learning—certainly measurable, but of doubtful value.

In this chapter, three structured systems for peer tutoring in literacy are described that strive toward structure with flexibility. They aim to efficiently scaffold the interactive learning process and also enable student self-management of learning and the development of greater meta-cognitive awareness.

These methods are Paired Reading, Cued Spelling, and Paired Writing. Paired Reading is suitable only for cross-ability tutoring (whether same- or cross-age), whereas Cued Spelling and Paired Writing can be used for both fixed role cross-ability tutoring and reciprocal role same-ability tutoring. In each case, the method is elaborated, its organization in practice detailed, and research evidence on effectiveness briefly summarized. Further information about all three methods is in Topping (1995).

PAIRED READING

Method

A problem with the label *Paired Reading* is that it is all too easily misapplied to anything that two people do together with a book. What is described here is a very specific structured method that has been the subject of much research. It is common to encounter people who say, "Oh yes, we do Paired

Reading," when what they are actually doing is nothing like this specific structured method.

Of course, the positive research findings do not apply to these variations and deviations. Because of this confusion, the structured method has recently been renamed *Duolog Reading,* especially when used in conjunction with the additional accountability of computer-based self-assessment of reading comprehension (Topping, 1997).

Selecting Material.   The tutee chooses high interest reading material from school, the community library, or home. Newspapers and magazines are fine. Because Paired Reading is a kind of supported or assisted reading, tutees are encouraged to choose material above their independent readability level. Of course, the material must not be above the independent readability level of the tutor!

Contact Time.   Pairs commit themselves to an initial trial period of at least 15 minutes per day, at least three times per week for about 8 weeks. At least some of this should be in regular scheduled class time, with the possibility of doing more during recess if the pair wishes. This frequency of usage enables the pair to become fluent in the method and is sufficient to begin to see some change in the tutee's reading.

Position and Discussion.   Finding a relatively quiet and comfortable place is desirable—not easy in a busy school with many other pairs also at work. It is important that both members of the pair can see the book equally easily—tutors who get neckache become irritable. Pairs are encouraged to talk about the book, to develop shared enthusiasm, and to ensure the tutee really understands the content. (In Duolog Reading, additional checking on comprehension is done through the computer). Of course, discussion makes noise.

Correction.   A very simple and ubiquitously applicable correction procedure is prescribed. When the tutee says a word incorrectly, the tutor just tells the tutee the correct way to say the word, has the tutee repeat it correctly, and the pair carry on. Saying "No!" and giving phonic or any other prompts is forbidden.

Pause.   However, tutors do not jump in and correct the word immediately. The rule is that tutors pause and give the tutee 4 seconds to see if they will correct it themselves. Tutees will not learn to self-correct if not allowed the opportunity to practice this. Waiting for 4 seconds is not easy. Tutors can be encouraged to count slowly to four in their heads before allowing themselves to interrupt. (The exception to this rule is with the rushed and impulsive reader. In this case earlier intervention and a finger point from the tutor to guide racing eyes back to the error word is necessary.)

Praise. Praise for good reading is essential. Tutors must look pleased as well as saying positive things. Praise is particularly required for good reading of hard words, getting all the words in a sentence right and putting wrong words right before the tutor does (self-correction). Paired Reading is designed so that undesirable behaviors are eliminated by engineering in incompatible positive behaviors.

Reading Together. So how can the tutee manage this difficult book they have chosen? Tutors support tutees through difficult text by reading together—Both members of the pair read all the words out loud together, with the tutor modulating his or her speed to match that of the tutee, giving a good model of competent reading. The tutee must read every word and errors are corrected as described previously.

Signaling for Reading Alone. When an easier section of text is encountered, the tutee may wish to read a little without support. Tutor and tutee agree on a way for the tutee to signal for the tutor to stop reading together. This could be a knock, a sign, or a squeeze. When the tutee signals, the tutor stops reading out loud right away, and praises the tutee for being so confident.

Return to Reading Together. Sooner or later while reading alone, the tutee will make an error that they cannot self-correct within 4 seconds. Then, the tutor applies the usual correction procedure and joins back in reading together.

The Paired Reading Cycle. The pair go on like this, switching from reading together to reading alone, to give the tutee just as much help as is needed at any moment. Tutees should never grow out of reading together; they should always be ready to use it as they move on to increasingly difficult books.

When the book has been completed, if a computer comprehension test is available, both members of the tutorial partnership can independently self-assess their comprehension of what they have jointly read (Topping, 1997). Duolog Reading thus incorporates cooperative learning with independent accountability, as recommended to maximize effectiveness by Slavin (1990).

The framework of the Duolog Reading technique is outlined in Fig. 5.1. Of course there is relatively little new about the Paired Reading elements of it—some aspects of long-standing practice have merely been put together in a particularly successful package. However, it is this precise combination that has been proven.

Recall that Paired Reading does not constitute the whole reading curriculum, but is designed to complement professional teaching without interfering with it. Further details are in Topping (1995). Details of how to use this and the associated spelling and writing methods in a family literacy context are in Topping and Wolfendale (1985) and Wolfendale and Topping (1996).

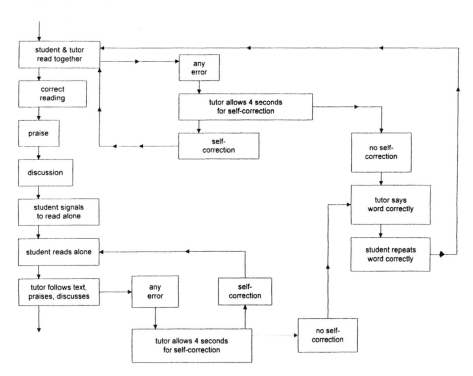

FIG. 5.1. Duolog Reading.

Organization

Paired Reading is widely used and effective with tutees of all reading abilities, but is not recommended in its pure form for students who do not have a sight vocabulary of at least 100 words. It makes sense for teachers to try it out initially on a range of students, rather than attempt to solve all their worst reading problems overnight. This will also help teachers avoid peer group stigmatization of their first effort. To start, a small group of volunteers should be selected, but not so small or so scattered that there is no sense of group ethos or solidarity.

Selection and Matching of Students.   Same-age tutoring within one class is the easiest to organize, although the quality of tutoring might not be as good as in cross-age projects. The reading ability of the students is the critical factor in selection and matching of pairs. There should be a differential of about 2 years' reading level between tutors and tutees. This ensures the reading material is challenging enough for the tutor, and the tutor's reading skill is also likely to improve.

For same-age tutoring in a whole class, all the students can be ranked in terms of reading ability and a line drawn through the middle of the ranked list to separate tutors at the top from tutees at the bottom. Then the most able tutor is paired with the most able tutee, and so on.

Social Factors.   Children should not be paired with their current friends, nor should a child be paired with another with whom there is a preexisting poor relationship. The gender balance in the class can represent a problem, particularly if there are more girls than boys, or more of the able readers are girls, because some boys express extreme reluctance at the prospect of being tutored by a girl. The teacher should allocate pairings and instruct them to proceed. A valuable side-effect is learning to relate to the opposite gender (or indeed students of different ethnic or social origin).

Dealing With Absence.   One of the organizational difficulties with peer tutoring is the impact of absence from school of a tutor or tutee. If the entire class is not involved, it is worthwhile for teachers to nominate a spare, stand-by, or supply tutor or two. Additionally, teachers should be prepared to rematch partnerless children—possibly with a change of role.

Contact Time and Space.   A minimum of three 15-to-20 minute class time contact sessions per week should be spaced preferably Monday, Wednesday, Friday, but there should be an opportunity for pairs to do additional reading in their own break time if they so wish.

Finding the physical space can be a problem. In a cross-age tutor project within a school, particularly where two full classes are involved, it is possible for half the pairs to work in the tutees' classroom and the other half in the tutors' classroom. Reading space can also be problematic during recess time.

Access to Materials.   Tutees must have easy and frequent access to a wide range of books. It helps strategic choice if the readability level of books is color-coded or otherwise evident. Pairs should also be taught a simple way of checking the readability of books themselves. Where interests are very disparate between tutee and tutor, the tutor might occasionally or alternately choose the reading material.

Training.   Pairs are trained together from the outset, most efficiently in groups. The group should be informed about the basic structure of the technique and given a demonstration. The demonstration can be on video, live by role-play between teachers or by a teacher with user-friendly tutee, or by a graduate pair from a previous program. Reading together and reading alone should be demonstrated separately to start with, then in normal alternation. Special care should be taken to highlight the correction procedure, the 4-second pause, and lots of praise.

Practice.   The pairs should now proceed to practice the technique. They should be offered necessary space and privacy. To practice reading together, the pair will need a book above the tutee's current independent readability level. It is highly desirable to have the tutees choose books for the practice in school before the meeting, so teachers can keep an eye on this. Left to themselves, the tutees would choose easy books to make a good impression.

Coaching.   As the pairs practice, the teacher should circulate to check on technique, offer further advice, coaching, or redemonstration with the individual tutee where necessary as well as praise. Teachers can not advise or coach unless *they* have tried out the technique first on a few tame children.

Questions and Administrative Issues.   After the practice, teachers should feed back their observations to the group, take questions, and outline the day-to-day organization of the project. Pairs should keep a reading diary or log, noting the date, what was read, for how long, with whom and any comments about how well the tutee did. Peer group brainstorming of new vocabulary of praise is useful. Pairs should be advised about the different places from which they may borrow books. An easy read handout should be distributed to remind them of the technique. Some schools offer badges, balloons, and other promotional materials—all helping to advertise the program.

Monitoring Tutoring.   During subsequent tutoring sessions, the teacher should circulate to monitor the quality of technique, appropriateness of book choice, and how the partner relationship is developing.

Feedback.   After the initial period of commitment, the teacher should gather all the pairs together for a feedback meeting. They should be told how the teacher thinks things have gone and their opinions should be sought on the technique and organization of the project. Some present will say little, so teachers might also wish to use feedback questionnaires for the participants (see Topping & Whiteley, 1990, for examples).

Evaluation.   Teachers might wish to test the tutors' and tutees' reading before and after the project, so they can feed back the overall results to the participants. They might also want to offer the group further tangible indicators of the school's approval at this point, but intrinsic motivation will usually have taken over.

Effectiveness

Paired Reading has been the subject of a very large amount of research, starting in the United Kingdom and now internationally, and this has been the subject of reviews by Topping and Lindsay (1992) and Topping (1995). Much of the evaluation has been in terms of gains on norm-referenced tests of reading before and after the initial intensive period of involvement. Published studies do not always reflect the reality of ordinary life in the classroom, but with Paired Reading it is possible to compare the results of 60 published (and therefore selected) studies of projects with outcome data from 155 unselected projects operated in one school district.

Literature Versus Real Life.   In the published studies, involving 1,012 tutees, in each passing month, the average paired reader gained 4.2 months in reading age for accuracy (oral decoding) and 5.4 months for comprehension. In the 155 unselected projects, involving 2,372 tutees, for each month of time passed, the average paired reader gained 3.3 months in reading age for accuracy and 4.4 months for comprehension. This still represents a very substantial effect size. More data were available for parent-tutored than peer-tutored projects, but no significant difference in outcomes between the two was found. The evidence suggested that tutors tended to gain more than tutees (e.g., Topping, 1987).

Control Groups and Follow-Up.   Of the published studies, 19 included control or comparison groups, whereas of the unselected projects, 37 included control groups. Although the control groups often also made gains greater than would normally be expected, the Paired Reading groups overall did far better. Do these gains last? It seems that although the initial startling acceleration does not continue indefinitely, the gains certainly do not 'wash out' or disappear subsequently. Follow-up data from control group projects confirm this (Topping, 1987, 1992), although there is less follow-up research on peer tutoring than parent tutoring.

Participant Feedback.   Taking another approach to evaluation, the subjective views of tutors, tutees, and teachers in the unselected projects were also gathered by structured questionnaire (Topping & Whiteley, 1990). In a sample of more than 1,000 tutors, after Paired Reading, 70% considered their tutee was now reading more accurately, more fluently, and with better comprehension. Greater confidence in reading was noted by 78% of tutors. Teachers reported generalized reading improvement in the classroom in a slightly smaller proportion of cases. Of a sample of 964 tutees, 95% felt that after Paired Reading they were better at reading and 92% liked reading more. Of the sample, 87% found it easy to learn to do, 83% liked doing it, and 70% said they would continue.

CUED SPELLING

Method

Turning from reading to spelling, the basic structure of the Cued Spelling technique comprises 10 steps, 4 points to remember, and 2 reviews. The 10 steps and 4 points apply to every target word worked on by the pair, whereas the speed review covers all target words for a particular session, and the mastery review covers all the target words for 1 week or a longer period if desired.

The 10 Steps.   The tutee chooses high interest target words irrespective of complexity (Step 1) from any curricular or interest area. The pair check the spelling of the word, put a master version in their cued spelling diary and usually also add it to the top of a piece of paper on which subsequent attempts are to be made (Step 2). The pair then read the word out loud synchronously, then the tutee reads the word aloud alone, ensuring tutee capability of accurate reading and articulation of the word (Step 3).

The tutee then chooses cues (prompts or reminders) to enable him or her to remember the written structure of the word (Step 4). These cues may be phonic sounds, letter names, syllables, other fragments or chunks of words, or wholly idiosyncratic mnemonic devices. Tutees are encouraged to consider and choose cues that fit well with their own cognitive structures (i.e., make sense and are memorable to them).

Once cues are decided, the pair say the cues out loud simultaneously (Step 5). The tutee then says the cues out loud as the tutor writes the word down on scrap paper to this dictation (Step 6). Thus, the tutee is provided with a demonstration or model of the required behavior. At Step 7, the tutor says the cues out loud as the tutee writes the word. At Step 8, the tutee says the cues and writes the word simultaneously.

Then, the tutee is required by the tutor to write the word as fast as possible (Step 9). The tutee may or may not decide to recite the cues out loud, but may well recite them subvocally. At Step 10, the tutee again reads the word out loud as a reminder of the meaningful context and purpose of the exercise.

The 4 Points.   The four points cover aspects of the technique relevant to its practical application:

1. At every attempt at writing a target word, the tutor is required to cover previous attempts on the work paper, to avoid the possibility of direct copying, although in fact some tutees prefer to do this themselves.

2. Every time there is a written attempt on a target word, the tutee checks the attempt and the tutor only intervenes if the tutee proves unable to check their own attempt accurately.

3. If tutees have written a word incorrectly, they are encouraged to cross it out very vigorously to assist its deletion from their memory.

4. At an incorrect attempt, the correction procedure is merely that the pair return to the step preceding the one at which the error was made. Tutors are also required to praise at various junctures that are specified quite clearly.

The 2 Reviews.   At the end of each tutoring session, there is a *speed review,* wherein the tutor requires the tutee to write all the target words for that session as fast as possible from dictation in random order. The tutee then self-checks all the words with the master version in the Cued Spelling diary. Target words that are incorrect at speed review have the 10 steps applied again, perhaps with the choice of different cues. In fact, tutees make only a small proportion of errors at speed review, and the requirement to reapply the 10 steps is not as onerous as it sounds.

At the end of each week, a *mastery review* is conducted, wherein the tutee is required to write all the target words for the whole week as fast as possible in random order. No specific error correction procedure is prescribed for mastery review, and it is left to the pair to negotiate for themselves what they wish to do about errors. Many pairs choose to include failed words in the next week's target words.

Underlying Principles.   The technique has been designed and structured to be highly interactive, but in operation appears as democratic rather than didactic. Cued Spelling features swift error correction and support procedures to eliminate the fear of failure; it is flexible and appropriate for a wide age and ability range. The self-selection of target words and self-management of many of the procedures is designed to increase motivation; it incorporates modeling and praise.

The steps are finely task-analyzed (are in small incremental stages) to reduce frustration on very difficult words—but they can be worked through very quickly on easier words. The emphasis in the later steps on speeded performance is to promote generalization over time and contexts. Otherwise there is a danger that the tutee will merely have learned spelling tricks, while continuing to spell the same words incorrectly in continuous free writing. Although the method may seem complex on first reading, 7-year-old tutees have been successfully trained in its use in about 1 hour.

Organization

Cued Spelling projects follow many of the organizational guidelines for Paired Reading projects. For fixed role, cross-ability tutoring, selection and matching proceeds much as for Paired Reading. For reciprocal role, same-ability tutoring, students immediately adjacent on a list ranked by spelling ability are selected, and the time scale for role change specified.

Training. Pairs are trained together. A talk on the method is best accompanied with a demonstration on video, as a live demonstration of Cued Spelling often lacks clarity of small detail. An additional practical demonstration of cueing using a chalkboard and soliciting from the group different words and different cueing strategies for each word is helpful in making the point that there are no right cueing strategies, only effective and ineffective ones. Pairs are given a 10-Steps chart to refer to while practicing the method with the tutee's own words (chosen before the meeting), using the paper, pencils, and dictionaries provided. Individualized feedback and further coaching are given as necessary.

Self-Recording. Cued Spelling diaries are given to each pair, each page including space to write the master version of up to 10 words on all days of the week, together with boxes to record daily speed review and weekly mastery review scores and spaces for comments from tutor (daily) and teacher (weekly). The pair are asked to use the technique on about five words per day (implying a minimum time of 15 minutes) for 3 days a week for the next 6 weeks.

Sources. The tutees are encouraged to choose words from their school spelling books, graded free writing, relevant project work, or special Cued Spelling displays of common problem words, and collect these (in a Cued Spelling collecting book), so they always have a pool of suitable words from which to choose. The teacher should keep watch on the words chosen, because some students choose words they already know, and others choose extremely difficult words of very doubtful utility. In this latter case you might need to prescribe a formula of "three for everyday use and two just for fun."

Checking. Where the pair are of equal spelling ability, it is especially important that the teacher ensures that the master version of the word is looked up in the dictionary and copied correctly into the Cued Spelling diary. In reciprocal tutoring, the fact that everyone gets to be a tutor is good for the self-esteem of both members of the pair, who learn their partner's words as well as their own.

Effectiveness

The initial reports on Cued Spelling were of a descriptive nature. Emerson (1988) used the technique with parents who tutored their own children at home. Scoble (1988) described how an adult literacy student was tutored by his wife and subsequently reported on the progress of 14 similar pairs (Scoble, 1989). All three reports noted excellent results at mastery review. Harrison (1989) described the extension of the method to peer tutoring between adult literacy students in a class situation.

Cross-Ability Tutoring.   However, the most popular application of Cued Spelling became peer tutoring in school. Subsequent research also looked increasingly at whether Cued Spelling resulted in generalized improvements in spelling beyond the specific words studied.

Oxley and Topping (1990) described how eight 7- and 8-year-old pupils were tutored by eight 9-year-old pupils in the same class in a small, rural school. Striking social benefits were noted and the children spontaneously generalized peer tutoring to other curricular areas. Subjective feedback from both tutors and tutees was very positive and the self-concept as a speller of both tutees and tutors showed a marked positive shift compared to that of nonparticipant children. Results on norm-referenced tests of spelling were equivocal, because although the scores of both tutees and tutors were strikingly improved at posttest, so were those of nonparticipant children in the same class.

Reciprocal Same-Ability Tutoring.   Peer-tutored Cued Spelling in a classwide, same-age, same-ability reciprocal tutoring format was reported by Brierley, Hutchinson, Topping, and Walker (1989). Overall, 75 children aged 9 to 10, in three classes, participated. Tutor and tutee roles changed each week. All the children were trained in a single group meeting. Mastery review scores averaged 80%, and the average norm-referenced test gain was .65 years of spelling age in 6 weeks. Subjective feedback from the children was very positive. Improved spelling self-concept was reported by 84% of the children. In a study of parent tutored Cued Spelling with 8-year-old mixed-ability children, France, Topping, and Revell (1993) found the 22 cued spellers gained at 2.8 times the rate of a comparison group of more able spellers.

Effect cn Free Writing.   To control for the possible effects of extra attention and time on-task, Watt and Topping (1993) compared Cued Spelling with traditional spelling homework (involving equal tutor attention and equal time on spelling tasks). They also compared parent- and peer-tutored Cued Spelling and assessed the generalization of Cued Spelling effects into continuous free writing.

Cued spellers gained more than 2 months of tested spelling age per calendar month, whereas the comparison group gained only half a month. Mastery review scores averaged 93% correct. Parent and peer tutoring seemed equally effective. Improved spelling self-concept was reported by 85% of the cued spellers, and 91% reported a higher rate of self-correction. Better tutee self-correction was also reported by 88% of the tutors and three out of four class teachers.

In samples of writing collected before and after the project, the average number of spelling errors per page reduced from 8.5 to 4.6 for the cued spellers and from 3.7 to 2.1 for the comparison children. The Cued Spelling group averaged 1.7 specific improvements in free writing per child, and the comparison group averaged 1.2.

Cued Spelling with Younger Children

An alternative training method for younger children was reported in Arizona by Parisek (1996). She modeled alternative cueing strategies for high frequency words on a whole class basis for some weeks, before progressing to regular Cued Spelling with completely individualized student management. This approach (akin to reciprocal teaching) worked well with these second graders and was associated with raised test scores and improved free writing. Other teachers have simply abbreviated the Cued Spelling procedure for use with younger children, but evaluations have not been reported.

PAIRED WRITING

Method

Spelling is one component of writing, which Paired Writing addresses in a more global way. Writing can be a lonely business, and a blank piece of paper waiting to be filled is strangely daunting. Paired Writing is a framework for a pair working together to generate (or co-compose) a piece of writing for any purpose they wish. The guidelines are designed to structure interaction between the pair so that a higher proportion of time is spent on-task—hopefully reducing dithering, head-scratching, staring out of the window, and blind panic to a minimum.

Underlying Principles. There is great emphasis on continuity—the pair stimulating each other to keep going at any threatened hiatus. There is also constant inbuilt feedback and cross-checking—what is written must make sense to both members of the pair. The system is designed to be supportive and eliminate the fear of failure. Anxiety about peripheral aspects of writing such as spelling or punctuation should thereby be reduced to an appropriate level, and dealt with in an orderly way. As the best copy is a joint effort of the pair, criticism as well as praise from external evaluators is shared.

Peer Evaluation.   Peer evaluation is incorporated, relieving the supervising professional of the burden of grading innumerable scripts after the event (sometimes so long after that the feedback given is totally ineffective). Research has indicated that peer evaluation is at least as effective as teacher evaluation.

Formats.   Paired Writing usually operates with a more able writer (the helper) and one less able (the writer) in the pair, but can work with a pair of equal ability so long as they edit carefully and use a dictionary to check spellings. In this latter case, it is possible to reciprocate roles from time to time to add variety. However, this should not be too frequent and the two roles should always be kept clearly separate.

Applications.   The system may be used in creative writing or English composition, or in descriptive or technical writing, or as part of cross-curricular work, employment, or other life needs. A Paired Writing project may be designed to mesh in with, or follow on from, direct instruction from a professional teacher on structural aspects of the writing process or a Paired Reading or Cued Spelling project. The method may equally be used on an ad hoc basis as the need arises once pairs are trained and practiced in its use.

Structure.   The structure of the system consists of 6 steps, 10 questions (ideas), 5 stages (drafting), and 4 levels (editing). Helpers should not be overly didactic, nor too supportive. Helpers are there to help writers to help themselves, not to do everything for them. As there are no right answers about what constitutes good writing, helpers should avoid direct criticism of the writer's efforts. Instead, they should make comments about their own subjective reaction (e.g., "I find that bit hard to understand—Can we think of a clearer way to write it?"). More praise for good bits than comment on doubtful bits is the rule, and praise must be given at least at the end of each step.

Steps, Stages, and Levels.   Step 1 is *ideas generation*. The helper stimulates ideas by raising stimulus questions with the writer, from a provided prompt list of 10 or using their own initiative. As the writer responds, the helper makes one-word notes. As this proceeds, the helper might recapitulate previous ideas before presenting the next stimulus word.

Step 2 is *drafting*. The notes should be placed where both members of the pair can easily see them. Sometimes visual mapping, linking, or numbering is used. Drafting then proceeds without concern for either spelling or punctuation. However, legibility is desirable, as is double-spaced writing to allow for subsequent editing. Most pairs will do better with lined paper. The writer considers the notes and dictates, sentence by sentence, what they wish to communicate.

Generally a pair chooses one of five stages of support to operate in for the session:

1. Tutor writes it all, tutee copies it all.
2. Tutor writes hard words in for tutee.
3. Tutor writes hard words in rough, tutee copies them in.
4. Tutor dictates hard words, tutee writes them in.
5. Tutee writes it all.

For a harder piece of writing, the pair are likely to choose a lower (numbered) stage, for an easier assignment a higher (numbered) stage.

However, they might go back one stage (or more) when encountering a particularly hard section. In any event, if the writer cannot proceed within 10 seconds, the helper must go back a stage on that problem word to give more support. There is a great emphasis on keeping going (with support as necessary) and not getting bogged down.

Step 3 is *reading*. The helper then reads the draft out loud, with as much expression and attention to punctuation (real or imagined) as possible, as the pair look at the text together. The writer then reads the text out loud. If a word is read incorrectly, the helper says that word correctly for the writer.

Step 4 is *editing*. The pair look at the draft together, and the writer considers where he or she thinks improvements are necessary. Problem words, phrases, or sentences might be marked with colored pen, pencil, or highlighter. The most important criterion of need for improvement is where meaning is unclear. The second most important is to do with the organization of ideas within the text—the order in which meanings are presented, whether phrases or sentences. The next consideration is whether spellings are correct, and the last is whether punctuation is helpful and correct. Meaning, order, spelling, and punctuation are the edit levels.

The helper praises the writer, then marks any areas the writer has missed, while bearing in mind the subjective nature of some aspects of quality in writing. The writer then suggests changes, the pair discuss the best correction to make, and when agreement is reached, the new version is inserted in the text (preferably by the writer). Spellings over which there is the slightest doubt should be referred to the dictionary.

Step 5 is the *best copy*. The writer (usually) then copies out a neat or best version of the corrected draft. Sometimes the helper may write or type or word-process the piece, however, depending on the skill and stamina of the writer.

Step 6 is *evaluation*. The pair should inspect and consider the best copy. External evaluation by more objective assessors is also highly desirable. Peer evaluation is a useful mutual learning experience, and assessment by another pair can proceed by reference to the criteria encompassed in the edit levels, again hopefully with positive comments outnumbering negative.

As with Paired Reading, there is nothing new in this, including as it does many of the traditional elements of process writing. More elaborate versions with more editing options have been developed for older tutees.

Organization

For training purposes (and indeed subsequently) each pair must have a system flowchart (Topping, 1995), two pens or pencils, scrap paper, easy access to a dictionary of an appropriate level, and good quality paper for the best copy. Most pairs will do best with lined paper. It is recommended that the use of erasers is strongly discouraged. A colored pen or pencil for editing might be found helpful.

Training Demonstration. At a training meeting, participants should sit at tables in their pairs, with a hard copy of the flowchart, which could also be projected. Talking through the flowchart should always be accompanied by a demonstration of the system in operation, and the most visible way of doing this is usually by live role play between teachers writing on an acetate sheet that is continuously overhead (retro) projected.

Practice Tasks. Practice, monitoring, and coaching follow. Some simple topic may be specified for all pairs for the practice, but this should be common to all and preferably functional (e.g., how to use a coin-operated telephone or how you should brush your teeth). At least 40 minutes and preferably 1 hour should be allowed for the meeting.

Onward Usage. After training, the system must be used as frequently as possible for the next few weeks, to ensure consolidation and promote fluency in its use and enable any problems to be picked up. Paired Writing for three sessions of 20 minutes a week for 6 weeks is a usual pattern.

Effectiveness

Most of the usage of Paired Writing since its recent inception has been on a same-age cross-ability basis in classes of mixed-ability students. Pairs often prefer the sociability and supportiveness of Paired Writing to the traditional approach. The objective of peer-tutored Paired Writing is to produce an increase in the quality and quantity of written output that generalizes to the solo writing situation and endures over time—for both tutors and tutees. A more complex issue arises—Is the final product better than if the members of the pair worked separately?

Comparative Research. To date, most of the evaluations of Paired Writing have been descriptive and anecdotal. However, a more substantial study by Sutherland and Topping (in press) compared same-ability and cross-ability pairing in 8-year-olds, in each case with a nonparticipant control group, considering effects in relation to solo writing. For same-ability pairs, combined performance proved better than pretest solo performance. For cross-ability pairs, combined performance was associated with significantly improved posttest solo performance. Controls showed no change. Subjects also expressed positive attitudes to Paired Writing.

FUTURE DIRECTIONS

What is important for the future? More implementation of what is already known. Quality implementation, with a minimum of dilution. Acceptance by teachers of an enhanced role as organizers of effective learning, rather than deliverers of curriculum content. Greater familiarity among teachers with a wider range of types of structured method, enabling better choice of the most effective method for the local objectives and context.

Further research is needed into the long-term and generalized effects of Cued Spelling and Paired Writing, in different formats. Other new methods will undoubtedly be developed, and should be carefully evaluated before being promoted as the latest educational fashion. The current political agenda is strongly in favor of peer tutoring, not least because of the high level of cost-effectiveness it shows. Of course, this alone is not enough to increase take-up rates. Fortunately, the methods outlined here can also make life easier and more satisfying for the busy teacher, and this will also help to lower the threshold of innovation.

The focus here has been on literacy, and this is indeed an excellent place to start, but the possibilities are endless. A great deal of work has been done on peer tutoring of mathematics, and there is great potential in other areas of the curriculum such as mathematics and science (see, e.g., Topping, 1998; Topping & Bamford, 1998a, 1998b).

REFERENCES

Brierley, M., Hutchinson, P., Topping, K., & Walker, C. (1989). Reciprocal peer tutored cued spelling with ten year olds. *Paired Learning, 5,* 136–140.

Cohen, P. A., Kulik, J. A., & Kulik, C-L. C. (1982). Educational outcomes of tutoring: A meta-analysis of findings. *American Educational Research Journal, 19*(2), 237–248.

Emerson, P. (1988). Parent tutored cued spelling in a primary school. *Paired Reading Bulletin, 4,* 91–92.

France, L., Topping, K., & Revell, K. (1993). Parent tutored cued spelling. *Support for Learning, 8*(1), 11–15.

Harrison, R. (1989). Cued spelling in adult literacy in Kirklees. *Paired Learning, 5,* 141.

Oxley, L., & Topping, K. (1990). Peer-tutored cued spelling with seven- to nine-year-olds. *British Educational Research Journal, 16*(1), 63–78.

Parisek, R. (1996). *Cued spelling: Positive effects on attitudes, test scores and student writing.* Glendale, AZ: Sunburst Elementary School.

Scoble, J. (1988). Cued spelling in adult literacy—A case study. *Paired Reading Bulletin, 4,* 93–96.

Scoble, J. (1989). Cued spelling and paired reading in adult basic education in Ryedale. *Paired Learning, 5,* 57–62.

Sharpley, A. M., & Sharpley, C. F. (1981). Peer tutoring: A review of the literature. *Collected Original Resources in Education, 5*(3), 7–C11.

Sutherland, J. A., & Topping, K. J. (in press). *Collaborative creative writing in eight year olds: Comparing cross ability fixed role and same ability reciprocal role pairing.* Paper submitted for publication.

Slavin, R. E. (1990). *Co-operative learning: Theory, research and practice.* Englewood Cliffs, NJ: Prentice-Hall.

Topping, K. J. (1987). Peer tutored paired reading: Outcome data from 10 projects. *Educational Psychology, 7*(2), 133–144.

Topping, K. J. (1992). Short- and long-term follow-up of parental involvement in reading projects. *British Educational Research Journal, 18*(4), 369–379.

Topping, K. J. (1995). *Paired reading, spelling and writing: The handbook for teachers and parents.* London & New York: Cassell.

Topping, K. J. (1997). *Duolog reading: A video training pack.* Madison, WI: Institute for Academic Excellence.

Topping, K. J. (1998). *The paired science handbook: Parental involvement and peer tutoring in science.* London: Fulton; Bristol, PA: Taylor & Francis.

Topping, K. J., & Bamford, J. (1998a). *The paired maths handbook: Parental involvement and peer tutoring in mathematics.* London: Fulton; Bristol, PA: Taylor & Francis.

Topping, K. J., & Bamford, J. (1998b). *Parental involvement and peer tutoring in mathematics and science: Developing Paired Maths into Paired Science.* London: Fulton; Bristol, PA: Taylor & Francis.

Topping, K. J., & Lindsay, G. (1992). Paired reading: A review of the literature. *Research Papers In Education, 7*(3), 1–50.

Topping, K. J., & Whiteley, M. (1990). Participant evaluation of parent-tutored and peer-tutored projects in reading. *Educational Research, 32*(1), 14–32.

Topping, K. J., & Wolfendale, S. W. (Eds.). (1985). *Parental involvement in children's reading.* London: Croom Helm.

Watt, J. M., & Topping, K. J. (1993). Cued spelling: A comparative study of parent and peer tutoring. *Educational Psychology in Practice, 9*(2), 95–103.

Wolfendale, S. W., & Topping, K. J. (Eds.). (1996). *Family involvement in literacy: Effective partnerships in education.* London and New York: Cassell.

6

Classwide Peer Tutoring

Carmen Arreaga-Mayer
Barbara J. Terry
Charles R. Greenwood
University of Kansas

Research concerning effective instruction has revealed several classroom processes that are related to improved academic outcomes for students of all ability levels and of culturally and linguistically diverse backgrounds. For example, students' engagement during instruction (e.g., Greenwood, 1991a), time spent actively learning a subject (e.g., Leinhardt & Pallay, 1982; Rosenshine & Berliner, 1978), how teachers organize lessons (e.g., Arreaga-Mayer & Greenwood, 1986; Brophy, 1983; Rosenshine & Stevens, 1986), and teachers' instructional behaviors (e.g., Arreaga-Mayer & Perdomo-Rivera, 1996; Brophy, 1979; Good & Grouws, 1979). Brophy and Good (1986), in their third handbook of research on teaching, pointed out that the greatest contribution of the teacher effectiveness research during the 1970s and 1980s was the clear demonstration that teachers and classroom instructional processes make a difference in student achievement (Anderson, Evertson, & Brophy, 1979; Leinhardt, Zigmond, & Cooley, 1981).

Since the 1980s, parallel lines of research have emerged within special education (e.g., Christenson, Ysseldyke, & Thurlow, 1989; Fuchs & Fuchs, 1990; Greenwood, 1991a; Kaufman, Kameenui, Birman, & Danielson, 1990; Sindelar, Smith, Harriman, Hale, & Wilson, 1986). Collectively, this literature indicates that what teachers and students do every day in the classroom (i.e., teacher and classroom processes) does make a difference in terms of academic achievement gains and oral language usage.

A practice widely known to orchestrate effective processes and to increase student achievement is classwide peer tutoring (CWPT), the focus of this chapter (Greenwood, Delquadri, & Carta, 1988; Greenwood, Maheady, & Carta, 1991). Over the past 17 years, research has illustrated and validated the potential for CWPT learning strategies in the instruction of children who are challenging to teach (e.g., Arreaga-Mayer, in press; Carlton, Litton, & Zinkgrof, 1985; Chapman & Leach, 1991; Cooke, Heron, & Heward, 1983; Delquadri, Greenwood, Stretton, & Hall, 1983; Delquadri, Greenwood, Whorton, Carta, & Hall, 1986; Fuchs, Fuchs, Bentz, Phillips, & Hamlett, 1994; Greenwood, 1991a, 1991b). These studies have been directed at answering questions regarding what is done and what needs to be done during instruction to produce optimal growth in students' learning. CWPT is a peer-assisted instructional procedure by which the elements of effective instruction and classroom processes just discussed can be orchestrated in the classroom. The purpose of this chapter is to review what is known about CWPT and to provide a perspective on the method, applications in the classroom, and evidence supporting its effectiveness. We also provide a succinct statement of the planning steps needed for successful replication. Specific emphasis in this chapter is devoted to students with limited English proficiency (LEP).

CLASSWIDE PEER TUTORING AS AN EFFECTIVE INSTRUCTIONAL ALTERNATIVE

CWPT is a specific type of same-age, intraclass, peer-assisted instruction developed by researchers at the Juniper Gardens Children's Project, University of Kansas, in collaboration with regular classroom teachers, to improve the acquisition and retention of basic academic skills (Delquadri, Greenwood, Stretton, & Hall, 1983). It has been successfully applied to passage reading, reading comprehension, sight-words reading, mathematics, spelling, language arts, science, and social studies instruction. It has been implemented effectively with regular, special education, and low-achieving students as well as with LEP students from kindergarten through high school levels (see reviews by Delquadri et al., 1986, and Greenwood, Carta, Kamps, & Hall, 1988).

Effectiveness

Classroom-based research studies since the early 1980s have demonstrated that students are able to learn more in less time using CWPT when compared to conventional forms of teacher-directed instruction (Greenwood, Carta, & Kamps, 1990; Greenwood, Maheady, & Carta, 1991; Mathes & Fuchs, 1993). The positive effects of CWPT on several measures of academic achievement in the areas of reading, spelling, vocabulary, and math have been documented and replicated extensively (e.g., Delquadri, Greenwood,

Whorton, Carta, & Hall, 1986; Harper, Mallette, Maheady, Parkes, & Moore, 1993). For example, in a study spanning 2 years, 211 students in Chapter I schools were found to be significantly more accurate on their spelling tests in comparison to students under teacher-designated instruction (Greenwood, Dinwiddie, et al., 1987). A study by Maheady and Harper (1987) replicated positive tutoring effects in spelling with low-income minority youngsters and these effects were further replicated to content area courses (e.g., social studies) at the secondary level (Maheady, Harper, & Sacca, 1988; Maheady, Sacca, & Harper, 1988). They reported improved performance of entire classrooms, often by as much as two letter grades (i.e., from D to B average).

Research has indicated that CWPT improves the rate of accurate responding to basic math facts. Harper, Mallette, Maheady, and Clifton (1990) assessed the rate and accuracy performance of 17 Grade 2 children with 100 subtraction problems. Results showed high rates of responding and an average of 98% accuracy over a 10-week period.

A number of studies demonstrated improvements in the oral reading rates and comprehension of students with learning disabilities and academic delays (Greenwood, Delquadri, & Hall, 1989; Madrid, Terry, Greenwood, Whaley, & Webber, 1991; Mathes, Fuchs, Fuchs, Henley & Sanders, 1994) and with mild retardation in integrated settings (Mortweet, 1995; Sideridis, 1994). Similarly, CWPT has been reported more effective than conventional instructional methods with secondary students with mild disabilities (Maheady, Sacca, & Harper, 1988), students with autism (Kamps, Barbetta, Leonard, & Delquadri, 1994) and children with attention deficit hyperactivity disorders (ADHD) in regular classrooms (Du Paul & Henningson, 1993; Fiore & Becker, 1994).

A series of research studies have concentrated on the academic, language learning, and social benefits of CWPT adapted for students with LEP and mild disabilities (Arreaga-Mayer, Greenwood, & Utley, 1994). Overall, results documented that English language use and academic engagement as well as achievement gains were increased significantly in CWPT classrooms when compared to traditional teacher-mediated instruction for LEP students with and without disabilities. Spelling and vocabulary CWPT test scores averaged 80% to 98%, reading fluency improved an average of 11 words per minute, errors dropped an average of 3 to 4 words, and comprehension percentage scores averaged 85% (an average increase of 35%) for LEP students. Their oral engagement during CWPT increased an average of 33%, and their academic engagement rate increased an average of 24% when compared to teacher-mediated procedures.

In a longitudinal project spanning 4 years and Grades 1 to 4 (Greenwood, Delquadri, & Hall, 1989), students in urban schools whose teachers employed CWPT each year, performed significantly better on the reading, mathematics, and language subtests of the Metropolitan Achievement Test in comparison to an equivalent control group. Effect sizes were .38 in mathematics, .58 in reading, and .60 in language. By the end of Grade 4, the CWPT group students approached the national normative level in these three subject areas, whereas controls were nearly one standard deviation below this level. Direct observation data corroborated that CWPT group students, in comparison with controls, increased their levels of oral and silent reading, writing, and academic talk and reduced their time spent in task management (e.g., looking for materials) and in competing inappropriate behaviors (e.g., disrupting, looking around, moving around during instruction time). Results from an 8-year, experimental, longitudinal follow-up study of the above mentioned students indicated that CWPT, when compared to at-risk and nonrisk groups that did not receive CWPT (a) increased growth in students' achievement at Grades 2, 3, 4, and 6 (Greenwood et al., 1989; Greenwood, 1991b; Greenwood, Terry, Utley, Montagna, & Walker, 1993), (b) reduced the number of CWPT students needing special education services by Grade 7 (Greenwood, Terry, et al., 1993), and (c) reduced the number of CWPT students dropping out of school by Grade 11 (Greenwood & Delquadri, 1995).

FEATURES OF THE CLASSROOM CWPT PROGRAM

CWPT involves the entire class in tutoring. Depending on instructional goals, students are paired either randomly, matched by ability (i.e., same level or adjacent skill levels), or matched by language proficiency to partners each week (e.g., Greenwood & Delquadri, 1995; Heron, Heward, Cooke, & Hill, 1983). In the case of the culturally diverse students who have LEP, it is recommended that initially they be paired with students that speak their native language, but that have a higher level of English proficiency. Once LEP students have a working knowledge of the English language they can be paired at random with bilingual or native English-speaking peers. Pairs are assigned to one of two teams that compete for the highest point total resulting from daily scheduled tutoring sessions in which individual students earn points for performance. Thus, the motivational component of CWPT combines both competitive and cooperative features.

Each tutoring pair consists of a tutor (teacher role) and a tutee (student role). Students' roles are switched within the daily tutoring session (reciprocal tutoring roles), allowing each child to be both the tutor–teacher and the tutee–student. New content to be learned, teams, and tutoring pairs are changed on a weekly basis. Students are trained in the procedures necessary to act as both tutor and tutee. In a given session, the students know who their partner is, the material to be covered, how to correct errors, how to award points for correct responding, and how to provide positive feedback for correct responding and participation.

Teachers organize the academic content to be tutored into daily and weekly units and prepare these materials for use within the peer teaching format. Unit mastery is checked at least weekly using teacher prepared tests in a pretest–posttest sequence, providing feedback to the students on their level of mastery. Tutoring occurs simultaneously for all tutor-tutee pairs involving the entire class at the same time, thus the term, *classwide*. This leaves the teacher free to supervise and monitor students' responding during sessions.

A major advantage of CWPT is that it empowers the students with a highly effective learning strategy to approach new learning tasks, independent of the CWPT classroom sessions (Delquadri, Greenwood, Stretton, & Hall, 1983). Students serving as tutors learn to effectively create learning opportunities and increase engagement time in academics for their partners, correct their errors, and give feedback and reinforcement. Students serving as tutees are trained to use auditory, visual, and writing modalities to practice and learn the new concepts.

CWPT for Spelling and Math: A Typical Day Format

At the beginning of each week, all students in a class are re-paired for tutoring, and these tutor–tutee pairs are assigned to one of two competing teams. One student in each pair serves as the tutor or teacher for 10 minutes, and the other student is the tutee. After the first 10 minutes have expired (signaled by a timer), the tutoring pairs reverse roles for an equivalent amount of time. The CWPT procedure focuses on students tutoring each other on prepared information in a reciprocal fashion, but the correct answers are provided by the tutor. Materials are prepared in advance by the teacher. Tutoring content lists or study guides consist of material either briefly introduced or not previously covered by the teacher (e.g., new list of spelling words). CWPT allows the teacher to introduce a lesson (e.g., phonics) to the whole class or small group and then to elaborate through independent practice the concepts during the peer tutoring sessions (e.g., selection of words following a specific phonetic rule for spelling tutoring).

As the students are working in pairs, they must follow the precise teaching procedure delineated by CWPT. That is, the tutor presents an instructional item orally and/or visually (e.g., vocabulary word, spelling word, math fact, social study question from a study guide) and the tutee must respond orally and in writing. If the answer is correct (tutor has the answer sheet), the tutor awards two points. However if the answer is incorrect, the tutor conducts an error correction procedure: (a) stops the tutee as soon as the error is made, (b) provides the correct response (modeling), (c) requires the tutee to write and say the correct answer three times (practice), and (d) awards one point to the tutee for correcting the mistake (reinforcement). If the tutee fails to provide the correct answer (three times), the tutor orally and visually provides the tutee with the correct response and proceeds to the next item, and no points are awarded. Repeated practice is provided when the length of the task is correctly set so that tutees cover the material at least two times in each 10-minute session.

The use of CWPT avoids direct competition between tutor-tutee pairs, but creates competition between teams. Both members of the tutoring pair are on the same team and work toward the common goal of winning with the highest point total. The object of CWPT is to complete as many items as possible, correctly, in the allotted tutoring time. The tutee is to proceed through the tutoring list or reading passage as many times as possible (during the 10 minutes). The more correct items the students complete, the more points they earn for themselves and their team, and the more active learning is taking place. Teams are rewarded with recognition (e.g., clapping of hands, stickers, privileges) and point posting on a classroom chart.

As the students are tutoring, the teacher moves about the classroom and awards bonus points for appropriate tutoring behaviors: (a) clear presentation of materials, (b) contingent awarding of points, (c) correct use of the error correction procedure, and (d) positive comments and reinforcers to the tutoring partner. Immediately after the tutoring session, students total their daily points, and these are recorded on a laminated team points chart posted in the front of the classroom. This provides another opportunity for the teacher to verbally reinforce students for their daily progress by evaluating their previous day's performance. Each day a team is announced as the daily winner. Students clap to congratulate the winner and quietly transition to the next class period.

Tutoring sessions typically occur 4 to 5 days during the week (30 minutes each for most subject areas; for reading, 40 to 45 minutes). At the end of the week, students' progress is assessed with a teacher prepared test covering the same material tutored during that week. Some teachers choose to tutor 4 days and allocate Fridays as a testing day. Students take tests individually, and earn 5 to 10 tutoring points for each correct answer. These points are also recorded on the team point charts. At the end of the week all points, including bonus and test points, are totaled and the winning team of the week is announced. The team is rewarded with a clapping of hands as well as through achievement certificates or special privileges. The second team is rewarded with a clapping of hands for their efforts and sportsmanship.

CWPT for Reading

The CWPT for reading follows basically the same procedures, with some minor variations. It uses the basal text or supplementary reading material (e.g., novels, newspapers) for the daily tutoring content. Two points are awarded for correct reading of complete sentences, one point for a corrected sentence, and no points are awarded when two errors occur in the same sentence reading. At the end of the first 10 minutes (reading passage tutoring), the tutor conducts a reading comprehension check (5 minutes) by asking the tutee five or more questions based on the passage, using who, what, where, when and why question formats. Students are trained in how to make these queries. Two points are awarded for correctly answered questions. A variation that has been implemented with culturally and linguistically heterogeneous classrooms is the provision of written comprehension questions by the teacher, using wall charts or overhead projectors. This provides LEP students with a correct model of how to compose and ask questions. After the first 15 minutes, the tutor–tutee pair changes roles and CWPT for: reading begins again.

Another variation of CWPT for reading is on the Friday test. Instead of a pretest and posttest format, a 1-minute reading rate check on one of the passages read that week, followed by five comprehension questions is used. A words-per-minute rate, error rate, and oral comprehension scores are calculated and charted on graphs. The graphs can be posted in the classroom or kept by the individual students. The teacher either chooses three low-achieving students and two average-achieving students to monitor on a weekly basis or assesses every student in the class.

In summary, core CWPT procedures include unit content development, peer pairing, reciprocal roles in each session, group and individual contingencies, immediate error correction procedures, public posting of individual team and group scores, social reward for the winning team, and weekly pretests and posttests.

BASIC PROCEDURAL COMPONENTS OF CWPT

Content Development

The goal of content preparation is to define a set of materials appropriate for the class that has not yet been mastered. The content selected to be taught in CWPT is based directly on the curriculum currently employed in the classroom through (a) reviewing grade-level scope, sequence, and students' individualized educational plans (IEPs); (b) organizing a hierarchical sequence of material to be learned; and (c) updating this sequence based on students' weekly pretest and posttest performance.

The tutoring content in spelling or math is a set of item lists sequenced in the same order as material that would be taught by traditional teacher format. For example, a list of 10 to 20 spelling words from the spelling book or reading content for the week or a list of multiplication facts. In reading, passages of text are used. The teacher selects the story or chapter to be read for the week and divides it into daily passages of equal or comparable length. This material is read aloud by the tutee to the tutor, a new short passage each day. It is also the basis for weekly oral reading rate and comprehension checks by the teacher. In social studies, passages of text are used in the same format of reading CWPT. The material is read aloud by the tutee to the tutor, and then they review the material using teacher-developed study guides. The study guides are composed of questions, fill-in-the-blank, or fill-in-a-map, based on the daily content.

In CWPT, the length of the material to be used is determined so that sufficient practice occurs in each session. A functional rule-of-thumb is that the length of material must be set so that the lowest ability student can practice through the entire material at least twice in a single, 10-minute tutoring session.

Weekly Assessments

In CWPT, pretest and posttest are used to monitor the academic effects of weekly tutoring sessions and mastery of the material. These weekly assessments are used by the teacher to make optimal adjustments in the difficulty of new material and demonstrate that CWPT consistently improves mastery and/or fluency levels compared to previous instructional formats. These data are charted each week and can be displayed publicly in the classroom, allowing students the opportunity to evaluate their performance. The pretest data assists the teacher in determining if the material for the week is appropriately new and challenging. If the class average in the pretest is above 50%, the teacher is advised to delete the most frequently correct items and to replace them with more difficult items. The posttest data are used to assess the mastery of the material tutored that week.

Mastery is demonstrated if the class average is at least 80% or above on the posttest. In reading, 1-minute reading rate checks are utilized. The rate of correct or incorrect words read per minute are computed and charted. An evaluation of the students' oral reading comprehension is recorded in the form of percent correct.

Teacher Training

Teachers learn to use the program through the CWPT manual (Greenwood, Delquadri, & Carta, 1988) and if available, structured training and interaction with a CWPT consultant (refer to the resources section). Typically a half day (4 to 6 hours) session is used to introduce the basics of the procedure to new teachers and to develop the basic charts. In addition, three consultant visits are desirable to assist teachers in selecting the specific content to be taught in tutoring, preparing the necessary materials, and in answering specific questions about fitting the program to the class. Then, the teacher is ready to train students in implementing the tutoring procedures.

In one investigation of the training required of CWPT, Maheady, Harper, Mallette, and Winstanley (1991) found that eight elementary school teachers reached a predetermined criterion (i.e., three consecutive sessions with fidelity of implementation ratings of 90% or above without consultant assistance) with an average training time of 178 minutes (2.96 hours). Subsequent fidelity checks indicated that implementation accuracy remained high (above 90%) without further consultant involvement.

Student Training

Students are taught by their classroom teacher to implement the tutoring procedures in four short lessons in which procedures are described, modeled, role played, and then practiced in isolation as directed in the manual. The lessons covered prior to the full CWPT session are the CWPT game, winning and losing teams–good sportsmanship, working with a partner, and being a peer tutor/tutor–tutee roles.

The full CWPT program is implemented when the teacher and students performance rates are 90% or above without consultant assistance. An implementation checklist is used by a consultant to provide feedback to the teacher on the accuracy of the implementation (see Greenwood, Delquadri,

& Carta, 1988) and serves as the basis for retraining during the next tutoring session.

Peer Pairing

There are various formats in which to achieve pairing in CWPT based on the content area and the characteristics of the students: random, modified random, and matching skill levels. A random or a modified random system of pairing can be employed for spelling, math, vocabulary, science, and/or social studies as these content areas provide the tutor with the written responses for accuracy. In the random system of pairing, the teacher draws students names from a hat for assignment to partners and partners to teams. In the modified random system, each pair includes a higher and a lower performing student. Teachers rank-order their students, then split the group in half. A top-ranked student in the higher performing half is paired with a top performer in the lower performing half. This matching process is continued until all students have a partner. Pairs are assigned to one of two teams for which they earn points. Teachers should be careful to ensure that both teams are equally balanced with high- and low-performing students. For LEP students, tutoring pairs are preferably composed of a student with no or limited English skills, and a student who speaks the same native language and that is more proficient in the English language. Pairing of students randomly is not recommended for culturally and linguistically diverse students with no or limited English skills, but is advisable for English-speaking peers and bilingual English-proficient students.

When the subject content area relies on the tutors' unaided ability to identify errors (i.e., when the correct answers are not available to the tutor), ability matching is recommended. Students in CWPT for reading are paired according to their placement in the reading program. Students are paired from within the same or adjacent reading levels. Only in the case of a very low-skilled student, a student with a disability, or a student for whom English is a second language and is LEP, would nonadjacent pairings or modified random pairings will be considered as a means of temporary support for instruction. In such cases, the higher performing reader reads first for each activity and serves as a model for the lower performing student.

Group and Individual Contingencies

Both group and individual contingencies are utilized in CWPT to maintain motivation and the quality of the implementation. Tutees are awarded 2 points for each correct first-time response, and 1 point for correctly practicing the correct response following an error. Individual points are recorded on a laminated point sheet that can be erased and reused. Students also receive bonus points from the teacher for following correct tutoring behaviors. At the end of each session, students report their total points earned. Individual points are added for each of the two teams and the winning team for the day is determined. The winning team is congratulated with applause and the weekly winning team receives a team of the week certificate (optional). The losing team after each session is also applauded for their good effort and it is challenged to work harder in the next session.

CWPT Tutoring Sessions

At the beginning of each CWPT session, the teacher directs the students attention to the "move–stay chart" posted in the classroom for their partner assignment. This chart displays the partners for the week, their team membership, which of the students need to move to their partners during tutoring, and which partner serves as tutor first. The teacher then instructs the students to get their tutoring materials and to move to their partners. Teacher sets the timer for the first 10-minute tutoring session. Each tutor presents the first item (e.g., word, equation, question) from the list to be learned by the tutee. The tutee then responds orally and in writing. The tutor checks the response by comparing it to the correct answer on the list. When an error occurs, the tutor immediately stops the tutee, provides the correct answer (orally and visually) and requires the tutee to practice by writing it three times. Tutees earn 2 points for correct answers and 1 point for correcting an error. These points are recorded in the individual point sheet by the tutor. The students go through the list of items as many times as possible during the 10-minute period.

At the end of the first 10-minute period, the tutor–tutee pair trades roles and a second 10-minute period is completed. In CWPT, for reading the tutoring sequence consists of a 10-minute period for oral reading followed by a 5-minute period for oral comprehension questions for each student. Following the second period, a 5-minute period is used by students to report orally the total points earned during CWPT. This information is posted on their team's chart. Individual points are summed and team totals announced. The winning team is congratulated with applause, and the losing team is encouraged to work harder in the next session. The teacher then transitions to the next activity of the day.

FUTURE DIRECTIONS AND CONCLUSIONS

In this chapter we presented empirical evidence in support of CWPT as an instructional procedure that enables the classroom teacher to orchestrate instructional processes know to accelerate and maintain the academic learning of students with diverse problems. CWPT provides the opportunity for sufficient practice, high levels of student active engagement, immediate error correction with feedback and the integration of students with heterogeneous abilities including students with disabilities and students for whom English is their second language. Beyond its effectiveness in the areas of academic achievement, CWPT represents an activity that can lead to a more positive classroom and learning atmosphere, in which all students can succeed, can learn effective learning strategies, and can become more socially acceptable.

The effectiveness of CWPT depends on how it is implemented. Although there are essential components to the CWPT program, it has proven flexible enough to be adapted to different content areas and diverse groups, allowing for teacher individualization and modifications without affecting the integrity of the procedure. Teachers' as well as students' satisfaction with the procedure have consistently rated high (80% to 98%). There is an initial time investment in training and preparation of materials (4 to 6 hours), after which, the time required for material preparation is minimal (average of 30 minutes per content, per week).

However, although CWPT is now an effective and validated procedure in a number of subject areas, it is not yet a complete, comprehensive system of instruction (Greenwood, Terry, Delquadri, Elliott, & Arreaga-Mayer, 1995). More research and validations are needed and are underway, including (a) curriculum and curriculum-based assessments uniquely designed for CWPT and PAL, (b) dissemination of the school building and system model for whole districts' adoption, and (c) improved software packages and technology to facilitate the implementation and monitoring of CWPT in classrooms.

CWPT is consistent with many recent developments in effective instruction, inclusion, and school reform. It presently has much to offer teachers and students looking for interesting, fun, and cost and time effective approaches to instruction and to accelerating learning.

REFERENCES

Achi-Dror, N. (1990). *Field replication of ClassWide Peer Tutoring in Israel.* Unpublished doctoral dissertation, Department of Human Development and Family Life, University of Kansas, Lawrence, KS.

Algozzine, B., & Maheady, L. (1986). In search of excellence: Instruction that works in special education classrooms (Special Issue). *Exceptional Children, 52,* 487–589.

Anderson, L., Evertson, C., & Brophy, J. (1979). An experimental study of effective teaching in first-grade reading groups.

Arreaga-Mayer, C. (in press). Effective strategies for teaching language minority students in the intermediate elementary grades. In R. Gersten (Ed.), *Language sensitive instruction.* Cleveland, OH: Lachina Publishing Services.

Arreaga-Mayer, C., Carta, J. J., & Tapia, Y. (1994). Ecobehavioral assessment of bilingual special education settings: The opportunity to respond revisited. In R. Gardner, III, D. Sainato, J. Cooper, T. Heron, W. Heward, J. Eskleman, & T. Grossi (Eds.), *Behavior analysis in education: Focus on measurably superior instruction* (pp. 225–240). Brooks/Cole.

Arreaga-Mayer, C., Carta, J. J., & Tapia, Y. (1995). Ecobehavioral assessment: A new methodology for evaluating instruction for exceptional culturally and linguistically diverse students. In S. B. Garcia (Ed.), *Addressing cultural and linguistic diversity in special education: Issues and trends* (pp. 10–29). Council for Exceptional Children.

Arreaga-Mayer, C., & Greenwood, C. R. (1986). Environmental variables affecting the school achievement of culturally and linguistically different learners: An instructional perspective. *Journal of the National Association for Bilingual Education, 10*(2), 113–135.

Arreaga-Mayer, C., Greenwood, C. R., & Utley, C. (1994). *Promoting literacy though ecobehavioral assessment and ClassWide Peer Tutoring for racial ethnic limited English proficient minority students with disabilities* (OSEP grant CFDA No. 84.023C). Kansas City, KS: Juniper Gardens Children's Project, University of Kansas.

Arreaga-Mayer, C. & Perdomo-Rivera, C. (1996). Ecobehavioral analysis of instruction for at-risk language minority students. *The Elementary School Journal, 96*(3), 245–258.

Berliner, D.C. (1988). The half-full glass: A review of research on teaching. In E.L. Meyen, G. A. Vergason, & R. J. Whelan (Eds.). *Effective instructional strategies for exceptional children* (pp. 7–31). Denver, CO: Love.

Brophy, J. E. (1983). Classroom organization and management. *The Elementary School Journal, 83,* 265–286.

Brophy, J. E. (1979). Teacher behavior and its effects. *Journal of Educational Psychology, 71,* 733–750.

Brophy, J. E., & Good, T. L. (1986). Teacher behavior and student achievement. In M. C. Wittrock (Ed.), *Handbook of research on teaching* (3rd ed., pp. 328–375). New York: Macmillan.

Carlton, M. B., Litton, F. W., & Zinkgrof, S. A. (1985). The effects of an interclass peer tutoring program on the sight-word recognition ability of students who are mildly mentally retarded. *Mental Retardation, 23,* 74–78.

Chapman, E., & Leach, D. (1991). Classwide peer tutoring: A comparison of "Tutor Huddle" and teacher-directed procedures. *The Australian Educational and Developmental Psychologist, 8,* 2–7.

Christenson, S. L., Ysseldyke, J. E., & Thurlow, M. I. (1989). Critical instructional factors for students with mild handicaps: An integrated review. *Remedial and Special Education, 10,* 21–31.

Cooke, N. L., Heron, T. E., & Heward, W. L. (1983). *Peer tutoring: Implementing classwide programs in the primary grades.* Columbus, OH: Special Press.

Delquadri, J., Greenwood, C. R., Stretton, K., & Hall, R. V. (1983). The peer tutoring game: A classroom procedure for increasing opportunity to respond and spelling performance. *Education and Treatments of Children, 6,* 225–239.

Delquadri, J., Greenwood, C. R., Whorton, D., Carta, J. J., & Hall, R. V. (1986). Classwide peer tutoring. *Exceptional Children, 52,* 535–542.

DuPaul, G. J., & Henningson, P. N. (1993). Peer tutoring effects on the classroom performance of children with attention deficit hyperactivity disorder. *School Psychology Review, 22,* 134–142.

Fiore, T. A., & Becker, E. A. (1994). *Promising classroom interventions for students with attention deficit disorders.* Research Triangle Park, NC: Center for Research in Education, Research Triangle Institute.

Fuchs, D., & Fuchs, L. S. (1990). Making educational research more important. *Exceptional Children, 57,* 102–108.

Fuchs, L. S., Fuchs, D., Bentz, J., Phillips, N. B., & Hamlett, C. L. (1994). The nature of student interactions during peer tutoring with and without prior training and experience. *American Educational Research journal, 31,* 75–103.

Good, T. L., & Grouws, D. A. (1979). The Missouri mathematics effectiveness project: An experimental study in fourth-grade classrooms. *Journal of Educational Psychology, 71,* 355–362.

Greenwood, C. R. (1991a). A longitudinal analysis of time, engagement, and achievement in at-risk versus non-risk students. *Exceptional Children, 57,* 521–535.

Greenwood, C. R. (1991b). Classwide peer tutoring: Longitudinal effects on the reading, language, and mathematics achievement of at-risk students. *Journal of Reading, Writing, and Learning Disabilities International, 7,* 105–123.

Greenwood, C. R., Carta, J. J., & Kamps, D. (1990). Teacher versus peer-mediated instruction. In H. Foot, M. Morgan, & R. Shute (Eds.), *Children helping children* (pp. 177–206). London, England: Wiley.

Greenwood, C. R., Carta, J. J., Kamps, D., & Hall, E. V. (1988). The use of classwide peer tutoring strategies in classroom management and instruction. *School Psychology Review, 17,* 258–275.

Greenwood, C. R., & Delquadri, J. (1995). Classwide peer tutoring and the prevention of school failure. *Preventing School Failure, 39*(4), 21–25.

Greenwood, C. R., Delquadri, J., & Carta, J. J. (1988). *Classwide peer tutoring (CWPT): Teacher manual.* Kansas City, KS: Juniper Gardens Children's Project, University of Kansas.

Greenwood, C. R., Delquadri, J., & Hall. R. V. (1989). Longitudinal effects of classwide peer tutoring. *Journal of Educational Psychology, 81,* 371–383.

Greenwood, C. R., Dinwiddie, G., Bailey, V., Carta, J. J., Dorsey, D., Kohler, F., Nelson, C., Rotholz, D., & Shulte, D. (1987). Field replication of classwide peer tutoring. *Journal of Applied Behavior Analysis, 20,* 151–160.

Greenwood, C. R., Maheady, L., & Carta, J. J. (1991). Peer tutoring programs in the regular classroom. In G. Stoner, M. R. Shinn, & H. M. Walker (Eds.), *Intervention for achievement and behavior problems* (pp. 179–200). Washington, DC: National Association fro School Psychologists (NASP).

Greenwood, C. R., Terry, B. J., Delquadri, J., Elliott, M., & Arreaga-Mayer, C. (1995). *ClassWide Peer Tutoring (CWPT): Effective teaching and research review.* Kansas City, KS: Juniper Gardens Children's Project, University of Kansas.

Greenwood, C. R., Terry, B., Utley, C. A., Montagna, D., & Walker, D. (1993). Achievement, placement, and services: Middle school benefits of ClassWide peer tutoring used at the elementary school. *School Psychologist, 22*(30), 497–516.

Harper, G. F., Mallette, B., Maheady, L., & Clifton, R. (1990). Responsive Research: Applications of peer tutoring to arithmetic and spelling. *Direct Instruction News, 9,* 34–38.

Harper, G. F., Mallette, B., Maheady, L., Parkes, V., & Moore, J. (1993). Retention and generalization of spelling words acquired using a peer-mediated instructional procedure by children with mild handicapping conditions. *Journal of Behavior Education, 3,* 25–38.

Heron, T. E., Heward, W. L., Cooke, N. L., & Hill, D. S. (1983). Evaluation of classwide peer tutoring system: First graders teach each other sight-words. *Education and Treatment of Children, 6,* 137–152.

Kamps, D., Barbetta, P. M., Leonard, B. R., & Delquadri, J. (1994). Classwide peer tutoring: An integration strategy to improve reading skills and promote peer interactions among students with autism and general education peers. *Journal of Applied Behavior Analysis, 27,* 49–61.

Kaufmann, M. J., Kameenui, E. J., Birman, B., & Danielson, L. (1990). Special education and the process of change: Victim or master of educational reform? *Exceptional Children, 57,* 109–116.

Leinhardt, G., & Pallay, A. (1982). Restrictive educational settings: Exile or haven? *Review of Educational Research, 52,* 557–578.

Leinhardt, G., Zigmond, N., & Cooley, W. W. (1981). Reading instruction and its effects. *American Educational Research Journal, 23,* 161–190.

Madrid, D., Terry, B., Greenwood, C. R., Whaley, D., & Webber, N. (1991). *Active versus passive peer tutoring: Focus on spelling performance.* Manuscript submitted for publication.

Maheady, L., & Harper, G. (1987). A classwide peer tutoring program to improve the spelling performance of low income third- and fourth- grade students. *Education and Treatment of Children, 10,* 120–133.

Maheady, L., Harper, G., Mallette, B., & Winstanley, N. (1991). Training and implementation requirements associated with the use of a classwide peer tutoring system. *Education and Treatment of
Children, 14,* 177–189.

Maheady, L., Harper, G., & Sacca, M. K. (1988). Classwide peer tutoring programs in secondary
self-contained programs for the mildly handicapped. *Journal of Research and Development in
Education, 21*(3), 76–83.

Maheady, L., Sacca, M. K., & Harper, G. (1988). The effects of a classwide peer tutoring program on
the academic performance of mildly handicapped students enrolled in 10th grade social studies
classes. *Exceptional Children, 55,* 52–59.

Mathes, P. G., & Fuchs, L. S. (1993). Peer-mediated reading instruction in special education resource
rooms. *Learning Disabilities Research & Practice, 8,* 233–243.

Mathes, P. G., Fuchs, D., Fuchs, L. S., Henley, A.M., & Sanders, M. (1994). Increasing strategic reading
practice with Peabody classwide peer tutoring. *Learning Disabilities Research & Practice, 9*(1),
44–48.

Mortweet, S. (1995). *Classwide peer tutoring effects on the social interactions of students with mild
disabilities and their typical peers across multiple settings.* Unpublished doctoral dissertation.
Department of Human Development and Family Life, University of Kansas, Lawrence, KS.

Rosenshine, B., & Berliner, D. C. (1978). Academic engaged time. *British Journal of Teacher Education,
4,* 3–16.

Rosenshine, B., & Stevens, R. (1986). Teaching functions. In M. C. Wittrock (Ed.), *Handbook of
research on teaching* (pp. 376–391). New York: Macmillan.

Sideridis, G. (1994). *Classwide peer tutoring: Effects on the social interactions and spelling performance of students with mild disabilities and their typical peers.* Unpublished doctoral dissertation.
Department of Human Development and Family Life, University of Kansas, Lawrence, KS.

Sindelar, P. T., Smith, M. A., Harriman, N. E., Hale, R. L., & Wilson, R. J. (1986). Teacher effectiveness
in special education programs. *Journal of Special Education, 20,* 195–207.

Reciprocal Peer Tutoring: Developing and Testing Effective Peer Collaborations for Elementary School Students

John Fantuzzo
Marika Ginsburg-Block
University of Pennsylvania

Reciprocal peer tutoring (RPT) is a peer-assisted learning (PAL) intervention that was developed originally for pairs of low-achieving urban, elementary school students (Fantuzzo, King, & Heller, 1992). This intervention comes in response to the growing need to discover effective strategies to help children in high-risk environments feel academically competent and make achievement gains.

In contrast to a mixed-ability peer tutoring strategy where the emphasis is placed on supporting the higher ability student's efforts to help the lower functioning student, RPT employs same-age student pairs (dyads) of comparable ability with the primary objective of keeping both peer student (tutee) and peer teacher (tutor) engaged in constructive academic activity.

RPT provides student dyads with the opportunity to alternate between peer student and peer teacher roles in the context of a structured format that guides them through the learning process. RPT uses both a reciprocal peer teaching structure and a peer-managed incentive system, designed to enhance learner control and peer cooperation. It was designed to incorporate the most effective learning strategies informed by the literature on peer teaching, academic achievement motivation, and classroom group-reward strategies.

The purpose of this chapter is to present the RPT intervention; the learning concepts that informed the development of this intervention; and the existing body of empirical, school-based studies documenting its effectiveness.

THE RPT INTERVENTION

The steps involved in implementing the RPT intervention in urban elementary schools include teamwork training, RPT training, and the supervision of the RPT intervention.

Prior to receiving specific training in RPT, participating students are introduced to the RPT classroom setting and the concept of teamwork over the course of two 45-minute sessions. During the introductory sessions, teaching aides present concepts such as *teamwork, partnership,* and *cooperation* and ask students to give concrete examples of these concepts, discuss how students help each other in school and play cooperative games that illustrate these concepts. The introduction to teamwork provides students with the opportunity to become familiar with their peer partners, receive instruction in the fundamentals of effective teamwork, and work successfully with their partners as a team. Providing all students with an introduction to teamwork assures that they are entering the program with a comparable understanding of teamwork, because students may vary in their prior exposure to collaborative learning strategies.

During these sessions, the dyads are told that they will learn how to make school more fun by discovering how they can win by using teamwork. Teaching aides provide dyads with instruction in basic teamwork concepts: goal setting, working together to attain goals (teamwork), attaining team goals. A velcro dart game is used to concretize these concepts. Each dyad sets a goal for their score and works under a time limit to attain their goal. The teaching aides help them identify some teamwork strategies that will increase their score. After these exercises, they discuss how working as a team is more useful in attaining their goal than working independently. The teaching aides conclude these sessions by complementing the students on their performance and emphasizing the concepts of goal setting, teamwork, and winning.

Training in the RPT intervention consists of two to three 45-minute training sessions, used to instruct students on the procedures for participating in structured peer teaching sessions and implementing their own interdependent group reward contingency. During these training sessions, teaching aides model the RPT procedures for student dyads until the students can follow the procedures without assistance.

RPT sessions are held twice weekly for 45 minutes and have been carried out over periods ranging from 10 weeks (Fantuzzo, Davis, & Ginsburg, 1995) to 5 months (Fantuzzo, King, & Heller, 1992) with positive results. RPT has been applied primarily to the mathematics education of low-achieving, upper elementary school children in Grades 3 through 6 and ranging in age from 8 to 13. Efforts are currently under way to modify RPT for use with additional student populations and areas of the curriculum and evaluate its efficacy in these varied contexts. Based on its effectiveness in promoting positive student outcomes for elementary students in mathematics and its foundation in many overarching learning principles, Fantuzzo and his associates are confident that RPT will be shown to be effective in its application to alternate student populations and areas of the curriculum. These endeavors are addressed in greater detail later.

Each RPT session follows an established routine that includes 20 minutes of dyads working on computational problems according to a teaching framework where they alternate roles as peer teacher and peer student. At the beginning of each session, children are instructed to decide who will act as peer teacher first. The student then opens their folder and hands their mathematics flash cards to their peer teacher. The flash cards are selected for each student, according to the mathematical computation areas in which they need strengthening. These areas are identified during curriculum-based assessment, conducted prior to implementing RPT. Each flashcard has one computation problem printed on one side with the computational steps and answer provided on the reverse side.

Peer teachers present flashcards to their students and instruct them to compute the problems on a structured worksheet. The worksheets (try sheets) are divided into sections: "Try 1," "Try 2," "Help," and "Try 3." Peer students then compute the problems as their peer teachers observe. Peer teachers check the peer student's work against the answer provided on the back of each flashcard. When peer students answer a problem correctly, peer teachers praise them and present the next problem. If the solution is incorrect, peer teachers instruct their students to try the problems again in the box marked "Try 2." If students are unable to answer a problem after the second try, peer teachers are permitted to help them in the space provided on the worksheet. Teaching aides are available to assist peer teachers if they have difficulty answering their students' questions. Students then continue working on the problem in the space labeled "Try 3" on the worksheet. After

10 minutes, participants switch roles, continuing to work in the same fashion, as peer teacher and student, for an additional 10 minutes.

RPT dyads choose their group rewards from a menu of available options and select team goals for mathematics performance from a predetermined range of choices representing improvements over baseline performance levels. Prior to the first RPT intervention session, teaching aides meet with classroom teachers to discuss the range of classroom rewards available to students. Rewards consist of special privileges such as the opportunity for students to act as teacher's helper, messenger, or work on a special project. A master list is compiled of the rewards approved by each teacher for students in individual classrooms. All of the rewards are rewards that teachers are already using in their classrooms.

Team goals are selected by dyads from a list of recommended choices during a weekly meeting with teaching aides, recording both their goal and reward on their team goal sheet. During each session, dyads have an opportunity to work toward meeting their team goal. Following the 20-minute reciprocal peer-tutoring session, a problem drill sheet consisting of 16 mathematics problems is distributed. Drill sheets are individualized for each child based on that child's previously determined level of mathematics proficiency. After completing the drill sheets, children switch papers with their partners and use an answer sheet to score and correct their partner's work. Dyads compute their team's total score by counting the number of problems each team member completed correctly. Therefore, each member of the dyad contributes to the team's total score, creating interdependence and individual accountability within the dyad. Children then compare the team score with their team goal to determine whether they have met their goal and if the team has won. After a predetermined number of wins, the team earns their team reward. Each dyad generally receives a reward once weekly. All of these rewards are administered by the students' classroom teachers.

In cases where students achieve a score of 13 or greater on their problem sheets, they are moved up one level of difficulty, in order to assure that students are sufficiently challenged by the problem sheets. In cases where students score 8 or less on their problem sheets, they are moved down one level of difficulty, in order for success to be attainable.

All of the mathematics materials (flash cards and problem sheets) used to implement RPT are easily produced from the school's current mathematics curriculum. Examples of the generic materials (try sheets and goal sheets) have been reproduced for the reader in the appendix.

CURRENT THINKING AND PRACTICE INFORMING RPT DEVELOPMENT

The RPT intervention was informed by the literature on peer teaching, achievement motivation, and group reward contingencies. The following sections summarize these current theories and their supporting research, and illustrate how RPT incorporates the most effective strategies from these bodies of literature.

Peer Teaching

Numerous studies have documented the benefits of PAL strategies (Greenwood, Carta, & Hall, 1988; Slavin, 1990). Peer-assisted methods have been linked to a wide range of student outcomes including increases in students' academic achievement, time on task, motivation, classroom behavior, and students' self-report of social, behavioral, and academic competence (Fantuzzo, King, & Heller, 1992; Greenwood, Terry, Utley, Montagna, & Walker, 1993; Slavin, 1990).

Proponents of cognitive elaboration theory (Slavin, 1990) or the text mediational view (Webb & Farivar, 1994; Webb & Palincsar, 1996; Wertsch & Bivens, 1992) of interpreting the mechanism by which social processes give rise to cognitive processes, have emphasized the academic value of enabling children to explain or teach concepts to one another. Empirical evidence supporting this theory shows that peer tutors display more gains than the students they teach (Greenwood, Carta, & Hall, 1988) and that providing explanations increases students' retention of information (Webb, 1985).

Although much is known about the outcomes of peer tutoring interventions, little is known about the mechanisms of the peer tutoring process in these popular intervention methods or what elements of peer teaching programs promote them (Ginsburg-Block & Fantuzzo, 1997). Therefore, research is needed to clarify the links between specific intervention components and peer interactions and positive student outcomes in well-defined peer tutoring interventions.

Several studies, however, provide a direction for further investigations of peer tutoring strategies. Webb and Farivar (1994) studied the effects of instruction and practice in academic helping skills on student achievement in mathematical operations and the use of elaborated help in small, mixed-ability learning groups, in a middle school setting. The findings indicated that giving and receiving elaborated help and providing answers, in the context of small, mixed-ability groups, was associated with mathematics achievement.

A study, involving seventh-grade students, was conducted by Webb, Troper, and Fall (1995) to investigate the conditions necessary for help received to be effective for learning. These researchers found that the level of constructive activity was the strongest predictor of achievement and the level of help that students received predicted constructive activity, but not achievement. This finding is consistent with previous research that found that students benefit from increased opportunities for practice in academic areas, yet often lack the skills or opportunities required to remain academically engaged (Stanley & Greenwood, 1983).

Based on theories of sociocognitive development and research related to peer teaching, opportunities to explain concepts to peers and practice these academic skills contribute to academic achievement. RPT was designed to promote student success by providing a learning environment that supports student dyads in maintaining their involvement in academic activity. The role of RPT peer teachers is to help their peer students successfully solve problems by keeping them on task, giving them instructional prompts, and providing them with praise and encouragement. Outside of these general guidelines, peer teachers and peer students are encouraged to be creative in assisting one another through the learning process, allowing them to benefit from articulating concepts and the exposure to new and challenging ideas from their same-age peers. RPT is designed to allow each student the opportunity to perform the role of peer teacher and peer student, drawing on the educational value of both providing and receiving assistance from a peer.

Academic Achievement Motivation

The academic achievement motivation literature focuses on ways that the learning environment either promotes or hinders intrinsic academic motivation, thereby affecting academic performance. The literature supports classroom structures that guide learning while providing students with the opportunity to contribute to the learning process.

Deci and Ryan (1985) made a distinction among classroom structures, using the terms *controlling, informational,* or *permissive* to describe the learning environment. Controlling structures tightly script all student activities, demanding that students follow a detailed, rigid format. In contrast, informational structures provide students with enough information to guide and sequence their learning activity, while allowing room for student creativity. Permissive classroom formats refrain from imposing external regulation or providing informational structures, leaving students with no academic structure or support.

Research findings indicate that controlling structures inhibit students' academic motivation, creativity, and long-term retention of academic material, whereas informational structures are associated with higher levels of intrinsic motivation, perceived competency, exploration, and self-worth (Koestner, Ryan, Bernieri & Holt, 1984; Ryan & Stiller, 1991).

Achievement goal theory draws attention to the purpose of achievement as it is defined in the classroom (Ames, 1992). Ames and Archer (1987; 1988) identified two contrasting achievement goal constructs to describe the learning environment, mastery and performance goals. A mastery goal is characterized by the belief that academic effort will result in achievement. In contrast, a performance goal reflects the belief that ability alone leads to success.

Ames (1992) suggested that the structure of classroom-tasks, authority, and evaluation can be modified to support a mastery goal, leading to increases in academic motivation (Schunk, 1996), and positive educational outcomes (Ames & Archer, 1988; Butler, 1987; Elliot & Dweck, 1988). In order to promote a mastery goal orientation, tasks should offer a reasonable challenge to students and place emphasis on self-referenced standards and opportunities for self-directed learning. The authority structure in mastery-oriented classrooms should provide students with choices, allowing them to participate in the decision-making process. In addition, students should be supported in the use of self-management and monitoring skills, providing them with opportunities to develop responsibility and independence. Evaluation or reward procedures should be based on improvement, progress and mastery of material, rather than social comparison or norm-based performance (Ames, 1992; Stipek, 1996).

In summary, the academic achievement literature links structure and achievement goal orientation to the development of academic motivation in students. Optimal learning conditions include the implementation of an informational classroom structure and the establishment of mastery learning objectives. The informational structure provided by RPT provides students with useful materials, such as flash cards and work sheets, and a structure to follow as each student assumes the role of peer teacher and peer student, while allowing for creativity and independence. Although teaching aides do not control student interactions, they provide support and encouragement throughout the PAL process. A mastery orientation is promoted by RPT through the autonomy that is provided to students by allowing them to choose their team goals and rewards and administer their own group reward contingencies. Tasks are designed to provide these low-achieving students with practice in basic skills that they need to master. Relative improvement is emphasized and rewarded rather than norm-based performance, promoting the belief among students that success is attainable and results from effort, not necessarily ability.

Group Reward Contingencies

The use of reward contingencies or extrinsic motivators to promote academic achievement has been studied with much enthusiasm and debate in the literature (Cameron & Pierce, 1994, 1996; Kohn, 1996; Lepper, Keavney, & Drake, 1996; Ryan & Deci, 1996). Group reward contingencies that target and reward academic effort have been found to promote academic achievement and even reductions in inappropriate classroom behaviors (Fantuzzo, King, & Heller, 1992; Pigott & Heggie, 1986).

Empirical study has identified several conditions under which the use of rewards is most effective in promoting positive student outcomes. These conditions include the use of group as opposed to individual rewards, the most cooperative group interdependent contingencies where each member contributes to obtaining the reward, contingencies that call for individual accountability and finally, the use of peer-managed reward contingencies (Pigott & Heggie, 1986; Slavin, 1983, 1990).

Slavin (1990) attributed the success of cooperative learning strategies in part to the establishment of group versus competitive or individual reward structures. Working toward a common goal, as in the case of group reward contingencies, promotes peer encouragement, reinforcement of effort, and the establishment of norms emphasizing academic achievement (Slavin, 1990). In contrast, traditional reward structures (i.e., individualistic and competitive) promote competition among students. These structures create a classroom environment in which academic achievement is not promoted by the peer group (Slavin, 1990).

There is a literature that recognizes the differences among students of various ethnic and racial backgrounds with regard to their learning styles and the most effective educational strategies. In a review of the theories, research, and models of the learning styles of African-American children, Willis (1992) concluded that African-American children generally learn in ways characterized by factors of social–affective emphases, harmony, holistic perspectives, expressive creativity, and nonverbal communication.

Widaman and Kagan (1987) conducted a study to determine the differential impact of several cooperative and competitive classroom organizations and the interaction of student characteristics with learning methods. They found that social orientation (cooperative or competitive) and ethnic status interact with classroom structure to determine achievement gains. Their findings support the hypothesis that competitive classroom structures fail to benefit minorities, who generally hold cooperative social orientations, yet cooperative classroom structures are associated with positive educational outcomes for individuals of minority status.

In their review of 20 empirical studies comparing the effectiveness of individual and group reward contingencies, Pigott and Heggie (1986) identified cooperative behavior and interdependence as factors likely to contribute to the increased effectiveness of group over individual reward contingencies. Interdependence is achieved when the administration of reinforcers is contingent on the performance of all group members, restricting the effect of any one student's performance on the group's outcome and subsequent reward attainment.

In a review of 60 studies of cooperative learning (CL) methods, Slavin (1990) found that methods that emphasized group goals and individual accountability were more effective in increasing student academic achievement than other methods. Slavin hypothesized that both conditions are necessary to provide incentives for students to help one another learn. For example, in situations where there is a group goal with no individual accountability, stopping and explaining concepts to a group member may delay the group and inhibit the group's ability to accomplish their task (Slavin, 1990). In cases where the success of each group member contributes to the success of the group, assisting a group member would contribute to the overall success of the group.

The literature on student-managed reward contingencies or self-management suggests that peer management fosters more student involvement, promoting academic achievement (Fantuzzo & Rohrbeck, 1992). In contrast to teacher-managed procedures, research on student-managed interventions documents the superior qualities of these interventions in promoting positive classroom behaviors and generalization of effects. Peer-managed interventions are more cost-effective and less intrusive than adult-directed interventions, because they employ students in managing their own academic behavior change programs (Fantuzzo & Polite, 1990).

In a review of 42 empirical studies of classroom-based, self-management strategies, Fantuzzo and Polite (1990) found a positive relationship between the degree of self-management employed in the intervention and the treatment effect size. In another study, Schunk (1996) found that fourth graders who were provided with opportunities to engage in self-evaluation in the context of a learning environment that emphasized effort over ability evidenced increases in their self-efficacy, skill, motivation, and task–goal orientation. (For additional information on Schunk's work, refer to chap. 10, this volume.)

In summary, the group reward literature points to the inclusion of structures that include interdependence, individual accountability, and peer management. The reward component of the RPT intervention was based on this literature and designed to maximize student choice and participation. The necessity for implementing a classroom reward strategy must be determined for each student population. Classroom group reward strategies should be designed specifically for the context in which they will be used with students. The strategy used in RPT was designed specifically for academically at-risk students in a large, urban school district in the United States. The distinct feature of RPT's reward component is the use of dyads to manage their own reward contingencies through selecting their team rewards and goals, monitoring and recording their performance, and evaluating and rewarding goal attainment. Each member of the dyad contributes to achieving the team goal and subsequent reward, fostering interdependence and individual accountability within the dyad.

EMPIRICAL INVESTIGATION CHARTING
THE DEVELOPMENT OF RPT

Development of the Peer-Mediated Group
Reward Contingency

In the early stages of developing the RPT intervention, a series of single-subject design studies was conducted to evaluate the effects of peer-managed group reward contingencies on student outcomes (Pigott, Fantuzzo, & Clement, 1986; Pigott, Fantuzzo, Heggie, & Clement, 1984; Wolfe, Fantuzzo, & Wolter, 1984; Wolfe, Fantuzzo, & Wolfe, 1986; Wolter, Pigott, Fantuzzo, & Clement, 1984) and to identify the intervention components responsible for effecting these changes (Fantuzzo, Polite, & Grayson, 1990).

A peer-administered group reward contingency was established that was based on combining peer-management procedures, interdependent group reward contingencies, and individual accountability procedures. A series of studies conducted to evaluate this intervention documented the effectiveness of the intervention in increasing arithmetic performance and decreasing disruptive behaviors of low-achieving elementary school students in both experimental (Wolfe, Fantuzzo, & Wolter, 1984; Wolter, Pigott, Fantuzzo, & Clement, 1984) and natural classroom settings (Pigott, Fantuzzo, & Clement, 1986; Pigott, Fantuzzo, Heggie, & Clement, 1984; Wolfe, Fantuzzo, & Wolfe, 1986).

Additionally, the social validity, maintenance, and social impact of treatment gains have been evaluated empirically by these studies. During the treatment and maintenance phases, the arithmetic performance of the low-achieving students who received the intervention was raised to the level of average-achieving students in their classroom. These findings validate the social significance or validity of the magnitude of improvement exhibited by students receiving the intervention. Assessment of the maintenance of treatment effects indicated that the average performance of treatment group students remained at or above treatment levels during the maintenance phase. Sociometric data (peer rankings) revealed that students who participated in the treatment groups remained constant (Wolfe et al., 1986) or increased (Pigott et al., 1986) in their amount of peer affiliation with other treatment group participants, yet remained stable relative to control group students.

The final study of this phase, conducted by Fantuzzo, Polite, and Grayson (1990), represents a partial component analysis of the teamwork (teaming and positive attention) and group reward contingency components of the peer-managed group reward contingency to determine the respective contribution of each aspect to student outcomes. Twenty-eight academically at-risk elementary school students from seven fourth- and fifth-grade classes across three public elementary schools participated. Participants were assigned randomly to either treatment or control conditions. A multiple-baseline design across children was used, where the teamwork component was isolated to determine the singular benefits of teamwork and the additive benefits of a group reward contingency.

Findings of this study indicated that merely teaming students and providing them with positive attention for cooperative, nonacademic behavior had no effect on mathematics performance, whereas training and practice in implementing group contingencies significantly increased mathematics performance and attendance rates for participating students. From this work, it became evident that the way in which peers worked together required modification in order to yield positive results from the peer teaming as well as the group reward contingency aspects of the intervention.

Development of the Structure and Process of RPT

The preliminary RPT studies served to document the efficacy of a strategy employing teamwork and a peer-managed group reward contingency in the context of single-subject design studies conducted under experimental and regular classroom conditions with small groups of students. Following this work, several studies were conducted to further develop and examine the process of peer tutoring.

Fantuzzo, King, and Heller (1992) conducted the first large-scale study implementing a completely randomized experimental design to examine the relative contributions of the two operative components of RPT: the structured, PAL format and the interdependent, group reward contingency. A second study conducted by Ginsburg-Block and Fantuzzo (1997) examined the peer teaching behaviors associated with RPT training and their relationship to student outcomes.

Important changes in the peer-managed group reward contingency intervention were made at this stage, leading to the development of the RPT intervention: First, the teamwork aspect of the intervention was enhanced to include structured reciprocal peer tutoring, rather than simply coaching on the implementation of strategies prior to completing a worksheet. Second, dyads, rather than groups of four or more students, became the targeted unit, allowing each student to perform all of the roles required to manage their own reward contingency.

The Fantuzzo, King, and Heller (1992) study evaluated the individual and combined effects of receiving structured PAL and an interdependent group reward contingency on mathematics performance, teacher reports of conduct, and child self-report of academic and behavioral competence. For this study, 64 students were selected randomly from a pool of 80 academically at-risk fourth- and fifth-grade students in an urban elementary school. These students were then assigned to one of four treatment conditions: structure only, reward only, structure plus reward, and no structure, no reward.

Fantuzzo et al. (1992) found that students who received both components of the RPT intervention displayed the highest levels of accurate mathematics computations. Regarding the unique role of each intervention component, analyses revealed that students in the structured conditions reported significantly higher levels of academic and behavioral competence. These findings are consistent with the literature on classroom structures that has found controlling structures to inhibit motivation and creativity, in contrast to informational structures that have been associated with student assessments of competency and exploration and increases in intrinsic motivation (Koestner et al., 1984). The informational structure provided by RPT equipped students with materials, such as flash cards and work sheets, and a structure to follow as each student performed the role of peer teacher and peer student. This structure enhanced students' confidence by guiding their interactions while promoting initiative, resulting in significantly higher levels of academic and behavioral competence reported by students.

Students who received the interdependent group reward contingency earned higher conduct reports from their classroom teachers than students who received no group reward contingencies. Students in the interdependent group reward condition were rewarded for their academic efforts, which would most likely compete with disruptive, off-task behavior. These findings are consistent with a subgroup of studies from the group reward literature that found targeting and reinforcing academic effort to be associated with collateral reductions in inappropriate classroom behaviors (Pigott & Heggie, 1986).

Impressive, however, is the fact that in the Fantuzzo, King, and Heller (1992) study, positive behavior patterns were generalized to the regular classroom. The reward selection and administration procedures in this study are believed to have enhanced the process of generalizing these behaviors to the classroom by using rewards that were already being used in the students' classrooms and having regular classroom teachers administer them to their students.

Stemming from the components study, which isolated the effects of structure and reward on student outcomes, a study was conducted to specifically examine the peer interaction process and the extent to which specific peer tutoring behaviors were associated with academic gains in the context of RPT (Ginsburg-Block & Fantuzzo, 1997). Further analysis of these RPT peer interactions enhances our knowledge of the peer teacher–peer student behaviors involved in increasing student academic outcomes and may be used to guide the development of more effective peer-tutoring strategies.

Forty academically at-risk fourth- and fifth-grade African-American public elementary school children participated in this study. Individual participants were assigned randomly to one of two experimental conditions, RPT or practice control (PC). The RPT condition was identical to the RPT intervention described earlier. The PC condition was structured identically to RPT; however, students worked alone, they were not paired in dyads and no reward contingencies were established. Opportunities for PC students to practice mathematics problems were identical to those for students in the RPT condition.

Findings of this study revealed significant group differences between students who had training and experience in RPT and PC participants in peer teacher and peer student peer tutoring interactions. Direct observation revealed that the RPT intervention was associated with significantly higher peer teacher and peer student rates of active task-related behavior as compared to controls. Peer students and peer teachers were actively engaged when they were productively involved in the academic task assigned to the dyad.

For peer teachers, this meant that they were providing task-specific assistance (presenting problems, focusing their peer student with questions, providing feedback, answers, or explanations in reference to their peer student's work) or nontask-specific support (providing praise, general instructions, or attending) to their peer student. For peer students, being actively engaged meant that they were working to solve a problem or interacting with their peer teacher in relation to the academic task (requesting assistance, listening to their peer teacher). These results support previous research in collaborative learning that found high levels of academically engaged behavior among students participating in collaborative learning programs (Greer & Polirstok, 1982; Slavin, 1990).

Unique to the literature on peer tutoring interactions is this study's examination of the relationship between observations of student interactions and student self report of social acceptance and conduct, as well as academic outcomes. Observations of peer teachers providing general instructions, praise, and attention to their peer students were associated with positive self-appraisals of behavioral conduct made by peer teachers. Observations of peer teachers insulting their peer students were associated with lower self-appraisals of social acceptance and conduct by peer teachers. The links between observational findings and student self-report lend significant support to the validity of the results found in this study.

An examination of student behaviors and their relationship to academic outcomes revealed that active engagement in the academic activity was positively related to mathematics computation scores, consistent with the literature (Stanley & Greenwood, 1983; Webb & Farivar, 1994). In contrast, observations of students assuming the role of the peer teacher, indicating problematic peer student–peer teacher interactions, were negatively associated with mathematics outcomes.

Together, these studies demonstrate the distinct roles of the structure, group reward, and peer teaching aspects of the RPT intervention in promoting positive student outcomes. The informational structure was linked to higher levels of academic and behavioral competence in students; the interdependent group reward contingency was linked to higher conduct reports from classroom teachers; and active engagement in academic activity in the context of peer teaching was linked to mathematics achievement. The combination of these RPT components produces promising academic, social, and behavioral outcomes for low-achieving students.

These studies have increased our understanding of the intervention components and the peer tutoring mechanisms at work in the RPT intervention. Studying the role that specific components of the RPT intervention play in promoting these positive peer teaching behaviors would be an important next step. Careful study of the intervention components of RPT and other published peer tutoring interventions believed to be responsible for specific peer teaching behaviors would allow educators to select and customize interventions to the special needs of their target populations.

Developing Parental Support for RPT

The benefits of employing students as active partners in the learning process have been documented clearly in the literature (Greenwood, Carta, & Hall, 1988; Slavin, 1990). Parent partnerships are another potent, but underutilized resource available to enhance student learning. Parents exert the earliest and most lasting influences on their children. For the first 18 years of life, children spend approximately 13% of their waking hours in school and 87% exposed to their families (National School Boards Association, 1988).

Research provides empirical support for the role that parents play in promoting their children's academic motivation, positive self-concept (Fantuzzo, Davis, & Ginsburg, 1995), cognitive development and school achievement (Comer, 1989; Cotton & Savard, 1982; Epstein & Dauber, 1991; Gottfried, 1984; Henderson, 1987; Walberg, 1984). Additionally, the body of literature is growing that documents the importance of school–family connectedness, linking the extent of overlap among school and family influences to the degree of resulting benefits (Epstein, 1987).

Epstein showed that when teachers regularly include parent involvement activities in their teaching practices, parents feel more positively about their ability to help their children, and student achievement and attitudes improve (Epstein, 1987, 1991). Studies addressing methods of enabling and empow-

ering parents to become involved in the schools suggest that it is important
to provide parents with choices regarding their participation and a role in
decision-making processes, creating an atmosphere in which parents feel
like valued partners in their children's education (Dunst & Trivette, 1987;
Fisher, Nadler, & Whitcher-Alagna, 1983; Hobbs et al., 1984). Designing
flexible parent involvement methods that are sensitive to cultural differences that may affect home–school partnerships (Powell, 1991) is particularly essential for educators who are interested in enhancing educational
outcomes for vulnerable students in urban areas.

Based on the value of employing parents in educational strategies, a
parent involvement component was designed for the RPT intervention,
calling for the active involvement of parents in the development of their
own strategies for participation. The PI intervention was based on a model
that stressed the importance of shared responsibility between families and
schools (Epstein, 1990). The PI intervention contained three main features:
co-construction of PI methods, celebration of student academic effort, and
regular personal contacts between school and home that were exclusively
positive.

A set of studies examining the individual and additive benefits of
home-based PI in conjunction with the RPT intervention was conducted
(Fantuzzo, Davis, & Ginsburg, 1995; Heller & Fantuzzo, 1993). Treatment
integrity data from both studies demonstrated the effectiveness of the
intervention in achieving PI. In both studies, all of the parents who agreed
initially to provide home-based support for their children's academic efforts
followed through with this activity.

Heller and Fantuzzo (1993) examined the effects of RPT and a home-
based PI intervention on the mathematics achievement, school adjustment,
and social confidence of academically at-risk fourth- and fifth-grade students. In this study, 84 students evidencing poor performance in mathematics were selected from a pool of 180 students in an urban elementary school
and randomly assigned to one of three conditions: RPT-plus-PI, RPT-only,
or wait-list control.

Findings of this study indicated that students who received the RPT
intervention in conjunction with a PI intervention evidenced the highest
rates of accurate computations on a curriculum-based measure. School
adjustment measures revealed that students who participated in the RPT-
plus-PI intervention were rated by their teachers as having significantly
better work habits, levels of motivation, organizational skills, independence, levels of interpersonal confidence, and less disruptive behavior

than control students. Students in the treatment groups that received RPT had significantly higher standardized computation scores than control students and perceived themselves as more socially confident in their interactions with peers than did controls.

Fantuzzo, Davis, and Ginsburg (1995) extended Heller and Fantuzzo's (1993) study by examining the unique effects of a home-based, parent-support PI intervention and the combined effects of PI-plus-RPT on self-concept and mathematics achievement for low-achieving, low-income, urban, elementary school students. Seventy-eight academically at-risk students from a population of 180 African-American fourth- and fifth-grade students were assigned randomly to one of three experimental conditions: PC, PI-only, or PI-plus-RPT.

Results of this study indicated that students who experienced the PI-only and the PI-plus RPT interventions reported significantly higher scholastic and behavioral self-concept ratings than did students in the PC condition. The evaluation of mathematics achievement showed that students in the PI-plus RPT condition exhibited significantly higher gains in curriculum based computation than students in either the PI-only or control conditions, and significantly higher scores in standardized achievement than control students.

Taken together, these studies link PI to higher teacher ratings of student readiness to learn in the classroom (i.e., more task-oriented, more motivated, and less disruptive than students who received RPT alone; Heller & Fantuzzo, 1993), and increases in students' academic and behavioral self-concept (Fantuzzo, Davis, & Ginsburg, 1995). The PI intervention in these studies programmed regular opportunities for parents to provide their children with acceptance, encouragement, and reinforcement for daily academic endeavors. The parenting styles and achievement motivation areas of research provide empirical support for the links between parent involvement and students' academic motivation and positive self-concept (Fantuzzo, Davis, & Ginsburg, 1995).

Maccoby and Martin (1983) reviewed the literature on the impact of parental behaviors on children and found that parental expectations in combination with warmth and responsiveness result in the development of self-esteem in children. Steinberg, Dornbusch, and Brown (1992) found that students exposed to this *authoritative* (Baumrind, 1971) parenting style evidenced higher self-esteem and fewer behavior problems when compared with other children. This parental pattern of behaviors provides children with a supportive environment to internalize both their parents' high expectations of academic success and their parents' belief that success is attainable for their children.

Returning to the achievement motivation literature, teacher or parent styles that emphasize effort rather than performance or level of ability are linked to the highest levels of student academic motivation (Ames, 1992; Ames & Archer, 1987). This mastery orientation involves teachers and parents providing students with rewards based on their effort and progress toward achieving goals. The parenting styles and achievement motivation literature connect parent support for academic effort with increased self-esteem and academic motivation among students.

In the Heller and Fantuzzo (1993) and Fantuzzo, Davis, and Ginsburg (1995) studies, the home-school communications were designed to report only good news about a student's academic effort. Therefore, parents learned to have positive expectations about their child's academic effort and progress. Parents then responded to these reports in a warm and enthusiastic manner, reinforcing their child's hard work. It is not surprising that confidence-building occurred within children as they experienced positive feedback from their parents, and that this confidence was associated with more assertive academic behaviors. More research is needed to identify and categorize the parent-child interactions that have the strongest impact on student academic achievement.

Returning to the outcomes associated with RPT, these studies (Fantuzzo, Davis, & Ginsburg, 1995; Heller & Fantuzzo, 1993) linked the RPT intervention to significant gains in mathematics achievement and positive reports of student social competence and peer acceptance, replicating prior research (Fantuzzo et al., 1992; Heller & Fantuzzo, 1993). RPT provides students with a positive opportunity to give and receive academic peer assistance. These positive reciprocal opportunities are responsible for higher self-ratings of social competence.

Finally, the Heller and Fantuzzo (1993) and Fantuzzo, Davis, and Ginsburg (1995) studies documented the potency of expanding partnerships to include both parents and peers as collaborators in student learning. In both studies, the PI-plus-RPT interventions resulted in the best combination of student outcomes. Analyses of a recent national database by Keith et al. (1993) suggested that there is a reciprocal relationship between PI and mathematics achievement. These researchers found that previous achievement affects PI, and PI affects current achievement. In a combined parent and peer intervention, peer tutors possibly raise student achievement levels, thereby enhancing the quality of parental involvement, which in turn fosters greater student achievement. A replication of the Fantuzzo et al. study (1995) with measurement of the intensity and nature of the parent support offered during PI intervention sessions could empirically address the reciprocal relationship question.

CONCLUSIONS

RPT is an intervention designed to address the needs of low-achieving, urban elementary students by incorporating the most effective learning strategies documented in the peer teaching, academic achievement motivation, and group reward contingency literature. RPT is implemented through a partnership-directed approach that includes developing a teacher–consultant partnership, field-testing strategies, and expanding the partnership to include parents. Currently, work is being done to extend the RPT procedures to additional areas of the curriculum and special student populations.

For example, Fantuzzo and his research associates are investigating methods of applying RPT to other facets of mathematics education. Recent trends in mathematics education (NCTM, 1989), are moving toward implementing a more conceptual elementary mathematics curriculum. Driving this reform is the assumption that children should be actively involved in thinking and reasoning mathematically through a curriculum that emphasizes real-world applications of mathematics and the utilization of technology, such as calculators and computers, in the classroom. As progressive schools begin to implement these new standards, innovative teaching methods, such as those involving peer collaboration, are needed to incorporate the new standards into the elementary mathematics curriculum. By definition, peer teaching methods require the active involvement of students in the learning process. By engaging peers in communicating mathematical concepts to one another, students will spend more time engaged in active learning and develop a more conceptual understanding of mathematics.

Research on the RPT intervention is currently being conducted to develop peer tutoring methods that can be incorporated into state-of-the-art mathematics curricula. In one study, the individual and combined effects of RPT and a problem-solving curriculum modeled after the new standards for mathematics education will be evaluated. Results of this study will inform the development of RPT for the recent innovations in elementary mathematics curriculum as well as provide information regarding the impact of this new curriculum on multiple student outcomes. The efficacy and utility of RPT strategies for achieving positive student outcomes in urban, public school settings has been demonstrated empirically and shows great promise for future applications. Partnerships are now being developed to investigate how RPT strategies can be used to facilitate the inclusion of students with serious behavioral disorders into mainstream classroom settings.

REFERENCES

Ames, C. (1992). Classrooms: Goals, structures, and student motivation. *Journal of Educational Psychology, 84,* 261–272.

Ames, C., & Archer, J. (1987). Mother's beliefs about the role of ability and effort in school learning. *Journal of Educational Psychology, 79,* 409–414.

Ames, C., & Archer, J. (1988). Achievement goals in the classroom: Students' learning strategies and motivation processes. *Journal of Educational Psychology, 80,* 260–267.

Baumrind, D. (1971). Current patterns of parent authority. *Developmental Psychology Monographs, 4* (1, Pt. 2).

Butler, R. (1987). Task-involving and ego-involving properties of evaluation: Effects of different feedback conditions on motivational perceptions, interest, and performance. *British Journal of Educational Psychology, 58,* 1–14.

Cameron, J., & Pierce, W. D. (1994). Reinforcement, reward, and intrinsic motivation: A meta-analysis. *Review of Educational Research, 64,* 363–423.

Cameron, J., & Pierce, W. D. (1996). The debate about rewards and intrinsic motivation: Protests and accusations do not alter the results. *Review of Educational Research, 66,* 39–51.

Comer, J. P. (1989). Child development and education. *Journal of Negro Education, 58,* 125–139.

Cotton, K., & Savard, W. G. (1982). *Parent involvement in instruction, K–12: Research synthesis.* Portland, Oregon: Northwest Regional Educational Lab. (ERIC Document Reproduction Service No. ED 235 397).

Deci, E. L., & Ryan, R. M. (1985). *Intrinsic motivation and self-determination in human behavior.* New York: Plenum.

Dunst, C. J., & Trivette, C. M. (1987). Enabling and empowering families: Conceptual and intervention issues. *School Psychology Review, 16,* 443–456.

Elliot, E. S., & Dweck, C. S. (1988). Goals: An approach to motivation and achievement. *Journal of Personality and Social Psychology, 54,* 5–12.

Epstein, J. L. (1987). Toward a theory of family–school connections: Teacher practices and parent involvement across the school years. In K. Hurrelmann, F. Kaufman, & F. Losel (Eds.), *Social intervention: Potential and constraints* (pp. 121–136). New York: deGruyter.

Epstein, J. L. (1990). School and family connections: Theory, research, and implications for integrating sociologies of education and family. *Marriage and Family Review, 15,* 99–126.

Epstein, J. L. (1991). School and family connections: Theory, research, and implications for integrating sociologies of education and family. In D. G. Unger & M. B. Sussman (Eds.), *Families in community settings: Interdisciplinary perspectives* (pp. 99–126). New York: Haworth.

Epstein, J. L., & Dauber, S. L. (1991). School programs and teacher practices of parent involvement in inner-city elementary and middle schools. *The Elementary School Journal, 91*(3), 289–305.

Fantuzzo, J., & Atkins M. (1992). Applied behavior analysis for educators: Teacher centered and classroom based. *Journal of Applied Behavior Analysis, 25*(1), 375–388.

Fantuzzo, J. W., Davis, G. Y., & Ginsburg, M. D. (1995). Effects of parent involvement in isolation or in combination with peer tutoring on student self-concept and mathematics achievement. *Journal of Educational Psychology, 87,* 272–281.

Fantuzzo, J. W., King, J. A., & Heller, L. R. (1992). Effects of reciprocal peer tutoring on mathematics and school adjustment: A component analysis. *Journal of Educational Psychology, 84,* 331–339.

Fantuzzo, J. W., & Polite, K. (1990). School-based self-management interventions with elementary school children: A component analysis. *School Psychology Quarterly, 5,* 180–198.

Fantuzzo, J. W., Polite, K., & Grayson, N. (1990). An evaluation of reciprocal peer tutoring across elementary school settings. *Journal of School Psychology, 28,* 309–323.

Fantuzzo, J. W., & Rohrbeck, C. A. (1992). Self-managed groups: Fitting self-management approaches into classroom systems. *School Psychology Review, 21,* 255–263.

Fisher, J. D., Nadler, A., & Whitcher-Alagna, S. (1983). Four theoretical approaches for conceptualizing reactions to aid. In J. D. Fisher, A. Nadler, & B. M. DePaulo (Eds.), *New directions in helping: Vol. 1. Recipient reactions to aid* (pp. 3–14). New York: Academic Press.

Ginsburg-Block, M. & Fantuzzo, J. (1997). Reciprocal Peer Tutoring: an analysis of "teacher" and "student" interactions as a function of training and experience. *School Psychology Quarterly, 12*(2), 134–149.

Gottfried, A. W. (Ed.). (1984). *Home environment and early cognitive development: Longitudinal research.* New York: Academic Press.

Greenwood, C. R., Carta, J. C., & Hall, R. V. (1988). The use of peer tutoring strategies in classroom management and educational instruction. *School Psychology Review, 17,* 258–275.

Greenwood, C. R., Terry, B., Utley, C. A., Montagna, D., & Walker, D. (1993). Achievement, placement, and services: Middle school benefits of classwide peer tutoring used at the elementary school. *School Psychology Review, 22,* 497–516.

Greer, R. D., & Polirstok, S. R. (1982). Collateral gains and short-term maintenance in reading and on-task responses by inner-city adolescents as a function of their use of social reinforcement while tutoring. *Journal of Applied Behavior Analysis, 15,* 123–139.

Heller, L. R., & Fantuzzo, J. W. (1993). Reciprocal peer tutoring and parent partnership: Does parent involvement make a difference? *School Psychology Review, 22,* 517–534.

Henderson, A. (1987). *The evidence continues to grow: Parent involvement improves student achievement.* Columbia, MD: National Committee for Citizens in Education.

Hobbs, N., Dokecki, P. R., Hoover-Dempsey, K. V., Moroney, R. M., Shayne, M. W., & Weeks, K. H. (1984). *Strengthening families.* San Francisco: Jossey-Bass.

Keith, T. Z., Keith, P. B., Troutman, G. C., Bickley, P. G., Trivette, P. S., & Singh, K. (1993). Does parental involvement affect eighth-grade student achievement? Structural analysis of national data. *School Psychology Review, 22,* 474–496.

Koestner, R., Ryan, R. M., Bernieri, F. & Holt, K. (1984). Setting limits on children's behavior: The differential effects of controlling versus informational styles on intrinsic motivation and creativity. *Journal of Personality, 52,* 233–248.

Kohn, A. (1996). By all available means: Cameron and Pierce's defense of extrinsic motivators. *Review of Educational Research, 66,* 1–4.

Lepper, M. R, Keavney, M., & Drake, M. (1996). Intrinsic motivation and extrinsic rewards: A commentary on Cameron and Pierce's claim that rewards do not undermine intrinsic motivation. *Review of Educational Research, 66, 5–32.*

Maccoby, E., & Martin, J. (1983). Socialization in the context of the family: Parent child interaction. In E. M. Hetherington (Ed.), *Handbook of child psychology: Vol. 4. Socialization, personality, and social development* (pp. 1–101). New York: Wiley.

The National Council of Teachers of Mathematics Commission on Standards for School Mathematics. (1989). *Curriculum and evaluation standards for school mathematics.* Reston, VA: Author.

National School Boards Association. (1988, November). *First teachers: Parental involvement in the public schools.* Alexandria, VA: Author.

Pigott, H. E., Fantuzzo, J. W., & Clement, P. W. (1986). The effects of reciprocal peer tutoring and group contingencies on the academic performance of elementary school children. *Journal of Applied Behavior Analysis, 19,* 93–98.

Pigott, H. E., Fantuzzo, J. W., Heggie, D. L., & Clement, P. W. (1984). A student-administered group-oriented contingency intervention: Its efficacy in a regular classroom. *Child and Family Behavior Therapy, 6,* 41–45.

Pigott, H. E., & Heggie, D. L. (1986). Interpreting the conflicting results of individual versus group contingencies in classrooms: The targeted behavior as a mediating variable. *Child and Family Behavior Therapy, 7*(4), 1–15.

Powell, D. R. (1991). How schools support families: Critical policy tensions. *The Elementary School Journal, 91,* 307–319.

Ryan, R. M., & Deci, E. L. (1996). When paradigms clash: Comments on Cameron and Pierce's claim that rewards do not undermine intrinsic motivation. *Review of Educational Research, 66,* 33–38.

Ryan, R. M., & Stiller, J. (1991). The social contexts of internalization: Parent and teacher influences on autonomy, motivation, and learning. In M. L. Maehr & P. R. Pintrich (Eds.), *Advances in motivation and achievement* (Vol. 7, pp. 115–149). Greenwich, CT: JAI Press.

Schunk, D. H. (1996). Goal and self-evaluative influences during children's cognitive skill learning. *American Educational Research Journal, 33,* 359–382.

Slavin, R. E. (1983). When does cooperative learning increase student achievement? *Psychological Bulletin, 94,* 429–445.

Slavin, R. E. (1990). *Cooperative learning: Theory, research and practice.* Englewood Cliffs, NJ: Prentice Hall.

Steinberg, L., Dornbusch, S. M., & Brown, B. B. (1992). Ethnic differences in adolescent achievement: An ecological perspective. *American Psychologist, 47,* 723–729.

Stanley, S. O., & Greenwood, C. R. (1983). How much "opportunity to respond" does the minority disadvantaged student receive in school? *Exceptional Children, 49,* 370–373.

Stipek, D. (1996). Motivation and instruction. In D. C. Berliner & R. C. Calfee (Eds.), *Handbook of educational psychology* (pp. 85–113). New York: Macmillan.

Walberg, H. J. (1984). Improving the productivity of America's schools. *Educational Leadership, 41,* 91–125.

Webb, N. (1985). Student interaction and learning in small groups: A research summary. In R. E. Slavin, S. Sharan, S. Kagan, R. Hertz-Lazarowitz, C. Webb, & R. Schmuck (Eds.), *Learning to cooperate, cooperating to learn* (pp. 147–172). New York: Plenum.

Webb, N., & Farivar, S. (1994). Promoting helping behavior in cooperative small groups in middle school mathematics. *American Educational Research Journal, 31,* 369–395.

Webb, N. M., & Palincsar, A. S. (1996). Group processes in the classroom. In D. C. Berliner & R. C. Calfee (Eds.), *Handbook of educational psychology* (pp. 841–873). New York: Macmillan.

Webb, N. M., Troper, J. D., & Fall, R. (1995). Constructive activity and learning in collaborative small groups. *Journal of Educational Psychology, 87,* 406–423.

Wertsch, J. V., & Bivens, J. (1992). The social origins of individual mental functioning: Alternatives and perspectives. *Quarterly Newsletter of the Laboratory of Comparative Human Cognition, 14*(2), 35–44.

Widaman, K. F., & Kagan, S. (1987). Cooperativeness and achievement: Interaction of student cooperativeness with cooperative versus competitive classroom organization. *Journal of School Psychology, 25,* 355–365.

Willis, M. G. (1992). Learning styles of African American children: A review of the literature and interventions. In A. K. H. Burlow, W. C. Banks, H. P. McAdoo, & D. A. Azibo (Eds.), *African American psychology: Theory, research and practice* (pp. 260–278). Newbury Park, CA: Sage.

Wolfe, J. A., Fantuzzo, J. W., & Wolter, C. F. (1984). Student-administered group-oriented contingencies: A method of combining group-oriented contingencies and self-directed behavior to increase academic productivity. *Child and Family Behavior Therapy, 6,* 45–60.

Wolfe, J. A., Fantuzzo, J. W., & Wolfe, P. K. (1986). The effects of reciprocal peer management and group contingencies on the arithmetic proficiency of underachieving students. *Behavior Therapy, 17,* 253–265.

Wolter, C. F., Pigott, H. E., Fantuzzo, J. W., & Clement, P. W. (1984). Student-administered group-oriented contingencies: The application of self-regulation techniques in the context of a group to increase academic productivity. *Techniques: A Journal for Counseling and Remedial Education, 1,* 14–22.

Appendix A1: Try Sheet

	TRY 1	TRY 2	HELP	TRY 3
#1				
#2				
#3				

PROJECT P.L.U.S.   NAME: _____   GROUP: _____

143

PROJECT P.L.U.S.
GOAL SHEET

GROUP _____

NAME _____

_____'S GOAL   _____'S GOAL   TEAM GOAL

_____ + _____ = _____

We will earn our reward when we get

_____ successes

The reward we want is _____

___/ _____ + _____ = _____   TRY AGAIN   SUCCESS

___/ _____ + _____ = _____   TRY AGAIN   SUCCESS

___/ _____ + _____ = _____   TRY AGAIN   SUCCESS

8

Disruptive Students as Tutors: A Systems Approach to Planning and Evaluation of Programs

Charles A. Maher
Brian C. Maher
Cynthia J. Thurston
Rutgers University

Students with behavioral and conduct disorders (CDs) are increasing in number in educational settings, especially in public schools. This increase has been documented even in special education programs, and recently in regular education settings (Danielson & Malouf, 1994). Legal, political, and curricular issues all have contributed to these increases. Moreover, emphases on inclusion and integration of disruptive students into mainstream educational settings in the United States, Great Britain, and elsewhere have helped create the current state of affairs (Fish & Evans, 1995).

Students with behavioral problems and emotional CDs are undoubtedly disruptive to others in schools. Such students hinder teaching and learning in classrooms and other school settings (Brophy, 1996). This is the case no matter what the student's level of schooling (e.g., elementary), degree of functional development (e.g., mentally retarded), or chronological age (CA; e.g., older adolescent). In this regard, disruptive students exist in schools despite the experience and competence of teachers. As such, disruptive students in schools are educational obstacles to other students, their teachers, and also to themselves (Goldstein, Harootunian, & Conoley, 1994).

The most obvious challenge for classroom teachers is how to provide instruction to disruptive students so that these students can benefit from their education. A related challenge is helping disruptive students to improve in behavioral and emotional areas. A more fundamental task is to improve the abilities of these students to effectively manage their own behaviors and emotions (Weinstein & Mignano, 1993). Meeting these challenges, however, is not a straightforward assignment for teachers. It can be even more difficult for educators in mainstream educational settings who may have had little or no prior contact with students who manifest severe behavior and emotional problems (Cartledge & Millburn, 1995).

Classroom teachers cannot be expected to help disruptive students meet important educational goals and social standards alone; appropriate organizational and programmatic resources, are necessary, no matter what the school or its setting. In this regard, various psychoeducational intervention programs and practices exist that may be used with disruptive students (Maher & Zins, 1988). These interventions can be implemented by classroom teachers either alone or in conjunction with other school-based professionals, such as school psychologists, or by those school specialists themselves.

More conventional psychoeducational programs and interventions that have proven effective in various school situations with specific types of disruptive students include behavior management procedures, individual counseling, group counseling, and work study programs (Larivee, 1992). These approaches are routinely attempted with disruptive students in various educational settings. However, one often overlooked approach to providing educational assistance to disruptive students is that of using them as tutors of other students. This programmatic alternative is the focus in the current chapter.

The notion of using disruptive students as tutors, however, may seem nonsensical to educators, because one reason these students are considered disruptive is because they interfere with other students' abilities to learn. However, some research and program evaluation evidence exists (reviewed later) to support planned use of disruptive students as tutors in school settings. Under carefully created conditions, using disruptive students as tutors may enhance their learning and development, as well as benefit the individuals who are being provided the tutoring. Available evidence suggests that educators and administrators in educational settings should not overlook the use of disruptive students as tutors but should consider it as a potentially effective psychoeducational intervention for benefiting all students. However, the method may be beneficial only if the initiative is carefully designed, precisely monitored as to implementation, and diligently evaluated as to outcomes for participants.

The purpose of this chapter follows:

1. Review current thinking and practice pertinent to the use of disruptive students as tutors in schools.
2. Provide guidelines to classroom teachers, school psychologists, and others in how to effectively design, implement, and evaluate tutoring programs using disruptive students as tutors.
3. Delineate advantages and limitations of using disruptive students as tutors, in relation to available research and program evaluation data.
4. Discuss future directions for using disruptive students as tutors.

REVIEW OF CURRENT THINKING AND PRACTICE

Key Terms and Concepts

In order to understand how disruptive students may benefit from participation in programs wherein they function as tutors, it is important to define and describe key terms and concepts. Definition and description of key terms and concepts serve as a basis for precise thinking and action about the task. When teachers have a clear concept and plan for a tutoring program, they are likely to be more motivated and confident.

Disruptive Student. A disruptive student is defined as any member of an elementary, secondary, or special classroom setting whose presence limits instruction. The disruptive student's actions and emotions limit classroom instruction through: (a) preventing effective teaching; (b) hindering learning of other class members; and (c) affecting the disruptive student's own academic development.

To illustrate this concern, recently, in a large midwestern school district, an assessment was conducted of the needs of teaching staff as a basis for a districtwide project having to do with inclusion (Maher, 1995). As part of the needs assessment, more than 200 elementary school teachers were asked to identify students who were of most concern to them. Consistently, across educational levels, teachers described students with behavior, conduct, and emotional disorders as most disruptive to the educational process and of concern to them. The following themes reflected the most frequently reported descriptions:

- Students who call out in class consistently, particularly when teaching is taking place.
- Students who hit other children, creating a concern for safety and well-being of others.
- Students who routinely verbally abuse others, especially during class time.
- Students who consistently, and purposely drop books, pencils, and other materials during instruction.
- Students who verbally confront teachers and others regarding classroom policies, procedures, and practices.

Disruptive Student as Tutor.   A disruptive student as tutor is defined as follows: "a student in an elementary school or secondary school who possesses behavioral and emotional problems and who is given the opportunity to tutor another student, typically in an academic subject matter area such as reading or mathematics."

When a disruptive student is engaged in the process of tutoring another student who is their same educational grade level, this disruptive student functions as a *peer tutor* to the other student. When a disruptive student tutors another student who is younger than themselves, and at a lower educational grade level, the disruptive student as tutor functions as a *cross-age tutor.*

Tutoring Program.   A tutoring program is considered as an organized configuration of resources that allows a disruptive student to function effectively as a tutor to another individual and defined by its program design elements (Maher & Bennett, 1984). These program design elements include the following:

- Purpose and goals of the program for the tutor (disruptive student) and the tutee (the student being tutored) are described.
- Explicit tutoring process in which the tutor is supervised by a school professional (e.g., classroom teacher, school psychologist) is delineated.
- Training of the disruptive student in the particular tutoring process is provided.
- Procedures are in place so that the disruptive student can monitor his or her involvement and performance as a tutor.
- A program evaluation plan is formulated that allows data to be collected on how the tutoring program is benefiting the tutor (disruptive student) and the tutee (peer, younger student).

Without a tutoring program that includes these elements, the likelihood of it being successfully implemented and beneficial to a disruptive student is minimal.

ORGANIZATIONAL READINESS FACTORS

As is the case with any educational program, there are a number of organizational readiness factors that may facilitate and inhibit the use of disruptive students as tutors. In this regard, Maher (1996) documented such factors as part of the *A VICTORY* framework.

A VICTORY is an acronym that denotes eight organizational readiness factors: ability, values, idea, circumstances, timing, obligation, resistance, and yield. These factors are assessed in terms of the readiness of a school organization (e.g., elementary school), for a possible program, in this case, using disruptive students as tutors.

Ability.   Ability has to do with the extent to which the school organization can commit resources to the tutoring effort. This includes the ability to conduct a selection, orientation, and training process for disruptive student tutors, classroom teachers, tutees, and parents. With respect to this factor, consultation with the classroom teacher on the program by a school psychologist or counselor is a particularly important resource that the school or educational setting must be able to provide. This is so because for the tutoring program to be successful, an outside consultant and supervisor need to oversee the implementation of the program and provide an outside opinion on its benefits and effectiveness.

Values.   Values has to do with the tradition in the school setting, or larger educational agency, regarding innovative approaches for educating disruptive students, such as using them as tutors. For instance, has there been a tradition of using students as tutors in the school to support the proposed tutoring venture? Relatedly, it is important to consider the tradition for using innovative approaches with other students, because the tutees involved may not be disruptive themselves.

Idea.   Idea has to do with the necessity of determining whose idea it is to use disruptive students as tutors, and why the notion was developed and put forth. It is also necessary to assess the thinking of others in the setting or agency in relation to this idea. How clear is the task perceived to be? By whom? What aspects of the idea are not clear? To whom?

Circumstances. Circumstances has to do with the prevailing factors pressing for or detracting from the tutoring program's integration into the school or educational setting? For example, will available school personnel be remaining in the school or school district during the program, or be available to follow through on its implementation? Or, will some of the key personnel be assuming other educational responsibilities, thereby limiting their attention to the program?

Timing. Timing refers to the synchronicity of the tutoring program's installation with significant events occurring within the school or educational setting. For example, is the current time the most opportune to proceed with implementation of the tutoring program? Why or why not? Is grant funding available to support the effort? Another important question is: Does sufficient time exist to design and implement the program?

Obligation. Obligation refers to the degree to which members of the school organization, particularly classroom teachers, have a stake in the tutoring program. Do these individuals feel obligated to assist disruptive students by addressing their needs through a tutoring program? Who wants to use disruptive students as tutors, and who is going to champion the effort?

Resistance. Resistance concerns the existence of any individuals in the school building or school district who may resist the tutoring effort and why this is so. Typically, such resistance is the result of these individuals possessing a fear that there is something to lose by adopting the tutoring program, such as time for them to perform other educational functions.

Yield. Yield has to do with the rewards or benefits that may result for the disruptive students involved as a consequence of their having been involved in the tutoring program. The rewards or benefits that may result for other students, classroom teachers, and other school personnel should also be considered, particularly educational benefits and learning experiences.

To illustrate, the application of the A VICTORY framework in relation to organizational readiness, Table 8.1 summarizes two elementary schools, drawn from files that had different degrees of readiness for using disruptive students as tutors (Maher, 1996). An A VICTORY analysis of both schools, outlined in Table 8.1, shows School *R* to be sound on almost all of the factors. This was not the case with School *NR*. As seen in the footnotes of

Table 8.1, successful implementation occurred only in School R, not in the other school.

ORGANIZATION

Utilization of disruptive students as peer tutors, or cross-age tutors, is a complex, challenging task. In this regard, students who are disruptive in classroom and school settings are known to be inconsistent in their behaviors, even volatile. This unpredictability suggests that the involvement of such students in a tutoring program occur cautiously, in a step-by-step manner.

Relatedly, the welfare of the individuals to whom tutoring will be provided—the tutees—also is of utmost concern. More specifically, it is important to make sure that the students being tutored are not put into situations

TABLE 8.1

Summarized Examples of an A VICTORY Analysis of the Readiness of Two Elementary Schools
for Using Disruptive Students as Tutors

A VICTORY Factor		School R^a		School NR^b
Ability		• Supervisor selected		• No supervisor available
		• Teachers had targeted time for the tutoring initiative		• Teachers indicated little space in schedule for the tutoring initiative
Values		• School had routinely used peer and cross-age tutoring approaches in the past		• Tutoring had been used very infrequently in the school
Ideas		• Teachers and principals were not clear about the idea		• Teachers and principals were not clear about the idea; some were confused
Circumstances		• School principal was on tenure		• Teachers were experienced
		• Low teacher turnover		• Cuts in instructional aides that year
Timing		• School psychologist was willing to assume responsibility to oversee the program		• No discernible *champion* or leader for the approach
Obligation		• Particular teachers were interested		• Particular teachers were interested
Resistance		• None discernible		• A few teachers resisted
Yield		• Teachers valued use of innovation; interested in inclusion		• Not clear

^{a}School R was considered ready for using disruptive students as tutors. Subsequently, such a program was designed and implemented, with success.

^{b}School NR was considered not ready (low on A,C,T factors; high on R factors). Subsequently, there were several attempts at implementing a tutoring program for disruptive students; efforts, though, could not sustain a successful program.

where they may be exposed to negative behaviors, actions, or other experiences of the tutor. This is especially relevant if the tutee also possesses behavior disorders. Again, the importance of a step-by-step approach to planning and evaluation of these programs is emphasized in matters of organization of the program. Such an approach is now considered.

Systems Approach

The recommended systems approach to program planning and evaluation consists of four separate, yet interrelated phases. A program planning and evaluation team can use this approach. The four phases follow:

1. Clarification Phase—Deciding about the specific disruptive students who will serve as tutors; to whom they will provide tutoring; in what school setting; and why tutoring is expected to be a valuable experience for each tutor (disruptive student) and their tutee (peer student, younger student).
2. Design Phase—Deciding exactly what is the nature and scope of the tutoring program in terms of its purpose and goals; supervisory personnel and responsibilities, orientation and training of the tutors; the tutoring process; timelines; and program evaluation procedures.
3. Implementation Phase—Deciding to what extent the tutoring program is being implemented as planned; and what adjustments, if any, are appropriate to make.
4. Evaluation Phase—Deciding about the extent to which each tutor (disruptive student) and tutee (peer student; younger student) are benefiting from the experience; and whether it is worthwhile to continue the program and/or expand it to other disruptive students.

Each of these phases consists of a set of procedural guidelines. These procedural guidelines can be best applied by a program planning and evaluation team. This team can consist of one or more classroom teachers, a program coordinator or supervisor such as a school psychologist or guidance counselor, and a school building administrator.

Each phase and its constituent procedural guidelines are discussed next. Please note that these procedural guidelines are only an overview summary.

Clarification Phase

By following the procedural guidelines that comprise this phase, it will become clear as to what disruptive students may benefit from serving as a tutor, why, with what types of tutees (same-age, cross-age), and in what school setting.

Procedural guidelines for the clarification phase follow:

1. Identify each disruptive student in the classroom or school building who may benefit from serving as a tutor to a same-age student (peer) or a younger student (cross-age). In this regard, it is recommended that disruptive students within the 10- to 18-year-old age range be considered as tutors. Typically, disruptive students who are younger than 10 have not reaped positive benefits from serving as tutors.

2. Spend some time considering the cognitive, emotional, and social needs of the identified disruptive students. In conjunction with other team members, discuss why these students may benefit from tutoring program participation. In particular, do these students need to improve their perspectives on school, how to prevent their emotions from getting out of control, specific behavioral self-management skills, or other psychoeducational needs?

3. Based on this kind of needs assessment, select one or two disruptive students to initiate the tutoring sentence. Discuss each student possibility with relevant staff, the parents of each student, and the students. During these discussions, emphasis should be placed on how involvement as a tutor is likely to help address important cognitive, emotional, and social needs of the student.

4. Seek to procure the interest and commitment of all these parties, as a basis for proceeding to the task of designing a potentially worthwhile tutoring program. If such interest and commitment cannot be obtained, it is strongly suggested that the disruptive students under consideration not be involved in the program.

Design Phase

By following the procedural guidelines that comprise this phase, it is possible to design a tutoring program that is likely to have two distinguishing features. One feature is that the program will be successfully implemented and completed. Second, the program will have proven educationally valuable for the tutor (disruptive student) and the tutee (same-age peer; cross-age peer).

The procedural guidelines for the design phase follow:

1. Develop a written statement of purpose for the tutoring program. A statement of program purpose also can be referred to as a mission statement. This information will make three important points clear to all concerned. These points are: who will be involved in the program; how the tutoring will occur in terms of steps and activities; and what benefits are expected to accrue to participants (tutor, tutee).

One example of a statement of one program's purpose follows:

"The purpose of the tutoring program is to assist middle school students who manifest conduct problems to improve their school behaviors by serving as tutors of other, younger middle school students. This purpose will be realized by means of a tutoring program held over a 10 week period in which two one-half hour tutoring sessions will be held in designated academic areas. As a result of their participation in the program, each tutor will become more productive in the classroom (in terms of behaviors); each tutee will receive worthwhile instructional support."

2. Based on the particular disruptive students who will serve as tutors, specify several goals for them that can be measured, that they can attain within the time frame of the program, and that are relevant to their school performance. In order to maximize motivation and follow through, these students should be actively involved, to the extent possible, in this goal-setting process.

Examples of the kinds of goals that have been found to be applicable for disruptive students as tutors include:

- Increase in the number of class assignments completed by the tutor.
- Increase in the number of homework assignments completed by the tutor.
- Positive ratings by teachers as to classroom behavior of the tutor.
- Positive reactions by the tutor to their involvement in the program

3. Identify each student, either same age, or younger, who can benefit from individual tutoring in an academic subject matter area. Each one of these students is referred to as a *tutee*. To be of assistance to the tutee, however, the tutor must have sufficient knowledge in the subject matter area to serve in that capacity, given the age and skill level of the tutee (peer, cross-age).

4. Discuss the tutoring possibility with the parents and teachers of the individual who will be tutored. Seek and obtain necessary approvals. Naturally, if these discussions do not occur and if necessary approvals are not obtained, the student should not be involved as a tutee.

5. Involve the tutor in a series of three half-hour meetings in which they are trained as a tutor. This can be accomplished by the school psychologist or counselor who is a member of the program planning and evaluation team and who has created a detailed tutoring process. It is at this time that the tutor (disruptive student) is trained in the following steps:

1. Purpose of tutoring.

2. Setting tutoring goals for the student being tutored.

3. Getting acquainted with the student to be tutored.

4. Implementing the tutoring process with the student.

5. Providing feedback to the classroom teacher.

6. Participating in supervisory sessions.

Table 8.2 provides an outline of training content that has been used by a qualified individual (e.g., school psychologist; guidance counselor) to train disruptive students in the previous steps.

Implementation Phase

By following the procedural guidelines that comprise this phase, the likelihood is increased that the tutoring program will be implemented as

TABLE 8.2

Training Program Content for the Disruptive Student as Tutor

Category	Description
1. Purpose of tutoring	A. To assist the student to do better in a subject (e.g., reading, mathematics)
	B. To help the student do better by teaching them a specific skill, fact, or approach
	C. To be supervised in tutoring
	D. To learn to be a better student and person through tutoring
2. Setting tutoring goals for the student being tutored	A. Goals for the student to be tutored and why these are important (rationale)
	B. Goals for the tutor and why these are important (rationale)
3. Getting acquainted with he student to be tutored	A. Meeting the student before tutoring (orientation)
	B. Starting each tutoring session (establishing rapport and focus)
4. Implementing the tutoring process with the student	A. Stating the goal to be accomplished with the student for the day (e.g., work on addition of two digit numbers)
	B. Working with the students on the steps and activities to accomplish the goal (e.g., take each column separately)
	C. Giving the student feedback on how he or she is working and accomplishing the goal
	D. Using praise and encouragement with the student
5. Providing feedback to the classroom teacher	A. Meeting with the teacher
	B. Getting the next tutoring sessions assignment
6. Participating in supervisory sessions	A. Who the supervisor is
	B. Supervision process and schedule

designed. It will thus become clear what adjustments, if any, need to be made in the tutoring program's design.

The procedural guidelines from the implementation phase follow:

1. Monitor the following activities of the tutoring program to make sure that they are occurring as planned:
   - Supervisory sessions (attendance of tutor).
   - Tutoring sessions (attendance of tutor and tutee).
2. Seek to detect any side effects that seem to be associated with the program. These side effects may be positive (e.g., a particular tutor seems very enthusiastic) or negative (e.g., teacher of a tutee finds the involvement in tutoring to be impractical). Positive and negative side effects can be detected by periodic discussions with the relevant stakeholders involved in the program. These stakeholders include tutors, tutees, parents, teachers, and so on.
3. Make necessary adjustments in program activities or tutoring schedules, based on the program monitoring information.

Evaluation Phase

By following the procedural guidelines for this phase, judgments can be made reguarding how each tutor and tutee is benefiting from the tutoring experience. In addition, overall judgments can be made reguarding the worth or merit of the tutoring program. This includes evaluation of whether the tutoring program should be expanded for use with other disruptive students.

The procedural guidelines to follow for the evaluation phase follow:

1. Have the tutor (disruptive student) monitor him or herself on the progress being made toward his or her own program goals (e.g., increased homework, sense of satisfaction with being in school). A self-monitoring form can be provided to each tutor for that purpose, each week, as part of supervision. Have each tutor complete the form weekly; then, review and discuss the results with the individual. Table 8.3 is an example of a self-monitoring form that has been used with disruptive students for this purpose.
2. Collect data or other products that are associated with the tutoring program. These products include number of sessions completed, work completed by the tutee, number of incidents of poor classroom behavior manifested by the tutor, and other such indicators.
3. Interview each of the key participants as to their reactions to the program. This may include each tutor, his or her parents, the tutee, the tutor's teacher, the tutee's parents, and the tutee's teachers. Key interview questions include:
   - What did you like best about the tutoring?

TABLE 8.3
Tutor Self-Monitoring Form

Name of Student:	Week:
I. My goals for this week/program:	Rating:

   1.

   2.

   3.

For this week, rate myself on how I am attaining each one of my goals. Use this scale: 1 = Outstanding; 2 = Above Average; 3 = Satisfactory; 4 = Poor; 5 = Unsatisfactory

II. Things that are going well for me this week (list).

III. Problems that I am facing that I need to discuss with my supervisor (list).

IV. What have I learned about myself as a student and person this week (describe).

- To what extent were you satisfied with it?
- Were you involved sufficiently in the program? Why/Why not?
- What did you like least about the program? Why?
- What can be done to make the program better?

4. Using the evaluation information that has been gathered, the program planning and evaluation team can meet to discuss and identify the following:
   - The current *strong points* of the tutoring program.
   - The current *limitations* of the tutoring program.
   - *Recommendations* for continuous program development and improvement.

The identification and documentation of tutoring program strong points, limitations, and recommendations, as suggested previously, can occur through a scheduled meeting of the program planning and evaluation team.

Table 8.4 is an outline of a suggested plan for evaluation of a tutoring program in which disruptive students are used as tutors. This plan has been used in many instances and has been considered by classroom teachers and school specialists as practical and as providing useful information for decision making about the program.

EFFECTIVENESS

There are both advantages and disadvantages to using disruptive students as tutors as a form of PAL. These advantages and disadvantages occur in

TABLE 8.4

Outline of a Plan for the Evaluation of a Tutoring Program in Which Disruptive Students Have Been Used as Tutors

Program Evaluation Analysis Questions	Methods for Data Collection	Procedures for Data and Reporting
1. Who has participated in the tutoring program (tutors; tutees)?	*Collection of demographic information and needs assessment data	*Comparison of participants to expected needs and eligibility criteria
	*Preprogram data collection	
2. How were training and supervision of tutors implemented?	*Training and supervisory logs	*Qualitative analysis
	*Data collection during the program	*Comparison to program design expectations
3. In what manner was the tutoring program implemented?	*Interviews and logs	*Qualitative analysis
	*Data collection during the program	*Comparison to program design expectations
4. What benefits accrued to tutors through their program participation?	*Questionnaires	*Descriptive statistics
	*Interviews	
	*Goal attainment ratings	
	*Data collection before, during, and after the program	
5. What benefits accrued to tutees?	*Questionnaires	*Qualitative analysis
	*Interviews	
	*Goal attainment ratings	
	*Data collection before, during, and after the program	
6. What have been reactions of teachers and parents to the program?	*Interviews	*Descriptive statistics
	*Questionnaire	

relation to classroom teachers, school professionals, disruptive students themselves, and other students. Some advantages have been documented in the PAL literature. Particular disadvantages are inherent in the conditions of behaviorally disordered students.

Researchers have often found that PAL results in gains for both the tutor and the tutee (Maheady, Harper, & Mallette, 1991). Such gains have been found for both regular and handicapped student populations (Cook, Scruggs, Mastropieri, & Casto, 1986; Scruggs, Mastropieri, Veit, & Osguthorpe,

1986). Early research on PAL focused primarily on the academic benefits of the intervention (Gerber & Kauffman, 1981). However, more recent literature has reflected a focus on more than just the academic benefits of PAL. For example, PAL has become a recommended practice in efforts to mainstream handicapped students (see, e.g., Maheady et al., 1991).

The emotional and social benefits that could result from PAL are also very important to consider, especially for handicapped students. Maheady et al. (1991), for instance, stated that PAL is an appealing instructional approach to enhance both academic and social functioning of handicapped students as well as low-performing students. In relation to handicapped populations, some of the documented benefits of PAL have been improvements in self-concept and self-perception (Franca, Kerr, Reitz, & Lambert, 1990; Yasutake, Bryan, & Dohrn, 1996), promotion of academic functioning and social integration (Franca et al., 1990; Osguthorpe & Scruggs, 1986), and improvements in impulse control (Nelson & Behler, 1989).

Cook et al. (1986) conducted a meta-analysis that demonstrated that handicapped students have the ability to be effective tutors of other handicapped, as well as nonhandicapped students. It has also been shown that PAL can result in improvements in students who are low-achieving (Cochran, Feng, Cartledge, & Hamilton, 1993), at risk for academic failure (Fantuzzo, King, & Heller, 1992), and at risk for placement in a special education program (Greenwood, Terry, Utley, Montagna, & Walker, 1993).

The research findings for PAL with behaviorally disordered populations, however, is not as definitive as the research conducted on regular education populations. The findings for the behaviorally disordered are much more varied. Many of the studies that do exist have been criticized for their reliance on informal observations and anecdotal reports in relation to social benefits (e.g., Franca et al., 1990; Scruggs et al., 1986). In one study (Maher, 1982), some social benefits of PAL were reported for behaviorally disordered students who tutored elementary school students with special needs. Behaviorally disordered students in a tutoring condition in this study received higher grades in social science and language art classes, were absent less often, and had fewer behavioral referrals than students in other conditions. Students who received the tutoring also were reported by teachers as benefiting in terms of improved classwork.

Maher's program was part of a school districtwide effort to involve special education students, including disruptive students, in positions of leadership. The behaviorally disordered students in Maher's study received training, supervision on their tutoring performance, and opportunities to be involved in self-monitoring of their behavior as a tutor in their classrooms. The systems approach to program planning and evaluation described earlier was the means to make sure that the program was implemented as designed and that the investigation was carefully conducted.

In a review of the literature, Scruggs, Mastropieri, and Richter (1985) concluded that PAL resulted in positive effects on the academic functioning of tutees. However, they also indicated that positive academic effects were only observed with tutors when the materials provided for fluency building in an appropriate academic area. Scruggs et al. (1985) also indicated that PAL with behaviorally disordered students can improve the social relations of the tutoring pair and create more positive attitudes toward the content being tutored.

An investigation by Franca et al. (1990) displayed positive academic benefits of PAL with behaviorally disordered students. They also demonstrated positive changes in self-concept scores for tutors, a significant increase in positive social interactions between tutor and tutee in each dyad, and less frequent negative social interactions between tutors and tutees. The authors did not, however, discover any significant changes in sociometric measures for tutors or tutees. As well, they did not report any increase in positive attitudes toward the content being tutored despite the inherent academic gains.

In an expanded version of Maher's (1982) study, Scruggs et al. (1986) found some anecdotal evidence that a PAL intervention was liked by, and perceived to be helpful to, behaviorally disordered students. According to the authors, quantitative analysis of more objective measures indicated that the PAL intervention that was employed (cross-age) was not effective in improving the general social functioning of the sample of behaviorally disordered students. This is somewhat contrary to Maher's (1982) findings. However, Scruggs et al. (1986) indicated that there are some discrepancies between the design of each study.

Bell, Young, Blair, and Nelson (1990) showed significant academic gains for behaviorally disordered students through the used of classwide PAL. In a single case design, Nelson and Behler (1989) demonstrated that, when taught to use cognitive–behavioral, self-instructional training, one impulsive child could teach another to use the same process. This procedure was evaluated as being beneficial to both the tutor and the tutee.

It is important to note here that investigations of PAL with disruptive students are scarce in relation to the overall PAL literature. Procedures can be borrowed or adapted, however, from this other literature and applied to disruptive populations. For instance, in an investigation by Roswal et al. (1995) with regular education students, data indicated that a collaborative peer tutor teaching program could be effective in eliciting improvements in self-concept and attitudes toward school. Yasutake et al. (1996) conducted a study using students with learning disabilities and students at risk for special education assessment as tutors. These students were taught a PAL strategy and were provided attribution training. Results indicated that students in the attribution-plus-strategy training group became more positive in their self-perceptions than students in the strategy-only condition.

In studies involving nonhandicapped students who were considered to be disliked before a tutoring program, results showed that, when used as tutors, these students were liked at the end of tutoring (Garcia-Vazquez & Ehly, 1992; Garcia-Vazquez, Ehly, & Vazquez, 1993). Fantuzzo et al. (1992) found that academically at-risk students who participated in structured peer tutoring possessed better self-control at the end of training than those who did not participate. These findings are important, because the elements being studied are problem areas for disruptive students, who are extremely likely to act out against their peers, and to be perceived as socially unacceptable.

In summary, the reader is reminded that caution should be taken when implementing any type of PAL intervention with disruptive students. Despite any positive gains shown by research, it is stressed that disruptive students can be very volatile. This is why the organizational factors discussed earlier in the chapter regarding the readiness for such an intervention are so important to assess before initiating a program. It is also extremely important to determine if anticipated gains made by particular students from PAL are needed by them.

DISCUSSION AND CONCLUSIONS

The use of disruptive students as tutors is a PAL approach that may have value for use with particular students, in schools that are ready for such an initiative. For a tutoring program of this type, however, careful attention must be paid by classroom teachers and other school professionals to specific aspects of program planning and evaluation. These aspects include (a) clarification of the students who may be participants including tutor (disruptive student) and tutee (same as peer; younger student), (b) actual design of the tutoring program, (c) how the program has been implemented, and (d) evaluation of the program with respect to tutor and tutee. Without systematic attention to these matters, the likelihood of a worthwhile tutoring endeavor of the kind discussed in this chapter is likely to be minimal for all concerned.

Clearly, additional research needs to occur about the use of disruptive students as tutors in public schools. First, a set of action research questions should be delineated as part of an action research agenda. The seemingly important questions follow:

1. What psychological and educational needs of disruptive students can be reasonably addressed through their participation in a tutoring program?
2. What organizational readiness factors of schools relate to successful tutoring program implementation?
3. What training and supervision is required for disruptive students in order for them to function effectively as tutors?
4. To what extent does an explicit tutoring process contribute to goal attainment for tutors and tutees?

In answering these questions, carefully planned and documented case studies should be implemented initially in the form of program evaluations. Then, based on those results, more comparative studies of alternative programs can be undertaken.

In the future, classroom teachers, school psychologists, guidance counselors, and school building principals will be called on to provide quality education. These school professionals will be asked to do so, more often than not, with limited and even shrinking resources. In essence, school professionals will be required to work harder and smarter. The use of disruptive students as tutors, under appropriate organizational conditions, coupled with a systematic program planning and evaluation approach, may well be a viable program option.

REFERENCES

Bell, K., Young, K. R., Blair, M., & Nelson, R. (1990). Facilitating mainstreaming of students with behavioral disorders using classwide peer tutoring. *School Psychology Review, 19*, 564–573.

Brophy, J. (1996). *Teaching problem students.* New York: Guilford.

Cartledge, G., & Millburn, J. (1995). *Teaching social skills to children and youth: Innovative approaches.* Elmsford, NY: Pergamon.

Cochran, L., Feng, H., Cartledge, G., & Hamilton, S. (1993). The effects of cross-age tutoring on the academic achievement, social behaviors, and self-perceptions of low-achieving African-American males with behavioral disorders. *Behavioral Disorders, 18*, 292–302.

Cook, S. B., Scruggs, T. E., Mastropieri, M. A., & Casto, G. C. (1986). Handicapped students as tutors. *The Journal of Special Education, 19*, 483–492.

Danielson, L. C., & Malouf, D. B. (1994). Federal policy and educational reform: Achieving better outcomes for students with disabilities. *Special Services in the Schools, 9*, 11–19.

Fantuzzo, J. W., King, J. A., & Heller, L. R. (1992). Effects of reciprocal peer tutoring on mathematics and school adjustment: A component analysis. *Journal of Educational Psychology, 84*, 331–339.

Fish, J., & Evans, J. (1995). *Managing special education: Codes, charters, and competition.* Buckingham, England: Open University Press.

Franca, V. M., Kerr, M. M., Reitz, A. L., & Lambert, D. (1990). Peer tutoring among behaviorally disordered students: Academic and social benefits to tutor and tutee. *Education and Treatment of Children, 13*, 109–128.

Garcia-Vazquez, E., & Ehly, S. W. (1992). Peer tutoring effects on students who are perceived as not socially accepted. *Psychology in the Schools, 29*, 256 266.

Garcia-Vazquez, E., Ehly, S. W., & Vazquez, L. A. (1993). Examination of tutor and tutee interactions and attitudes: What happens during peer tutoring. *Special Services in the Schools, 7*, 1–20.

Gerber, M., & Kauffman, J. M. (1981). Peer tutoring in academic settings. In P. S. Strain (Ed.), *The utilization of classroom peers as behavior change agents* (pp. 155–187). New York: Plenum.

Goldstein, A., Harootunian, B., & Conoley, J. (1994). *Student aggression: Prevention, management, and replacement training.* New York: Guilford.

Greenwood, C. R., Terry, B., Utley, C. A., Montagna, D., & Walker, D. (1993). Achievement, placement, and services: Middle school benefits of ClassWide Peer Tutoring used at the elementary school. *School Psychology Review, 22*, 497–516.

Larivee, B. (1992). *Strategies for effective classroom management: Creating a collaborative climate.* Boston: Allyn & Bacon.

Maheady, L., Harper, G. F., & Mallette, B. (1991). Peer-mediated instruction: A review of potential applications for special education. *Reading, Writing, and Learning Disabilities, 7*, 75–103.

Maher, C. A. (1982). Behavioral effects of using conduct problem adolescents as cross-age tutors. *Psychology in the Schools, 19*, 360–364.

Maher, C. A. (1995). *Needs assessment for program planning in the Madison Public Schools.* Madison, WI: Author.

Maher, C. A. (1996). *Resource guide: Planning and evaluation of human services programs.* Piscataway, NJ: Graduate School of Applied and Professional Psychology, Rutgers University.

Maher, C. A., & Bennett, R. E. (1984). *Planning and evaluating special education services.* Englewood Cliffs, NJ: Prentice-Hall.

Maher, C. A., & Zins, J. E. (1988). *Psychoeducational interventions in the schools.* Elmsford, NY: Pergamon.

Nelson, W. M., & Behler, J. J. (1989). Cognitive impulsivity training: The effects of peer teaching. *Journal of Behavior Therapy and Experimental Psychiatry, 20*, 303–309.

Osguthorpe, R. T., & Scruggs, T. E. (1986). Special education students as tutors: A review and analysis. *Remedial and Special Education, 7*, 15–26.

Roswal, G. M., Mims, A. A., Evans, M. D., Smith, B., Young, M., Burch, M., Croce, R., Horvat, M. A., & Block, M. (1995). Effects of collaborative peer tutoring on urban seventh graders. *Journal of Educational Research, 88*, 275–279.

Scruggs, T. E., Mastropieri, M. A., & Richter, L. (1985). Peer tutoring with behaviorally disordered students: Social and academic benefits. *Behavioral Disorders, 10*, 283–294.

Scruggs, T. E., Mastropieri, M., Veit, D. T., & Osguthorpe, R. T. (1986). Behaviorally disordered students as tutors: Effects on social behavior. *Behavioral Disorders, 12*, 36–44.

Weinstein, C., & Mignano, A., Jr. (1993). *Elementary classroom management: Lessons from research and practice.* New York: McGraw-Hill.

Yasutake, D., Bryan, T., & Dohrn, E. (1996). The effects of combining peer tutoring and attribution training on students' perceived self-competence. *Remedial and Special Education, 17*, 83–91.

Tutoring and Students With Special Needs

Thomas E. Scruggs
Margo A. Mastropieri
Purdue University

Investigations of the facilitative effects of peer tutoring involving students with special needs have been conducted since the 1970s. In this chapter, we describe the accumulated evidence of the utility of peer tutoring involving students with special needs, and discuss several generalizations that can be made about the various uses of students with special needs in tutoring roles.

TUTORING AND SPECIAL NEEDS

Peer tutoring and other peer-mediated learning interventions have long been recommended as effective approaches to promoting school achievement (Topping, 1988). Research over the years has demonstrated the potential effectiveness of these approaches in a variety of educational situations.

In this chapter, we describe peer tutoring and review research on tutoring and students with special needs, drawn from research conducted since the 1970s, and offer some overall generalizations regarding the positive effects, and limitations, of tutoring. Although much of this research involves students with special needs as tutees—those receiving tutoring—a surprising amount also involves the use of students with special needs as tutors—those providing tutoring. Moreover, several studies have employed students in cross-tutoring configurations in which tutors and tutees exchange roles frequently throughout tutoring interventions.

TUTORING PROGRAMS

Many advocates of tutoring interventions have described the importance of systematic training, implementation, and monitoring procedures to ensure that the intervention is successful (Ehly & Larsen, 1980; Jenkins & Jenkins, 1981; Osguthorpe & Scruggs, 1986; Topping, 1988). Topping, noted:

> There is no doubt that peer tutoring can work. That is unequivocally demonstrated by the research evidence. However, the evidence also shows that peer tutoring can fail to work, and failure you cannot afford. Careful planning is necessary to ensure that you are successful. (p. 27)

For example, Jenkins and Jenkins (1981) described the important roles of such variables as content, curriculum selection, establishing mastery levels, frequency and duration of tutoring sessions, and tutor training and supervision, in implementing effective tutoring programs. Topping (1988) described the organization of peer tutoring programs with respect to the educational context, selection and matching of participants, curriculum and materials, contact, techniques, training, and evaluation. One example of a tutoring program to improve functioning in social studies is given in the case study.

TUTORING CASE STUDY

Mrs. Goodwin, the seventh-grade special education teacher, knew that her learning disabled students needed additional practice learning information from their general education social studies class. This year, Mr. Halleran, the general education social studies teacher, gave weekly quizzes requiring students to provide the factual recall of important people, events, and geographic locations from the readings in the textbook. The students with learning disabilities had a difficult time learning and remembering this information, as it was all so unfamiliar to them. Moreover, their performance to date on the weekly quizzes was abysmal at best, so something had to be done soon.

After examining the students' schedules, Mrs. Goodwin decided that during seventh period study hall she could set up a peer tutoring program during which the students could practice studying and reviewing social studies with one another. Her first step was to determine the specific information that Mr. Halleran wanted the students to know. Her second step included devising instructions and a plan for tutoring sessions. Then, she needed to train her students to become tutors and tutees. After that, the implementation of the tutoring program could begin. Finally, she could evaluate the tutoring program by measuring growth of her students in Mr. Halleran's class and asking for feedback from the students regarding perceived benefits of the tutoring.

Step 1: Determining the Specific Content for Tutoring Material

Mrs. Goodwin met with Mr. Halleran weekly and generated a listing of the important information from each social studies chapter. For example, the information on the World War I chapter included some of the following: Woodrow Wilson, president of the United States; William Jennings Bryan, a pacifist and secretary of state; definition of alliance system; names of countries in the Central and Allied Powers alliance systems; incidents leading up to the U.S. involvement in World War I, such as the Zimmermann Note and the sinking of the Lusitania; and famous individuals and their accomplishments, including Eddie Rickerbacker and George M. Cohan.

Step 2: Devising a Tutoring Plan

Next, Mrs. Goodwin designed for tutoring a plan that included specific instructions for students to use while tutoring each other and rules for appropriate behavior during tutoring sessions.

She decided that students would be tutors and tutees during sessions, because they all needed review and practice with the materials. Furthermore, she decided that the best way to practice learning the information would be to have the students ask each other questions concerning the important pieces of information. She planned to put the questions and answers on index cards, which could be used as tutoring materials. Questions would be on one side, with answers on the reverse.

The guidelines she established for tutoring behavior included the following:

1. Be nice to your partner, and sit facing each other.
2. Decide who will be the tutor first, then take turns asking and answering questions in an orderly fashion, and reverse roles when all questions have been answered correctly.
3. Speak in a pleasant tone, when asking questions or when responding.
4. Encourage your partner, by using statements like "great job, good answer" or "not quite, can you think of something else?"

5. Record the correct and incorrect responses.

6. Review any incorrect questions several times.

Instructing Students in Tutoring Roles and Behaviors

Next, Mrs. Goodwin planned a couple of sessions to review the tutoring roles and behaviors with her students with learning disabilities. She selected some materials from a previously covered social studies chapter, and she modeled both the tutor and tutees roles for her students. She then provided them with opportunities to practice both roles and provided any corrective feedback during the practice session. When she decided students had mastered the tutoring behaviors and understood their roles, she began the tutoring sessions during study hall.

Monitoring Performance

During the implementation of the tutoring sessions, Mrs. Goodwin began to collect systematic data on the efficacy of the tutoring. She was interested in knowing whether or not tutoring improved students' scores on weekly quizzes in Mr. Halleran's social studies class and whether or not students enjoyed the tutoring. She began to collect students' weekly quiz scores and charted them. She also devised a questionnaire for students to answer periodically. Sample questions included: Do you like being a tutor? Do you like being a tutee? Do you think tutoring helps you perform better on social studies quizzes? Again, she recorded student responses systematically. After a month of tutoring and collecting data, she was able to state that students' quiz scores had increased an average of 30 points and that all students reported enjoying being both tutors and tutees.

Most recently, comprehensive tutoring materials have been designed and implemented in reading and math (e.g., Fuchs, Fuchs, Karns, & Phillips, 1995; Fuchs, Mathes, & Fuchs, 1995). These materials, the Peabody Peer-Assisted Learning Strategies (PALS) have been implemented on a wide-scale basis, and positive benefits have been reported consistently for mainstreamed students with learning disabilities, low-achieving students without disabilities, as well as for average and high-achieving students (e.g., Fuchs, Fuchs, Phillips, Hamlett, & Karns, 1995). PALS appears unique in several important ways. First, training materials include more sophisticated strategic instructional techniques, rather than only rehearsal or repetition strategies. For example, the PALS reading methods include partner reading, a paragraph-shrinking strategy for summarizing main ideas, a prediction relay for predicting what will happen next, and a story mapping strategy designed to have students identify the main characters, the settings, the problems, story outcomes, and major events. The PALS math materials include coach's (tutor) instructions for guiding students through math problem solving (e.g., "Look at the sign. What kind of problem is it? Where do you start?" Fuchs, Fuchs, Karns, & Phillips, 1995, p. 4).

PALS training materials also include comprehensive instructions for teachers to use in teaching their students how to become effective tutors and tutees. Information on scheduling tutoring sessions is provided, and it is recommended that teachers implement PALS for 35 minutes three times a week. Furthermore, guidelines are presented on how to pair students into dyads. Then, scripted lessons and accompanying overhead transparencies are provided as models for teachers to use in teaching their students how to become coaches and how to implement the specific strategies during tutoring. Because students assume roles of both tutors (coaches) and tutees (readers) throughout tutoring sessions, practice is provided for both roles during the initial training sessions. In addition, specific instructions for selecting reading materials and providing ongoing monitoring of progress are provided.

Finally, PALS integrates a point reward system and employs a competitive game format to increase students' motivation. Students award each other daily points based on coaching and reading performance, and the class is divided into two teams comprised of the individual dyads.

A variety of other tutoring projects involving students with disabilities have also been described. In the following sections, research evidence on these projects is summarized, and conclusions are drawn regarding the results that can be expected from well-designed tutoring programs that involve students with disabilities.

TUTORING AND ACADEMIC ACHIEVEMENT

Effects on Achievement

One conclusion that can be drawn from research literature on tutoring is that students with special needs generally benefit academically from tutoring interventions (Mathes & Fuchs, 1994; Osguthorpe & Scruggs, 1986). For example, Top (1984) employed students with learning and behavioral disabilities as tutors in reading to younger, nonhandicapped elementary age students, for four 20-minute sessions per week over a 14-week period. Tutors and tutees alike performed better than control group students on reading tests. Gable and Kerr (1980) reported that tutees with learning problems gained substantially in math computation skills after being tutored by older students with behavioral disorders.

Tutors, however, gained little academically from the intervention, perhaps because they had already acquired most of the skills that they were tutoring. Kane and Alley (1980) found that incarcerated tutors and tutees (the latter with learning disabilities) learned math skills, but did not gain relative to comparison condition students who received teacher-directed instruction. Wingert (1980) reported that 20 elementary students with learning and behavioral disabilities made greater gains than controls on curriculum-based tests, but not on a standardized reading test. Truesdale (1976) reported that tutors and tutees with mild mental retardation performed significantly better than controls on spelling measures after a tutoring intervention. Generally, it can be stated that tutors and tutees with special needs very frequently make academic gains as a consequence of tutoring interventions. This appears to be true whether the student with special needs serves as tutor or tutee (Cook, Scruggs, Mastropieri, & Casto, 1985–1986).

Classwide peer tutoring (CWPT), in which an entire classroom participates in tutoring activities, has been promoted as an intervention strategy for promoting mainstreaming or inclusion of students with disabilities (Delquadri, Greenwood, Whorton, Carta, & Hall, 1986). Recently, Fuchs, Fuchs, Phillips, Hamlett, and Karns (1995) examined the effects of a CWP program (PALS) in math on the academic achievement of elementary students. In that investigation, 20 classrooms were assigned at random to CWPT or comparison conditions that controlled for allocated time on-task. Students in the tutoring condition underwent a 25-week CWPT project. Curriculum-based measurement (CBM) was conducted once per week. Twice monthly, these data were used to make decisions about which students to pair and what skills to work on. During twice-weekly tutoring sessions, students worked on 12 instances of the target problem type. The tutor modeled a series of questions, based on the type of problem, leading to the problem solution.

Results suggested that average-achieving students, low-achieving students, and students with learning disabilities all made gains in mathematics relative to the comparison classrooms. These results are significant in they impacted on various types of learners, and improved mathematics functioning relative to regular class instructional methods with the same overall time allocation (see also Fuchs et al., in press). Similar programs have resulted in academic gains in reading, across ability groups (Fuchs, Fuchs, Mathes,

& Simmons, in press); such programs have also been positively regarded by teachers (Phillips, Fuchs, & Fuchs, 1994). Positive academic gains from CWPT programs have also been reported by Maheady and Harper (1987), for a spelling program involving elementary classes of students receiving compensatory special education; and Maheady, Sacca, and Harper (1988) for three mainstream social studies classes that included students with learning disabilities and behavioral disorders.

One reason that has been given for the positive academic effects of tutoring is that it increases academic engaged time over what may ordinarily be available (Hall, Delquadri, Greenwood, & Thurston, 1982). For example, rather than students waiting their turn to read aloud for a teacher, they can gain additional practice reading continuously with a peer tutor. Research has suggested that peer tutoring can double or triple the engagement rates in a classroom on practice activities in areas such as reading (Greenwood, Delquadri, & Hall, 1989; Mathes, Fuchs, Fuchs, Henley, & Sanders, 1994). In the Fuchs, Fuchs, Phillps, Hamlett, and Karns (1995) investigation, it was found that one-on-one instruction was seven times more frequent in the PALS classrooms than in the contrast classes. Because most students with mild disabilities can benefit greatly from increased academic engagement and additional practice in basic skills areas (Mastropieri & Scruggs, 1994), tutoring could be expected to be an important intervention strategy for students with special needs.

Another possible reason for the success of tutoring interventions is the sense of ownership of academic endeavors conferred on the tutor. Such a supposition suggests that control of the learning situation may instill responsibility and a desire for learning to take place. The notion that students serving as tutors would gain in such areas as responsibility and ownership is the basis for the assumption that students could gain in socioemotional ways from the tutoring experience. This could be of particular benefit to students with disabilities, who may feel disconnected from the educational enterprise (Mastropieri & Scruggs, 1994). And, in fact, tutoring has been seen to impact positively in these areas, as discussed later in this chapter.

Comparison Groups

Scruggs and Richter (1988) reviewed the literature on tutoring and students with learning disabilities and concluded that treatments were more likely to be found to be effective if pre- post or no-treatment comparison groups were employed (e.g., Lamport, 1982; Lane, Pollack, & Sher, 1972). Nonsignificant differences were more likely to be observed when tutoring was compared to a specific alternative intervention, such as teacher-led small group instruction (e.g., Sindelar, 1982; but for an exception see Russell & Ford, 1983). Mathes and Fuchs (1994) reviewed tutoring investigations in the area of reading and concluded, "Unfortunately, none of the studies [reviewed] compared peer tutoring to other empirically validated methods ... [and] it remains unclear whether peer tutoring interventions with students with disabilities are equally or more effective than other validated interventions" (p. 77; see also Scruggs & Osguthorpe, 1986). These conclusions are supported by a meta-analysis of effects of students with disabilities as tutors (Cook, Scruggs, Mastropieri, & Casto, 1985–1986), in which it was reported that the mean standardized effect sizes associated with tutoring as a supplement to instruction were .96 and .69, for tutors and tutees, respectively, whereas those for tutoring as a substitute for instruction were .63 and .66.

Nevertheless, it is important to consider that tutoring has nearly always produced academic gains, particularly for tutees, and very often for tutors. That it has not always produced more positive results than, for example, small-group, teacher-directed instruction is not surprising, in that students are not expected to be more effective instructors than teachers. However, in situations where class size is large, or the teacher is not able to interact directly or frequently with all students, tutoring may be one effective strategy for increasing academic engagement. When assessing the potential effectiveness of tutoring, it is important to consider the range of alternative instructional interventions that are possible to implement in a given setting. In those settings when extended individual engagement with a teacher is not feasible, tutoring may be an effective alternative.

Different tutoring methods also have been compared in tutoring research. Sindelar (1982) reported that "hypothesis/test" instruction from elementary grade peer tutors resulted in higher reading comprehension performance than tutors using word recognition instruction with students with learning disabilities. Mathes and Fuchs (1993) compared level of text difficulty as well as two different tutoring methods—repeated reading and sustained reading—and a traditional teacher-led instructional control. Text difficulty (instructional vs. independent) exerted no apparent influence on outcomes. However, the sustained reading tutoring condition outperformed the teacher-led condition on fluency, but not comprehension. The repeated reading condition scored between the other two conditions. Clearly, the manner in which instruction is delivered in tutoring interventions is of significant importance; however, little comparative research has been completed to date in this area.

Types of Outcomes

Effects of peer tutoring have also depended to a certain extent on the type of outcome measure collected. Effects have generally been more pronounced on direct criterion tests of the content being tutored than on more general standardized measures of the academic area in general. Cook et al. (1985–1986), in a meta-analysis of effects of students with disabilities as tutors, reported standardized mean effect sizes of .91 and .89 for criterion measures, and .41 and .45 for standardized measures, for tutors and tutees, respectively. Such findings suggest that tutoring interventions, as they have been previously employed, can be expected to impact most strongly on specific skills, rather than more general abilities.

Cook et al. (1985–1986) reported that tutoring appeared to produce tangible effects on reading, writing, language, and math. King (1982) observed that Grade 6 students with learning disabilities learned more social studies content when tutored by same-age peers than a control group studying independently. Gains were observed in spelling for tutees but not tutors (see also Jenkins, Mayhall, Peschka, & Jenkins, 1974). Such findings suggest that tutors may not gain in areas in which they have already demonstrated mastery of skills they are tutoring (e.g., specific spelling words).

Research has also suggested that tutoring groups generally make more progress in basic skill areas than broader comprehension areas. Thus, Scruggs and Osguthorpe (1986) reported that cross-age and peer tutoring improved decoding, but not reading comprehension. Although this may have been due to the use of a phonics-based curriculum, Mathes and Fuchs (1993) also reported improvement relative to controls on decoding, but not comprehension, when the curriculum included a substantial comprehension component. Both of these investigations took place in special education settings. Although comprehension objectives may be generally more difficult to influence than decoding objectives (Mastropieri & Scruggs, 1997; Scruggs & Mastropieri, 1986), and tutoring interventions have most frequently addressed basic skills areas, it could be that more expert teachers may be better, in general, at implementing comprehension-type objectives. However, in recent regular education classwide tutoring programs, Fuchs, Fuchs, Phillips, Hamlett, and Karnes (1995) demonstrated that students did improve on concepts/applications subtests of math tests when tutoring included structured strategy training components. Fuchs, Fuchs, Mathes, and Simmons (in press) reported gains on tests of reading comprehension after a CWPT program, relative to comparison condition students (see also Sindelar, 1982). Further research can provide additional information on the extent to which tutoring can achieve results in more cognitive- conceptual domains.

Tutees versus Tutors

It has generally been seen that tutoring interventions can benefit tutors as well as tutees academically. Cook et al. (1985–1986), in a meta-analysis of handicapped students as tutors, reported a mean academic effect size of .59 for tutors with special needs and .65 for tutees. It seems logical to suggest that students are less likely to benefit directly from tutoring in subjects they have already mastered. Thus, Gable and Kerr (1979) reported that tutees with behavioral disorders improved in criterion math skills as a result of tutoring, but tutors with behavioral disorders did not improve. However, in most investigations, tutors also gained academically from the tutoring experience (e.g., Maher, 1982, 1984; Mellburg, 1980). Higgins (1982) reported that both peer tutoring and independent study increased spelling skills relative to a no-treatment control condition; in this investigation, tutees gained more than tutors from the program.

It is also possible that the generalized effects of tutoring may impact on academic achievement in other areas. However, Scruggs, Mastropieri, Veit, and Osguthorpe (1986) reported that students with behavioral disorders did not benefit significantly relative to controls on standardized academic achievement measures as a consequence of tutoring severely handicapped, younger students in basic language skills. However, in that investigation, tutors exhibited a descriptive advantage over controls in academic achievement.

As suggested by Scruggs, Mastropieri, and Richter (1985), it seems likely that tutors are likely to benefit academically to the extent tutoring promotes increased fluency-building and practice for academic areas in which tutors have already gained some initial competence. Thus, Singh (1982) reported that secondary-level tutees with learning disabilities made gains relative to nontutored controls on both math computation and math concepts/applications tests; while tutors made relative gains on concepts/applications tests, but not computation tests. Because virtually all tutoring studies with students with disabilities have involved basic skills areas, this seems to be an appropriate area for achieving academic results. However, it should be noted that tutoring interventions have rarely been attempted in areas where thinking skills and comprehension have been emphasized. Some recent evidence suggests that students with mild disabilities can benefit from constructing explanations for scientific facts (e.g., Scruggs, Mastropieri, & Sullivan, 1994), so using tutors in such a capacity may prove advantageous.

TUTORING AND SOCIAL–EMOTIONAL FUNCTIONING

Attitudes Toward School and Academic Subject

Many researchers have reported improved attitude toward school as a consequence of tutoring interventions. Lamport (1982) reported that attitude toward school improved in 24 students with learning disabilities who tutored younger students with learning disabilities. Similarly, Top (1984) reported that 39 students with learning and behavioral disorders improved in attitude toward school after tutoring younger students. Franca (1983) reported that tutoring improved attitude toward math for both tutors and tutees with behavior disorders. However, Scruggs, Mastropieri, Veit, and Osguthorpe (1986) reported that a tutoring program involving students with behavioral disorders as tutors of lower functioning, younger students did not improve scores on an attitude toward school measure, relative to control condition students. In that investigation, however, tutors generally reported positive attitudes toward their tutees.

Effects on Social Interactions

Much research involving students with special needs examined the effects of tutoring on social interaction between students with disabilities and nondisabled students. Osguthorpe, Eiserman, and Shisler (1985) trained 17 elementary students with mild mental retardation in sign language over an 8-week period. Over the following 10 weeks, these students tutored non-disabled age peers in sign language, during 15-minute afternoon sessions that met three times a week (see also Custer & Osguthorpe, 1983). During this time, observations were made of playground interactions between students with and without disabilities. It was reported that positive interactions increased from 4% to 11% of the interaction time, a statistically significant difference. In contrast, comparison groups in another school exhibited no change in positive interactions, remaining at or near zero throughout the same period (see also Osguthorpe, Eiserman, Top, & Scruggs, 1985). In the Scruggs, Mastropieri, Veit, and Osguthorpe (1986) investigation, number of positive interactions between tutor and tutee increased by about 56%, although this difference was not found to be statistically significant.

Asper (1973) employed eight Grade 6 and 8 students as tutors of eight withdrawn Grade 1 and 4 children. Compared with a no-tutoring control condition, social interactions increased between tutees and peers, but frequency of social contact with teacher was not affected. Similar to the Osguthorpe, Eiserman, and Shisler (1985) investigation, increases in social interactions were modest. The authors recommended use of tutoring in conjunction with other therapies.

Other investigations revealed similar findings. Csapo (1976) reported that "juvenile delinquent" tutors and younger tutees with reading disabilities increased in positive interactions after tutoring. Franca (1983) reported improvement in positive social interaction between tutors and tutees, including less frequent negative social interactions, in an investigation of tutoring in math. Most recently, Locke and Fuchs (1995) reported that marked improvement in academic engagement and positive comments between peers corresponded to the implementation of peer-mediated reading instruction.

However, these generally positive outcomes should not be taken to mean that peer interactions are always positive between students with disabilities and nondisabled students. Positive peer interactions should be prompted and carefully monitored. As an example of unproductive interactions on a group learning task, O'Connor and Jenkins (1996) provided the following report:

> Toby, a fifth-grade boy with [learning disabilities], rarely received productive help from his partners, although he frequently requested it. By this point in our observation, Toby's partner had long since ceased to follow Toby's reading or correct his errors. Toby stopped reading and announced, "I need help." The partner supplied a word, but it was not the word in the text. Toby used it anyway, and they both laughed. This game escalated until each time Toby needed decoding help, his partner said, "I'm a dumbo," which Toby inserted into the sentence.... Eventually, Toby tired of the game. "I need help," he said again, but from this partner he would not receive it. (p. 36)

Positive Social Behavior

The evidence that tutoring improves positive social behavior outside the tutoring context is less consistently documented. Most of the positive outcomes were obtained on samples for which there was no control condition. Maher (1984) reported a decrease in disciplinary referrals of students with emotional handicaps during a program in which they served as tutors of students with mild mental handicaps. Csapo (1976) reported that juvenile delinquents who served as tutors decreased in adjudicated delinquencies during the tutorial period, and increased in the number of nights the tutors arrived home before midnight. Lane, Pollack, and Sher (1972) reported that tutors with "maladaptive behavior" decreased in disruptive behavior and reported more self-confidence and responsibility.

However, research employing control conditions has yielded less consistent outcomes. Maher (1982) reported that students with emotional–behavioral disorders randomly assigned to experimental and control conditions were absent from school less often and exhibited fewer disciplinary problems while tutoring and being tutored. Scruggs, Mastropieri, Veit, and Osguthorpe (1986), however, reported no differences in absences, disciplinary referrals, or positive changes in target behaviors between elementary students with behavioral disorders assigned at random to a tutoring or control condition; and Swenson (1975) reported that students with learning disabilities randomly assigned to tutoring conditions did not improve in social acceptance relative to controls.

Self-Esteem

Reviews of tutoring research with special populations have concluded that tutoring exerts little or no effect on global self-esteem measures (Mathes & Fuchs, 1994; Osguthorpe & Scruggs, 1986; Scruggs & Richter, 1988). Cook, Scruggs, Mastropieri, and Casto (1985–1986) reported mean overall effect sizes of -.06 for tutors and .12 for tutees on self-esteem measures, a negligible effect in either case. This finding is also supported by the literature involving nondisabled students (Cohen, Kulik, & Kulik, 1982; Sharpley, Irvine, & Sharpley, 1983).

The fact that many researchers chose to include self-esteem measures (e.g., Kreutzer, 1973; Lazerson, 1980; Swenson, 1975) suggests that many view the process of tutoring as something likely to lead students to "feel better about themselves"; and, in fact, anecdotal evidence from teachers supports this view (e.g., Scruggs, Mastropieri, Veit, & Osguthorpe, 1986; Top, 1984). One possible explanation for this discrepancy is that teachers perceive tutoring as helpful in improving self-esteem—presumably because of the roles of responsibility and authority it confers on the tutor—but that the tutors themselves do not perceive tutoring as helpful in this way; that, in fact, the expectations often attributed to tutoring are simply overstated in this area. Another possibility is that students with disabilities may not necessarily exhibit low self-esteem at the onset of tutoring programs. Top (1984) for example, argued that self-esteem scores of students selected for tutoring were found to be high at the onset of treatment, and therefore could not be expected to increase greatly as a consequence of tutoring. It is probably important to consider that, although most students with disabilities exhibit deficits in basic academic functioning (Heward, 1996), they do not necessarily exhibit low self-esteem.

A third possibility is that conventional self-esteem measures are simply too general to reflect the positive social influences of tutoring interventions. Many of the items on these tests have little or nothing to do with perceptions of school functioning, or perceptions of interactions with school peers. Given that tutoring often does positively impact on more narrowly focused measures (e.g., social interaction, attitude toward school), it seems very possible that conventional self-esteem measures are less appropriate for assessing the outcomes of tutoring interventions.

CONCLUSIONS

Since the 1970s, a substantial number of studies have been conducted in the area of tutoring interventions involving students with disabilities. Reviewing the results of research in tutoring interventions, a number of general conclusions can be drawn. These are summarized next.

Generalization 1: Students with Special Needs Generally Benefit Academically From Tutoring.   This is apparently true whether students with disabilities function as tutors, tutees, or both. Students do not always benefit relative to other alternative conditions, such as small-group, teacher-led instruction, or structured independent study, but they nearly always make some gain. Tutors and tutees alike benefit; but tutors may benefit less if they have already fully mastered the content tutored. Gains are more likely to be obtained on criterion tests than achievement tests. Tutoring generally also has favored tests of specific skills rather than tests of comprehension, although more recent research, including strategy training components, has reported more positive results in comprehension/conceptual domains. Tutees nearly always gain something from appropriately structured tutoring, although tutors are somewhat less certain to benefit. Overall, tutoring can be expected to benefit tutors and tutees academically when (a) alternative means for delivering one-on-one or small group instruction are not feasible, (b) students are appropriately selected and trained in their roles,

(c) content being tutored is likely to benefit both tutor and tutee, and (d) progress toward prespecified goals is continuously monitored.

Generalization 2: Students with Special Needs Often Benefit in Socioemotional Domains From Tutoring.   Students with special needs very often demonstrate improvement in socioemotional domains of functioning as a result of tutoring, although these effects are somewhat less predictable and more variable than academic benefits. Improved attitudes toward the academic areas being tutored, and improved social interactions between tutors and tutees are very frequently observed. Improved attitudes toward school are also often observed. Less consistently observed are more generalized interactions between tutoring groups, or attitudes toward generalized groups (e.g., individuals with mental retardation). Reductions in disciplinary referrals have sometimes been reported. Improvements on global self-esteem measures are rarely observed. Observed benefits such as improved attitudes toward authority, more cooperative behavior, fewer antisocial acts, friendlier play, and dressing more neatly—although sometimes documented—are more often described anecdotally without documentation. Overall, positive socioemotional benefits are more likely to be obtained when:

1. Students are selected and trained systematically.
2. Efforts are made to keep the tutoring intervention successful for all participants.
3. Tutors and tutees are provided with appropriate positive support for their good performance.
4. Expectations are more specifically focused on the attitude toward the content being tutored and interactions between tutor and tutee.
5. Progress toward prespecified goals is continuously monitored.

Although there is much more to be learned about the effectiveness of tutoring interventions, sufficient evidence now exists about the efficacy of tutoring in special education to draw general conclusions. Nevertheless, tutoring—although clearly an effective instructional intervention overall—cannot be regarded as a panacea for special education. In fact, the comments from an earlier review of tutoring review still bear repeating. Krouse, Gerber, and Kauffman (1981) cautioned, "Although it has been demonstrated that academic and social gains are frequently obtained by the tutor, this in itself is not sufficient justification for the child to be a tutor.

Instead it must be shown that by being a tutor specific needs are being met" (p. 112). Given that systematic planning, implementation, monitoring, and documentation are being undertaken, however, it is likely that tutoring can be an extremely effective and significant component of a special education.

REFERENCES

Asper, A. L. (1973). *The effects of cross-age tutoring on the frequency of social contacts initiated by withdrawn elementary school children.* Unpublished doctoral dissertation, University of South Dakota, Vermillion.

Cohen, P. A., Kulik, J. A., & Kulik, C. C. (1982). Educational outcomes of tutoring: A meta-analysis of findings. *American Educational Research Journal, 19,* 237–248.

Cook, S., Scruggs, T. E., Mastropieri, M. A., & Casto, G. C. (1985–1986). Handicapped students as tutors. *Journal of Special Education, 19,* 483–492.

Csapo, M. (1976). If you don't know it, teach it! *Clearinghouse, 12,* 365–367.

Custer, J. D., & Osguthorpe, R. T. (1983). Improving social acceptance by training handicapped students to tutor their nonhandicapped peers. *Exceptional Children, 50,* 173–174.

Delquadri, J., Greenwood, C. R., Whorton, D., Carta, J. J., & Hall, R. V. (1986). Classwide peer tutoring. *Exceptional Children, 52,* 535–542.

Ehly, S. W., & Larsen, S. C. (1980). *Peer tutoring for individualized instruction.* Boston: Allyn & Bacon.

Franca, V. M. (1983). *Peer tutoring among behaviorally disordered students: Academic and social benefits to tutor and tutee.* Unpublished doctoral dissertation, George Peabody College for Teachers of Vanderbilt University, Nashville, TN.

Fuchs, D., Fuchs, L. S., Mathes, P. G., & Simmons, D. C. (in press). Peer-assisted learning strategies: Making classrooms more responsive to diversity. *American Educational Research Journal.*

Fuchs, L. S., Fuchs, D., Hamlett, C. L., Phillips, N. B., Karns, K., & Dutka, S. (in press). Enhancing students' helping behavior during peer-mediated instruction with conceptual mathematical explanations. *Elementary School Journal.*

Fuchs, L. S., Fuchs, D., Karns, K., & Phillips, N. (1995). *Peabody peer-assisted learning strategies (PALS): Math methods.* Nashville, TN: Peabody College, Vanderbilt University.

Fuchs, L. S., Fuchs, D., Phillips, N. B., Hamlett, C. L., & Karns, K. (1995). Acquisition and transfer effects of classwide peer-assisted learning strategies in mathematics for students with varying learning histories. *School Psychology Review, 24,* 604–620.

Fuchs, D., Mathes, P. G., & Fuchs, L. S. (1995). *Peabody peer-assisted learning strategies (PALS): Math methods.* Nashville, TN: Peabody College, Vanderbilt University.

Gable, R. V., & Kerr, M. M. (1980). Behaviorally disordered adolescents as academic change agents. In R. B. Rutherford, Jr., A. G. Prieto, & J. E. McGlothlin (Eds.), *Severe behavior disorders of children and youth* (Vol. 4, pp. 117–124). Reston, VA: Council for Children with Behavioral Disorders.

Greenwood, C. R., Delquadri, J. C., & Hall, R. V. (1989). Longitudinal effects of classwide peer tutoring. *Journal of Educational Psychology, 81,* 371–383.

Hall, R. V., Delquadri, J., Greenwood, C. R., & Thurston, L. (1982). The importance of opportunity to respond to children's academic success. In E. Edgar, N. Haring, J. Jenkins, & C. Pious (Eds.), *Mentally handicapped children: Education and training* (pp. 107–140). Baltimore: University Park Press.

Heward, W. L. (1996). *Exceptional children: An introduction to special education* (5th ed.). Columbus, OH: Merrill.

Higgins, T. S. (1982). *A comparison of two methods of practice on the spelling performance of learning disabled adolescents.* Unpublished doctoral dissertation, Georgia State University, Atlanta.

Jenkins, J. R., & Jenkins, L. M. (1981). *Crossage and peer tutoring: Help for children with learning problems.* Reston, VA: Council for Exceptional Children.

Jenkins, J. R., Mayhall, U. R., Peschka, C. M., & Jenkins, L. M. (1974). Comparing small group and tutorial instruction in resource rooms. *Exceptional Children, 40,* 245–250.

Kane, B. J., & Alley, G. R. (1980). A peer-tutored, instructional management program in computational mathematics for incarcerated, learning disabled juvenile delinquents. *Journal of Learning Disabilities, 13,* 39–42.

King, R. T. (1982). Learning from a PAL. *The Reading Teacher, 35,* 682–685.

Kreutzer, V. O. (1973). *A study of the use of underachieving students as tutors for emotionally disturbed children.* Unpublished doctoral dissertation, Brigham Young University, Provo, UT.

Krouse, J., Gerber, M. M., & Kauffman, J. M. (1981). Peer tutoring: Procedures, promises, and unresolved issues. *Exceptional Education Quarterly, 1*(4), 107–115.

Lamport, K. C. (1982). *The effects of inverted tutoring on reading disabled students in a public school setting.* Unpublished doctoral dissertation, Oklahoma State University, Stillwater.

Lane, P., Pollack, C., & Sher, N. (1972). Remotivation of disruptive adolescents. *Journal of Reading, 15,* 351–354.

Lazerson, D. B. (1980). I must be good if I can teach!—Peer tutoring with aggressive and withdrawn children. *Journal of Learning Disabilities, 13,* 152–157.

Locke, W. R., & Fuchs, L. S. (1995). Effects of peer-mediated reading instruction on the on-task behavior and social interaction of children with behavior disorders. *Journal of Emotional and Behavioral Disorders, 3,* 92–99.

Maheady, L., & Harper, G. F. (1987). A classwide peer tutoring program to improve the spelling test performance of low income, third- and fourth-grade students. *Education and Treatment of Children, 10,* 120–133.

Maheady, L., Sacca, M. K., & Harper, G. F. (1988). Classwide peer tutoring with mildly handicapped high school students. *Exceptional Children, 55,* 52–59.

Maher, C. A. (1982). Behavioral effects of using conduct problem adolescents as cross-age tutors. *Psychology in the Schools, 18,* 360–364.

Maher, C. A. (1984). Handicapped adolescents as cross-age tutors: Program description and evaluation. *Exceptional Children, 51,* 56–63.

Mastropieri, M. A., & Scruggs, T. E. (1994). *Effective instruction for special education.* Austin, TX: ProEd.

Mastropieri, M. A., & Scruggs, T. E. (1997). Best practices in promoting reading comprehension in students with learning disabilities: 1976–1996. *Remedial and Special Education, 18,* 197–213.

Mathes, P. G., & Fuchs, L. S. (1993). Peer-mediated reading instruction in special education resource rooms. *Learning Disabilities Research & Practice, 8,* 233–243.

Mathes, P. G., & Fuchs, L. S. (1994). The efficacy of peer tutoring in reading for students with mild disabilities: A best-evidence synthesis. *School Psychology Review, 23,* 59–80.

Mathes, P. G., Fuchs, D., Fuchs, L. S., Henley, A. M., & Sanders, A. (1994). Increasing strategic reading practice with Peabody Classwide Peer Tutoring. *Learning Disabilities Research & Practice, 9,* 44–48.

Mellburg, D. B. (1980). *The effect of the handicapped and nonhandicapped tutor on the academic achievement of the economically disadvantaged adolescent tutor and the elementary age tutee.* Unpublished doctoral dissertation, University of Wisconsin, Madison.

O'Connor, R. E., & Jenkins, J. R. (1996). Cooperative learning as an inclusion strategy: A closer look. *Exceptionality, 6,* 29–51.

Osguthorpe, R. T., Eiserman, W. D., & Shisler, L. (1985). Increasing social acceptance: Mentally retarded students tutoring regular class peers. *Education and Training of the Mentally Retarded, 20,* 235–240.

Osguthorpe, R. T., Eiserman, W., Top, B., & Scruggs, T. E. (1985). Handicapped children as tutors: Final Report (1984–1985). Provo, UT: Department of Educational Psychology, Brigham Young University. (ERIC Document Reproduction Service No. 267 545)

Osguthorpe, R. T., & Scruggs, T. E. (1986). Special education students as tutors: A review and analysis. *Remedial and Special Education, 7*(4), 15–26.

Phillips, N. B., Fuchs, L. S., & Fuchs, D. (1994). Effects of classwide curriculum-based measurement and peer tutoring: A collaborative researcher–practitioner interview study. *Journal of Learning Disabilities, 27,* 420–434.

Russell, T., & Ford, D. F. (1983). Effectiveness of peer tutors vs. resource teachers. *Psychology in the Schools, 20,* 436–441.

Scruggs, T. E., & Mastropieri, M. A. (1986). Improving the test-taking skills of behaviorally disordered and learning disabled students. *Exceptional Children, 53,* 63–68.

Scruggs, T. E., Mastropieri, M. A., & Richter, L. L. (1985). Peer tutoring with behaviorally disordered students: Social and academic benefits. *Behavioral Disorders, 10,* 283–294.

Scruggs, T. E., Mastropieri, M. A., & Sullivan, G. S. (1994). Promoting relational thinking skills: Elaborative interrogation for mildly handicapped students. *Exceptional Children, 60,* 450–457.

Scruggs, T. E., Mastropieri, M. A., Veit, D. T., & Osguthorpe, R. T. (1986). Behaviorally disordered students as tutors: Effects on social behaviors. *Behavioral Disorders, 12,* 36–44.

Scruggs, T. E., & Osguthorpe, R. T. (1986). Tutoring interventions within special education settings: A comparison of cross-age and peer tutoring. *Psychology in the Schools, 23,* 187–193.

Scruggs, T. E., & Richter, L. (1988). Tutoring learning disabled students: A critical review. *Learning Disability Quarterly, 11,* 274–286.

Sharpley, A. M., Irvine, J. W., & Sharpley, C. F. (1983). An examination of the effectiveness of cross-age tutoring program in mathematics for elementary school children. *American Educational Research Journal, 20,* 103–111.

Sindelar, P. T. (1982). The effects of cross-age tutoring on the comprehension skills of remedial reading students. *The Journal of Special Education, 16,* 199–206.

Singh, R. K. (1982). *Peer tutoring: Its effects on the math skills of students designated as learning disabled.* Unpublished doctoral dissertation, American University, Washington, DC.

Swenson, S. H. (1975). *Effects of peer tutoring in regular elementary classrooms on sociometric status, self-concept and arithmetic achievement of slow learning tutors and learners in a special education resource program.* Unpublished doctoral dissertation, Indiana University, Bloomington.

Top, B. L. (1984). *Handicapped children as tutors: The effects of cross-age, reverse-role tutoring on self-esteem and reading achievement.* Unpublished doctoral dissertation, Brigham Young University, Provo, UT.

Topping, K. (1988). *The peer tutoring handbook: Promoting co-operative learning.* Cambridge, MA: Brookline Books.

Truesdale, E. L. (1976). *The effects of assigned tutorial responsibilities on mildly retarded students.* Unpublished doctoral dissertation, Florida State University, Tallahassee.

Wingert, D. A. (1980). *The use of high school paraprofessional tutors with programmed tutorial materials to instruct elementary learners with handicaps.* Unpublished doctoral dissertation, Utah State University, Logan.

III

PEER FACILITATION
AND EDUCATION

Peer Modeling

Dale H. Schunk
Purdue University

Modeling is an important means for acquiring skills, beliefs, attitudes, and behaviors (Bandura, 1986; Rosenthal & Zimmerman, 1978). Teachers, parents, and other adults serve as powerful models for children, but equally important are the many peers with whom children interact. Research shows that peer models play an important role in children's cognitive, social, and emotional development (Schunk, 1987).

In this chapter, the concept of how peer modeling affects students' learning and motivation is discussed. Important definitions are as follows:

Peer: One who is roughly equivalent in development to the observer and who may be similar in other ways (e.g., gender, level of competence).

Model: A person whose actions, verbalizations, and expressions are attended to by one or more observers and serve as cues for modeling.

Modeling: The process by which observers pattern their thoughts, beliefs, strategies, and actions after those displayed by one or more models.

Peer modeling: Modeling that occurs as a function of observing peers (Bandura, 1986; Berger, 1977; Field, 1981; Hartup, 1978; Schunk, 1987).

In the next section I discuss observational learning through modeling to include influential factors and forms of modeling. A theoretical explanation for the effects of peer models on learning and motivation is offered. Important considerations in incorporating peer models into instruction are described. Research evidence is presented on the effects of peer models in learning settings to include generalization of effects, concluding with suggestions for future research. To focus the chapter, emphasis is given to learning cognitive skills and strategies, although some attention is given to social skills.

OBSERVATIONAL LEARNING THROUGH MODELING

Social Cognitive Theory

An important contribution of Bandura's (1977, 1986) social–cognitive theory is to elucidate the process of observational learning through modeling and to identify influences on observational learning. Observational learning occurs when observers display new behaviors that prior to modeling are not demonstrated, even with motivational inducements to do so (Schunk, 1987). Observational learning is especially important, but there are other forms of modeling. Bandura (1969) discussed response facilitation, or performance of previously learned behaviors due to prompting (e.g., looking upward in response to a crowd looking upward), and inhibition–disinhibition, which refers to strengthening or weakening of behavioral inhibitions due to observing models (e.g., students who stop misbehaving when they observe other misbehaving students punished by the teacher).

Observational learning comprises attention, retention, production, and motivation (Bandura, 1986). Observer attention to relevant environmental events is necessary for them to be perceived meaningfully. Retention requires coding and transforming modeled information for storage in memory, as well as organizing and rehearsing information cognitively. Production involves translating mental conceptions of modeled events into actual behaviors. Many actions may be learned in rough form through observation, but practice and feedback are necessary for skill refinement.

Motivation influences observational learning because students are likely to attend to, retain, and produce modeled actions that they feel are important. Students who believe that models possess a skill that is useful to know are likely to attend to them and attempt to retain what they learn. Students do not demonstrate all the knowledge, skills, and behaviors they learn through observation. Outcome expectations are important: They perform actions they believe will result in rewarding outcomes and avoid those they expect to be followed by negative outcomes (Schunk, 1987). Students also perform activities they value and avoid those they find dissatisfying.

Observation of models also can raise observers' self-efficacy, or beliefs about their capabilities to learn or perform behaviors at designated levels (Bandura, 1986, 1997). Seeing a successful model may lead observers to believe that if the model can learn, they can as well. As students perform actions and note their learning progress, their sense of self-efficacy is substantiated, which maintains motivation for further skill-learning.

Learner motivation is a critical process that teachers attempt to promote in various ways including making learning interesting, relating learning to students' interests, having students set learning goals and monitor their progress, providing students with feedback that indicates increased competence, and showing students how skills can be applied in different ways. Peer models can assist teachers with many of these types of motivational activities.

Factors Affecting Observational Learning

Simply observing models is no guarantee that learning will occur. Several factors affect learning through their influence on attention, retention, production, and motivation. Important factors are developmental status of learners, model prestige and competence, vicarious consequences, outcome expectations, self-efficacy, and goal setting (Schunk, 1987).

Students' abilities to learn from models depend on level of development. Young children have difficulty attending to modeled events for long periods, distinguishing relevant from irrelevant cues, and organizing information. With development, children acquire more extensive knowledge and become better capable of handing complex modeled events. With respect to production, development produces greater physical capabilities. Motivational influences also change with development. Young children are easily swayed by immediate consequences of their actions, whereas older students can keep long-range goals in mind and are more likely to perform modeled actions consistent with their goals and values.

Especially when there are multiple models, students are more likely to attend to those with prestige and competence. In most instances, high-status models have ascended to their positions because they are competent. High-status models for students are persons who have achieved success; (e.g.,well-respected teachers, business and community leaders, published writers, student leaders). Their actions have functional value for observers, who are apt to believe that rewards will be forthcoming if they act accordingly. Interestingly, the effects of model prestige often generalize to areas in which models have no particular competence, as when children adopt the commercial food preferences of prominent athletes.

Vicarious consequences of modeled actions affect modeling. Peer modeling depends in large part on perceived similarity between model and observer. Modeling is a form of social comparison, or comparing oneself with others. Festinger (1954) postulated that observers often evaluate themselves through comparisons with others and that the best (most accurate) evaluations derive from comparisons with those who are viewed as similar in the ability or characteristic being evaluated. Peer models are most influential in situations where perceived similarity provides information about one's abilities or the appropriateness of behaviors.

Observation of models can be informative and motivating. Observing competent models perform actions that lead to success conveys information about the sequence of actions to use to succeed. Students learn new skills and strategies by observing models. Models are informative in another way. Most social situations are structured so that the appropriateness of behaviors depends on such factors as age, gender, or status. By observing modeled behaviors and their consequences, people form outcome expectations about which behaviors are likely to be rewarded or punished, and people act based on their expectations.

Similarity to models helps one gauge behavioral appropriateness and formulate outcome expectations (Schunk, 1987). Children who perceive the actions of same-age peers to be more appropriate for themselves than the actions of younger or older models are apt to emulate the peers. Brody and Stoneman (1985) found that in the absence of competence information, children were more likely to model actions of same-age peers. When children were given competence information, modeling was enhanced by similar competence, regardless of model age.

No strong evidence suggests that children consistently learn any better from peers or adults. Evidence does show that peers and adults use different teaching strategies. Child teachers often use nonverbal demonstrations to show how to perform specific tasks; adults typically employ more verbal instruction and relate information to be learned to other material (Ellis & Rogoff, 1982). Peer instruction may be especially beneficial with students with learning problems who do not process verbal material well. Similarity seems most important in situations where observers have little information about functional value (i.e., tasks with which observers are not familiar or those not immediately followed by consequences).

Vicarious consequences serve a motivational function. Seeing others succeed or fail, or be rewarded or punished, creates outcome expectations, and students are more likely to perform actions when they believe they will be successful or rewarded than when they expect to fail or be punished. These motivational effects depend in part on observers' self-efficacy. Observing similar peers succeed can raise observers' self-efficacy and motivate them to try the task because they are apt to believe that if their peers can succeed, they can as well. Observing similar others fail or have difficulty may lead students to believe they lack the competence to do well, which can lead to avoidance. Model attributes often predict performance capabilities. Peer models who observers believe are similar in competence to themselves can have strong motivational effects when students are uncertain about their capabilities, are unfamiliar with the (new) task, or have previously experienced difficulties learning and now doubt whether they can succeed (Bandura, 1986).

Goal setting is influential because observers are likely to attend to peer models who demonstrate behaviors that help observers attain goals. Goals enhance learning through their effects on students' attention, task activities, perceptions of learning progress, and self-efficacy. Initially, students make a commitment to attempt to attain a goal (Locke & Latham, 1990). As they work on the task, they compare their current performances with goals. Positive self-evaluations of progress raise self-efficacy and sustain motivation. Many goals are acquired through modeling (e.g., students decide to work on a computer task that they observe others attempting).

Forms of Modeling

Modeling can take many forms. Those that lend themselves to portraying perceived similarity include cognitive modeling, mastery and coping modeling, and self-modeling.

Cognitive Modeling. Cognitive modeling incorporates modeled explanation and demonstration with verbalization of the model's thoughts and reasons for performing actions (Meichenbaum, 1977). In teaching division skills, a model might verbalize the following while solving the problem 276 divided by 4:

> First decide what number to divide 4 into. I take 276, start on the left and move toward the right until I have a number the same as or larger than 4. Is 2 larger than 4? No. Is 27 larger than 4? Yes. So my first division will be 4 into 27. Now I need to multiply 4 by a number that will give an answer the same as or slightly smaller than 27. How about 5? $5 \times 4 = 20$. No, too small. Let's try 6. $6 \times 4 = 24$. Maybe. Let's try 7. $7 \times 4 = 28$. No, too large. So 6 is correct.

Teachers commonly use cognitive modeling during instruction, but peers make excellent cognitive models. For example, a teacher might ask a student to solve a problem on the board and verbalize aloud while the class observes. Peers' verbalizations can include task and other types of statements (i.e., affective statements such as, "I can do this"). When errors occur, students can be shown how to deal with them. Errors may heighten perceptions of similarity between observers and models because students often make errors while learning. Self-reinforcing statements (e.g., "I'm doing well") also are useful, especially for students who encounter learning difficulties and doubt whether they are capable of learning.

A procedure that incorporates cognitive modeling is self-instructional training (Meichenbaum, 1986). Meichenbaum and Goodman (1971) used this five-step procedure to teach impulsive second graders to slow down and thereby make fewer errors:

1. Cognitive modeling: Model verbalizes while performing the task and child observes.
2. Overt guidance: Child performs under direction of model's instruction.
3. Overt self-guidance: Child performs while instructing him- or herself aloud.
4. Faded overt self-guidance: Child whispers instructions while performing task.
5. Covert self-instruction: Child performs task while guided by inner silent speech.

Research shows that modeling combined with verbalized thoughts is more effective than modeling alone (Rosenthal & Zimmerman, 1978). Cognitive modeling has been used to teach various tasks to many types of students (Fish & Pervan, 1985). It is especially valuable for teaching students to work on tasks strategically (Schunk, 1981). In teaching reading comprehension, the model might state, "What is it I have to do? I have to find the topic sentence of the paragraph. The topic sentence is what the paragraph is about. I start by looking for a sentence that sums up the details or tells what the paragraph is about" (McNeil, 1987, p. 96). Statements for coping with difficulties (e.g., "I haven't found it yet, but that's all right") can be easily included.

Mastery and Coping Modeling.   Mastery and coping models teach skills and help develop students' self-efficacy for learning. These models differ in how rapidly they demonstrate skill attainment and in the types of statements they verbalize.

Mastery models perform competently and demonstrate high skill from the outset. In addition to task-relevant statements, they also may verbalize statements of high confidence (e.g., "I can do that"), high ability ("I'm good at this"), and positive attitudes ("This is fun"). Mastery models demonstrate rapid learning and make no errors.

In contrast, coping models illustrate how determined effort and positive self-thoughts overcome difficulties. They initially demonstrate learning difficulties and possibly fears, but gradually improve their performances and gain confidence. At first they might verbalize statements of task difficulty and low confidence (e.g., "This is tough," "I don't know if I can do this"), but they shift to coping statements indicating high effort ("I'll have to work hard"), persistence ("I might be able to do it if I don't give up"), and concentration ("I need to pay attention to what I'm doing"). Eventually their performances improve to the level portrayed by mastery models, and their verbalizations reflect confidence, high ability, and positive attitudes.

Although mastery models teach skills, coping models may be better with students who often experience problems because they may view themselves more similar to coping models given the initial difficulties and gradual progress. The heightened similarity can raise self-efficacy in observers, who are likely to think that since their peers could learn, they can too (Schunk & Hanson, 1985).

Self-Modeling. The highest degree of model–observer similarity occurs when one is one's own model. Behavioral change that results from observing one's own behaviors is called self-modeling (Dowrick, 1983). In a typical procedure, one is videotaped while learning or performing a task and subsequently views the tape. For example, a teacher might videotape a student working on an ecology project during science. Observing a self-model tape is a form of review and is especially informative for skills that one cannot watch while performing (e.g., golf swing).

Self-model tapes that contain errors may discourage some students (Hosford, 1981). Commentary from a knowledgeable individual (e.g., teacher) while students view their tapes helps to prevent them from feeling less efficacious; the teacher can explain how to perform better the next time. Errorless performances can be portrayed by videotaping a skillful performance or by editing the tape to remove sequences with errors. It helps to videotape on different occasions to show progress in learning, which conveys that one is capable and raises self-efficacy and motivation.

Distinguishing Features of Modeling

Modeling requires the following elements: one or more models, one or more observers (learners), and a task to be performed. If the skill is complex, it is unlikely to be mastered through observation. Instead, following the modeled demonstration, learners must practice the task and receive corrective feedback.

It helps to accentuate those features of the modeled display to which learners should attend. This can be done through physical means (e.g., distinctive colors), by verbalizing their importance ("Watch carefully now"), or by repeating the sequence. Making features distinctive holds student attention, which aids retention.

If self-modeling is to be used, videotaping equipment and a private viewing area are needed. While viewing the tape, students must be able to clearly see their performances; thus, the taping area must have adequate lighting and their work must be captured on tape. The latter may require zooming in on those aspects of their performances that will be highlighted during the subsequent viewing.

ORGANIZATION OF PEER MODELING

Using peer models during instruction requires careful planning of the content and of what the models will demonstrate. These organizational aspects are discussed next.

Content

An important consideration is whether the content can be easily modeled by peers. Questions such as the following should be addressed: What is to be learned? What materials and equipment are necessary? How long will be needed for learning to occur?

Content should ideally be not too complex and be able to be clearly displayed by peers. At the same time, the learning could present some difficulties; this allows for coping modeling. The advice is to choose content that will allow student success with some effort.

This type of modeling is appropriate for much school learning. For example, peers can be used effectively to model learning of various skills in mathematics (e.g., adding fractions, solving long division problems), reading comprehension (e.g., finding main ideas, locating details), writing (e.g., constructing topic sentences, filling in details), science (e.g., mixing chemicals, balancing equations), and so forth. If the skill is complex, it may be necessary to break the unit into subunits that can be modeled separately. It is not desirable to ask peers to work on complex skills; if they make many mistakes, this conveys that the task is hard and will lower self-efficacy for learning among observing students.

Models

A key point is to select peer models whom students perceive as similar to themselves in important characteristics. Similarity can be based on gender, age, competence, learning style, and the like. If much diversity exists in the class, it is helpful to use multiple models who differ in these attributes. Multiple models allow students to perceive themselves as similar to at least one model.

Another important point is to show models learning. By observing peers learn, students are apt to experience a sense of self-efficacy for learning themselves (Schunk, 1987). Material should be selected such that if models encounter difficulty, they will be able to cope with problems and eventually portray the desired behaviors.

Sustained attention to models is necessary. A good way to gain and sustain student attention is to keep modeled displays short and interest-ing—especially for young children who have limited attention spans. To further enhance attention, teachers can verbalize the usefulness of the material to be learned (e.g., "This skill is important since we will be using it throughout the next few months when we work on math").

As an example, consider a teacher who wishes to model ways to construct a topic sentence for a paragraph. Initially the teacher might select four or five peers with varying levels of writing skill. Students then could go to a chalkboard individually and be given a topic on which they will write a short paragraph (e.g., describe a bird). Each student could write down several things about birds and then decide how best to summarize these points in one (topic) sentence (e.g., "A bird is an amazing creature"). In this fashion, students are exposed to multiple models who have different expe-riences with birds and construct different topic sentences for paragraphs with the same theme.

EVIDENCE FOR EFFECTIVENESS

Next is research on peer modeling, including advantages of peer models, along with some drawbacks. Evidence is presented on their effects relative to other forms of modeling and instruction. This research focuses on the cognitive domain, although some research on social outcomes is reported. Methods for conducting research on peer modeling are described, and finally a discussion on the generalization of peer modeling effects is presented.

Advantages of Peer Models

A major advantage is that students often can better identify with the skills and learning strategies of peers than with the demonstrated competence of an adult teacher. Higher perceived similarity raises self-efficacy and motivation (Schunk, 1987). Teachers may unwittingly convey that a task is easy to learn by performing flawlessly. Although modeled teacher competence can raise students' self-efficacy, that increase will be short-lived if students subsequently have difficulty (Schunk, 1987). Students may develop the belief that the teacher's success does not guarantee theirs. Students are more swayed by peer successes.

Peer models have other advantages. Peers can model ways to deal with problems in terms that student observers can understand (e.g., "Here's what to do when this happens"). This point relates to the idea that peers teach differently than adults. Peers are more likely to focus on the practical ("how to do") aspects and be less concerned with general principles than are teachers. Initial success boosts efficacy, and students can be taught principles better later on. Finally, there are many benefits of having students serve as their own models (self-modeling).

One potential drawback is that peers may model incorrectly. Improper learning can be minimized if teachers carefully select tasks to be modeled such that students can master them with reasonable effort. If peers display incorrect operations, then teachers can quickly offer constructive feedback that emphasizes what is correct and what needs reworking. It is not desirable to have models struggle with learning as this can lower observers' self-efficacy. Another potential problem is that peer modeling takes time. When time available is short, it may be better for teachers to correctly demonstrate the skills and have students practice. Peer models also may be unnecessary if skills are easy to learn and thus students' self-efficacy already is high.

Research Methods

To evaluate the effects of peer models on students' achievement outcomes, researchers typically include groups of students that are exposed to peer models and other groups that are not. For example, assume that a researcher wished to determine the effects of peer models on students' skills in composing expository paragraphs. In one condition (Group 1), students might be exposed to a peer model who explained and demonstrated composition principles. In another condition (Group 2), students might observe an adult teacher provide comparable instruction. All students might then practice composing and be tested to determine whether one group wrote better compositions.

Comparing Groups 1 and 2 would indicate how effective peer models are relative to adult models. The researcher might add Group 3, in which students studied material on their own that described and exemplified principles of expository paragraph composition. Comparisons of Groups 1 and 2 to Group 3 would reveal how effective models are relative to no model.

It usually is not sufficient to include only Groups 1 and 3. If Group 1 students outperform Group 3 students, it is not clear whether the advantage stems from being exposed to a model or from the model's characteristics (i.e., peer). A condition that includes a nonpeer model also is needed.

Besides student learning, researchers are also interested in how peer models affect other achievement outcomes. Peers may influence student motivation including choice of activities, effort, and persistence. Peers also can affect students' achievement beliefs about their capabilities (self-efficacy), perceived causes of outcomes (attributions), and interests. Researchers often assess diverse achievement outcomes to better understand the scope of peer modeling effects.

Research Evidence

Schunk and Hanson (1985) showed that peer models can enhance self-efficacy for learning better than adult models. Elementary school children who had experienced difficulties learning to subtract observed either a videotaped peer model learn subtraction with regrouping operations, a videotaped adult model demonstrate the operations, or no model. Children in the peer-model conditions observed either a mastery or a coping model. The mastery model solved problems correctly and verbalized statements reflecting high self-efficacy and ability, low task difficulty, and positive attitudes. The coping model initially made errors and verbalized negative statements, but then verbalized coping statements (e.g., "I need to pay attention to what I'm doing") and eventually verbalized and performed as well as the mastery model. Following the videotaped modeling, all children received instruction and practice in subtraction and were posttested on self-efficacy and subtraction skills.

Mastery and coping models increased self-efficacy and subtraction achievement better than the adult model or no model; adult-model children outperformed no-model students. These results suggest that model–observer age similarity can raise self-efficacy among low-achieving children. Higher self-efficacy developed through peer observation likely was substantiated by children's subsequent successes during instruction and led to higher posttest skill. Children who observed the adult model may have wondered whether they were capable of becoming as competent.

The lack of differences between the coping and mastery model conditions may have arisen because children had previously experienced success with subtraction. They might have reflected on those successes and thought that since the peer learned to regroup, they could as well. Schunk, Hanson, and Cox (1987) further explored the coping–mastery model distinction and found that observing coping models enhanced children's self-efficacy and skills more than did observing mastery models. Unlike Schunk and Hanson (1985), Schunk et al. (1987) used a task (fractions) with which children had no prior success. Coping models may be more beneficial when students work on unfamiliar tasks or have experienced learning difficulties. Schunk et al. (1987) also found that multiple models (coping or mastery) promoted outcomes as well as a single coping model and better than a single mastery model. With multiple models, learners are apt to perceive themselves as similar to at least one.

Schunk and Hanson (1989a) investigated variations in coping modeling. Children observed either one or three same-sex peer mastery, coping-emotive, or coping-alone models, learn to solve fraction problems. Mastery models learned quickly; coping-emotive models initially experienced difficulties learning and verbalized negative emotive statements (e.g., "I don't think I can do this") but then displayed coping behaviors and eventually performed as well as mastery models; coping-alone models performed in identical fashion to coping–emotive models but never verbalized negative statements. Coping–emotive models led to the highest self-efficacy for learning among observers. Mastery and coping–alone children perceived the model as competent and themselves as equally competent; coping-emotive subjects viewed themselves as more competent than the model. All children received instruction and practice on fractions; on the posttest, the three conditions did not differ in self-efficacy or skill.

The differences in self-efficacy for learning did not affect problem solving during instruction or posttest outcomes, perhaps because children were able to learn the operations. Coping–emotive children overestimated their learning efficacy. Overly high efficacy brought about by exposure to coping-emotive models is not instructionally desirable if children subsequently encounter difficulty learning and feel less motivated to learn.

Schunk and Hanson (1989b) found support for the notion that viewing self-model tapes raises self-efficacy and achievement. Children were videotaped solving mathematical problems and later viewed their tapes. Following an instructional program, these children demonstrated higher self-efficacy, motivation, and learning than did students who had been videotaped but did not observe their tapes and those who had not been videotaped. Self-model tapes highlight progress in skill acquisition, which promotes self-efficacy, motivation, and learning.

Much research shows that observing peer models affects other behaviors. Significant effects of peer models on observers have been obtained in the following domains: food preferences (Brody & Stoneman, 1981, 1985), aggression (Hicks, 1965), coping with snakes (Kornhaber & Schroeder, 1975), communication (Sonnenschein & Whitehurst, 1980), Piagetian conservation (Robert, 1983; Robert & Charbonneau, 1977), expressive behavior (Hayes, 1973), adoption of behavioral standards (Davidson & Smith, 1982), self-rewards (Akamatsu & Farudi, 1978), and prosocial behaviors (Becker & Glidden, 1979), and block construction (Barry & Overmann, 1977), with educable mentally retarded children.

Strain, Kerr, and Ragland (1981) trained peers to initiate social interactions with socially withdrawn children by using verbal signals (e.g., "Let's play blocks") and motor responses (handing child a toy). Initiations increased students' social initiations and gains often generalized to other classroom aspects, although gains related to children's entry-level social repertoires. Training of peer initiators is time-consuming but is cost-effective compared with methods of remedying social withdrawal that require near-continuous teacher involvement (i.e., prompting, reinforcement).

Peer modeling occurs when a socially competent peer is paired with a less competent child to work on a task. The opportunity for social interaction within the dyad typically promotes the less competent child's social skills (Mize, Ladd, & Price, 1985).

Generalization of Effects

An important question is whether peer modeling effects generalize beyond the research or intervention context to other settings. Most studies do not address generalization, but there are some positive results. Strain et al. (1981) obtained evidence of generalization to other facets of classroom life.

Schunk et al. (1987) found that peer modeling increases in motivation and self-efficacy led to skill gains on types of problems not included in the original modeling.

To promote generalization it may be necessary to have peer models conduct refresher sessions with students after the initial modeling. These sessions could include new types of situations to which behaviors should generalize. Peer helpers are especially useful in working with students who have severe cognitive and social skill deficiencies (Peck, Cooke, & Apolloni, 1981). Effective social skills training is particularly important given the educational emphasis today on inclusion of special needs students in regular classrooms.

More research is needed on generalization, especially on long-term maintenance. Using nonhandicapped children, Oden and Asher (1977) found that increases in peer acceptance maintained themselves after 1 year; however, most research examining maintenance has employed short periods (up to 1 month).

A promising means of promoting generalization is by having peers demonstrate effective strategies for learning and coping with difficulties (Schunk & Hanson, 1985). Such strategies as rehearsing information to be learned, setting goals, checking work, maintaining positive beliefs about learning, and using self-reinforcement (e.g., "I'm doing better") could generalize to new content and settings. Research not employing peer models shows that strategy training effects maintain themselves and generalize to new content (Graham & Harris, 1989a, 1989b; Sawyer, Graham, & Harris, 1992); however, strategy generalization is not automatic (Pressley et al., 1990). Students may believe that the strategy is not useful on other content, think that the old strategy works better, fail to understand how to modify the strategy for use on other tasks, or feel incapable of using the strategy effectively (Schunk & Rice, 1993). Demonstration of strategy use on different tasks by peer models can facilitate generalization. A detailed example of peer modeling to include generalization appears in Table 10.1.

CONCLUSION AND FUTURE DIRECTIONS

This chapter shows that peer models affect students' learning and motivation, but more research is needed to understand better how modeling effects occur and how to effectively incorporate models into instruction. Research on the topics of inclusion, motivation, and self-regulation is recommended.

TABLE 10.1

Using Peer Models to Teach Strategy Learning and Generalization

Context: A fifth-grade classroom teacher wants to teach students a simple, general problem-solving strategy and how to adapt it for application to different academic content.

Strategy: The components of the strategy and the statements to be verbalized by models are as follows:

(Goal) — What is it I have to do?

(Given) — What do I know?

(Subgoals) — What steps do I follow?

(Perform) — Perform the steps

(Check) — Check my work to see if it looks OK

Initial Learning

The initial learning occurs during mathematics instruction on solving word problems. Students are given problems such as the following:

Shaun has 16 pieces of candy. He wants to give twice as many pieces to Lisa as he gives to Kelly and still have 4 pieces left for himself. How many pieces of candy should he give to Lisa and Kelly?

The teacher asks a student to exemplify the strategy at the board while solving the problem. Previously the teacher and student met and the teacher explained and demonstrated the strategy for the student. Thus, the teacher has prepared the model to ensure that the model will be successful.

The model verbalizes the following while solving the problem:

What is it I have to do? I need to figure out how many pieces of candy to give to Lisa and Kelly. *What do I know?* I know that there are 16 pieces of candy and that after giving candy to Lisa and Kelly I must have 4 pieces left for myself. *What steps do I follow?* First I should figure out how many pieces of candy I will give away. Then I can divide that total so that Lisa gets two times as many as Kelly. *Perform the steps.* There are 16 pieces, and I will keep 4. 19 minus 4 is 12. So I will give away 12 pieces. Now I will divide 12 so Lisa gets two times as many as Kelly. I'll start with 2. 2 times 2 equals 4. 2 plus 4 equals 6; no, too low. I'll try 3. 3 times 2 equals 6. 3 plus 6 equals 9, still too low. I'll try 4. 4 times 2 equals 8. 4 plus 8 equals 12. I think that's right. *Check my work to see if it looks OK.* I'll add all the pieces of candy to make sure the total is 16. 4 for me plus 4 for Kelly plus 8 for Lisa equals 16. Yes, OK.

Next the teacher selects one or more other students to model the strategy for the class. Eventually the teacher forms small groups of 4 students. In each group, students take turns being the model for solving a problem until all students can successfully use the strategy. Following this session, the teacher provides students periodically with review sessions where they use the strategy to solve word problems.

Generalization

The teacher encourages generalization in two ways:

(a) by having students apply the strategy to other types of word problems, and (b) by teaching students how to modify the strategy to fit other tasks.

To illustrate the latter, assume that the teacher decides to teach a unit on writing an informative paragraph. For example, the goal might be to write a paragraph describing a forthcoming school event and make it sound so interesting and worthwhile that community members will want to attend. The teacher could initially work with a peer

What is it I have to do? Write a paragraph that informs community people about our fund-raising event and makes them want to attend it. *What do I know?* I know when, where, and why it will be held. I know that people will want to come if I make my description sound like people will enjoy the event. *What steps do I follow?* First I should describe the event and why we are holding it. Then I can ask people to come and support us and tell them why they will enjoy being there. *Perform the steps.* (At this point the model will compose the paragraph at the board while verbalizing aloud.) *Check my work to see if it looks OK.* (The model can reread the paragraph to make sure it tells people about the event and makes it sound interesting so they will be likely to attend.)

Inclusion

The present emphasis on inclusion means that classes have large variations in student cognitive, motor, language, and social skills. This situation presents challenges and a unique opportunity to have peers assist in learning. Research needs to explore ways to use peer models effectively to foster successful inclusion. For example, researchers could test the idea that perceived similarity is important and that special-needs students benefit more from exposure to models who themselves have special needs than from peers who have no special needs.

Motivation

Research is needed is on the influence of peer models on students' motivation to learn and perform competently. Theories of learning increasingly are emphasizing the importance of motivational processes (Schunk, 1996). Research demonstrates the effects on learning of such processes as setting goals, believing in the value of learning, perceiving oneself capable of learning, and believing that positive outcomes will result from learning (Schunk, 1996). Models can demonstrate these processes and verbalize positive beliefs. The research by Schunk and Hanson (1985) and Schunk et al. (1987) is illustrative of ways to incorporate motivational processes into modeled displays, but more studies conducted during actual classroom learning are needed.

Self-Regulation

A final area of emphasis is self-regulation, or the process whereby students activate and sustain cognitions, behaviors, and emotions that are systematically oriented toward the attainment of goals (Zimmerman, 1989; 1994). Self-regulation includes such activities as attending to and concentrating on instruction; organizing, coding, and rehearsing information to be remembered; establishing a productive work environment and using resources effectively; holding positive beliefs about one's capabilities, the value of learning, the factors influencing learning, and the anticipated outcomes of actions; and experiencing pride and satisfaction with one's efforts (Schunk, 1994). Self-regulation research is in its infancy, but early efforts show that models can affect self-regulatory development (Graham & Harris, 1989a; 1989b). Future research should examine the role of peer models in fostering self-regulation.

In summary, peers are a valuable instructional resource. They typically command students' attention and raise their self-efficacy for learning. When using peers, teachers should select tasks that models can learn or perform successfully or work with peers to ensure that they will model the desired behaviors. When properly structured, peer modeling can be a useful adjunct to a sound instructional program and enhance student learning in various domains.

REFERENCES

Akamatsu, T. J., & Farudi, P. A. (1978). Effects of model status and juvenile offender type on the imitation of self-reward criteria. *Journal of Consulting and Clinical Psychology, 46,* 187–188.

Bandura, A. (1969). *Principles of behavior modification.* New York: Holt, Rinehart & Winston.

Bandura, A. (1977). *Social learning theory.* Englewood Cliffs, NJ: Prentice-Hall.

Bandura, A. (1986). *Social foundations of thought and action: A social cognitive theory.* Englewood Cliffs, NJ: Prentice-Hall.

Bandura, A. (1997). *Self-efficacy: The exercise of control.* New York: Freeman.

Barry, N. J., Jr., & Overmann, P. B. (1977). Comparison of the effectiveness of adult and peer models with EMR children. *American Journal of Mental Deficiency, 82,* 33–36.

Becker, S., & Glidden, L. M. (1979). Imitation of EMR boys: Model competency and age. *American Journal of Mental Deficiency, 83,* 360–366.

Berger, S. M. (1977). Social comparison, modeling, and perseverance. In J. M. Suls & R. L. Miller (Eds.), *Social comparison processes: Theoretical and empirical perspectives* (pp. 209–234). Washington, DC: Hemisphere.

Brody, G. H., & Stoneman, Z. (1981). Selective imitation of same-age, older, and younger peer models. *Child Development, 52,* 717–720.

Brody, G. H., & Stoneman, Z. (1985). Peer imitation: An examination of status and competence hypotheses. *Journal of Genetic Psychology, 146,* 161–170.

Davidson, E. S., & Smith, W. P. (1982). Imitation, social comparison, and self-reward. *Child Development, 53,* 928–932.

Dowrick, P. W. (1983). Self-modelling. In P. W. Dowrick & S. J. Biggs (Eds.), *Using video: Psychological and social applications* (pp. 105–124). Chichester, England: Wiley.

Ellis, S., & Rogoff, B. (1982). The strategies and efficacy of child versus adult teachers. *Child Development, 53,* 730–735.

Festinger, L. (1954). A theory of social comparison processes. *Human Relations, 7,* 117–140.

Field, T. (1981). Early interactions. In P. S. Strain (Ed.), *The utilization of classroom peers as behavior change agents* (pp. 1–30). New York: Plenum.

Fish, M. C., & Pervan, R. (1985). Self-instruction training: A potential tool for school psychologists. *Psychology in the Schools, 22,* 83–92.

Graham, S., & Harris, K. R. (1989a). Components analysis of cognitive strategy instruction: Effects on learning disabled students' compositions and self-efficacy. *Journal of Educational Psychology, 81,* 353–361.

Graham, S., & Harris, K. R. (1989b). Improving learning disabled students' skills at composing essays: Self-instructional strategy training. *Exceptional Children, 56,* 201–214.

Hartup, W. W. (1978). Children and their friends. In H. McGurk (Ed.), *Issues in childhood social development* (pp. 130–170). London: Methuen.

Hayes, M. E. (1973). *A study of the relationship between the type of behavior to be modeled and the model's similarity to the observers.* Dissertation Abstracts International, *34*(4B), 1723.

Hicks, D. J. (1965). Imitation and retention of film-mediated aggressive peer and adult models. *Journal of Personality and Social Psychology, 2,* 97–100.

Hosford, R. E. (1981). Self-as-a-model: A cognitive social learning technique. *The Counseling Psychologist, 9*(1), 45–62.

Kornhaber, R. C., & Schroeder, H. E. (1975). Importance of model similarity on extinction of avoidance behavior in children. *Journal of Consulting and Clinical Psychology, 43,* 601–607.

Locke, E. A., & Latham, G. P. (1990). *A theory of goal setting and task performance.* Englewood Cliffs, NJ: Prentice-Hall.

McNeil, J. D. (1987). *Reading comprehension: New directions for classroom practice* (2nd ed.) Glenview, IL: Scott, Foresman.

Meichenbaum, D. (1977). *Cognitive behavior modification: An integrative approach.* New York: Plenum.

Meichenbaum, D. (1986). Cognitive behavior modification. In F. H. Kanfer & A. P. Goldstein (Eds.), *Helping people change: A textbook of methods* (3rd ed., pp. 346–380). New York: Pergamon.

Meichenbaum, D., & Goodman, J. (1971). Training impulsive children to talk to themselves: A means of developing self-control. *Journal of Abnormal Psychology, 77,* 115–126.

Mize, J., Ladd, G. W., & Price, J. M. (1985). Promoting positive peer relations with young children: Rationales and strategies. *Child Care Quarterly, 14,* 221–237.

Oden, S. L., & Asher, S. R. (1977). Coaching low-accepted children in social skills: A follow-up sociometric assessment. *Child Development, 48,* 496–506.

Peck, C. A., Cooke, T. P., & Apolloni, T. (1981). Utilization of peer imitation in therapeutic and instructional contexts. In P. S. Strain (Ed.), *The utilization of classroom peers as behavior change agents* (pp. 69–99). New York: Plenum.

Pressley, M., Woloshyn, V., Lysynchuk, L. M., Martin, V., Wood, E., & Willoughby, T. (1990). A primer of research on cognitive strategy instruction: The important issues and how to address them. *Educational Psychology Review, 2,* 1–58.

Robert, M. (1983). Observational learning of conservation: Its independence from social influence. *British Journal of Psychology, 74,* 1–10.

Robert, M., & Charbonneau, C. (1977). Extinction of liquid conservation by observation: Effects of model's age and presence. *Child Development, 48,* 648–652.

Rosenthal, T. L., & Zimmerman, B. J. (1978). *Social learning and cognition.* New York: Academic Press.

Sawyer, R. J., Graham, S., & Harris, K. R. (1992). Direct teaching, strategy instruction, and strategy instruction with explicit self-regulation: Effects on the composition skills and self-efficacy of students with learning disabilities. *Journal of Educational Psychology, 84,* 340–352.

Schunk, D. H. (1981). Modeling and attributional effects on children's achievement: A self-efficacy analysis. *Journal of Educational Psychology, 73,* 93–105.

Schunk, D. H. (1987). Peer models and children's behavioral change. *Review of Educational Research, 57,* 149–174.

Schunk, D. H. (1994). Self-regulation of self-efficacy and attributions in academic settings. In D. H. Schunk & B. J. Zimmerman (Eds.), *Self-regulation of learning and performance: Issues and educational applications* (pp. 75–99). Hillsdale, NJ: Lawrence Erlbaum Associates.

Schunk, D. H. (1996). *Learning theories: An educational perspective* (2nd ed.). Englewood Cliffs, NJ: Prentice-Hall.

Schunk, D. H., & Hanson, A. R. (1985). Peer models: Influence on children's self-efficacy and achievement. *Journal of Educational Psychology, 77,* 313–322.

Schunk, D. H., & Hanson, A. R. (1989a). Influence of peer-model attributes on children's beliefs and learning. *Journal of Educational Psychology, 81,* 431–434.

Schunk, D. H., & Hanson, A. R. (1989b). Self-modeling and children's cognitive skill learning. *Journal of Educational Psychology, 81,* 155–163.

Schunk, D. H., Hanson, A. R., & Cox, P. D. (1987). Peer model attributes and children's achievement behaviors. *Journal of Educational Psychology, 79,* 54–61.

Schunk, D. H., & Rice, J. M. (1993). Strategy fading and progress feedback: Effects on self-efficacy and comprehension among students receiving remedial reading services. *Journal of Special Education, 27,* 257–276.

Sonnenschein, S., & Whitehurst, G. J. (1980). The development of communication: When a bad model makes a good teacher. *Journal of Experimental Child Psychology, 3,* 371–390.

Strain, P. S., Kerr, M. M., & Ragland, E. U. (1981). The use of peer social initiations in the treatment of social withdrawal. In P. S. Strain (Ed.), *The utilization of classroom peers as behavior change agents,* (pp. 101–128). New York: Plenum.

Zimmerman, B. J. (1989). A social cognitive view of self-regulated academic learning. *Journal of Educational Psychology, 81,* 329–339.

Zimmerman, B. J. (1994). Dimensions of academic self-regulation: A conceptual framework for education. In D. H. Schunk & B. J. Zimmerman (Eds.), *Self-regulation of learning and performance: Issues and educational applications* (pp. 3–21). Hillsdale, NJ: Lawrence Erlbaum Associates.

Peer Education For Health

Elspeth Mathie
Nick Ford
University of Exeter

More education is routinely prescribed as the panacea to cure all the social ills of contemporary society. Yet, increasing traditional school-based personal and social education have proved largely ineffective in ameliorating these ills. Peer education is a complementary approach. Peer educators are not intended to replace certified professionals but to serve as an extension to the education already provided.

Peer education is defined by Finn (1981a, p. 91) as "the sharing of information, attitudes or behaviors by people who are not professionally trained educators but whose goal is to educate" (also see chap. 1, this volume). It involves training people to carry out informal or organized educational activities with individuals, small groups or classes over a period of time (AHRTAG, 1994). The peer educators are usually of an age similar to the group they are educating, although some programs involve older students working with younger ones (Phelps, Mellanby, Crichton, & Tripp, 1994). Much of the recent popularity of peer education has been in health behavior education, which is the main focus for this chapter.

Peer education has primarily been used to address issues such as smoking (Perry, Klepp, Halper, Hawkins, & Murray, 1986; St. Pierre, 1983), contraception and sexuality (Baldwin & Staub, 1976), sexually transmitted diseases (Jordheim, 1976), AIDS (Richie & Getty, 1994), and alcohol consumption (McKnight & McPherson, 1986; Perry et al., 1989).

The approach has also been used to address problem areas such as diet and nutrition, drug abuse, drinking and driving, oral English language proficiency, violence prevention, suicide prevention, gang membership, dealing with divorce and loss, drop-out prevention, coping with chronic/

terminal illness, rape awareness, sexual harassment, and posttraumatic stress syndrome.

Other interesting applications include a rubella control peer education program operating in a college setting (Clark & Clark, 1985) and Lobato's (1985) program of peer education and support for the siblings of handicapped children. The long standing Child-to-Child initiative demonstrates the extension of the concept to the village community (Somerset, 1987). A number of interesting case studies in peer education can be found in McNeill (1995).

It is worth remembering that peer education is not just for young people. For example, the Home-Start scheme involves parent-to-parent peer education through home visits. The University of the Third Age in the United Kingdom engineers peer education between senior citizens. The Teenage Parenthood network promotes peer education among very young mothers. The applications are potentially endless.

Returning to the focus on health, recent years have seen an increasing recognition of the multidimensional nature of sexual health, and consequently the need to include in health education skills and values clarification as well as information. Sexuality is socially shaped and an area of great concern to young people, about which they are bombarded by images and information from many sources. These characteristics make sexual health promotion a particularly appropriate field for peer-assisted learning (PAL) strategies. The aim is to provide a setting in which young people can work out their own feelings and values and develop the skills with which to protect themselves and enhance their personal relationships.

This chapter outlines the rationale for peer education with a particular focus on health, followed by a discussion of the underlying theories. Key organizational issues are identified from the literature relevant to setting up peer education. Finally, the issue of evaluation is discussed, with examples from the literature.

WHY PEER EDUCATION?

Traditional Techniques Have Proved Unsuccessful

In the area of health education, traditional teaching methods have not been very successful in bridging the gap between knowledge and behavior (Finn, 1981a). Many health education projects have succeeded in increasing knowledge, but failed to make much impact on actual behavior. Friedman (1992) believed that in order to influence behavior and attitudes, both formal and informal learning is essential. Chesler (1990) stated that in addition to obtaining information about contraception, teenagers need to clarify their values so that their social behaviors are congruent with their moral codes. Sex education therefore demands a varied approach. The education strategy has to be flexible and involve skill development. The interaction between the educator and the educated has to be nonthreatening, and peer education can assist in this process.

Teachers Are Often Seen as Authority Figures

Teachers are in authority roles and consequently the power relationship between teacher and pupil is unequal. Teachers are often seen as part of the establishment and there is likely to be a certain amount of distance between the teenager and the teacher. It may be difficult for young people to be in a geography class and then talk honestly about personal subjects with the same teacher, who they see on a daily basis. In addition teachers are often asked to conduct sessions on sex education without relevant or recent training, and in an area where they themselves may feel uncomfortable and embarrassed. In any event, teenagers are unlikely to perceive teachers as experts in the field of adolescent social decision making, because they are not experiencing the same real life problems and decisions as the young people.

Peers Speak the Same Language

Peer educators can be credible role models for young people. They also use the same social language (Perry et al., 1989). Peers are a "readily accessible forum ... for young people to connect easily with persons who will discuss with them in an open, nonjudgmental and supportive fashion the kinds of problems and concerns which are common to both parties" (Carrera, 1976, p. 54). The educators and the peers use the same vocabulary, which is very important when discussing sensitive issues. Language is gender, age, social class, and area-specific. Peers who use similar language have a foundation for relating to each other.

Peer Interaction Already Takes Place

The process of transference of information from one peer to another already takes place informally. In the majority of studies that examined sources of sexual health information, friends were often rated as an important source (e.g., Abraham, Sheeran, Abrams, Spears, & Marks, 1991). However, the information is not always accurate (Thornburg, 1981). In the past, "this closed communication system has generated much misinformation" (Steinhausen, 1983, p. 7). The existing channels of communication provide an opportunity for educators to strengthen the accuracy of the information in the system through proper training. In addition, peer education is valuable not only for changing harmful health behavior, but also for reinforcing existing healthful behavior so that it is continued (Finn, 1981b).

The Importance of the Peer Influence

Adolescents are highly sensitive to the influence of peer pressure (Rubenstein, Panzarine, & Lanning, 1990). Any educators who make recommendations that go against the norms, ethics, and ethos of the peer community may find it difficult to persuade (Quackenbush, 1987). However, a peer educator may have more credibility if challenging some of the existing peer values. Rosati (1991) believed that peers "can play a critical role in changing the potentially self-destructive rites of passage that exist in many countries throughout the world" (p. 13).

CURRENT THINKING AND PRACTICE IN PEER HEALTH EDUCATION

Peer education has developed a substantial literature. Steinhausen (1983) offered a review of peer education programs in secondary schools. Baldwin (1995) reviewed a number of HIV/AIDS peer education programs in *The Peer Facilitator Quarterly*. Sciacca and Appleton (1996) reviewed a number of smoking, alcohol, stress reduction, eating behavior, and HIV/AIDS peer projects in the same journal.

Peer education has become particularly popular in recent health promotion campaigns. Each peer education program varies in size, format, and content; and one of the main issues facing health education today is to examine what messages the programs are aiming to convey.

Theoretical Basis

The theoretical foundations of peer education are said to be social inoculation and social learning theory. McGuire's social inoculation model (1964) suggested that an individual's resistance to social pressure (e.g., to start using drugs) would be stronger if the individual has already developed arguments with which to counter such pressure (Perry et al., 1986). The model is premised on the belief that individuals do not want to engage in unhealthy behaviors, but they lack the negotiating skills to resist social pressure to do so. It has been argued that peer educators can assist in realistic practice of these counterarguments. McGuire identified pressure from peer groups, the media, and parents as significant in this context.

Social learning theory proposes that to change behavior, individuals must have the opportunity not only to observe the desired behavior, but also to practice it until they feel confident in their ability to perform it effectively (Bandura, 1986). This suggests that an action such as using a contraceptive method is determined by a young person (a) understanding what must be done to avoid a pregnancy, (b) believing that he or she will be able to use the method, (c) believing that the method will be successful in preventing pregnancy, and (d) understanding the anticipated benefit for accomplishing the behavior (Kirby, 1992a, 1992b). This theory also suggests that use of attractive role models (such as peer educators) with whom the audience can identify is critical.

Contexts and Difficulties

Initially, many peer education programs in the United Kingdom and United States were carried out in the informal settings of youth clubs rather than schools (Clements & Buckiewicz, 1993). Peer education has also occurred in nightclubs and pubs. The Torbay Sea, Sand, and Safer Sex project took the peer educators into these leisure venues (Mathie & Ford, 1996). This project was based on a survey that showed that many young people on holiday go to clubs, drink alcohol, and then fail to practice safe sex (Ford, Inman, & Mathie, 1996).

Health education in schools is subject to specific constraints and is an especially contentious issue, because of education legislation, the problems of gaining authorization when teaching those under age 16 and the constraints of the formal setting (Wilton, Keeble, Doyal, & Walsh, 1995). However, despite these constraints, numerous peer education projects have operated apparently successfully during school hours with captive audiences. Relatively few of the school-based sexual health projects have been reported in detail in the literature, but two such successful projects are described next.

Two U.K. Projects

In Plymouth in southwestern England, a peer education project ran for 3 years (1992 to 1995). The peer educators were recruited through advertisements in schools, colleges, pubs, and a local youth magazine. They were then selected on the basis that they should display nonjudgmental attitudes, be able to relate well to each other, and also be able to meet the needs of the diverse range of young people in the area (in terms of social class, geographical area, gender, and sexuality). The content of the peer education was HIV/AIDS, sexual health, gender issues, and substance misuse.

Fifteen peer educators attended 14 evening training sessions, one residential weekend, and a Saturday workshop. The peer educators were paid as sessional workers. Five schools were involved with the project. Two received a series of four peer education sessions and three acted as control groups.

Comments from the students aged 16 to 17 years included: "Because they were young they were on the same wavelength,"; "Made better and easier learning than teacher preaching,"; "They teach you as if you were the same as them," (Blacksell, Ford, Taylor, Buckley, & Stidson, 1995, p. 59).

By the end of the first year, the peer educators had participated in 84 events (59 peer sessions; 15 roadshows; 7 presentations; exhibitions and media interviews, and 3 consultancy sessions).

The evaluation results showed that there were small but consistent measurable improvements in knowledge and attitudes in the intervention group compared to the control group (Blacksell et al., 1995). This was a good example of an intensively trained group of peer educators who were motivated and committed to the project. In fact, all but one of the first year (1993) peer educators were still involved at the end of 1995.

A second project was carried out in Somerset (again in southwest England) in two "sixth form colleges" (for those aged 16 to 18) in 1992 to 1994 (Mathie & Ford, 1994). Following a residential weekend, 14 self-selected male and female students created a play that dealt with issues surrounding HIV/AIDS and relationships. A pretest questionnaire was completed by 122 students, measuring knowledge, attitudes, and behavior in sexual health at the start of the project. The play was then performed in each college. A further 2 days of training was held in which the peer educators were exposed to participatory small group exercises, including brainstorming the meaning of safer sex, practicing putting condoms on carrots, and negotiating condom use. They then spent time planning and practicing their peer education sessions.

In the first year, 14 peer educators ran 11 peer-led sessions for students within their own colleges. In the second year, 17 peer educators led 18 sessions within college and 5 outside college (for other colleges and youth groups). In total, 273 young people received a peer education session. The peer educators did not get paid but received a certificate. Some of the students used the work towards their accredited social care project work.

The project was evaluated as a whole and also by each individual session (Mathie, 1994; Mathie & Ford, 1993). In the first year, six areas were positively identified as being affected by the peer education: increase in communication surrounding HIV/AIDS, wider definition of safer sex, increase in confidence and knowledge surrounding condom use, increase in negotiation skills for condom use, increase in perceived vulnerability to HIV/AIDS and increased empathy for people living with HIV. The findings clearly illustrated that young people are very capable of undertaking innovative, participatory education strategies in the area of sexual health.

ORGANIZATION OF PEER EDUCATION

Organizing a peer education program in your own school is a challenging task but very rewarding. Following are some of the issues arising.

Selection of Peer Educators

There has been some debate as to whether peer educators should be self-selected. There are arguments on both sides. Professional staff can recommend students who demonstrate competence in human relations and communication skills. In some schools, there has been specific recruitment of those with leadership skills or academic qualifications. Teacher selection has the disadvantage of establishing an elite corps of students, who may not be representative of, or acceptable to, the general school population (Carrera, 1976). Self-selection allows students to identify themselves and ensures that they are motivated. Carrera stated: "as the essential character of the program is 'for students by students,' self-selection is recommended" (p. 2). The peer educators should ideally come from the same social group as the target group.

The Center for Population Options (CPO; 1990) identifed the following as necessary qualities for peer educators: possessing communication skills, developmentally mature, aware of comfort level of subjects, committed and already in *in* groups. Peer educators themselves might have different criteria: popularity, enthusiasm for the project, and the ability to keep secrets (AHRTAG, 1994). It is important to remember different strengths (and weaknesses) can complement each other in the team of peer educators.

The Role of a Peer Educator

It is important that the role of peer educator is explained clearly from the outset, including the level of commitment expected, what the training will involve, number of sessions and time involved. It is better for students to drop out at this stage than after they have been trained. Ideally, previous peer educators are the best source for a realistic description of the role, tasks, and problems.

Number of Peer Educators Per Session

Peer educators often prefer to lead sessions in pairs, because running a group on one's own is fairly daunting. However, too many peer educators in sessions makes them difficult to coordinate, especially if peer educators have different timetables. It is preferable if the peer educators come from the same class or group, as this makes scheduling of sessions much easier. One or two extra peer educators should be recruited in case some drop out over the year.

Training Peer Educators

It is important that the training be extended as long as necessary for the peer educators to become confident to run the sessions. Therefore, it will depend largely on the type of peer educators who are recruited to the programs. Training sessions have lasted from 1 evening to more than 10 weeks. Much depends on the peer educators themselves and on the resources and time available.

Content of the Training

Naturally, the training should explore behaviors and attitudes as well as giving information. Content should be focused by what the peer educators will need for the planned peer session(s). Initially, small group discussions (or a questionnaire) with the peers will reveal existing knowledge and skills. Some will need a lot of correct health information themselves. Others will need training in small group work or other interactive and participatory techniques, communication skills, and how to time and plan sessions. There must be ample time for the peer educators to rehearse and practice in front of each other. There are many training manuals available (see listing of resources and contacts at the end of this volume).

Some professional educators hold the unfounded belief that young people can only employ basic learning strategies. Our work in the United Kingdom showed conclusively that with proper training, peer educators are more than able to employ a range of innovative learning approaches.

The Trainers

Teachers within the school, a youth leader, or staff from the local health authority may be able to assist in organizing training sessions or providing appropriate materials. Many prior projects showed that previous peer educators are also ideal trainers.

Gender of the Target Group

A key decision is whether to give the peer education sessions mixed- or same-gender groups. Many sessions have been given to same-gender groups, as the pupils feel less embarrassed and can discuss issues more openly. For some less sensitive topics, mixed groups can work very well. Peer education on sexual health issues needs to take into account the implications of gendered power relationships, as in mixed groups females are often "reluctant to talk and share opinions" and males "cover their embarrassment with bravado" (Hamilton, 1992, p. 30).

Gender of the Peer Educators

Many projects have used female peer educators. It appears females volunteer more than males. Therefore, it is important to try to motivate males to participate in the program. Peer education has been delivered successfully by female peer educators to male students and to mixed groups. Few projects have involved male peer educators delivering to female students, usually because of the limited availability of male peer educators. However, in a questionnaire survey of more than 3,000 school children ages 15 to 16, less than one third felt that sex education should be taught in same-gender groups (Mellanby, Phelps, & Tripp, 1996). Nevertheless, although students will not usually request them, in practice same-gender groups often seem to allow more open discussion. The Somerset project found that a higher percentage of students attending the same-gender peer education sessions rated the sessions "very useful" than those attending the mixed-gender sessions (Mathie, 1994).

Peer Involvement in the Program

There is always a practical concern regarding at what stage and to what extent the peer educators are to be involved in the program development and design. Obviously, top–down approaches with fixed specific objectives and curricula are potentially self-defeating. It has been recommended (AHRTAG, 1994) that peer educators be involved in defining their roles and responsibilities and with the planning and management. The philosophy of peer education is about empowering the young people, so they should be involved in the planning of their project. It is a matter of going beyond the rhetoric of empowerment to really work in such a way that it actually happens.

Objectives of Peer Education

It is important to be clear about what the sessions are ultimately trying to achieve (e.g., condom use, delay age of first intercourse, or abstention). As in any program, success depends crucially on the clarity with which core objectives are expressed and the appropriateness of strategies to attain them. It is essential that the peer educators are involved from an early stage in the formulation of objectives.

For example, The Health Promotion Agency in Plymouth reviewed with the potential peer educators the range of issues involved in sexual health and jointly identified specific elements for the program to address (Blacksell et al., 1995). During this process, peer educators developed increasing confidence and knowledge, enabling them to take an increasingly assertive role in the program. One of the strengths of the peer-assisted approach is that it can ensure that objectives are formed in ways meaningful and relevant to the audience. For instance, peers will be aware of the counterproductiveness of a program seeking to direct young people into prescribed behaviors and be better able to present training in ways that facilitate an open, personal appraisal and foster self-responsibility.

Synchronizing with the Timetable

Peer educators might have to miss lessons, and this has to be coordinated within the school timetable. It is best if the peer education sessions can take place as part of an already existing course such as personal, social and health education, but it can be brought into many areas of the curriculum, such as biology or geography.

Peer education also has to be organized around the holidays, exams, and other events. In an academic year during the first term (semester), select the peer educators and carry out training. In the second term, actually deliver the peer education sessions. It will take time to gain authorization within the school and organize teachers who are sympathetic (Blacksell et al., 1995).

Duration of the Sessions

Sessions can last 15 minutes to 2 hours. It depends on the nature of the activities and on the school timetable. It is often good for the peer educators to carry out short sessions at the beginning of a regular teacher-led lesson, as 1 hour with a whole class can seem a long time at first. Timing is important and the training should include consideration of clear structures for sessions. Activities may take longer than predicted. If the session is to be evaluated, time must be allowed for completing questionnaires or other measures. It is also useful to plan sessions to run before lunchtime or before a break, so that if the sessions run over it is not a problem. This also gives the peer educators some time to relax after the session. It must also be remembered that the peer educators have to get from their lessons to the allocated room and that small group work often means moving chairs that have to be replaced afterwards. Some rooms are better for these types of activities than others.

Support for Peer Educators

Successful projects have been characterized by the commitment of one or two members of staff who act as the coordinating and support tutors. Health authorities or other related agencies should also be in a position to provide such support and feedback. It is crucial for the peer educators to have debriefing, someone with whom to discuss the sessions and ask advice. The peer educators will need continual support throughout the project, and the assigned teacher must have the time available to provide this assistance. This time commitment may need to be assured by heads of departments.

Support From the Rest of the School

The support and coordinating tutors have to be responsible for informing the rest of the school about the peer education. Some heads of schools, school governors, and parents may need convincing of the appropriateness of having young people run sessions. Given the commitment that peer education demands from staff, it should be recognized in reviews for promotion.

Payment of Peer Educators

Some peer educators have been paid per session and others have been provided with traveling expenses. Most peer education projects have provided their peer educators with a certificate, which they could include as part of their curriculum vitae when applying for jobs. Some peer educators have also used the sessions as part of their required and accredited course work.

Length of Project

After the first year it is important the enthusiasm is maintained and the peer education continues. The second year is always easier, as much of the groundwork has been carried out in setting up the project. It is also beneficial if the peer education is part of a wider education campaign at school, which may include other speakers, posters, and trips. More research needs to be undertaken into the institutional factors that enhance the sustainability of peer-based programs (see chap. 15, this volume).

EFFECTIVENESS

Peer education projects have subjectively seemed to be very successful, although many have not been rigorously evaluated (Baldwin, 1995; Sciacca & Appleton, 1996; Steinhausen, 1983). Evaluation is vital to ensure that successful pilot peer education projects can continue into the future. Evaluation needs to be built (and budgeted) into the program from its inception. At the pilot stage, detailed process and outcome evaluation is necessary. Once a program is running smoothly, only limited outcome evaluation is required. Process evaluation can then be included in the tutor's feedback and support meetings with the peer educators.

Many projects have shown increases in knowledge and influence on attitudes, but few projects have been able to produce evidence of behavior change. As Sciacca (1995) noted, finding reliable, valid, and economical measures is not easy. Process indicators are more straightforward and measure what actually happened during the project. Process evaluation at the pilot stage should involve qualitative assessment of how the sessions actually function. This is usually undertaken by discussion with peer educators and educated, as well as by direct observation. It is important to define process objectives at the outset of the project so that these indicators can be measured.

A recent extensive international review of evaluations of HIV prevention programs has highlighted the effectiveness of peer-based strategies (Coleman & Ford, 1996). The World Health Organization involved four countries (Australia, Chile, Norway, & Swaziland) in a study on the effectiveness of school-based alcohol education. Twenty-five schools in four countries were randomly assigned to peer-led education, teacher-led education, and a control group. Pretest measures covered alcohol use knowledge, attitudes, skills, and friends' drinking patterns.

An important conclusion from this latter study was that a peer-led approach to adolescent alcohol education appeared to be effective across a variety of settings and cultures. Overall, students in the peer-led program subsequently reported significantly less use of alcohol than did students in the teacher-led program and control group, irrespective of whether they were drinkers or nondrinkers at the start. The students in the peer-led group gained more knowledge, acquired better attitudes and reported fewer friends drinking at posttest. The teacher-led and control groups did not demonstrate more positive outcomes than the peer education group in any of the countries (Perry et al., 1989).

A cross-age peer project in Exeter (England) involved 17- to 19-year-olds educating 13- to 14-year-olds. The project was evaluated using pretest and posttest questionnaires. The aims of the project were to "improve pupil's knowledge, tolerance and respect, to improve contraceptive use for those who are sexually active, and to enable those who are not to resist unwelcome pressures in relationships" (Phelps et al., 1994, p. 128). The evaluation showed that, after peer education, the pupils' knowledge had increased significantly and the pupils were aware of more strategies when experiencing unwelcome pressure to have sexual intercourse (Mellanby et al., 1996).

Evaluation is not easy, especially within a school setting. If the project intends to use an experimental peer education group and a control group (which does not receive the peer education), it is difficult to ensure the same students attend the pretest, the peer education, and the posttest. Paradoxically, given that peer education strategies seek to encourage discussion and related interaction outside the project sessions, there is an obvious danger of contamination between the supposed experimental and control groups. For this reason it is recommended that control groups be derived from other institutions (e.g., schools) that are broadly matched for socioeconomic and educational characteristics.

There are also constraints on time in administering questionnaires. If questionnaires are completed too soon after the peer session, there will be no possibility of evidence of behavioral change. However, knowledge and attitude changes can be measured in short and simple questionnaires. These can also provide useful feedback for the peer educators and those running the sessions. Examples of evaluation questionnaires can be found in many training manuals. Each project will naturally need an individually tailored questionnaire.

DISCUSSION AND CONCLUSIONS

Peer education has proved to be effective in the area of health-related behaviors, such as alcohol misuse, drug-taking, and unprotected sexual intercourse. Peer education has been used mainly by young people, but also by work colleagues and special groups such as prostitutes. It can be formally structured, but peer education is often informal. One of the major benefits is the increased communication this can encourage within and outside the school. Many peer education projects have shown that the sessions within the school curriculum have often sparked off other conversations with other peers and with parents. This ripple effect is an added benefit of peer education.

Health education deals with particularly sensitive topics, and parents and teachers may have some reservations about peers taking sessions. For this reason, clear objectives and explanations of the project must be available, and authorization within schools must be obtained, although this may take some time to achieve. The opportunity to follow peer education approaches is also limited by timetable, examination, and curriculum pressures. However, with a supportive teacher within the school and good quality training, these problems can easily be overcome. Teachers have been impressed by the skill of peer educators in handling a class of young people. Peer education can be undertaken by pupils in their own schools or by the peer educators visiting other schools. The literature suggests it is preferable if the peer educators are self-selected and the content of the sessions designed with or by the peer educators.

Bernard (1991) argued for a paradigm change that involves demystifying professional expertise and empowering young people to help themselves and each other. Finn (1981b) advocated for peer education to continue not only in school but throughout a person's life, so that friends and relatives continue to discuss issues and learn from each other.

Peer education projects benefit both the target group and the peer educators. The target group receive education and the peer educators gain in terms of their personal development. They develop skills in communication, design and planning which can been transferred into other situations such as future employment (Clements & Buckiewicz, 1993). Studies that have administered questionnaires to the peer educators before and after the project have also found an increase in confidence and assertiveness (Mathie & Ford, 1994). The peer educators themselves will continue to educate others. This means the informal communication channels will continue to convey good quality information.

The projects described here illustrate that peer educators are able to achieve complex participatory education techniques that many adults find difficult. They are able to discuss issues in a nonthreatening and informal manner. The benefits have been documented. More peer education projects are needed in all areas of health behavior. This necessitates funding, not only to establish such projects, but also to evaluate them properly and ensure their sustainability, so that peer education within schools becomes more common.

REFERENCES

Abraham, C., Sheeran, P., Abrams, D., Spears, R., & Marks, D. (1991). Young people learning about AIDS: A study of beliefs and information sources. *Health Education Research, 6,* 19–29.

Appropriate Health Resources and Technologies Action Group (AHRTAG).(1994). Youth to youth AIDS prevention. *AIDS Action* (supplement), *25,* 1–4.

Baldwin, B. A., & Staub, R. E. (1976). Peers as human sexuality outreach educators in the campus community. *Journal of the American College Health Association, 24*(5), 290–293.

Baldwin, J. (1995). Using peer education approaches in HIV/AIDS programs for youth. *The Peer Facilitator Quarterly, 12*(3), 34–37.

Bandura, A. (1986). Social foundations of thought and action: A social cognitive theory. Englewood Cliffs, NJ: Prentice-Hall.

Bernard, B. (1991). The case for peers. *The Peer Facilitator Quarterly, 8*(4), 20–27.

Blacksell, S., Ford, N., Taylor, L., Buckley, T., & Stidson, M. (1995). *The life skills initiative peer education project: The health promotion agency, Plymouth; evaluation 1993–1995.* Exeter: The Institute of Population Studies.

Carrera, M. A. (1976). Peer group sex information and education. *Journal of Research and Development in Education, 10*(1), 50–55.

Center for Population Options (CPO). (1990). *Guide to implementing TAP.* Washington, DC: Teens for AIDS Prevention Project.

Chesler, J. (1990). Twenty-seven strategies for teaching contraception to adolescents. *Journal of School Health, 1,* 18–21.

Clark, E., & Clark, A. (1985). Peer power: An educational model for the control of rubella. *Health Education, 16*(1), 23–24.

Clements, I., & Buckiewicz, M. (1993). *Approaches to peer-led health education.* London: Health Education Authority.

Coleman, L., & Ford, N. (1996). An extensive literature review of the evaluation of HIV prevention programs. *Health Education Research, 11*(3), 327–338.

Finn, P. (1981a). Institutionalizing peer education in the health education classroom. The *Journal of School Health, 51*(2), 91–95.

Finn, P. (1981b). Teaching students to be lifelong peer educators. *Health Education, 12,* 13–16.

Ford, N., Inman, M., & Mathie, E. (1996). Interactions to enhance mindfulness: Positive strategies to increase tourists' awareness of HIV and sexual health risks on holiday. In S. Clift, & S. J. Page (Eds.), *Health and the international tourist* (pp. 279–293). London: Routledge.

Friedman, J. (1992). *Cross-cultural perspectives on sexuality education.* Sex Information and Education Council of the United States Report, August/September, 5–11. (Publication Dept., 130 West 42nd Street, Suite 2500, New York, NY 10036).

Hamilton, V. (1992). HIV/AIDS: A peer approach. *Youth and Policy, 36,* 27–31.

Jordheim, A. (1976). A comparison study of peer teaching and traditional instruction in venereal disease education. *Journal of the American College Health Association, 24,* 286–289.

Kirby, D. (1992a). School-based programs to reduce sexual risk-taking behaviors. *Journal of School Health, 62*(7), 280–287.

Kirby, D. (1992b). School-based prevention programs: Design, evaluation and effectiveness. In R. J. Diclemente (Ed.), *Adolescents and AIDS, a generation in jeopardy* (pp. 159–180). London: Sage.

Lobato, D. (1985) Preschool siblings of handicapped children: Impact of peer support and training. *Journal of Autism and Developmental Disorders, 15*(3), 345–350.

Mathie, E. (1994). *Evaluation of the second year: An HIV and sexual health peer education project in Strode and Yeovil colleges, Somerset.* Exeter: Institute of Population Studies.

Mathie, E., & Ford, N. (1993). *Evaluation of a college-based HIV and sexual health peer education project in Somerset.* Exeter: Institute of Population Studies.

Mathie, E., & Ford, N. (1994). Evaluation of the Somerset peer education project. *The Peer Facilitator Quarterly, 12*(1), 14–17.

Mathie, E., & Ford, N. (1996). Sea, sand and safer sex messages. *Education and Health, 13*(4), 49–51.

McGuire, W. (1964). Inducing resistance to persuasion. In L. Berkowitz (Ed.), *Advances in experimental social psychology* (pp. 191–229). New York: Academic Press.

McKnight., A. J., & McPherson, K. (1986). Evaluation of peer intervention training for high-school alcohol safety education. *Accident Analysis and Prevention, 18*(4), 339–347.

McNeill, C. (1995) *Peer tutoring: A winning way for all.* Stafford, England: Network Educational Press.

Mellanby, A. R., Phelps, F. A., & Tripp, J. (1996). *A pause: Added power and understanding in sex education.* The project and results. Exeter: Department of Child Health, University of Exeter.

Perry, C. L., Grant, M., Ernberg, G., Florenzano, R. U., Langdon, M. C., Myeni, A. D., Waahlberg, R., Berg, S., Anderson, K., Fisher, K. J., Blaze-Temple, D., Cross, D., Saunders, B., Jacobs, D. R., & Schmid, T. (1989). WHO collaborative study on alcohol education and young people: Outcomes of a four country pilot study. *The International Journal of the Addictions, 24*(12), 1145–1171.

Perry, C. L., Klepp, K. I., Halper, A., Hawkins, K. G., & Murray, D. M. (1986). A process evaluation study of peer leaders in health education. *Journal of School Health, 56*(2), 62–67.

Phelps, F. A., Mellanby, A., Crichton, N. J., & Tripp, J. H. (1994). Sex education: The effect of a peer program on pupils (aged 13–14 years) and their peer leaders. *Health Education Journal, 53,* 127–139.

Quackenbush, M. (1987). Educating youth about AIDS. *Focus, 2*(3), 1.

Richie, N. D., & Getty, A. (1994). Did an AIDS peer education program change first year college students' behaviors? *Journal of American College Health, 42*(4), 163–165.

Rosati, M. J. (1991). Peer leadership in adolescent health promotion. *Entre Nous, 17,* 13.

Rubenstein, E., Panzarine, S., & Lanning, P. (1990). Peer counseling with adolescent mothers: A pilot program. *Families in Society, 71*(3), 136–141.

Sciacca, J. (1995) Evaluating peer resource programs: Which instrument is best? *The Peer Facilitator Quarterly, 12*(3), 3–4.

Sciacca, J., & Appleton, T. (1996). Peer helping: A promising strategy for effective health education. *The Peer Facilitator Quarterly, 13*(2), 22–28.

Somerset, T. (1987) *Child-to-child: A survey.* London: Child-To-Child Trust.

Steinhausen, G. W. (1983) Peer education programs: A look nationally. *Health Education, 14*(7), 7–8.

St. Pierre, R. W. (1983) Youth helping youth: A behavioral approach to the self-control of smoking. *Health Education, 14*(1), 28–31.

Thornburg, H. (1981). Adolescent sources of information on sex. *Journal of School Health, 4*(81), 274–277.

Wilton, T., Keeble, S., Doyal, L., & Walsh, A. (1995). *The effectiveness of peer education in health promotion: Theory and practice. An overview of the literature and an audit of projects in the South and West Region.* Bristol: South and West Regional Health Authority.

12

Peer Counseling

Stewart W. Ehly
University of Iowa
Enedina Garcia Vazquez
New Mexico State University

PEER COUNSELING: A DEFINITION

Peer counseling programs are increasingly common in school districts in the United States and are expanding elsewhere around the world (Ehly & Dustin, 1989). Definitions of *peer counseling* vary widely by author, but center around a core agenda involving students in the promotion of an affective support system. Topping and Ehly (chap. 1, this volume) consider peer counseling to involve "people from similar groupings who are not professional teachers or line managers who help clarify general life problems and identify solutions by listening, feeding back, summarizing and being positive and supportive. As with other forms of peer-assisted learning (PAL), this might occur on a one-on-one basis or in groups." D'Andrea and Salovey (1983) highlighted specific counseling techniques that can be used by students with peers: "Peer counseling is the use of active listening and problem-solving skills, along with knowledge about human grown and mental health, to counsel people who are our peers—peers in age, status, and knowledge" (p. 3). This chapter follows a similar emphasis on counseling techniques that promote affective awareness and coping, concentrating on school-aged populations from kindergarten to high school. References to university-aged students are limited to identifying resources.

We restrict use of the peer label to individuals without professional status in a school or community setting. Emphasis is directed at school-aged students who are identified as eligible for training in peer counseling techniques, and who commit to a coherent agenda of activities, bringing them into contact with fellow students requesting the assistance of a peer.

Peer counselors help students to explore feelings, plans, and decisions so that the individual seeking help perceives support and guidance. The American Psychological Association (APA; 1982) defined *peer counseling* to capture the restrictions we identify: "Peer counseling is defined as supervised performance of limited counselor functions by persons of approximately the same age or status as the counselee" (p. 124). Finally, there is increasing interest in developing peer counseling programs outside of schools, in youth and community centers and other neighborhood drop-in facilities (Carr, 1988).

Links to the PAL Literature

From the 1970s, when peer counseling interventions appeared with increasing frequency in the literature, the notion of peer self-help was present. Raubolt (1975), for example, considered the success of such programs as Alcoholics Anonymous and Synanon to stem from the peer support embedded in the components of both organizations. Earlier large group tutoring programs, reported by Gartner, Kohler, and Riessman (1971), were created during the Johnson administration to combine an academic agenda (help students learn) with an affective one (help students feel valued, work to increase motivation to attend school).

Guralnick (1981), in summarizing available literature, proposed that peer interactions are "a potentially powerful source of influence on development" (p. 34). Whether through interactions with siblings or children in the neighborhood or school, peers are important models, critics, and guides to a child's perceptions and actions. Guralnick additionally argued that children from an early age are capable of sophisticated adjustments to the actions of peers, and display a "sensitivity to relevant listener characteristics and feedback as well as to situational factors" (p. 38). Imitation of peers represents a "powerful instructional resource" available to educators to support children's growth and development (Peck, Cooke, & Apolloni, 1981, p. 69).

Berndt and Perry (1986) conducted a study involving children from Grades 2, 4, 6, and 8. The authors were interested in the children's perceptions of friendships and their experiences of peer social support. Children were able at all grade levels to distinguish between the social support offered by a friend versus an acquaintance, and become increasingly sophisticated with age in their attributions regarding the quality of their relationships. The extensive literature on peer counseling recognizes that children at different grade levels require training to enact peer interventions consistent with the children's maturity and understanding of peer support.

In the next sections, we consider peer counseling as an intervention of value to educators who support, whether formally or informally, an affective curriculum in the school. Reliance on peer assistants to complement the teacher's efforts with students provides a cost-effective and powerful extension to a school's counseling priorities.

Peer Counseling Since the 1980s

Peer counseling has been instituted in many schools to help ease the demand for counseling services at a time when students may be feeling disconnected from school or experiencing personal problems that influence school performance. Although peer counseling has been instituted in various school programs since the 1950s (Bowman & Myrick, 1987), peer counseling programs have gained impetus since the early 1980s. Initially, more documented programs could be found in high schools; however, since the early 1980s, peer counseling programs in elementary schools have received much needed attention (Bowman & Myrick, 1987).

Various benefits from peer counseling programs have been documented in the literature. Downe, Altmann, and Nysetvold (1986) suggested that peer counseling helps meet the growing affective needs of students at a time when the supply of counselors has decreased, making it difficult to meet the demands of all students. Aside from the emotional benefits to students, results of peer counseling programs have included increased academic performance and improvements in classroom behavior (Bowman & Myrick, 1987).

Students who receive peer counseling also gain by having a forum in which to share experiences and feelings. They experience understanding, social support, role models, and personal growth (Downe, Altmann, & Nysetvold, 1986). Psychological and interpersonal improvements have been noted among the peer counselors as well. Benefits include increases in self-esteem, skill building, social involvement with peers, and adult attention (Downe, Altmann, & Nysetvold, 1986). Peer counseling can assist in mentoring students to the helping professions. Training peer counselors can create a lasting relationship between counselors, teachers, and students.

Although peer counseling programs have been employed to provide assistance across a designated time period, they can be beneficial in crisis situations. For example Strip, Swassing, and Kidder (1991) indicated that gifted adolescents can be trained to provide immediate assistance when a peer experiences severe emotional trauma. Peer counselors can offer important forms of support for students experiencing strong emotions associated with death or divorce, relocation issues, problems in family relationships, pregnancy, and other challenges to daily life. Peer counseling programs can designed to provide both crisis and developmental support.

Peer counseling has received broad support from educators, but its effectiveness has not been documented with an abundance of empirically based research. Early studies followed a descriptive format, relying on anecdotal records to demonstrate program effectiveness. Recent efforts at documenting the success and benefits of peer counseling programs are more rigorous (Bowman & Myrick, 1987).

Peer Counseling in Elementary and Middle Schools

The trend in peer counseling programs for the majority of elementary schools has been directed toward remediation (Downe, Altmann, & Nysetvold, 1986). Peer counseling also can be designed to assist students with disruptive behavior. In a study by Bowman and Myrick (1987), sixth-grade students assisted third-grade students who were disruptive. Various criteria were employed in selection of their peer counselors including verbal ability, intelligence, motivation, responsibility, achievement, and availability (Bowman & Myrick, 1987).

An extensive and structured training component was provided to the peer counselors. Program effectiveness was assessed using several measures to obtain quantitative data. Results suggested that cross-age peer counseling was effective. The authors found that the peer counselors were able to use their knowledge and skills. Positive findings for the students with disruptive behaviors also were noted. Not as encouraging were their findings related to the peer helper's attitudes towards others or themselves. However, they did find that peer counseling microskills such as listening and communicating became more effective with experience.

Although this is only a single example, others can be cited in schools around the United States. Programs such as the one described by Mitchum (1983) suggest that peer counseling for middle school students is a possibility for any child. The Total Involvement Program (TIP) promotes the belief that any student can be involved and is not dependent on intelligence, leadership qualities, and other criteria. TIP is particularly effective in selecting and training peer facilitators (Mitchum, 1983). Whatever the program model, peer counseling has been shown to be effective for the peer counselor and the counselee at the elementary and middle grades levels.

Peer counseling programs in elementary and middle schools are best designed to include a strong training component that alerts peer counselors to expectations and intervention options. As children progress through the elementary and middle school grades, they will become ever more adept at understanding the verbal and nonverbal signals as well as needs of their peers. Although the literature is almost nonexistent on the experience of working with a peer counselor, educators and parents understand the importance of preparing children for the role of counselee. The younger the child, the greater the need to prepare children to understand what a peer counselor can and cannot do. Formal programs that support peer counseling are in very important ways competing with properly functioning support systems already familiar to children and used as they react to the stresses of life among peers and with adults. Adults responsible for the development of peer counseling programs are well advised to assess children's awareness and understanding of their opportunities for attention to their affective needs.

Peer Counseling in High Schools

Peer counseling programs for adolescents are greater in number and appear to be better documented. As early as the 1960s, secondary school programs were described by educators and researchers. Typical goals of training are that peer counselors become effective in understanding self and others and become capable of skills in communication and problem solving. With secondary programs, explicit claims for benefits to peer counselors have been made (Ayal & Beckerman, 1978; Rockwell & Dustin, 1979).

Williams (1983) stated that peer counseling programs within secondary schools involve preparing students to "work under a counselor's supervision and listen to, support, offer alternatives to, counsel, facilitate the growth and development of students" (p. 11). Williams proposed that such programs could be used to promote the effectiveness of the school's general counseling program, reach larger numbers of students than would be possible with professional services, contribute to the school's affective curriculum, function as a primary prevention component within mental health services, and promote the emotional development of adolescents.

Given the influence that adolescents have on equivalent-aged classmates, peer counseling in the secondary school setting would appear to be a significant force in mental health services to students. Programs can be implemented with students who volunteer for counselor roles, or be based on a selection process guided by self–teacher–counselor nomination or other objective screening criteria. Given that few rigorous early studies of peer counseling indicated statistically significant differences compared to control groups, research in the last decade has focused on establishing clear benefits for participants.

Morey, Miller, Fulton, Rosen, and Daly (1989) were interested in establishing, through training in empathic listening, a group of peer counselors to provide support and friendship to other students. The authors were interested in uncovering the characteristics of students who met with a peer counselor, the types of problems students discussed in meeting with peer counselors, the students' satisfaction with peer counseling, and the students' perceived helpfulness in responding to the presenting problems.

Students in Grades 10 through 12 participated. Questionnaire responses revealed that students gave an average rating of 3.22 on a 5-point scale for their self-reported level of general satisfaction with peer counseling. Students rated the peer counselors most helpful with discussing plans for the future (3.14) and school problems (3.06). Students revealed lowest levels of perceived helpfulness in the areas of alcohol and drug problems (2.25 and 2.11, respectively). Overall, only 38% of students perceived that what the peer counselor told them had an impact on their lives.

The results indicated that there may be a divergence between the school's goals for the training peer counselors receive, and what the students themselves expect to get out of peer counseling. Determining students' expectations regarding peer counseling can help shape the content for training peer counselors. Allowing students to clarify their expectations of peer counseling can help them to understand the merits as well as limitations of the experience.

Lynn (1986) was interested in getting students to take an interest in their school, by involving them in defining the educational, social, and philosophical goals of the school. The author set up a program that involved both peer tutoring and peer counseling. Participants were enrolled in a 1,600-student public high school. Students attended Grades 10 through 12. Approximately 2% of the students were minority.

Lynn (1986) chose 15 students to be resource tutors, whose main goal was to provide immediate, short-term classroom assistance to students and teachers who required the service. Another 100 students were selected to be long-term peer tutors. An additional 15 became peer counselors and received 30 hours of peer counselor training. Training provided to the student volunteers emphasized practicing specific counseling skills using immediate feedback during role play and real situations. Analysis of findings revealed that graduating peer helpers (tutors and counselors) rated the high school training they received, including the work they did in their roles as peer helpers, as the most satisfying experience of their high school years. Lynn's (1986) research showed that peer counselors can be a strong force for change and growth in high school, and can foster a sense of being important to those seeking help.

Robinson, Morrow, Kigin, and Lindeman (1991) were interested in evaluating peer counselors' training and its effects on students. Specifically, the authors wanted to meet the need for peer counselors in a large high school in a southwestern metropolitan region. The school contained 1,972 students who completed a survey in which they listed persons whom they would seek out whenever they had personal problems. Eight individuals, (5 White, 1 Black, 1 Mexican American, and 1 Asian) were trained over a 3-day weekend as peer counselors. Two follow-up sessions were held with the peer counselors in which professional counselors described their experiences in a formal helping role. Thirteen second-year students (8 boys and 5 girls), agreed to join the peer counselors and received more individualized training in the school setting, as well as communication skills that were covered with the previous year's peer counselors. Each of the second-year students also received weekly supervision from a doctoral student at the school site.

Results of the first year were limited to the peer counselors' perceptions of the effectiveness of training in communication skills. Peer counselors believed they had acquired important skills in empathic listening and reflection. At the end of the second year, analyses revealed that gender was a significant predictor of peer counseling contacts: Female peer counselors received more contacts than did male peer counselors. The authors hypothesized that students view females as more empathic listeners than males. Females may be judged to be less likely to reveal information to others than their male counterparts.

Morey, Miller, Rosen, and Fulton (1993) were interested in identifying factors that correlate with students' satisfactions with peer counseling. The sample included 159 students (84 male, 75 female) who had met with a peer counselor. Each participant completed the Peer Counseling Helping Style Technique and the Peer Counseling Consumer Satisfaction Questionnaire. Overall, students were slightly satisfied with peer counseling services. Self-referred students scored higher in satisfaction rate than did students who were referred by others (teachers, administrators, counselors). Results showed students had an overall satisfaction with the empathic listening skills displayed by their peer counselors, as well as with the relationship-improving problem solving they developed. There was a substantial gender difference among students, with female students showing more specific satisfaction with peer counselors' behaviors, as well as with the help they received in strengthening familial and school relationships. Overall, however, satisfaction between genders was not significant. The authors proposed that peer counseling must extend beyond empathic listening and understanding. Once rapport is achieved, peer counselors can help students devise a plan to systematically work through the problem the student is having.

In another study, Boehm, Chessare, Valko, and Sager (1991) were interested in assisting teenagers to provide peers with accessible and acceptable information and guidance services. The authors conducted a peer telephone listening service. Of 2,270 calls received at a peer counseling service, 1,532 were from females and 732 were from males. Peers were unable to determine the gender of 6 callers.

Most common reasons for calls to the service were, in descending order, peer relationships (831), just to talk (569), family problems (428), and sexuality (343). Although not related to school, the telephone counseling service provided a way to disseminate information to teenagers and provide a support for those experiencing difficulties.

An evaluation of a prototype counseling program using an outcome evaluation design was presented by Kim, McLeod, Rader, and Johnston (1992). Thirty-six peer counselors were surveyed. The peer counselors recorded a broad array of frequently encountered issues. Relationship problems with peer of opposite gender as well as those with family members were high on the list, as were disappointments in school and feelings of being left out and uninvolved in school. It should be noted that depression was noted as the second most frequent concern. As for peer counselors, the trainees showed significant improvements in self-esteem as well as improvement in social skills.

Additional studies have documented the success of peer counseling programs (Bowman & Myrick, 1987; Carr & Saunders, 1980). Implications of the research show that peer counseling can have a multidirectional effect. Peer counseling affects students who seek out peer counseling as well as those that provide the support.

PEER COUNSELING AND SPECIAL POPULATIONS

Consider the case of Miranda, an Hispanic high school student who became concerned when she noticed that her pregnant peers often dropped out of school in large numbers. She approached a school counselor and was successful in convincing her of the importance of a program to assist pregnant teens, especially Hispanic students who were not likely to return to school. Miranda and the counselor recruited the support of other educators, support professionals, and students. Together, they developed a peer counseling program that provided information on educational options plus affective support services.

The program sought out teens who had indicated that they were planning to withdraw from school because of a pregnancy. Each student was asked to speak with the counselor, who encouraged the students to remain in school and to consider the peer counseling program. If the student elected to remain enrolled, she was matched with a trained peer counselor. The students would meet with their peer counselor to monitor health (check how the pregnancy was proceeding, assess attitude) and to discuss their educational needs. Students typically met at least twice a week for 10 to 15 minutes to discuss their health with their peer counselor. Additional, longer sessions were common when a student needed the peer to listen or consider strategies that addressed educational needs.

The pregnant teens were appreciative of all forms of peer counselor support. They became more knowledgeable about resources and options for their education, and were excited to be able to plan for their future. The pregnant teens were encouraged to seek out family support and were couched in how best to approach family members. Consistent with the emphasis of the program to encourage continued enrollment in school, the teens were able to meet with the peer counselor after the birth of their child.

Miranda took the initiative, with the support of her counselor, to interview physicians and to seek out reading materials so that other peer counselors would be well informed on pregnancy and childrearing issues. She forwarded all materials to the counselor who used them during training of peer counselors. The school counselor consulted with and supervised every student serving as a peer counselor and led counseling groups for pregnant teens. The next stage of the school's peer counseling program will be to assist the male partners of the pregnant teens.

Peer counseling programs can be developed to respond to a broad range of needs within the schools. Peer-to-peer helping relations have been effective in enhancing ethnic and race relations (Downe, Altmann, & Nysetvold, 1986). For diverse populations, various factors are important to consider as peer counseling plans are developed and implemented. If peer similarity is to be achieved, socioeconomic factors, language issues, and stereotypes must be considered (Aponte, Rivers, & Wohl, 1995). Many students from ethnic backgrounds are familiar with high poverty rates. As a result they may not have the same experiences and opportunities as those who hail from higher economic strata. In pairing the peer counselor and counselee, the student may see the peer counseling experience as one of few opportunities to access support. A peer would be an excellent source of support to some help seekers. At the same time, credibility and effectiveness can be lost if the peer counselee does not believe that the peer counselor can relate to his or her experience. Regardless of ethnicity and socioeconomic position, the gap between students can be widened when the pair's backgrounds differ significantly. An important consideration is the language the students feel most comfortable using. Determining language use and preference for both participants becomes critical. Understanding can be increased if both can communicate effectively in the language they prefer.

Examining stereotypes is an important consideration in peer counseling programs (Aponte, Rivers, & Wohl, 1995). If the peer counselor has stereotypes about certain groups, whether negative or positive, the counseling experience can be affected. At the same time if the peer counseling intervention reflects stereotypes about certain groups, the counseling experience can be influenced. Although it would be beyond the scope of this chapter to consider the impact of all potential biases, assessment of potentially biasing factors is of vital importance to the peer counseling program.

Perhaps, though, the most critical variables to assess include the individuals' worldview, acculturation, and ethnic identity development. Worldview is important because it reflects how students perceive themselves and others in their environment. Worldview can incorporate views on gender, spirituality, disability, ethnicity, and ageism. Acculturation provides information on language, cultural identification, generational status, and perceived discrimination. Students can possess many of the western cultural traits as espoused in the schools or they could have few. If they are similar in their cultural views to those reflected in the school's curriculum, they will be considered highly acculturated and may see the peer counseling program positively. If not highly acculturated, the goals of the peer counseling may not be fully understood. At the same time, students who are not culturally similar to the school may find the peer counselor accessible and appropriate, if that counselor embodies similar acculturation and ethnic identity. Caution must be exercised in terms of the role the peer counselor will follow. Assessing acculturation will shed light on within-group differences, offering a more accurate prediction of which pairs would be most effective.

In terms of identity development, all children and adolescents engage in the process—achieving an identity is critical to development. For students from minority backgrounds, identity development differs in that the impact of one's ethnicity affects the process. Many students from ethnic minority backgrounds tend to score higher in disclosure than do their White counterparts (Aponte, Rivers, & Wohl, 1995). Negative and positive messages influence ethnic identity development, starting in childhood, affecting the student's potential experience during peer counseling. In general, assessment of student traits and needs is critical to the success of the peer counseling program, and can be especially true when students in peer counseling programs are from ethnic minority backgrounds.

Organizing Peer Counseling: Tips for Teachers

D'Andrea and Salovey's (1983) agenda for peer counseling training matches the priorities of elementary, middle, and high schools. The authors propose the following advice for implementation, and monitoring of peer counseling skills:

1. Be nonjudgmental. Peer counselors must be trained to listen closely to their partners, with emphasis on understanding what their partners are saying and showing with nonverbal signals. With children, especially at the elementary level, training is essential to avoid evaluating and labeling their peer's emotional displays and comments. With practice, peer counselors can master a response repertoire that paraphrases rather than judges. For example if the help-seeker says, "I'm having problems getting along with other kids and knowing what to do when I'm being picked on," the peer counselor can respond with a paraphrase ("You're uncertain what to do with the other children) or a perception check ("Are you feeling bad and uncertain how to get along?").

2. Be empathetic. Successful peer counselors can distinguish between empathy (understanding a classmate's feelings) and sympathy (feeling bad about the classmate's problems). Training peer counselors to engage in empathy involves preparing students to recognize one or more of the following—the peer's situation (e.g., pressures, difficulties, lack of awareness), feelings (e.g., sad, glad, scared), wants (e.g., to discuss a topic), or beliefs (e.g., have been unfairly treated). When the peer acknowledges the paraphrase of their perceived situation, the counselor can proceed with the recommended elements of the intervention.

3. Do not give personal advice. Advice-giving is a tactic that is quite easy for children and adults yet seldom has the payoff that effective counseling

attempts to insure. When a student agrees to be trained as a peer counselor, the school staff and students must be clear on the relevance of personal experience and advice within the counseling process. The distinction between "do what I would do" and "I've experienced some of what you are saying" can be built into training. Of course, when the counseling program is built on a specific theoretical approach (e.g., behavioral) with attendant specialized language and techniques, the students will be prepared to the point of mastery in the intervention.

4. Do not ask questions that begin with "why." D'Andrea and Salovey are in the counseling mainstream by advocating questions that clarify the help-seeker's comments, rather than probe for an explanation that might jump too quickly to explanations of thoughts and feelings. Instead, open questions ("How are you feeling?") and closed questions ("Are you upset with what he said?") are recommended.

5. Do not take responsibility for the help-seeker's problems. To be successful as a peer counselor, the student does not strive to solve the help seeker's presenting problems. Instead, the peer counselor offers a supportive context in which to clarify thoughts and feelings, to consider alternative responses to life's challenges, and to direct the help seekers to resources, especially when the challenges have overwhelmed the ability to cope. Being clear about relevant resources is an important outcome of the training phase of counseling.

6. Don't interpret when a paraphrase will do. Johnson's (1986) recommendation to adhere to paraphrasing with the goal of understanding another speaker is relevant here. Quick closure on identification of a problem has seldom resulted in an optimal counseling intervention. Consistent with Johnson, we support "understanding of the client" as the central characteristic of all forms of counseling.

7. Stick with the present day. Once again, D'Andrea and Salovey are in the mainstream with their emphasis on the importance of immediacy within the counseling relationship. By remaining in the present, peer counselors can strive for genuineness in expressions of emotions and perceptions. How to optimally train peer counselors to achieve immediacy is a separate matter. Young children especially are seldom sophisticated, particularly in the counselor role, in distinguishing between past and present influences on emotions. If immediacy is a priority with an elementary school level program, children will require clear guidelines and examples on what to say and do.

8. Deal with feelings first. Understanding feelings will precede attempts at problem solving. If problem solving is the priority, the relationship being promoted between peers would be consultation rather than counselor. A peer counseling agenda supports the expression of a help-seeker's feelings before attempting to direct the child toward coping strategies or resources.

An abundance of reports on peer counseling programs provide information that is useful in setting up a program. The references cited within the text as well as the additional resource list highlight the diversity of approaches possible within a peer counseling program. In general, it is important to determine the purpose and goals of the peer counseling programs before proceeding to develop activities.

A clear plan for the selection of peers (both counselors and counselees) is essential. The literature provides suggestions such as the use of sociometrics (Downe, Altmann, & Nysetvold, 1986); published and unpublished measures (Bowman & Myrick, 1987); and adult recommendations from teachers, parents, and principals (Downe, Altmann, & Nysetvold, 1986) to guide the selection process. Sources to query for potential participants include the students themselves, parents, and school staff members. Assessing students' strengths and personal characteristics can aid the selection of students who will succeed as peer counselors. Selection of students who will receive peer service may be conducted prior to implementing a program. The needs and presenting issues must be examined to make sure these can be met through the peer program and fit the goals and purpose of educators as well as the abilities of the peer counselors.

Although training emphases may differ across programs, the need for training is clearly evident. During training, actual skill building, role playing, and guided practice experiences can be critical in preparing students for the counselor role. Students must be trained as well on when to refer, how they will be evaluated, and the limits of confidentiality. Peer helpers are provided with significant power in the counseling relationship and must not be left without support.

Monitoring and evaluation procedures must be clearly delineated by counseling staff, and peer counselors alerted to the mechanics of adult supervision and input. Techniques to insure personal accountability can be part of the training process, and be linked to a support system (technical and emotional) to assist the peer helpers. Ongoing supervision is both ethical and necessary as students become responsible for their peers' lives. Of special importance will be the presentation of clear guidelines and instructions to helpers on how to proceed when situations become more serious that they can handle. Readers seeking further details on implementation will wish to consult reports by Garner, Martin, and Martin (1989) and de Rosenroll and Dey (1990).

CONCLUSIONS

Peer counseling can succeed at the elementary and secondary school levels as an extension of the counseling agenda of the school practitioner staff. When a school district commits to a peer counseling program, children and adolescents can benefit. Monitoring participants, following up on contacts, and evaluating the impact and relevance of services will assure educators that students are addressing issues of importance. Peer counseling is a viable subset of the broader category of PAL, and is likely to remain relevant to schools as long as they pursue an affective component to their agenda for student growth and development.

REFERENCES

American Psychological Association. (1982). *Thesaurus of psychological index terms* (3rd ed.). Washington, DC: Author.

Aponte, J. F., Rivers, R. Y., & Wohl, J. (Eds.). (1995). *Psychological interventions and cultural diversity.* Boston: Allyn & Bacon.

Ayal, H., & Beckerman, R. (1978). Peer counselling: A means of actualising adolescents' helping potential. *British Journal of Guidance and Counseling, 6,* 204–214.

Berndt, T. J., & Perry, T. B. (1986). Children's perceptions of friendships as supportive relationships. *Developmental Psychology, 22,* 640–648.

Bowman, R. P., & Myrick, R. D. (1987). Effects of an elementary school peer facilitator program on children with behavior problems. *The School Counselor, 34*(5), 369–378.

Boehm, K., Chessare, J. B., Valko, T. R., & Sager, M. S. (1991). Teen line: A descriptive analysis of a peer telephone listening service. *Adolescence, 26*(103), 643–648.

Carr, R. A. (1988). The City-Wide Peer Counseling Program. *Children & Youth Services Review, 10,* 217–232.

Carr, R. A., & Saunders, G. (1980). *Peer counseling starter kit.* Victoria, B.C.: University of Victoria.

D'Andrea, V. J., & Salovey, P. (1983). *Peer counseling: Skills and perspectives.* Palo Alto, CA: Science and Behavior Books.

de Rosenroll, D. A., & Dey, C. (1990). A centralized approach to training peer counselors: 3 years of progress. *School counselor, 37,* 304–312.

Downe, A. G., Altmann, H. A., & Nysetvold, I. (1986). Peer Counseling: More on an emerging strategy. *The School Counselor, 33*(5), 355–364.

Ehly, S., & Dustin, R. (1989). *Individual and group counseling in schools.* New York: Guilford.

Garner, R., Martin, D., & Martin, M. (1989). The PALS program: A peer counseling training program for junior high school. *Elementary School Guidance and Counseling, 24,* 68–76.

Gartner, A., Kohler, M., & Riessman, F. (1971). *Children teach children: Learning by teaching.* New York: Harper & Row.

Guralnick, M. J. (1981). Peer influences on the development of communicative competence. In P. S. Strain (Ed.), *The utilization of classroom peers as behavior change agents* (pp. 31–68). New York: Plenum.

Johnson, D. W. (1986). *Reaching out: Interpersonal effectiveness and self-actualization* (3rd ed.). Englewood Cliffs, NJ: Prentice-Hall.

Kim, S., McLeod, J. H., Rader, D., & Johnston, G. (1992). An evaluation of prototype school-based peer counseling program. *Journal of Drug Education, 22*(1), 37–53.

Lynn, D. R. (1986). Peer helpers—increasing positive student involvement in the school. *The School Counselor, 34*(1), 62–66.

Mitchum, N. T. (1983). Introducing TIP: The involvement program for peer facilitators. *The School Counselor, 31*(2), 146–149.

Morey, R. E., Miller, C. C., Fulton, R., Rosen, L. A., & Daly, J. L. (1989). Peer counseling: Students served, problems discussed, overall satisfaction, and perceived helpfulness. *The School Counselor, 37*(2), 137–143.

Morey, R. E., Miller, C. D., Rosen, L. A., & Fulton, R. (1993). High school peer counseling: The relationship between student satisfaction and peer counselors' style of helping. *The School Counselor, 40*, 293–300.

Peck, C. A., Cooke, T. P., & Apolloni, T. (1981). Utilization of peer imitation in therapeutic and instructional contexts. In P. S. Strain (Ed.), *The utilization of classroom peers as behavior change agents* (pp. 69–99). New York: Plenum.

Raubolt, R. R. (1975). Adolescent peer networks: An alternative to alienation. *Corrective and Social Psychiatry and Journal of Behavior Technology Methods and Therapy, 21*(4), 1–3.

Robinson, S. E., Morrow, S., Kigin, T., & Lindeman, M. (1991). Peer counselors in a high school setting: Evaluation of training and impact on students. *The School Counselor, 39*, 35–40.

Rockwell, L. K., & Dustin, R. (1979). Building a model for training peer counselors. *The School Counselor, 26*, 311–316.

Strip, C., Swassing, R., & Kidder, R. (1991). Female adolescents counseling female adolescents: A first step in emotional crisis intervention. *Roeper Review, 13*(3), 124–128.

Williams, B. K. (1983). *The relationship of peer counselor training to the self-esteem, interpersonal relations orientation, and attitudes toward school of adolescent trainees.* Unpublished doctoral dissertation, University of Iowa, Iowa City.

IV

PEER FEEDBACK

Peer Monitoring

Carlen Henington
Christopher H. Skinner
Mississippi State University

Perhaps the best way to define and describe peer monitoring is to borrow from the self-monitoring literature. Self-monitoring is often broken down into two behaviors: self observation and self-recording (Kanfer, 1971; Shapiro, 1996). In its most basic form, peer monitoring could also be limited to peer observation and peer recording. When self-monitoring is described in broader terms, (i.e., self-management), additional activities such as self-instruction, self-evaluation, and self-reinforcement are often included (Cole & Bambara, 1992). Similarly, peer evaluation, peer reinforcement, and peer instruction could be included in broader peer-assisted programs. Although some of these additional components are noted briefly, this chapter focuses on peer observation and recording.

The product of peer monitoring, recorded data, can serve an assessment function (e.g., student has completed assignment and is ready for next assignment). Peer monitoring procedures and processes should also impact students. In this chapter, these processes and procedures are described and analyzed with recommendations designed to enhance students' cognitive, social, and emotional development.

REVIEW OF CURRENT THINKING AND PRACTICE

In our society, more is being demanded from educators. Teachers are expected to teach, improve, and maintain appropriate social and academic skills and to decrease, eliminate, and prevent inappropriate social and academic behaviors. Furthermore, there is increasing demand that teachers be held more accountable. These expectations put pressure on teachers and limit the time they have available to perform all their professional duties (Skinner, Belfiore, & Watson, 1995; Witt, Elliott, & Martens, 1984).

Peer monitoring can be a time efficient and resource-efficient procedure used to collect data more frequently. Such data can be used to make a variety of decisions that can improve a student's educational programming. Peer monitoring data can be used to determine the nature of a student's problem (Kratochwill, Elliott, & Rotto, 1995). For example, a teacher may refer a student for academic difficulties. However, peer monitoring may provide data that show the difficulty is due to inattention and low on-task rates of behavior, rather than poor academic skills. Data collected over a series of days can be used as baseline data. Baseline data can be used to shape programs and establish goals (Fuchs, 1995). For example, data may show a child completes only 20% of assigned independent seat-work over the course of several days. This data would suggest that an initial goal of 50% independent seat-work completed would be more appropriate than 100% work completed.

Peer monitoring data may also be used to evaluate the effects of interventions by comparing the baseline data to data collected following intervention (Marston & Tindale, 1995). Educators can also use peer monitoring data to determine when students meet goals, when interventions need to be altered, and when interventions are detrimental or ineffective (Shapiro, 1996).

Characteristics and Limitations of Peer-Monitored Data

There are some problems associated with peer monitoring. If education personnel make important treatment or programming decisions based on peer-collected data, it is important that this data is accurate or reliable. The behavior(s) being monitored, the data-recording system, and training may all influence the reliability of peer monitored data.

A second problem with peer-collected data is reactivity. *Reactivity* is a term used to describe the behavior change that occurs in reaction to the monitoring process. Researchers have shown that reactivity is variable. Sometimes it occurs and at other times it does not. In fact, many possible outcomes could occur when monitors observe and record behaviors come of these outcomes follow:

1. No reactivity may occur.
2. Reactivity may increase or strengthen observed behavior.
3. Reactivity may decrease or weaken observed behavior.
4. Reactivity may stabilize or destabilize rates of observed behavior.

5. Reactivity may alter observed behavior (different form, intensity, duration, etc.).

Although researchers have identified a variety of variables that may influence reactivity including conspicuousness of the observer, rationale for observations, and personal attributes of the observer, the level or amount of reactivity is unlikely to be stable for an individual across behaviors, tasks, settings, or time (Johnson & Bolstad, 1973). It is not always possible to separate behavior caused by reactivity from behavior caused by current conditions, programs, and/or interventions. Therefore, even when data is collected in a reliable manner, reactivity can lead to erroneous decisions. For example, reactivity may increase on-task behavior, causing the teacher to conclude that failure to complete assignments is caused by academic deficits, rather than noncompliance.

Several things may be done to decrease reactivity. When visitors enter classrooms specifically to collect observation data, they are conspicuous and students are likely to behave differently (Saudargas & Fellers, 1986). Having a peer observe and record data may be less conspicuous, and should decrease reactivity. This in turn, should allow data to more accurately reflect in vivo behavior. Thus, covert peer monitoring may be an effective way to collect data without introducing reactivity. However, having a peer monitor observe and record another's behavior without that student's knowledge or consent may have adverse side effects. Although peer monitoring can be an effective way to obtain accurate information about a child's behavior, it is important to design a peer monitoring program that meets the needs of the teacher, but minimizes negative side effects.

ORGANIZING A PEER MONITORING PROGRAM

Peer monitoring can be broken down into several steps. The steps that follow are designed to be sequential. However, problems at later stages can sometimes be resolved by altering earlier stages. For example, sometimes altering operational definitions of target behaviors may be necessary in order to develop an acceptable data recording system or to allow students to collect data in a more reliable manner.

   1. Identify target behaviors and goals.
- Target appropriate behaviors rather than inappropriate behaviors.
- Unobservable behaviors can be targeted.
- Academic behaviors can include reading, writing, or mathematic skills.

2. Design a data-recording system.
  - Narrative recording.
  - Event recording.
  - Duration recording.
  - Interval recording.
3. Select the peer monitor.
4. Training the peer monitor.

DESIGNING AN EFFECTIVE
PEER MONITORING PROGRAM

This section describes each of the steps in designing and implementing a peer monitoring program. Recommendations designed to enhance reactivity, decrease the probability of negative side effects, and facilitate implementation in educational settings is provided.

Selecting Behaviors to Monitor

The first step in structuring a peer monitoring program is to identify behaviors to be monitored. Peers can observe and record data on a variety of behaviors including: appropriate and inappropriate behaviors, directly observable behaviors and correlates of unobservable behaviors, and social and academic behavior.

Appropriate Versus Inappropriate Behaviors. One key consideration when using peer monitors is that an important, but often overlooked step occurs between observing and recording behavior. When monitoring, observers must use evaluation to determine which behaviors to record.

Children spontaneously observe and evaluate each other's inappropriate behavior. One of the most salient forms of monitoring is tattling. Tattling involves observing, evaluating, and reporting another's inappropriate behavior. There are several advantages to using peer monitors to observe and collect data on inappropriate behavior. First, children often learn to avoid performing these behaviors when and where they can be directly observed by those in authority. Therefore, peers may be more likely to be able to observe these behaviors. Smoking in the bathroom is an example of a behavior more likely to be observed by peers than adults.

A second advantage of monitoring inappropriate behavior is that these behaviors are often discrete, obvious, and occur infrequently. These characteristics allow efficient and accurate peer monitoring. For example, students and teachers rarely take notice of a student working on independent seat-work. Rather, the student is merely doing what students are supposed to be doing. However, a student who is screaming profanities will rarely go unnoticed. Furthermore, because this behavior usually occurs infrequently and is discreet, recording often requires less time and attention on the part of the monitor.

There are also negative aspects associated with using peers to monitor inappropriate behavior. Children with high rates of inappropriate behavior are more likely to be rejected by peers (Coie, Dodge, & Kupersmidt, 1990). Peer monitoring of inappropriate behavior may draw attention to these behaviors and increase the probability of peer rejection. Peer monitoring and reporting of inappropriate behaviors may also increase physical and relational aggression. For example, children may threaten, physically injure, or socially manipulate another child to either prevent them from, or to punish them for, reporting inappropriate behaviors (Crick, 1995). Further, peers may falsely accuse each other in order to cause trouble for another.

Thus, peer monitoring of inappropriate behavior may lead to an increase in aggression, peer rejection, and other negative interactions in the classroom. Peer rejection and aggressive behaviors are likely to be stable across time (Eron & Huesmann, 1990), and have been shown to be related to serious, long term socioemotional difficulties (Coie, Lochman, Terry, & Hyman, 1992). Furthermore, when they experience high levels of negative interactions at school, students may come to distrust peers (Coie, Dodge, & Kupersmidt, 1990), as well as teachers, administrators, and the entire education system. These potential outcomes may explain why Turco and Elliott (1986) found that students preferred private, as opposed to public, interventions designed to decrease inappropriate behavior.

A focus on inappropriate behavior may also detract attention from appropriate behaviors. Students are more likely to learn in an environment that focuses on skill building and strengthening appropriate behaviors (Hoge & Andrews, 1987; Lentz, 1988). When classrooms revolve around the monitoring and punishing of inappropriate behaviors or rule violations, students may learn to avoid punishment by being quiet or docile (Winette & Winkler, 1972). Because effective learning requires students to engage in, rather than refrain from, behavior it may be more appropriate and preferable for peers to monitor appropriate behaviors (Daly, Lentz, & Boyer, 1996; Skinner, Fletcher, & Henington, 1996).

Unobservable Behaviors.   To monitor a peer's behavior, the behavior must be directly observable. Students cannot directly observe peers' thoughts or feelings. However, children can be trained to vocalize or report their private feelings or emotions (Walco & Varmi, 1991) and their thoughts as they solve social problems (Urbain & Savage, 1989) or academic problems. These verbal reports can then be monitored by peers.

Children's self-report of covert thinking or feelings are affected by their age and vocabulary. Older students may have the cognitive ability and vocabulary necessary to verbalize their thinking process while problem solving (e.g., giving self-directions for each step in solving a math problem). Although younger children may have difficulty vocalizing thoughts or feelings, researchers have shown that children as young as elementary school age can be taught to report their covert thoughts (Meichenbaum & Goodman, 1971; Shure & Spivack, 1979).

Another option when behaviors are not easily observed is to monitor broadly defined observable correlates or related behaviors. For example, although silent reading behaviors are not directly observable, it is possible to determine if a student is on-task (i.e., has head and eyes oriented toward reading material). Another advantage of monitoring broad correlates such as on-task behavior is that it may allow peer monitors to use the same definition of a behavior across environments. This may reduce the need to retrain peers to monitor behaviors across different students, settings, tasks, and activities (Lentz, 1988).

Caution is warranted when peers monitor correlates of unobservable behavior. For example, when students have their head and eyes oriented toward a text, they could be silently reading or they might be thinking about lunch. Any time correlates of covert behaviors are monitored, educators should periodically collect other data (e.g., comprehension questions on material assigned for reading) to confirm that students are engaging in the desired behaviors.

Academic Performance.   Peers can monitor academic performance in reading, writing, and mathematics. Because these skills are essential for long-term success, frequent peer monitoring of academic performance can be used to make important educational decisions. Peer monitoring can also address basic academic-related behaviors. For example, students can observe if peers have their name and the date on their assignment, have homework materials ready at the end of the school day, or have erased completely and neatly (Stern, Fowler, & Kohler, 1988). Although it is time consuming for teachers to monitor these behaviors, peers can quickly check their presence or absence, and cue when necessary.

Teachers often collect written independent seat- or home-work, summatively assess (i.e., evaluate or grade) it, provide written qualitative feedback, and return the work within a day or more (Leper, 1985). This practice does not allow for immediate feedback on academic performance. However, peer monitors can provide much more immediate feedback on the nature and effectiveness of learning processes as they are occurring. Peers who have mastered skills can easily evaluate responses and provide accurate responses. Even when monitors do not know the correct response, they can often identify errors (Greenwood, Delquadri, & Carta, 1988). Monitors can use answer-key responses (e.g., answers on the back of flashcards) to evaluate responses and provide correction (Skinner, Shapiro, Turco, & Brown, 1992).

Immediate peer feedback regarding accuracy can serve several functions. When responses are accurate, this peer-delivered immediate feedback may reinforce those responses, increasing the probability that future responses will also be accurate. Immediate feedback following errors may prevent students from practicing incorrect responses and may also serve as a cue to seek additional instruction. This instruction could then come from the peer monitor, the teacher, or even independent study to prevent further inaccurate responding (Skinner & Smith, 1992).

In order for peers to monitor academic responses, responses must only be public; they do not have to yield permanent products (e.g., answers written on paper). When teachers are the only ones evaluating academic responses that are not permanent products, they can only evaluate one student's response at a time. For example, during round-robin reading, only one student receives immediate corrective feedback. However, peers can take turns providing immediate corrective feedback for verbal responses. This allows for half the class to be receiving immediate feedback as opposed to one student. In this example, half the class can be reading aloud while the other half is monitoring (Greenwood et al., 1988).

Providing feedback on verbal responses can be useful in other situations. For example, if students verbalize the steps they will use in solving a problem (e.g., social problems, science problems, mathematics problems), monitors could listen to those steps (observe), evaluate them, and provide corrective feedback. The monitor could evaluate whether peers were leaving out steps or making errors *before* incorrect steps are used.

Teachers may provide higher quality feedback (e.g., more precise) than peers. Furthermore, some students, especially young students, may respond more readily to teacher, as opposed to peer feedback. However, the greater volume and immediacy of peer feedback can render it equally, if not more effectively than infrequent, delayed teacher feedback.

For some academic skills to be useful or functional, students must be able to perform them both quickly and accurately. Monitors can also observe and record speed of responding. For example, many educators want students to be automatic (accurate and quick) with their one-digit by one-digit multiplication. Hasselbring, Goin, and Bransford (1987) described a procedure for measuring automaticity using flashcards. Students were shown a flashcard and only when they responded accurately within two seconds were they considered automatic. It would be difficult and time consuming for a teacher to monitor each student's automaticity. However, if students monitored each others' automaticity, teachers would be able to quickly determine which specific problems require more training for each student.

Peers can also be used to collect fluency data (i.e., speed of accurate responding data across a broader class of behaviors). For example, peers could be given a fixed amount of time to complete as many single-digit multiplication problems as possible as a peer observed, evaluated, and recorded (and even corrected) errors. By keeping the amount of time fixed, monitors are able to calculate rate data (e.g., the number of problems completed accurately per minute). Using these procedures allows for monitoring of fluency. Fluency data can then be used to evaluate increases in students' skills across academic areas including reading (words correct per minute), mathematics (digits correct per minute), writing (words written per minute), and spelling (letter sequences correct per minute; Shapiro, 1996).

Designing Recording Procedures

There are many different procedures that can be used to record observations. Depending on characteristics of behaviors being measured, some recording procedures are more valuable than others. Advantages and disadvantages for some common data-recording procedures are described and illustrated.

Narrative Recording.   When narrative recording is employed, monitors provide written descriptions of observed events. An example would be to require the peer monitors to write down an observed positive or prosocial behavior or event. Teachers could then collect these observations at the end of the school day. Because these behaviors often go unnoticed, this type of procedure would make teachers and students aware of these behaviors, provide scheduled time for reinforcing these appropriate behaviors, and possibly increase the likelihood that the behaviors will occur in the future.

Although narrative recordings can be useful, they require subjective judgments and are difficult to verify. Furthermore, narrative reports do not translate well into empirical or numerical data. These characteristics make it difficult to evaluate the accuracy of narrative reports and to use narrative reports to make important programming decisions.

Event Recording.   Event or frequency recording requires a monitor to keep a tally of each observed event. Many behaviors are easily counted (e.g., number of problems completed, number of problems completed accurately, number of assignments completed at 80% or better). Tallies can be kept with paper and pencil, golf score counters, and so forth.

Event or frequency data may be more useful when converted to ratio data (e.g., percentage or rate data). For example, knowing the number of problems completed accurately may not be as important as knowing the percent of problems completed accurately. The only additional data required for ratio data is a record of problems completed inaccurately. Rates of occurrence may also be important. For example, some students read accurately, but slowly. This lack of fluency may hinder comprehension and success across curricula (Reutzel & Hollingsworth, 1993). By having peer monitors collect data on words read correctly per minute, teachers can evaluate the effects of interventions designed to increase fluency.

One difficulty with event recording is that some behaviors are not very discrete (i.e., lack a clear beginning and ending). This can be addressed by changing the operational definition of the behavior to include a temporal component. In the previous example, we used aggressive outburst to define a group of behaviors (i.e., hitting and kicking). If a child hits and kicks another child 15 times within 20 seconds, it could be defined as 15 aggressive acts or as one aggressive outburst. Because it is difficult to count rapidly occurring behaviors and teachers are probably more concerned with the number of outbursts, a monitor could collect data on outbursts. A single outburst could be defined as beginning when the first kick or hit occurs and ending when there is no hitting or kicking for 30 seconds.

Duration Recording.   Sometimes temporal characteristics of behaviors are important. For example, educators may want to increase the amount of time a student spends responding (persistence) before engaging in other behaviors. In other instances, educators may be concerned with how long an aggressive outburst lasts, rather than the number of outbursts. Continuous data collection (e.g., starting and stopping a stopwatch every time a student changes behaviors from on-task to off-task or vice versa) can also be used to collect data on temporal aspects of behavior. Continuous duration recording is used less frequently than event recording because it requires the use of a timing device and the behavior must be monitored constantly.

Time-Sampling Recording.

Partial interval, whole interval, and momentary time-sampling procedures allow estimates of time spent engaged in specific behaviors. These procedures are useful for high-rate and nondiscrete behaviors that do not lend themselves to event recording. For all three procedures, the observation period is divided into smaller intervals and the observer records the presence or absence of the behaviors during each interval.

If partial interval recording is used, the monitor records the behavior if it occurs any time during an interval. This procedure is useful when low-rate data is recorded over long intervals. For example, a student could record the presence of swearing for each class period. If the student swore one or more times during class, swearing is scored. Swearing is not scored if the student did not swear in class. During whole interval recording, the behavior is scored if it occurs throughout the entire interval. With momentary time sampling, the behavior is scored if it is observed at the exact moment the interval begins. Whole interval and momentary time sampling are useful when behaviors are continuous and intervals are fairly brief (e.g., on-task with 3-minute intervals).

However, in many instances, momentary time sampling may be preferable because it does not require observation for the entire interval. Time-sampling data is translated to percentage of intervals during which the behavior occurred. This percentage is an estimate of the percentage of time engaged in each behaviors. Educators using time-sampling procedures should be aware of the limitations of each procedure. Whole interval recording tends to underestimate, whereas partial interval recording tends to overestimate time engaged in observed behaviors (Powell, Martindale, Kulp, Martindale, & Bauman, 1977). Although momentary time sampling causes neither consistent overestimates or underestimates, it can result in poor estimates of time engaged in the behavior, particularly with long observation intervals (Test & Heward, 1984). Another limitation when using peer monitors to collect-time sampling data is that a method of marking intervals is necessary. Often, audiotapes with beeps or other audible cues are used to mark intervals (Shapiro, 1987). These audible cues can be distracting to the monitor who may also be engaged in other behaviors (e.g., their own schoolwork), as well as the peer being observed and classmates.

Selecting a Peer Monitor

Researchers have found that both cross-age (McCurdy & Shapiro, 1992) and same-age peers (Stern, Fowler, & Kohler, 1988) are effective in increasing a variety of academic behaviors (e.g., work completion, accuracy) in a variety of subject areas (e.g., reading, mathematics). Studies indicate that children with varying abilities (e.g., preschool children, children with developmental delays) can be trained to successfully monitor peers (Carden-Smith & Fowler, 1984). Researchers have also suggested that it is not necessary for the monitor to be accepted or preferred by peers (Kalfus, 1984). Thus, selection of the monitor is not limited by factors that might intuitively be considered problematic.

However, there are several important considerations when selecting a monitor. The most important consideration is that the monitor must be able to directly observe the peer (e.g., is seated nearby). If data is to be collected frequently, it is also important that the monitor attend school regularly. When a monitor is not consistently available, it may be necessary to change monitors. Researchers have found that randomly assigned peer monitors are effective (Greenwood, Delquadri, & Carta, 1988). In order to be a peer monitor, the student must have the necessary observation, evaluation, and recording skills. Although it may be easier to select monitors who already possess these skills, teachers can also train students in these prerequisite skills. There are several reasons why teachers should consider training students to be monitors when other students could monitor without training.

There is strong evidence that the process of observing and evaluating others' academic performance may improve the monitor's academic skills (McCurdy, Cundari, & Lentz, 1990; Salend & Nowak, 1988). However, the broader social gains that may occur when students monitor each others' behavior may be more significant than academic gains (McCurdy & Shapiro, 1992; Stern, Fowler, & Kohler, 1988). If all students can serve as monitors, then students can exchange roles. This may enhance the efficiency of peer monitoring and give a sense of equality within the classroom. Considering how often students classify and group each other based on variables such as gender, ability, race, and age, this sense of equality may be very important. For example, a neglected student who performs poorly in mathematics may have few opportunities to interact with other students or to evaluate their mathematics performance. Although teachers may be more likely to select this student to be monitored, this student may gain the most (e.g., socially, academically, emotionally) from serving as a monitor. Therefore, it would behoove the teacher to train this student to monitor.

A variety of curricula or programs (e.g., cooperative learning) require students to work and learn together (Slavin, 1991). In order to help each other succeed, these programs require students to monitor each others' behavior. Earlier, we suggested that peers often spontaneously monitor each others' inappropriate behavior. Students whose only experience with peer monitoring is focused on inappropriate behavior are likely to have difficulty forming cooperative relationships. By training all students to monitor peers' appropriate academic behavior, educators may shift the focus and attention from inappropriate behavior to appropriate behavior. This shift may improve the climate of the entire classroom, and enhance and encourage positive interactions among diverse students (Skinner, Cashwell, & Dunn, 1996). Cooperative learning (CL) programs may be more likely to succeed in a classroom where the focus is on increasing appropriate academic and social behaviors, as opposed to decreasing rule violations and other inappropriate behaviors. Furthermore, students who gain experience in working together through peer monitoring may develop the cooperative skills necessary to perform other important activities such as group goal setting, group problem solving, and conflict resolution.

Peers who learn the basic steps involved in monitoring other students (i.e., observe, evaluate, record) may apply these same procedures to their own behavior. These self-monitoring procedures may then be used to improve their own performance across academic and social/behavioral skills (Cole & Bambara, 1992).

Children often enjoy and value the role of monitoring (Carden-Smith & Fowler, 1984; Doughterty, Fowler, & Paine, 1985). Although students are often motivated to serve as monitors, teachers may need to enhance student motivation for peer monitoring to continue to be valued by students. Although providing individual reinforcement contingent on consistent and accurate peer monitoring is likely to be effective, teachers may find that group oriented contingencies are more effective and are more likely to encourage cooperation, as opposed to competition (Skinner, Cashwell, & Dunn, 1996).

Training the Peer Monitor

Accurate peer monitoring requires students to observe behavior, quickly evaluate whether it is within the limits of the operational definition or not, and accurately record the behavior. After it has been determined that the monitors can observe responses, the next step is to teach monitors the operational definitions (e.g., correct response, on-task) and the recording procedures.

Describing, modeling, role playing, and practice have all been used to train peer monitors (Skinner, Shapiro, Turco, & Brown, 1992). When learning to discriminate behaviors based on the operational definition, monitors should be provided with examples of behaviors that would and would not be recorded. Initially, it is best to provide examples that *clearly* fall within or outside operational definitions. Then, students should be given more difficult examples to discriminate and evaluate. Requiring monitors to supply their own examples of classroom behaviors to evaluate also enhances training.

After operational definitions are learned, modeling can be used to teach the recording procedure. All aspects of recording should first be broken down into small steps, then modeled as an entire monitoring situation. Once the monitor has had the opportunity to see the procedure modeled correctly, it is important to model difficult situations. For example, model those situations that involve difficult evaluations or rapidly occurring behaviors.

The peer monitors should role play with the teacher or trainer providing corrective feedback and encouragement. The role play should be conducted in the exact situation that the monitoring will occur (e.g., in the classroom during normal classroom activity). This in vivo experience will allow teachers to identify problems (e.g., settings or behaviors) when accurate peer recording does not occur and correct them. Furthermore, because monitors are not required to generalize skills across situations, in vivo training and practice will enhance the likelihood that accurate peer monitoring will occur. Sometimes inaccurate recording can be corrected with more training. Often, however, inaccurate recording is caused by poor operational definitions (e.g., too broadly defined behavior) or overly complex data-recording systems (e.g., too many behaviors being recorded at once) that may have to be altered.

Once the monitors have acquired the ability to record behaviors accurately, it is important that they practice monitoring. One effective method would be to have peers monitor each other. Because in vivo monitoring may be extremely time consuming, another useful procedure is to use videotapes to train monitors.

Before actual monitoring begins, it is important to evaluate the monitors and establish the accuracy of their recording. One way to do this is to compare two or more monitors engaged in simultaneous monitoring to determine if their recordings match. Using videotapes, comparison data can be preestablished. This preestablished data can be compared to that of the monitor, thus reducing the need for two monitors.

A simple and direct measure for determining monitors' accuracy would be to calculate the percentage of agreements between the monitor and the comparison data:

$$\frac{\# \text{ of agreements}}{\text{number of agreements } + \text{ disagreements}} \times 100\%$$

Researchers have required monitors to reach 85% or higher agreement across three consecutive trials before they consider them accurate (Suen & Ary, 1989). However, in some instances, decisions can be based on data where this high level of agreement may not be required. For example, if a student recorded three instances of fighting within a day and the teacher recorded five instances, then interobserver agreement was only 60%. However, even with this low agreement educators could safely conclude, based on either the student's or teacher's data, that the current fighting reduction intervention was not working and decide to alter the intervention. It is important to note that, although the accuracy of the monitors may initially be high, observer drift may cause decreases in accuracy over time (Shapiro, 1987). Therefore, it may be important to periodically recalculate monitors' accuracy (Barton & Ascoine, 1984). If accuracy has decreased to unacceptable levels, then retraining should be implemented until accuracy has been reestablished.

Researchers have trained monitors in as little as three 10-minute training sessions (e.g., Fowler, 1986). However, the amount of training required will depend on monitor variables (e.g., prerequisite skills), data-recording system complexity (e.g., multiple behaviors vs. single behaviors), and the behaviors themselves (e.g., out-of-seat vs. on-task).

DISCUSSION AND CONCLUSIONS

Researchers have found consistently that teachers prefer procedures that require less school time (Elliott, 1988). Although peer monitoring requires teacher's time up-front for training and teachers must continue to invest time to evaluate the accuracy of the peer monitoring, studies indicate that peer monitoring requires less teacher time than teacher monitoring (McCurdy & Shapiro, 1992).

Inconsistent results have been found when peer, self, and teacher monitoring have been compared. Different types of monitoring might be effective, or *more* effective, with different children in different situations (Skinner, Shapiro, Turco, & Brown, 1992; Stern, Fowler, & Kohler, 1988). Additionally, skills may be impacted differentially by the three types of monitoring (Knapczyk, Johnson, & McDermott, 1983; McCurdy & Shapiro, 1992). Future researchers should attempt to determine if specific student characteristics, ecological variables, and/or behaviors (e.g., on-task vs. work completed) are more likely to be influenced by interventions that employ peer monitoring as opposed to self- or teacher monitoring.

Although the process of self-monitoring can bring about change in behavior, and that change tends to be in the desired direction (e.g., appropriate behaviors tend to increase, whereas inappropriate behaviors tend to decrease), collecting peer monitoring data may not be sufficient to create improvement (Kanfer, 1971). Because the process of peer monitoring may not cause reactivity, teachers must actively use data generated by peer monitoring procedures (e.g., design or alter interventions; McCurdy & Shapiro, 1992) if students are to benefit. Even when reactivity does occur, it may not occur in the desired direction. For example, peers often engage in inappropriate behaviors because others are observing, evaluating, and possibly reinforcing those behaviors (e.g., the class clown). Therefore, educators should not expect peer monitoring, in and of itself, to alter or maintain behaviors. Rather, educators should use peer monitoring data as components of positive reinforcement procedures. Feedback, goal setting, public posting, self-graphing, contingent individual reinforcement, and group contingencies can all be combined with peer monitoring to reinforce, encourage, shape, teach, and maintain appropriate behaviors.

In summary, peer monitoring can bring about both positive and negative social, emotional, and cognitive changes in students who are being monitored, as well as in those students doing the monitoring. Educators who are careful in constructing their peer monitoring programs are likely to be rewarded with improved classroom social climate, decreased inappropriate behaviors, and increased learning rates. Furthermore, this change can be accomplished in a manner that reduces, rather than increases, demand on teacher time and available resources. Thus, the initial effort of developing peer monitoring programs is likely to have far reaching benefits.

REFERENCES

Barton, E. J., & Ascoine, F. R. (1984). Direct observation. In T. H. Ollendick & M. Hersen (Eds.), *Behavioral assessment of children* (pp. 166–194). Elmsford, NY: Pergamon Press.

Carden-Smith, L. K., & Fowler, S. A. (1984). Positive peer pressure: The effects of peer monitoring on children's disruptive behavior. *Journal of Applied Behavior Analysis, 17,* 213– 227.

Coie, J. D., Dodge, K. A., & Kupersmidt, J. B. (1990). Peer group behavior and social status. In S. R. Asher & J. D. Coie (Eds.), *Peer rejection in childhood* (pp. 17–59). New York: Cambridge University Press.

Coie, J. D., Lochman, J. E., Terry, R., & Hyman, C. (1992). Predicting early adolescent disorder from childhood aggression and peer rejection. *Journal of Consulting and Clinical Psychology, 60,* 783–792.

Cole, C. L., & Bambara, L. M. (1992). Issues surrounding the use of self-management interventions in the schools. *School Psychology Review, 21,* 193–201.

Crick, N. R. (1995). Relational aggression: The role of intent, attributions, feelings of distress, and provocation type. *Development and Psychopathology, 7,* 313–322.

Daly, E. J., Lentz, E. F., & Boyer, J. (1996). Understanding effective components of reading interventions. *School Psychology Quarterly, 11,* 369–386.

Doughterty, B. S., Fowler, S. A., & Paine, S. C. (1985). The use of peer monitors to reduce negative interaction during recess. *Journal of Applied Behavior Analysis, 18,* 141–153.

Elliott, S. N. (1988). Acceptability of behavioral treatments: Review of variables that influence treatment selection. *Professional Psychology Research and Practice, 19,* 68–80.

Eron, L. D., & Huesmann, L. R. (1990). The stability of aggressive behavior—Even into the third generation. In M. Lewis & S. M. Miller (Eds.), *Handbook of developmental psychopathology* (pp. 147–156). New York: Plenum.

Fowler, S. A. (1986). Peer-monitoring and self-monitoring: Alternatives to traditional teacher management. *Exceptional Children, 52,* 573–581.

Fuchs, L. S. (1995). Defining students goals and outcomes. In A. Thomas & J. Grimes (Eds.), *Best practices in school psychology-III* (pp. 539–546). Washington, DC: National Association of School Psychologists.

Greenwood, C. R., Delquadri, J. C., & Carta, J. J. (1988). Class Wide Peer Tutoring (CWPT). *Programs for spelling, math, and reading* [Training Manual]. Delray Beach, FL: Educational Achievement Systems.

Hasslebring, T. S., Goin, L. I., & Bransford, J. D. (1987). Developing automaticity. *Teaching Exceptional Children, 1,* 30–33.

Hoge, R. D., & Andrews, D. A. (1987). Enhancing academic performance: Issues in target selection. *School Psychology Review, 16,* 228–238.

Johnson, S. M., & Bolstad, O. D. (1973). Methodological issues in naturalistic observation: Some problems and solutions. In L. A. Hamerlynck, L. E. Handy, & E. J. Marsh (Eds.), *Behavior change: Methodology, concepts, and practice* (pp. 7–68). Champaign, IL: Research Press.

Kalfus, G. R. (1984). Peer mediated intervention: A critical review. *Child and Family Behavior Therapy, 6,* 17–43.

Kanfer, F. H. (1971). The maintenance of behavior by self-generated stimuli and reinforcement. In A. Jacobs & L. B. Sachs (Eds.), *The psychology of private events* (pp. 39– 58). New York: Academic Press.

Knapczyk, D. R., Johnson, W. A., & McDermott, G. (1983). A comparison of the effects of teacher and peer supervision on work performance and on-task behavior. *Journal of the Association for People with Severe Handicaps, 8*(4), 41–48.

Kratochwill, T. R., Elliott, S. N., & Rotto, P. C. (1995). School-based behavioral consultation. In A. Thomas & J. Grimes (Eds.), *Best practices in school psychology-III* (pp. 519–536). Washington, DC: National Association of School Psychologists.

Lentz, F. E. (1988). On-task behavior, academic performance, and classroom disruptions: Untangling the target selection problem in classroom interventions. *School Psychology Review, 17,* 243–257.

Leper, M. R. (1985). Microcomputers in education. *American Psychologist, 40*(1), 1–18.

Marston, D., & Tindale, G. (1995). Performance monitoring. In A. Thomas & J. Grimes (Eds.), *Best practices in school psychology-III* (pp. 597–607). Washington, DC: National Association of School Psychologists.

McCurdy, B. L., Cundari, L., & Lentz, F. E. (1990). Enhancing instructional efficiency: An examination of time delay and the opportunity to observe instruction. *Education and Treatment of Children, 13,* 226–238.

McCurdy, B. L., & Shapiro, E. S. (1992). A comparison of teacher-, peer-, and self- monitoring with curriculum-based measurement in reading among students with learning disabilities. *The Journal of Special Education, 26,* 162–180.

Meichenbaum, D. H., & Goodman, J. (1971). Training impulsive children to talk to themselves: A means of developing self-control. *Journal of Abnormal Psychology, 77,* 115–126.

Powell, J., Martindale, B., Kulp, S., Martindale, A., & Bauman, R. (1977). Taking a closer look: Time sampling measurement error. *Journal of Applied Behavior Analysis, 10,* 325–332.

Reutzel, D. R., & Hollingsworth, P. M. (1993). Effects of fluency training on second graders' reading comprehension. *Journal of Educational Research, 86,* 325–331.

Salend, S. J., & Nowak, M. R. (1988). Effects of peer previewing on LD students' oral reading skills. *Learning Disability Quarterly, 11,* 47–52.

Saudargas, R. A., & Fellers, G. (1986). *State-event classroom observation system: Research edition.* Knoxville, TN: University of Tennessee, Department of Psychology.

Shapiro, E. S. (1987). *Behavioral assessment in school psychology.* Hillsdale, NJ: Lawrence Erlbaum Associates.

Shapiro, E. S. (1996). *Academic skills problems: Direct assessment and intervention* (2nd ed.). New York: Guilford.

Shure, M. B., & Spivack, G. (1979). Interpersonal cognitive problem solving and primary prevention: Programing pre-school and kindergarten children. *Journal of Clinical Child Psychology, 2,* 89–94.

Skinner, C. H., Belfiore, B. J., & Watson, T. S. (1995) Assessing the relative strength of interventions in students with mild disabilities: Assessing instructional time. *Assessment in Rehabilitation and Exceptionality, 2,* 207–220.

Skinner, C. H., Cashwell, C. S., & Dunn, M. S. (1996). Independent and interdependent group contingencies: Smoothing the rough waters. *Special Services in the Schools, 12,* 61–78.

Skinner, C. H., Fletcher, P. A., & Henington, C. (1996). Increasing learning rates by increasing student response rates: A summary of research. *School Psychology Quarterly, 11,* 313 325.

Skinner, C. H., Shapiro, E. S., Turco, T. L., & Brown, D. K. (1992). A comparison of self-and peer-delivered immediate corrective feedback on multiplication performance. *Journal of School Psychology, 30,* 101–116.

Skinner, C. H., & Smith, E. S. (1992). Issues surrounding the use of self-management interventions for increasing academic performance. *School Psychology Review, 21,* 202–210.

Slavin, R. E. (1991). Cooperative learning and group contingencies. *Journal of Behavioral Education, 1,* 105–116.

Stern, G. W., Fowler, S. A., & Kohler, F. W. (1988). A comparison of two intervention roles: Peer monitor and point earner. *Journal of Applied Behavior Analysis, 21,* 103–109.

Suen, H., & Ary, D. (1989). *Analyzing quantitative behavioral observation data.* Hillsdale, NJ: Lawrence Erlbaum Associates.

Test, D. W., & Heward, W. L. (1984). Accuracy of momentary time sampling: A comparison of fixed- and variable-interval observation schedules. In W. L. Heward, T. E. Heron, D. H. Hill, & J. Trapp-Porter (Eds.), *Focus on behavior analysis in education* (pp. 177–196). Columbus, OH: Merrill.

Turco, T. L., & Elliott, S. N. (1986). Assessment of students' acceptability ratings of teacher-initiated interventions for classroom misbehavior. *Journal of School Psychology, 24,* 277–283.

Urbain, E. S., & Savage, P. (1989). Interpersonal cognitive problem solving training with children in schools. In J. N. Hughes & R. J. Hall (Eds.), *Cognitive behavioral psychology in the schools: A comprehensive handbook* (pp. 466–497). New York: Guilford.

Walco, G. A., & Varmi, J. W. (1991). Cognitive–behavioral interventions for children with chronic illnesses. In P. C. Kendall (Ed.), *Child and adolescent therapy: Cognitive–behavioral procedures* (pp. 209–244). New York, NY: Guilford.

Winette, R. A., & Winkler, R. C. (1972). Current behavior modification in the classroom: Be still, be docile. *Journal of Applied Behavior Analysis, 5,* 499–504.

Witt, J. C., Elliott, S. N., & Martens, B. K. (1984). Acceptability of behavioral interventions used in classrooms: The influence of amount of teacher time, severity of behavior problem, and type of intervention. *Behavioral Disorders, 10,* 95–104.

Peers Assessing Peers:
Possibilities and Problems

Angela M. O'Donnell
Rutgers University
Keith Topping
University of Dundee

It is midmorning on Friday in an elementary school classroom. The teacher dictates the last word in the regular weekly 20-item class oral spelling test. She has each child exchange his or her test paper with a partner. Then as she writes the correct spellings on the board, each child checks his or her partner's written attempts with the master version and marks it right or wrong. Finally, a score out of 20 is given and the papers are returned to their originators—many of whom double-check to make sure they have not gotten a raw deal. The teacher is cleverly maximizing student attention and time on-task, while saving herself some very tedious work.

Meanwhile, in a high school English class, *peer writing response groups* of three or four students are gathered. Each student has already read the draft written composition of every other group member. Now the students take turns giving qualitative verbal feedback to each writer. They have had prior class discussions about the complexities of establishing criteria for good and bad writing, so they are not surprised that there is some consistency and some disagreement in the group feedback. Each writer will subsequently reflect independently about how his or her writing can be improved and will revise his or her paper before turning it in to the teacher.

In both scenarios, peer assessment is operating—although neither teacher really thought to call it that before. Peer assessment is not a new idea. For example, George Jardine, a professor at the University of Glasgow from 1774 to 1826, described a pedagogical plan including methods, rules, and advantages of peer assessment of writing (Gaillet, 1992).

DEFINITION OF PEER ASSESSMENT

As noted in chap. 1, *assessment* is the determination of the amount, level, value, or worth of something. *Peer assessment* is an arrangement for peers to consider the level, value or worth of the work of their equal-status peers. Peer assessment focuses on the products or outcomes of learning, and should not be confused with *peer monitoring,* which is about peers keeping an eye on whether their partners are employing appropriate and effective processes and procedures of learning—effective study behaviors (see chap. 13, this volume). Peer assessment considers products or outputs of learning, whereas peer monitoring considers processes or procedures. However, in everyday practice, the distinction sometimes becomes blurred. Clearly, effective processes will most likely result in good products. The thoughtful and constructive assessment of products will most likely influence subsequent processes.

Peers often react to and evaluate the ephemeral products (Smith, 1993) generated during peer interaction, such as orally stated plans. Ephemeral products are ones that are generated during interaction and are not likely to be preserved in the records of the group. Examples of such products include verbal statements, brief personal notes, or demonstrations to illustrate a point. When products are intangible, assessment depends on memory of the event and is subject to error. However, the focus of this chapter is on peer reaction to tangible products involving some concrete records (Smith, 1993) that are observable by the peers involved. Tangible products from group interaction (such as a list of ideas, paper, outlines) are easier for members of an interacting group to inspect and reconsider or alter. Peer response groups in writing classrooms are illustrative of this sense of peer assessment.

WHY USE PEER ASSESSMENT?

When peers interact with the purpose of assessing one another's work, the expectation is that the quality of the work of all concerned will often improve as a result of the thinking involved and feedback provided. Students may also improve their own skills in critiquing or evaluating their own work (self-assessment) as a result of their interactions during peer assessment (Towler & Broadfoot, 1992). They may acquire new strategies for task performance or fine-tune existing strategies. Also, the practice of regulating the activities of others by commenting on the quality of peers' work may help students internalize techniques for self-regulation (Zimmerman, 1990; Zimmerman, Greenberg, & Weinstein, 1994). Students who engage in self-regulation set goals, decide on strategies for goal accomplishment, monitor progress toward those goals, and evaluate the outcomes of their efforts (Butler & Winne, 1995). When students assess the work of others, they have the opportunity and need to make these processes explicit. The potential benefits of peer assessment are explored in more detail later.

TYPES OF PEER ASSESSMENT

Peer assessment activities can vary in a number of ways. Peer assessment can operate in different curriculum areas or subjects. The product or output to be assessed can vary—writing, portfolios, oral statements, test performance, or other skilled behaviors. The peer assessment can be summative (judging a final product to be correct–incorrect, accept–reject, or assigning some quantitative mark or grade to the output by criterion matching). Alternatively, it can be formative (involving detailed qualitative feedback about better and worse aspects, with implications for making improvements to the current or subsequent products). The participant constellation can vary—the assessors may be individuals or pairs or groups; the assessed may be individuals or pairs or groups. Directionality can vary—peer assessment can be one-way, reciprocal, or mutual. Assessors and assessed may come from the same or different year of study, and be of the same or different ability. Place and time can vary—most peer assessment is formal and in class, but it can occur informally out of class. The objectives for the exercise may vary—the teacher may target cognitive or metacognitive gains, time saving, or other goals.

Chapter Overview

In this chapter, we already considered a definition and typology of peer assessment. The potential benefits of peer assessment are now reviewed. This is followed by discussion of common concerns about peer assessment, particularly regarding reliability and validity, the influence of purpose, and the distinction between summative and formative assessment. The importance of feedback in peer assessment and the cognitive and social demands of participation are described. Methodology and research on peer assessment of writing is discussed in relation to peer editing and peer response groups. Portfolio peer assessment is then considered. Other types of peer assessment are then discussed, including through marks, grades, and tests, and peer assessment in the group work or project setting. Important parameters in the organization of peer assessment are then listed. The conclusion is followed by a more detailed case study of peer assessment of writing.

THE BENEFITS OF PEER ASSESSMENT

Many theoretical approaches to peer learning are available that propose varied mechanisms for how peer learning benefits participants in group interaction (O'Donnell & O'Kelly, 1994; Slavin, 1992). A common theme in many of the approaches is the notion that peers can enhance the conceptual development of their partners, promoting a more student centered classroom (Stiggins, 1994). Assessment by peers can promote more active processing and result in elaborated or altered cognitive structures.

As professional teachers are well aware, carrying out assessment is a complex activity requiring a great deal of planning. Teachers must know what their learning goals are and then be able to assess students' work to determine if those learning goals have been accomplished. The cognitive challenge and development for peers in assessing others might operate particularly through gains in some of the following mechanisms and activities (see chap. 1, this volume):

> Time on-task, engagement, and practice
> Accountability, responsibility
> Questioning—Intelligent and adaptive
> Self-disclosure and thus assessment of understanding
> Error identification and analysis
> Diagnosis of misconception
> Identification of gaps and engineering closure
> Explaining
> Simplification, clarification, summarizing, and reorganization
> Cognitive restructuring
> Increased feedback—Corrective, confirmatory, suggestive
>   immediacy, timeliness, individualization of feedback
> Practice, fluency—Speed of response
> Post hoc reflection
> Generalization to new situations
> Self-assessment
> Metacognitive self-awareness

The key task for a teacher is to provide conditions under which these processes are likely to occur.

CONCERNS ABOUT PEER ASSESSMENT

The research on peer learning with respect to academic achievement provides strong support for a variety of methods of peer learning, including cooperative learning (Johnson & Johnson, 1989), collaborative learning

(Brown & Campione, 1995), and peer tutoring (Cohen, Kulik, & Kulik, 1982; Greenwood, 1991; see chap. 6, this volume; Fantuzzo, King, & Heller, 1992; see chap. 7, this volume). Although these various methods show achievement benefits, the mechanisms by which these techniques accomplish these goals differ (O'Donnell, in press). In contrast to the vast literature on the use of peers for directly promoting achievement, the literature on the use of peers for assessment is quite sparse. Why, if peer interaction can facilitate so many positive outcomes in and out of classrooms, do we not use it use more in the assessment process?

Reliability and Validity

The reliability and validity of peer assessments is a key concern for instructors who wish to use the method. If students' assessments of their peers are part of the grading practices, any inconsistency raises questions of fairness. Research findings on the reliability of peer assessments mostly emanate from studies of peer assessment between students in colleges and universities. A majority of such studies found adequate reliability, and a minority found it variable (Topping, 1998). Findings generated in university or college settings may not apply in other contexts. However, a number of other studies have found quite encouraging consistency between peer and teacher assessments in the school setting itself (Karegianes, Pascarella, & Pflaum, 1980; Lagana, 1972; MacArthur, Schwartz, & Graham, 1991; Pierson, 1967; Weeks & White, 1982).

Contradictory findings might be explained in part by differences in the outcomes being evaluated, the contingencies associated with those outcomes, the training, and the support provided for assessment in the form of checklists or other rating guides. The use of checklists or rating guides helps students understand the teacher's criteria, and the reliability of assessments can be greatly improved by the clear articulation of criteria for success. Generally, student assessments are less reliable when judgment of the quality of the outcome is more subjective or unsupported by teacher assistance or checklists (e.g., Pond, Ul-Haq, & Wade, 1995, in the college setting). Many teachers provide such checklists or response sheets, but beyond this, discussion, negotiation, and joint construction of assessment criteria with the class is likely to deepen understanding and give a greater sense of ownership. In a study with undergraduates, Pond et al. (1995) showed that students were more satisfied with a peer review process when they had an opportunity to participate in developing the criteria for assessment. Students at the high school level also understand criteria for grading better when they participate in developing those criteria and selecting examples that illustrate stronger and weaker examples (Lawrence, 1996).

The Influence of Purpose

All forms of assessment should be fit for their purpose, and the purpose of the peer assessment is a key element in determining its validity and/or reliability. The purposes of assessments influence many facets of student performance including anxiety (Wolfe & Smith, 1995), goal orientation (Dweck, 1986), and perceived controllability (Rocklin, O'Donnell, & Holst, 1995). The influence of purpose on peer assessment can be seen in a number of studies conducted in the university or workplace setting (Bernadin & Beatty, 1984; Farh, Cannella, & Bedeian, 1991; Fedor & Bettenhausen, 1989). Farh et al. (1991) informed some subjects that their ratings would be used to provide developmental feedback to team members but would not be used for grading purposes, whereas other participants were informed that their ratings of their peers would be used to make adjustments to grades. Participants rated their peers on a number of dimensions after working with them on a project. Farh et al. (1991) found that students were more lenient in assigning ratings to peers when the ratings were to be used for grading purposes than when ratings were to be used to improve performance. Peer assessments under such conditions do not yield information that is useful in improving performance.

Summative Assessment

Summative assessments are intended to evaluate the level of accomplishment attained by students after a period of instruction. Typically, summative assessments rely on traditional measures such as multiple-choice tests or set essays or reports. The feedback is likely to be categorical or quantitative—certainly simplistic. Concerns about the objectivity of the evaluator are higher when assessment is summative and consequences follow from judgments of accomplishments. However, it is worth distinguishing summative assessment by multiple-choice or other structured tests where a master version is available to the assessor from those situations where the peer assessor is asked to give a quantitative mark or grade to a piece of work (e.g., writing) where there is no single correct response. Clearly, the latter is much less safe, as well as not particularly helpful to the assessed peer. Additionally, students' intrinsic motivation may be undermined by an excessive focus on grades and concerns about the quality of assessment may be heightened thereby.

The assessment of students' work is usually the sole province of the teacher in the classroom. Many teachers successfully involve students collaboratively in the task of learning and thereby relinquish some of the control of classroom content and management (Brown & Campione, 1995; Scardamalia, Bereiter, & Lamon, 1995). However, many fewer teachers relinquish authority over the assignment of grades in the "unsafe" situation previously described. Teachers are also often reluctant to use group grades in which students risk being penalized by the failure of their peers to perform or being excessively rewarded by peer contributions to work. Parental influence on such decisions is significant. Involving students in assigning formal grades for anything other than structured tests with fixed criteria of correctness is unlikely to become widespread in schools, although it has been done and actually researched in colleges and universities. However, formative peer assessment holds greater promise, especially when coupled with nontraditional approaches such as portfolio assessment.

Formative Assessment

An alternative purpose of assessment is to inform or redirect instruction or effort and assist with more appropriate linking of content and outcomes. Formative assessments can provide much more qualitative detail about which content requires further explanation, consolidation, and development, not merely indicating the number of errors but indicating where they are, of what type and thereby cueing thoughts about ways in which they might be remediated. Many informal assessments that occur in response to homework or in-class activities are formative in nature, and peers can assist with much of this. In formative assessment, the role of feedback is obviously central.

The Role of Feedback

The role of feedback in learning has received a great deal of attention because the conditions under which it is effective are enormously complex (Bangert-Drowns, Kulik, Kulik, & Morgan, 1991; Butler & Winne, 1995; Kulhavy & Stock, 1989). Feedback can correct errors and seems to have potent effects on learning when a student receives it thoughtfully and positively (Bangert-Drowns et al., 1991; see chap. 1, this volume). Feedback is essential to the development and execution of self-regulatory skills (Paris & Newman, 1990). Butler and Winne (1995) frame their analysis of the utility of feedback within a model of self-regulated learning. Having set

goals for themselves, students identify strategies or tactics that are expected
to help them achieve the goals, monitor progress toward those goals, and
adjust their strategies or even their goals based on self-generated or externally provided feedback.

Feedback (either internal or external) serves five functions (Butler &
Winne, 1995). These functions are as follows:

1. Feedback can confirm that a student's understanding of what a task required
   was correct.
2. Feedback can help students to add information to their knowledge when they
   experience an information gap.
3. If elements of previously held information are incorrect, feedback can help
   to replace the erroneous information with more accurate information.
4. Even when students have correct information, the provision of feedback can
   help them learn when to apply their knowledge.
5. If students hold false theories that are incompatible with new information,
   the availability of feedback can help students to restructure their schemata.

Students react differently to feedback from peers and from adults (Bush
& Dweck, 1976; Cole, 1991; Henry, 1979). Bush and Dweck used peer and
adult evaluators to examine gender differences in the responses of 108 fifth
graders to failure feedback. Performance in boys improved with feedback
from adult agents but did not change with peer feedback. Performance in
girls improved with peer feedback but showed little improvement with adult
feedback. By contrast, Henry (1979) had first graders praised for successful
performance by a boy and girl or a man and woman. Boys were most
responsive to peer feedback and girls to adult feedback.

Peer assessment can indeed serve the functions described by Butler and
Winne (1995). Of course, peer feedback might be of poorer quality than that
provided by the teacher. However, peer feedback is usually available in
greater volume and with greater immediacy than teacher feedback, which
might compensate for any quality disadvantage. Peer assessment can contribute to such facilitation of learning by prompting the articulation of goals
and the explicit judgments of progress toward the accomplishment of those
goals. Such processes may promote cognitive restructuring.

Cognitive Demands

Providing effective feedback or assessment is a cognitively complex task
requiring understanding of the goals of the task and the criteria for success,

together with the ability to make judgments about the relationship of the product to both of these. The feedback should assist future performance. However, the efficacy of feedback depends on both the giver and the receiver.

Although help-giving and feedback are not identical constructs, many of the conditions under which they are effective are similar. Webb (1989) noted that the following conditions must be met for help to be effective:

1. The help given must be relevant to the particular misunderstanding or lack of understanding of the help-seeker.
2. The help given must be delivered at a level of elaboration that is appropriate to the level of help needed.
3. Help should be given in a timely manner and in close proximity to when it is needed.
4. The help-seeker must understand the help given.
5. The help-seeker must have an opportunity to act on the help given.
6. The help-seeker must be motivated to act on the help given.

Providing effective help requires sophisticated social and metacognitive skills. Furthermore, the benefits of help giving depend greatly on the help-seeker's willingness and ability to profit from help.

Webb and Farivar (1994, in press) provided further clarification of the relationships between help-giving, help-receiving, and achievement. Students in need of help must be able to receive elaborated explanations and must engage in constructive activity in the wake of such explanations. Students might require a great deal of assistance in learning how to give elaborated explanations and in learning how to benefit from them (Webb & Farivar, 1994, in press). Feedback is filtered by a learner's belief system and understanding of the goals of the task (Butler & Winne, 1995). As Webb (1989) pointed out, the learner must be able to see the feedback as relevant to his or her understanding of the goals of the task or must be able to accept an alternative interpretation of task goals.

Social Demands

Any group can suffer from negative social processes (Salomon & Globerson, 1989) such as social loafing, free rider effects, diffusion of responsibility, and interaction disabilities (Cohen, 1982). When peers are placed in the role of evaluator of the work of their peers, social processes might influence the reliability and validity of the assessments. Pond et al. (1995)

suggested a number of ways in which peer assessment can be contaminated by social processes. *Friendship grading* can occur when students assign high grades to peers as a consequence of friendship. Peers are often reluctant to criticize their peers where this could be perceived as constituting or inviting social rejection. *Collusive grading* results in a lack of differentiation between peers, especially likely with high stakes assessment. *Decibel grading* is when the most active students are awarded the highest scores. Additionally, the extent to which the teacher is directly monitoring the peer feedback is likely to affect its nature and quality. Thus, although there are significant benefits to be derived from peer involvement in assessment, care must be taken to limit the possibility of negative social influences and keep complexity within manageable limits. One area in which peer assessment is used widely is in the writing classroom.

PEER ASSESSMENT IN WRITING

Peer involvement in the writing process is a commonly accepted practice. A variety of studies have demonstrated the benefits of peer involvement in the development of writing skills, in both school and higher education settings (Brufee, 1984; George, 1984; Higgins, Flower, & Petraglia, 1992; Lynch & Golen, 1992; O'Donnell, Larson, Dansereau, & Rocklin, 1986). The involvement of peers in the writing process can result in improved attitudes toward writing (Benson, 1979; Cheatham & Jordan, 1979; Katstra, Tollefson, & Gilbert, 1987). Peers can be used to support many aspects of the writing process, including planning (Higgins, Flower, & Petraglia, 1992), editing (Bissland, 1980), revision (Benson, 1979), and cowriting (O'Donnell et al., 1985). Peer assessment in the form of peer response groups or as a component of peer editing is particularly common (Weaver, 1995).

There is some evidence for the effectiveness of peer editing. Bouton and Tutty (1975) reported one of the few studies of the effects of peer assessment of writing by itself, in this case with high school students. No details of training were given and a narrow spectrum of aspects of writing was assessed, highly focused on grammar. The experimental group did better than the control group in a number of areas. The effects of a computer spelling checker and peer assessment on fourth-grade students' editing, spelling, and writing performance were compared by Dalton (1991). After 6 weeks, the spell check group produced more accurately edited texts than the peer-edit group, but students tended to rely on the spelling checker to detect all their errors. Because the spelling checker missed errors frequently generated by young writers, only 45% of their errors were actually corrected. Both peer-edit and spell-check students preferred peer editing to self-editing.

Peer assessment of writing is also used with classes studying English as a second language (ESL) and foreign languages. Samway (1993) described the evaluation criteria that ESL children in Grades 2 to 6 naturalistically employed (without training) when evaluating writing. The students were critical evaluators, tended to focus on meaning regardless of their age, but were highly idiosyncratic in the range of evaluation criteria that they employed.

Peer Editing

Peer editing includes formative peer assessment, but goes beyond it—the assessor making specific recommendations for improvement, coupling assessment with intervention. There are a number of studies of peer editing in which a peer assessment component was included, but the contribution of that component to the overall success of the program is rarely partialed out.

The early work of Karegianes et al. (1980) examined the effects of peer editing on the writing proficiency of 49 low-achieving 10th-grade students. The peer-edit group had significantly higher writing proficiency than did students whose essays were edited by teachers. In a well-controlled study, Weeks and White (1982) compared groups of Grade 4 and 6 students in peer editing and teacher editing conditions. The results showed that differences were not significant, but the peer assessment group did show more improvement in mechanics and in the overall fluency of writing. Raphael (1986) gathered data from 159 fifth- and sixth-grade students and their teachers, comparing peer editing and teacher instruction. Similar improvements in composition ability resulted from both conditions. Califano (1987) made a similar comparison in classes of fifth and sixth graders. Again, no significant differences were found in the writing ability or in the attitudes toward writing of the teacher editing group and the peer editing group. Both groups of students improved their writing performance.

In a higher education setting, O'Donnell et al. (1986) showed that peers who edited instructions written by a peer improved the quality of the work and also wrote better instructions themselves on a subsequent task. This research showed that students could improve the quality of their peer's work and also derive personal benefit from the activity that carried over to another, individually performed writing task. Cover (1987) investigated peer editing with seventh graders, finding a statistically significant improvement in editing skills and students' attitudes toward writing. Wade (1988) combined peer feedback with peer tutoring for 17 sixth-grade students. Results clearly demonstrated that the experimental package improved the students' writing. After training, the children could provide reliable and correct feedback. By this time, peer editing was becoming commonplace, as indicated by the article title: "When the Principal Asks: 'Why Aren't You Using Peer Editing?'" (Harp, 1988).

Variations in procedure and applications became more adventurous (Leibnitz, 1989). Holley (1990) focused on peer editing of grammatical errors with Grade 12 high school students in Alabama, resulting in a reduction in such errors and greater student interest and awareness. Mac-Arthur, Schwartz, and Graham (1991) used peer editing in grades 4 to 6 in special education classrooms. Peer support proved more effective than regular teacher instruction only. Stoddard and MacArthur (1993) then demonstrated the effectiveness of peer editing with seventh- and eighth-grade students with learning disabilities. The quality of writing increased substantially from pretests to posttests, and the gains were maintained at follow-up and generalized to other written work. Byrd (1994) reported applications of peer editing in the foreign language classroom. It seems clear that students' writing improves as a result of responses to initial drafts of papers (Newell, 1994).

Peer Response Groups

Broadly defined, a *peer response group* is a group of students gathered together for the purpose of providing feedback on one another's work. Response groups are intended to foster collaborative thinking. Peer response groups allow students to check their perception of the task and strengthen their social skills. They also help students improve their writing by enhancing their motivation for revision and developing an awareness of audience (McManus & Kirby, 1988; Shriver, 1992; Zhu, 1995).

Typically, peer response groups engage in directed exercises that focus on revision. Brufee's (1985) exercises are dialogic in structure and involve increasing the complexity and sophistication of the critic's task in a peer response group as a semester progresses. This spiraling toward complexity works with many cognitive skills such as developing question-asking skills by young students (King, in press). An alternative method for directing peer response groups is provided by Elbow and Belanoff (1989). The exercises provided by Elbow and Belanoff focused on more specific actions such as identifying what is *almost* said. The techniques proposed by Brufee (1985) and Elbow and Belanoff (1989) provide support for the student assessors as they learn how to become good responders. Response groups provide the writer with an audience who provide immediate feedback, which clarifies

audience or writing goals. A key element of effective writing is the antici-
pation of reader's needs (Shriver, 1992) and peer response groups can
effectively communicate about readers' needs.

DiPardo and Freedman (1988) and Weaver (1995) noted the overwhelm-
ing acceptance of response groups in the writing classroom. Despite this,
there are relatively few actual studies of the effects. Gere and Abbot (1985)
analyzed the quality of talk in response groups whose members were directed
to read drafts aloud twice, with others in the group listening the first time,
taking notes on the second hearing, and then providing an oral response. The
results of the study showed that students did stay on-task and provided
content-related feedback. Younger students spent more time on content than
did older students, who attended more to the form of the writing. Nystrand
and Brandt (1989) found response groups very effective in the college
setting. In contrast, Newkirk (1984a, 1984b) described college students'
responses as lacking in many important respects. He suggested that students
were unwilling to be critical of their peers and often made inferences to fill
in the communicative gaps in their group members' writing.

Freedman (1992) analyzed response groups in two ninth-grade classrooms, in which the teachers deployed response groups in writing in quite
different ways and embedded in distinct instructional practices. She also
concluded that students in both classes suppressed negative assessments of
their peers. Peers in one of the classes almost never responded to requests
for help. The effects of revision instruction and peer response groups on the
writing of 93 sixth-grade students was compared by Olson (1986, 1990).
Students receiving instruction that included both teacher revision and peer
assessment wrote rough and final drafts that were significantly superior to
those of students who received instruction in revision only, while peer
assessment only students wrote final drafts significantly superior to revision
instruction only students. Rijlaarsdam (1987) and Rijlaarsdam and
Schoonen (1988) made similar comparisons with 561 ninth-grade students
in eight different schools. Teacher instruction and peer assessment proved
equally effective.

Practitioners are often enthusiastic about peer response groups but students do not necessarily share those reactions (Jacobs, 1987; Weaver, 1995),
and cultural and local differences can be expected. Weaver (1995) summarized the reactions of instructors and students to peer response groups as
reported by Freedman (1987). More than 500 instructors were surveyed
about peer response groups in writing. Regardless of the stage in the writing
process (early vs. late), instructors generally found peer responses to be

more helpful than the teacher's and used response groups relatively often. In contrast, students stated they found the teacher's responses to be more helpful in all stages of writing. Nevertheless, when students could seek peer responses at the Writing Center rather than in class, their writing improved (Weaver, 1995). Student acceptability clearly needs to be cultivated.

Most teachers of writing provided peer assessors with some sort of checklist or other predesigned instrument to guide their assessments. Although improving reliability and consistency, these instruments can have the effect of limiting student discourse through overdependency (Freedman, 1992). A number of researchers have suggested ways in which to promote better levels of feedback in groups without necessarily relying on written guidelines (e.g., Stanley, 1992). Benesch (1984) suggested that teachers can model the provision of effective feedback in their own practices as they respond to students' papers. In addition, they can monitor peer feedback by taping discussions in peer groups, feeding this back to the students and redirecting them as appropriate. There is evidence from higher education that teacher modeling and feedback to moderate and develop peer feedback is an effective training and maintenance procedure (Zhu, 1995).

A descriptive case study of peer response groups in action can be found as an appendix to this chapter.

PORTFOLIO PEER ASSESSMENT

The introduction of new forms of assessment in classrooms may provide an opportunity to involve peers more purposefully. These new forms of assessment (e.g., portfolios, exhibits) combine elements of both formative and summative assessment. Portfolio assessments provide an assessment of a student's work over a period of time in a content area. This feature of the assessment allows an evaluator to sample more than immediate performance. A *portfolio* is "a purposeful collection of student work that exhibits the student's efforts, progress, or achievement in one or more areas. The collection must include student participation in selecting contents, the criteria for judging merit, and evidence of the student's self reflection" (Paulson, Paulson, & Meyer, 1991, p. 60).

A student must be able to judge the quality of their own work in order to develop an effective portfolio. They must also be able to recognize gradations of performance quality and be able to comment on how and why improvement was or might be made (Hebert, 1992; Wilson, 1985). Students need a lot of help in learning how to evaluate their own work in this way, as such assessments place heavy demands on metacognitive skills.

Tierney, Carter, and Desai (1991) saw an important function for a portfolio in promoting self-assessment. They identified four prerequisites that must be in place for such self-assessment to occur: (a) student ownership, (b) student centeredness, (c) a noncompetitive environment, and (d) the ability to customize portfolios to fit the purposes of the class. One of the key elements of the process of maintaining a portfolio is to develop criteria for what should be included. Discussions about what counts among students can be very enlightening. Often students feel that assessment is something that is "done to them" (Tierney et al., 1991) and participating in the description of what a portfolio should include gives students a chance to understand the goals of the assessment and better direct their performance toward those goals (Reeve, 1996).

The symbiotic linkage between peer assessment and self assessment is clearly relevant here. Peer assessment of portfolios provides opportunities to engage in all of the five functions of feedback described by Butler and Winne (1995). The tangible nature of the products included in a portfolio make it possible for students to compare products and to evaluate development of skill. Students in one fourth grade class were confused when asked to select the "best" work (J. O'Kelly, personal communication, May 16, 1996). Because they had not experienced being in control of the criteria for success, they were unable to respond effectively. The task was reframed to them as "pick a paper that you liked and one that you didn't like." Given this second task, students were able to respond. Collaboration among students allows for the generation of multiple ideas about how to proceed with the task.

OTHER KINDS OF PEER ASSESSMENT

Despite the traditional example first presented here, any formative effects of peer assessment through the use of marks, grades, and tests appears to have received very little attention in the research literature. Thompson (1981) and Parris (1989) reported systems for peer grading of written compositions, but this is of little interest in schools, although common in higher education. McCurdy and Shapiro (1992) deployed peers to undertake curriculum-based measurement in reading among 48 elementary students with learning disabilities, comparing with teacher- and self-assessment. It was found that students in the self- and peer conditions could collect reliable data on the number of correct words per minute. No significant differences were found between conditions. This study hovers on the borderline between peer monitoring and peer assessment (see chap. 13, this volume).

A number of studies in the higher education setting have explored peer assessment as a device for clarifying proportionate individual contributions to group projects receiving group grades, but (perhaps surprisingly) there are few such studies in schools. Relatedly, Salend, Whittaker, and Reeder (1993) examined the efficacy of a consensus-based group-evaluation system with students with disabilities. The system involved (a) dividing the groups into teams (b) having each team agree on a common rating for the group's behavior during a specified time period (c) comparing each team's rating to the teacher's rating and (d) delivering reinforcement to each team based on the group's behavior and the team's accuracy in rating the group's behavior. Results indicated that the system was an effective strategy for modifying behavior. Ross (1995) explored the effects of audiotaped feedback with interpretation training on student behaviors in cooperative learning groups in a seventh-grade math class. Increases in the frequency and quality of help seeking and help giving and improved students' attitudes about asking for help resulted. Effective peer assessment of assertion skills in female adolescents was reported by Tillmann (1981).

In higher education, the beginnings of computer-assisted peer assessment are evident (Topping, 1998), but this is not yet reported in schools, although peer-assisted computer assessment has already arrived. Distance peer assessment through the Internet is already happening in universities, although not yet researched in schools. There are many possible novel applications of peer assessment awaiting exploration by enthusiastic practitioners.

ORGANIZATIONAL COMPONENTS OF PEER ASSESSMENT

The organization of peer assessment will obviously vary according to the type to be used (see typology discussed previously) and in particular the type of product or output to be assessed. Organizational issues are subsumed here under the headings objectives, criteria, matching and constellation, training, activity, monitoring, moderation, onward action, and evaluation.

Objectives. Those considering introducing peer assessment need to prepare the ground by fostering a collaborative ethos among the students and clearly explicating purposes or objectives, to clarify expectations. Acceptance of peer assessment is better if results are used for developmental rather than administrative purposes, ownership is seen to lie with the peer group, and detailed feedback is not directly accessed by authority figures. In any event, the objectives of the initiative should be considered thoroughly, and the professionals should seek to empathize with the likely objectives of the students, which may be very different from their own.

Criteria. Clarification of the assessment criteria for all concerned is essential, and student involvement in their development, elaboration, or simplification is generally accepted as highly desirable. Consideration also needs to be given to written guidance and visual prompts to remind the assessors. The nature of the criteria will of course vary greatly according to the curricular output to be assessed and the objectives of the exercise. Behaviorally defined, criterion-referenced performance dimensions are likely to better accepted by students, who may well dislike ratings without meaningful scales and generalized ratings directly comparing them to others. Consideration should be given to providing model answers where appropriate. Teachers must be alert to the possibility of students' using written criteria and pro formas very rigidly and procedurally, limiting the quality of discourse in the group and providing feedback that is rather sterile.

Matching and Constellation. Teachers should reflect on how peer assessors and the students they will assess should be matched, and in what size of group or other social constellation peer assessment should optimally occur. Information on this topic is rarely seen in the literature. It might imply matching students with peer assessors they find credible, or with whom they already had a friendly relationship. However, other workers have randomly allocated work to be assessed to peer assessors. Contact between assessor and assessed is not essential, as feedback does not have to be verbal and face to face—but most workers assume that this format will yield the greatest benefits.

Training. The availability of clear assessment criteria does not guarantee their successful application, which requires transfer from knowledge to skill. Providing effective assessment to a peer requires a complex battery of cognitive, metacognitive, and social skills. The evaluator must understand the goals of the task, recognize progress toward the goal, judge the potential efficacy of addressing gaps in knowledge or strategy in attaining that goal, and be sensitive to the person to whom feedback is given. Students do not perform this evaluative function well without support from their teachers. Training for participants will be needed in objectives, general organization, developing and using criteria and any associated materials, giving and receiving positive and negative feedback, action in response to feedback, arrangements for evaluation, and so on. Thereafter, continuous teacher modeling of the necessary features of effective feedback will be important.

Activity.   Especially initially, participants need a clear explanation and demonstration of exactly what they have to do. What, with whom, where, when, with what materials, and why are the key questions needing an answer—not necessarily in that order. Designating regular routine peer editing days or sessions might be helpful, involving specific tasks and questions for peer assessors to use that build on previous work in class and on previous peer sessions. Also recommended is a set time limit and having peer assessors give both verbal and written feedback. It is important that teachers are specific about how to give feedback about errors or flaws, as this is the point of greatest socioemotional challenge. Should the assessor indicate that an error has been made, where it has been made, and/or what type of error has been made? Should the assessor then go on to prompt their assessed partner to offer alternatives, and comment on those alternatives, or not? Should the assessor ever give their partner the right answer—or what they might think is the right answer?

Monitoring.   Professional staff should monitor the peer assessment activity while it is in process if at all possible, especially when the participants are inexperienced. There is no guarantee they will be doing what they have been trained to do, and further coaching and/or troubleshooting is likely to be necessary for at least some. A critical variable requiring close monitoring is the extent to which student errors are actually noticed by the assessor, let alone corrected correctly. This can be a special concern in ESL or special education classes. Teachers should look out for absent or faulty correction of grammatical errors, reinforcement of errors by peers, and the opportunity for cheating and plagiarism. Teachers might want to consider monitoring on a sampling basis (see chap. 13, this volume) or even audio or video recording of some sessions. However, they should not underestimate the potential of the peer group itself. They may appoint a particularly capable peer as assistant monitor, but in any event, students will probably learn a good deal from each other spontaneously.

Moderation.   Running checks on the reliability and validity of the peer assessments need to be arranged, even if only on a sample. Some teachers assess the peer assessments and give feedback on them to the assessors.

Onward Action.   Students should be clear about whether formative feedback is expected to impact their next effort or whether they should rework their current effort.

Evaluation.   Issues of reliability and validity of peer assessment are part of the evaluation of the procedure. Teachers might wish to include a peer assessor self-assessment component. Subjective feedback about student attitudes can be gathered verbally or via questionnaire. If one of the objectives was to increase achievement in both peer assessors and those assessed, consider how this can be measured objectively, and perhaps compared to the progress of a parallel or previous group.

CONCLUSIONS

The research evidence on the effectiveness of peer assessment in writing is substantial, particularly in the context of peer editing, and to a lesser extent in the context of peer response groups. Peer assessment seems to be at least as effective in formative terms as teacher assessment, and sometimes is more effective. Extension into portfolio assessment looks very promising. The research on peer assessment of other products of learning is as yet sparse, but merits exploration by innovative practitioners.

Teachers and students can derive great instructional benefits from the use of peer assessment in the classroom. However, there are caveats—this can be affected by the purpose, type, structure, and acceptability of the peer assessment procedures in relation to the specific target group of students. Furthermore, students need preparation in how to assess effectively. A combination of discussion and negotiation of assessment criteria, teacher modeling of feedback, and written prompts can be most effective in supporting student acquisition of the skills necessary to be a good assessor.

APPENDIX: CASE STUDY IN PEER ASSESSMENT OF WRITING

Johannessen (1995) described how to conduct a peer response group on descriptive writing and support students' evaluation of papers, responses to them, and revision activity. The teaching objective is to improve the quality of the students' descriptive writing. The students are assigned to small groups and provided with four to five stories that represent a range of quality, written by another group. (Students are more willing to be honest in their criticism when they know that the writer of a paper under review is not in the group.) To help students engage in evaluation, they are also provided with an evaluation sheet. Johannessen (1995) referred to this as "criterion-guided evaluation." Because he anticipated student difficulty in developing appropriate criteria unaided, he used an evaluation sheet with somewhat open-ended questions to guide the students' discussion of the papers. The evaluation sheet asks the students to identify which paper they think is best in describing a place or event so that the reader can see, feel, and hear what is being described. The students are then asked which paper is weakest. They are asked to identify which details in the best story make it interesting, and what overall impression is created. Finally, they are asked how to make it better.

Having the students comment on the best and weakest papers helps them to identify anchor points for other judgments. They identify which details included in the best story make the story interesting or memorable. They are asked to look for similar details in the paper they think is weakest. They explicitly compare and contrast the two papers and identify differences between them. Then they are asked to comment on the middle papers and compare them to the best and worst ones they have already identified. The students complete the evaluation sheets in groups, one sheet per group. They engage in very lively and animated discussion about which story or paper is best or worst. Once students have come to consensus about the best and worst papers, they then analyze the middle ones. Finally, students generate ideas about how to revise one of the papers and actually do so.

REFERENCES

Bangert-Drowns, R. L., Kulik, J. A., Kulik, C. C., & Morgan, M. (1991). The instructional effects of feedback in test-like events. *Review of Educational Research, 61,* 213–238.
Benesch, S. (1984, March). *Improving peer response: Collaboration between teachers and students.* Paper presented at the 35th annual meeting of the Conference on College Composition and Communication, New York, NY.
Benson, N. L. (1979). *The effects of peer feedback during the writing process on writing performance, revision behavior, and attitude toward writing.* Dissertation Abstracts International, *40*(4), 1987.
Bernadin, H. J., & Beatty, R. W. (1984). *Performance appraisal: Assessing human behavior at work.* Belmont, CA: Wadsworth.
Bissland, J. H. (1980). Peer evaluation method promotes sharper writing. *Journalism Educator, 34*(4), 17–19.
Bouton, K., & Tutty, G. (1975). The effect of peer-evaluated student compositions on writing improvement. *The English Record 3,* 64–69.
Brown, A. L., & Campione, J. C. (1995). Guided discovery in a community of learners. In K. McGilley (Ed.), *Classroom lessons: Integrating cognitive theory* (pp. 229–270). Cambridge, MA: MIT Press.
Brufee, K. A. (1984). Peer tutoring and the "conversation of mankind." *College English, 46,* 635–652.
Brufee, K. A. (1985). *A short course in writing: Practical rhetoric for teaching composition through collaborative learning* (3rd ed.). Boston, MA: Little.
Bush, E.S., & Dweck, C. S. (1976). Sex differences in learned helplessness: Differential debilitation with peer and adult evaluators. *Developmental Psychology 12*(2), 147–156.

Butler, D. L., & Winne, P. H. (1995). Feedback and self-regulated learning: A theoretical synthesis. *Review of Educational Research, 65,* 245–281.

Byrd, D. R. (1994). Peer editing: Common concerns and applications in the foreign language classroom. *Unterrichtspraxis 27*(1), 119.

Califano, L. Z. (1987). *Teacher and peer editing: Their effects on students' writing as measured by t-unit length, holistic scoring, and the attitudes of fifth and sixth grade students.* Dissertation Abstracts International, *49*(10), 2924.

Cheatham, T. R., & Jordan, W. J. (1979). Influence of peer evaluations on student attitudes and achievement. *Improving College and University Teaching, 27*(4), 174–177.

Cohen, E. G. (1982). Expectation states and interracial interaction in school settings. *Annual Review of Sociology, 8,* 209–235.

Cohen, P. A., Kulik, J. A., & Kulik, C. C. (1982). Educational outcomes of tutoring: A meta-analysis of findings. *American Educational Research Journal, 19,* 237–248.

Cole, D. A. (1991). Change in self-perceived competence as a function of peer and teacher evaluation. *Developmental Psychology, 27*(4), 682–688.

Cover, B. T. L. (1987): *Blue-pencil workers: The effects of a peer editing technique on students' editing skills and attitudes toward writing at the seventh grade level.* Dissertation Abstracts International. *48*(8), 1968.

Dalton, B. M. (1991). *Writing and technology: The effect of a computer spelling checker versus peer editor on fourth-grade students' editing, spelling and writing performance.* Dissertation Abstracts International. *52*(6), 2053.

DiPardo, A. M., & Freedman, S. W. (1988). Peer response groups in the writing classroom. *Review of Educational Research, 58,* 119–149.

Dweck, C. S. (1986). Motivational processes affecting learning. *American Psychologist, 41,* 1040–1047.

Elbow, P., & Belanoff, P. (1989). *Sharing and responding.* New York: Random House.

Fantuzzo, J. W., King, J. A., & Heller, L. R. (1992). Effects of reciprocal peer-tutoring on mathematics and school adjustment: A component analysis. *Journal of Educational Psychology, 84,* 331–339.

Farh, J., Cannella, A. A., & Bedeian, A. G. (1991). Peer ratings: The impact of purpose on rating quality and user acceptance. *Group and Organization Studies, 16,* 367–386.

Fedor, D. B., & Bettenhausen, K. L. (1989). The impact of purpose, participant preconceptions, and rating level on the acceptance of peer evaluations. *Group and Organization Studies, 14,* 182–197.

Freedman, S. W. (1987). *Response to student writing. Research Report 23.* Urbana, IL: National Council of Teachers of English.

Freedman, S. W. (1992). Outside-in and inside-out: Peer response groups in two ninth grade classes. *Research in the Teaching of English, 26,* 71–107.

Gaillet, L. I. (1992). *A foreshadowing of modern theories and practices of collaborative learning: The work of the Scottish rhetorician George Jardine.* Paper presented at the 43rd annual meeting of the Conference on College Composition and Communication, Cincinnati, OH, March 19–21, 1992.

George, D. (1984). Writing with peer groups in composition. *College Composition and Communication, 35,* 320–336.

Gere, A. R., & Abbot, R. D. (1985). Talking about writing: The language of writing groups. *Research in the Teaching of English, 19,* 362–379.

Greenwood, C. R. (1991). Classwide peer tutoring: Longitudinal effects on the reading, language, and mathematics achievement of at-risk students. *Reading, Writing, and Learning Disabilities, 7,* 105–123.

Harp, B. (1988). When the principal asks: "Why aren't you using peer editing?" *Reading Teacher, 41*(8), 828.

Hebert, E. A. (1992). Portfolios invite reflection—From students and staff. *Educational Leadership, 49,* 58–61.

Henry, S. E. (1979). Sex and locus of control as determinants of children's responses to peer versus adult praise. *Journal of Educational Psychology, 71*(5), 605.

Higgins, L., Flower, L., & Petraglia, J. (1992). Planning text together: The role of critical reflection in student collaboration. *Written Communication, 9,* 48–84.

Holley, C. A. B. (1990). *The effects of peer editing as an instructional method on the writing proficiency of selected high school students in Alabama.* Dissertation Abstracts International, *51*(9), 2970.

Jacobs, G. (1987). First experiences with peer feedback on compositions: Student and teacher reaction. *System, 15,* 325–333.

Johannessen, L. R. (1995, March). *Teaching descriptive/narrative writing: Strategies for middle and secondary students.* Paper presented at a Teacher's Institute Inservice at Indian Prairie Community Unit School District 204, Naperville, IL.

Johnson, D. W., & Johnson, R. T. (1989). *Cooperation and competition: Theory and practice.* Edina, MN: Interaction Book Co.

Karegianes, M. L., Pascarella, E. T., & Pflaum, S. W. (1980). The effects of peer editing on the writing proficiency of low-achieving tenth grade students. *Journal of Educational Research, 73*(4), 203–207.

Katstra, J., Tollefson, N., & Gilbert, E. (1987). The effects of peer evaluation on attitude toward writing and writing fluency of ninth grade students. *Journal of Educational Research, 80*(3), 168–172.

King, A. (in press). Discourse processes mediating peer learning. In A. M. O'Donnell & A. King (Eds.), *Cognitive perspectives on peer learning.* Mahwah, NJ: Lawrence Erlbaum Associates.

Kulhavy, R. W., & Stock, W. A. (1989). Feedback in written instruction: The place of response certitude. *Educational Psychology Review, 1,* 279–308.

Lagana, J. R. (1972). *The development, implementation and evaluation of a model for teaching composition which utilizes individualized learning and peer grouping.* Unpublished doctoral thesis, University of Pittsburgh, Pittsburgh, PA.

Lawrence, M. J. (1996). *The effects of providing feedback on the characteristics of student responses to a videotaped high school physics assessment.* Unpublished doctoral thesis, Rutgers University, New Brunswick, NJ.

Leibnitz, M. (1989). Writing workshop: Sharing and strategies. *Journal of Reading, 32*(8), 747–748.

Lynch, D. H., & Golen, S. (1992). Peer evaluation of writing in business communication classes. *Journal of Education for Business,* (Sept/Oct), 44–48.

MacArthur, C. A., Schwartz, S. S., & Graham, S. (1991). Effects of a reciprocal peer revision strategy in special education classrooms. *Learning Disabilities Research and Practice, 6*(4), 201–210.

McCurdy, B. L., & Shapiro, E. S. (1992). A comparison of teacher-monitoring, peer-monitoring, and self-monitoring with curriculum-based measurement in reading among students with learning disabilities. *Journal of Special Education, 26*(2), 162–180.

McManus, G., & Kirby, D. (1988). Research in the classroom using peer group instruction to teach writing. *English Journal, 77*(3), 78.

Newell, G. E. (1994). The effects of written between-draft responses on students' writing and reasoning about literature. *Written Communication, 11,* 311–347.

Newkirk, T. (1984a). Direction and misdirection in peer response. *College Composition and Communication, 35*(3), 301–311.

Newkirk, T. (1984b). How students read student papers: An exploratory study. *Written Communication, 1,* 283–305.

Nystrand, M., & Brandt, D. (1989). In C. M. Anson (Ed.), *Writing and response: Theory, practice, and research* (pp. 209–230). Urbana, IL: National Council of Teachers of English.

O'Donnell, A. M. (in press). Structuring dyadic interaction through scripted cooperation. In A. M. O'Donnell & A. King (Eds.), *Cognitive perspectives on peer learning.* Mahwah, NJ: Lawrence Erlbaum Associates.

O'Donnell, A. M., Dansereau, D. F., Rocklin, T., Lambiotte, J. G., Hythecker, V. I., & Larson, C. O. (1985). Cooperative writing: Direct effects and transfer. *Written Communication, 2,* 307–315.

O'Donnell, A. M., Larson, C. O., Dansereau, D. F., & Rocklin, T. R. (1986). Effects of cooperation and editing on instruction writing performance. *Journal of Experimental Education, 54,* 207–210.

O'Donnell, A. M., & O'Kelly, J. (1994). Learning from peers: Beyond the rhetoric of positive results. *Educational Psychology Review, 6,* 321–349.

Olson, V. L. B. (1986): *The effects of revision instruction and peer response groups on the revision behaviors, quality of writing and attitude toward writing of sixth grade students.* Dissertation Abstracts International, *47*(12), 4310.

Olson, V. L. B. (1990). The revising processes of sixth-grade writers with and without peer feedback. *Journal of Educational Research, 84*(1), 1.

Paris, S. G., & Newman, R. S. (1990). Developmental aspects of self-regulated learning. *Educational Psychologist, 25,* 87–102.

Parris, T. B. (1989). *Peer evaluation: Can it improve the writing ability of grade 12 students in the United States Virgin islands?* Dissertation Abstracts International, *53*(1), 89.

Paulson, E. L., Paulson, P. R., & Meyer, C. A. (1991). What makes a portfolio a portfolio? *Educational Leadership, 48*(5), 60–63.

Pierson, H. (1967). *Peer and teacher correction: A comparison of the effects of two methods of teaching composition in grade 9 English classes.* Unpublished doctoral thesis, New York University, New York.

Pond, K., Ul-Haq, R., & Wade, W. (1995). Peer review: A precursor to peer assessment. *Innovations in Education and Training International, 32,* 314–323.

Raphael, T. E. (1986). *The impact of text structure instruction and social context on students' comprehension and production of expository text.* East Lansing, MI: Institute for Research on Teaching, Michigan State University.

Reeve, J. M. (1996). *Motivating others: Nurturing inner motivational resources.* Needham Heights, MA: Allyn & Bacon.

Rijlaarsdam, G. (1987). *Effects of peer evaluation on writing performance, writing processes, and psychological variables.* Paper presented at the 38th annual meeting of the Conference on College Composition and Communication, Atlanta GA, March 19–21, 1987.

Rijlaarsdam, G., & Schoonen, R. (1988). *Effects of a teaching program based on peer evaluation on written composition and some variables related to writing apprehension.* Amsterdam: Stichting Centrum voor Onderwijsonderzoek, Amsterdam University.

Rocklin, T. R., O'Donnell, A. M., & Holst, P. M (1995). Effects and underlying mechanisms of self-adapted testing. *Journal Of Educational Psychology, 87,* 103–116.

Ross, J. A. (1995). Effects of feedback on student behavior in cooperative learning groups in a grade-7 math class. *Elementary School Journal, 96*(2), 125–143.

Salend, S. J., Whittaker, C. R., & Reeder, E. (1993). Group evaluation—A collaborative, peer-mediated behavior management system. *Exceptional Children, 59*(3), 203–209.

Salomon, G., & Globerson, T. (1989). When teams do not function they way they ought to. *International Journal of Educational Research, 13,* 89–99.

Samway, K. D. (1993). This is hard, isn't it—Children evaluating writing. *Tesol Quarterly, 27*(2), 233 257.

Scardamalia, M., Bereiter, C., & Lamon, M. (1995). The CSILE project: Trying to bring the classroom into the world. In K. McGilley (Ed.), *Classroom Lessons: Integrating Cognitive Theory* (pp. 201–228). Cambridge, MA: MIT Press.

Shriver, K. A. (1992). Teaching writers to anticipate readers' needs. *Written Communication, 9,* 179–208.

Slavin, R. E. (1992). When and why does cooperative learning increase achievement? Theoretical and empirical perspectives. In R. Hertz-Lazarowitz & N. Miller (Eds.), *Interaction in cooperative groups: The theoretical anatomy of group learning* (pp. 145–173). New York: Cambridge University Press.

Smith, J. B. (1993). *Collective intelligence in computer-based collaboration.* Hillsdale, NJ: Lawrence Erlbaum Associates.

Stanley, J. (1992). Coaching student writers to be effective peer evaluators. *Journal of Second Language Writing, 1,* 217–233.

Stiggins, R. J. (1994). *Student-centered classroom assessment.* New York: Macmillan.

Stoddard, B., & MacArthur, C. A. (1993). A peer editor strategy—Guiding learning-disabled students in response and revision. *Research in the Teaching of English, 27*(1), 76–103.

Thompson, R. F. (1981). Peer grading—Some promising advantages for composition research and the classroom. *Research in the Teaching of English, 15*(2), 172–174.

Tierney, R. J., Carter, M. A., & Desai, L. E. (1991). *Portfolio assessment in the reading–writing classroom.* Norwood, MA: Christopher Gordon.

Tillmann, G. Y. (1981). *The effects of peer feedback on assertive training outcomes with female adolescents.* Dissertation Abstracts International, *41*(11), 4278.

Topping, K. J. (1998). *Peer assessment between students in college and university.* Paper submitted for publication.

Towler, L., & Broadfoot, P. (1992). Self-assessment in the primary school. *Educational Review, 44*(2), 137–151.

Wade, L. K. (1988). *An analysis of the effects of a peer feedback procedure on the writing behavior of sixth-grade students.* Dissertation Abstracts International, *50*(5), 2181.

Weaver, M. E. (1995). Using peer response in the classroom: Students' perspectives. *Research and Teaching in Developmental Education, 12,* 31–37.

Webb, N. M. (1989). Peer interaction and learning in small groups. *International Journal of Educational Research, 13,* 13–40.

Webb, N. M., & Farivar, S. (1994). Promoting helping behavior in cooperative small groups in middle school mathematics. *American Educational Research Journal, 31,* 369–395.

Webb, N. M., & Farivar, S. (in press). Developing productive group interaction in middle-school mathematics. In A. M. O'Donnell & A. King (Eds.), *Cognitive perspectives on peer learning.* Mahwah, NJ: Lawrence Erlbaum Associates.

Weeks, J. O., & White, M. B. (1982, March). *Peer editing versus teacher editing: Does it make a difference?* Paper presented at Meeting of the North Carolina Council of the International Reading Association, Charlotte, NC.

Wilson, J. (1985). The role of metacognition in English education. *English Education, 17,* 211–220.

Wolfe, L., & Smith, J. K. (1995). The consequence of consequence: Motivation, anxiety, and test performance. *Applied Measurement in Education, 8,* 227–242.

Zhu, W. (1995). Effects of training for peer response on students' comments and interaction. *Written Communication, 12,* 492–528.

Zimmerman, B. J. (1990). Self-regulated learning and academic achievement: An overview. *Educational Psychologist, 25,* 3–17.

Zimmerman, B. J., Greenberg, D., & Weinstein, C. E. (1994). Self-regulating academic study time: A strategy approach. In D. Schunk & B. Zimmerman (Eds.), *Self-regulation of learning and performance: Issues and educational applications* (pp. 181–199). Hillsdale, NJ: Lawrence Erlbaum Associates.

V

EMBEDDING AND EXTENDING
PEER-ASSISTED LEARNING

Mutual Tutoring: Embedding and Extending Peer-Assisted Learning

Audrey Gartner
City University of New York

Students tend to learn when they are interested and involved, see purpose in learning, and have some control over it. One way of approaching the challenge of improving student learning would be to consider students as *prosumers*: education consumers who also produce learning. This refers to involvement in the roles of help-giving (producing) and help-receiving (consuming) by students. Of course, students cannot do it alone; teachers and other school staff are crucial in facilitating this process of converting children from passive receivers into producers of learning.

A critical aspect of this approach is peer-assisted learning strategies (PAL), where students function as peer tutors and educators and benefit from these experiences. Compared with tutoring programs that use adults to assist students, peer tutoring has several distinct advantages. Foremost, if properly structured, both the tutor and tutee gain from the intervention, achieving a double benefit.

Because peer tutoring is of value to both tutor and tutee, an ideal whole school approach would expose children to both roles. All children have some area of competence that can be imparted to a younger or less sophisticated child. Conversely, children can also benefit from tutoring in areas in which they are relative novices. In assuming both tutor and tutee roles, children also gain a highly informative experience in role reversal. Switching from expert to novice can impart to the child a deeper and more sympathetic under-standing of the educational endeavors of self and others (Damon, 1984).

At the same time, peer tutoring yields an exponential increase of help-giving resources in the schools, in a cost-effective way. This approach builds on students' strengths and mobilizes them as active participants in the learning process. All of this connects to the school ethos, developing and reflecting a cultural norm of helping and caring. This should serve to increase the meaningful participation of everyone involved in the educational experience, most particularly the students themselves.

Mutual tutoring emphasizes the special benefits for the tutors—learning through teaching. Giving all students the opportunity to teach others is at the core of the mutual tutoring design. Being a tutee is seen as a crucial developmental step toward becoming a tutor. Through the requirement that all tutors first be tutees, the experiential basis for continuing cycles of PAL is inherent.

Among the educational bonuses of this approach are the following:

1. As students are tutored in preparation for becoming tutors, their ambivalence about receiving help decreases and their motivation to learn increases.
2. All the students have the chance to participate and the opportunity to help, which makes them all feel equally valuable and worthwhile.
3. The asymmetry between tutor and tutee is reduced, and the stigma often associated with receiving help disappears.
4. An ethos of cooperation is built (Gartner & Riessman, 1994).

A TUTOR-CENTERED DESIGN

A study at Mobilization for Youth, in New York City, found that when high school students with limited reading skills tutored fourth graders who were behind in reading, the reading scores of the younger students advanced by 6 months. However, strikingly, the tutors made almost 2 years' more progress in reading than similar students in a comparison group (Cloward, 1976).

The significant point of the study is that tutoring produced a quantum leap in learning. For this to take place it is, of course, necessary that the tutors have room to improve—that they do not enter the tutoring relationship with ability way above the tutee's zone of proximal development. If the tutor is a below average or average student, a much greater growth potential for the tutor exists.

The *Harvard Education Letter* (1987) reported: "Tutors learn at least as much as the students they teach—and tutors who are far behind academically gain even more" (p. 2). "Preparing and giving the lessons ... benefits the tutors themselves because they learn more about the material they are teaching" (U.S. Department of Education, 1986, p. 36). Hedin (1987) described this phenomenon as follows: "The experience of being needed, valued, and respected by another person produces a new view of self as a worthwhile human being" (p. 43). As a result of their efforts to help others, tutors reinforce their own knowledge and skills, which, in turn, builds their self-confidence and self-esteem.

A sizable body of literature on peer tutoring approaches has found higher levels of academic and social development gains in PAL students when compared with students in conventional learning settings (Benard, 1990; Bloom, 1984; Goodlad & Hirst, 1989; Greenwood, Delquadri, & Hall, 1989; Swengel, 1991). A Stanford University study reported that in raising both reading and mathematics achievement, peer tutoring was two times more cost effective than computer-assisted instruction and three times more cost-effective than lengthened school day or reduced class size (Levin, Glass, & Meister, 1984). Both tutees and tutors had improved achievement scores for the same dollar input.

The following illustrates the effect of teaching someone else:

> WE LEARN:
> 10% of what we READ
> 20% of what we HEAR
> 30% of what we SEE
> 50% of what we both SEE and HEAR
> 70% of what we DISCUSS with others
> 80% of what we EXPERIENCE personally
> 90% of what we TEACH others

The important potential for tutor development accruing from PAL has long been recognized, but often regarded as a serendipitous by-product rather than an integral outcome of the tutoring intervention. Mutual tutoring, by focusing on symbiosis of the tutor and tutee roles, enables a broad range of students to be tutors. This is in contrast to traditional tutorial programs that use a starkly cross-ability approach, using tutors as surrogate professional teachers, in which tutees learn only by receiving and often experience dependency and powerlessness.

Mutual tutoring is intended to universalize the tutor role within tutoring schemes integrated fully into the school's educational program. Prior experience as a tutee is accepted as part of the normal apprenticeship for becoming a tutor. Thus, in one elementary school, sixth graders tutor third graders who, in turn, tutor first graders. As students are promoted, they have the opportunity of tutoring younger students. In intraclass tutoring, the roles of tutor and tutee may be alternated regularly to ensure that all students share the experience of giving and receiving tutoring. Teachers prepare half of the students to tutor the rest of the class on a one-on-one basis in a particular subject, then reverse the roles, teaching the former tutees how to review a different skill.

This developmental pattern is critical for the establishment of an ethos built around the values of equality, cooperation, and caring. Research suggests that experiencing a caring community provides the foundation for children's development of character, citizenship and intellect (Schaps, Lewis, & Watson, 1995). In schools experienced as caring communities, students show a greater liking for school, greater concern for others, greater enjoyment of helping others learn, and higher academic self-esteem.

Students come to recognize their importance as educational resources; they are not only receivers, but givers and helpers as well. Both tutors and tutees gain a greater understanding of the subject matter that is being tutored. They also learn how to tutor. Furthermore they learn how to listen and communicate effectively, and perhaps most importantly, they learn about learning.

This is a strength-based approach that emphasizes students' assets and skills to help themselves as well as others. Implicit in this approach is the acknowledgment that there is enormous potential in the youngsters that the school system as presently organized does not tap or unleash (Riessman & Gartner, 1995).

ORGANIZING A NEW TUTORING PROGRAM

The Peer Research Laboratory's approach to tutoring incorporates the following components:

1. A universal approach to tutoring as a central learning strategy for all students, integrated into the regular school program.
2. An emphasis on the significant benefits for both tutors and tutees, with special attention paid to the impact on the tutor.
3. In-depth preparation and training of peer tutors about learning strategies, the significance of indirect and informal learning, the relationship between cognitive and social development, and attuning material to the learner's interests.
4. Tutors' ongoing reflection, feelings, and thoughts of the tutoring process via journals and discussion.

5. Removal of the stigma or negativity usually associated with receiving help, because all students participate in giving and receiving help.

6. An effort to build a strong relationship between tutor and tutee, provide role models, and create more symmetry between students.

7. A recasting of the teacher's role from directing the action from the front of the classroom to one of facilitator or manager of the learning process.

8. Diminished teacher isolation by bringing teachers together regularly in mutual support and problem-solving forums where they can expand their pool of ideas, materials, and methods.

9. An in-school form of community service that strengthens classroom learning, contributes to a sense of community, and encourages personal and social development.

EFFECTIVENESS OF MUTUAL TUTORING

Mutual tutoring grew out of studies conducted by the Peer Research Laboratory that sought to minimize the hierarchical relationship that traditionally existed between tutor and tutee. This asymmetrical, "top–down" aspect of the traditional relationship takes on added importance if the tutees have been performing poorly in school, need remedial assistance, and have been identified as underachievers, thus increasing their ambivalence toward receiving help. By improving tutees' motivation to learn through participatory sharing with tutors, and increasing their self-esteem as they recognize the value of being tutored as preparation for their tutoring role in the future, their receptivity to being tutored may be enhanced.

To test whether access to this new tutoring model would have an impact on the learning of tutees, a two-semester program was developed by the Peer Research Laboratory and implemented in six, low socioeconomic status New York City public high schools with high student dropout rates (Gartner & Riessman, 1995).

Tutors and tutees were drawn from the general student population. Three program features were introduced in three randomly assigned treatment schools:

1. Tutees were involved in activities to promote joint program ownership, such as group meetings with tutors for planning, training, program assessment, and sharing of their experiences. These meetings were facilitated by an adult teacher–coordinator at each site.

2. Tutees were given an opportunity to become tutors the following semester, if they passed the course in which they were being tutored (with a grade of

75 or higher) and they were absent from the group meetings no more than two times.

3. Tutees were provided with a stipend for participation in the group meetings, but not for receiving tutoring.

In three control schools, tutees received a traditional tutorial program. To balance the weekly group meetings in the experimental schools, control school tutees met once a week with the teacher–coordinator to discuss their progress and needs.

The hypotheses in this experiment were that tutees in the treatment group would be more likely to remain in the program, have more positive attitudes toward school, achieve higher grade point averages for the semester, and pass the course(s) in which they were tutored. The findings in the experimental cohort showed higher program attendance (91% compared to 70% in the control schools), significantly higher grades in the first semester in tutored subjects (78.3 compared to 65.4), and higher rates of completion in tutored courses (14% of students in the fall semester and 7% of students in the spring semester had not completed their courses compared to 22% in the fall and 13% in the spring for students in control schools).

Through observations, interviews, and survey questionnaires, both cohorts of students reported that their tutoring experiences were generally positive; they indicated that tutoring was helpful with school work and provided them with a chance to learn new material. In contrast to the comparison group, the tutoring experience in the treatment schools was more collaborative and less tutor-directed and allowed for more extensive interactions between tutors and tutees. The findings suggested that relaxation of artificial barriers to full and equal participation in tutoring allows greater benefits for tutees.

IMPLEMENTING THE MODEL

To bridge the gap between research outcomes and everyday educational practice, the Peer Research Laboratory has implemented a number of programs designed to make more intensified use of students as tutors:

1. To help recruit minority youth into the teaching profession, students in two New York City high schools with largely African-American and Hispanic American populations are being offered a credit-bearing course called "Adventures in Teaching", in which they not only learn about issues in education, child development, and effective teaching, but participate in structured peer

tutoring field placements in nearby elementary schools. In-depth tutor training and reflection on their tutoring experiences form the underpinning of the course. This program was undertaken to address the growing disparity between the number of minority students in the city's schools (80%) and the overwhelmingly nonminority teaching staff (25%).

2. Twenty thousand new students, the majority from countries outside the United States, enter New York City schools each year. A pilot high school program, focusing on these new students, pairs them with a trained student tutor–mentor. In their mentor role, they guide their mentees through the intricacies of school rules and norms and acquaint them with their new community. In their tutor role, they help tutees with academic work and English-language acquisition.

3. In an elementary school in New York City's Chinatown, with more than 500 students, whole classes of students are tutors to younger students. All students in the school, regardless of academic ability and including those in special education classes, have the opportunity to tutor. As students progress through the grades, they tutor younger students, leading to an integrated system that spreads the tutoring experience. Teachers received intensive training in conducting a tutoring program and were provided with on-site assistance to help them initiate cross-age tutoring between classes. Teachers met together regularly as a support group and for inservice training. The school has become a demonstration training base for other teachers who want to learn about peer tutoring.

4. Another program paired student-tutors from low-, middle-, and high-achieving high schools with elementary and junior high school students in a structured in-school tutoring program. The study showed no significant differences in effectiveness among the tutors from the various schools.

5. The Peer Research Laboratory, in collaboration with the Time Dollar Institute of Washington, DC, is involved in an intensive after-school tutoring program with the Chicago Public Schools. In 10 elementary schools on Chicago's South Side, more than 500 tutors in Grades 6 to 8 are earning "service credits" for working one-on-one with an equal number of younger students. They tutor 4 hours each week, providing assistance in reading, math, social studies, and science. For each hour of tutoring or being tutored, students earn one Time Dollar; 100 hours of service credit earn the students a reconditioned computer with educational software for their own use at home.

EXPANDING THE USE OF MUTUAL TUTORING

It is evident that mutual tutoring can be conducted among different grades in a school, within one grade or level (intraclass), and among secondary-level students tutoring each other or younger pupils. Tutor-centered learning focuses on the power of learning through teaching and emphasizes the tutor role, and not just for those usually considered tutor material, (i.e., more able students). It seeks to universalize the tutor role within tutoring schemes integrated fully into the school's educational program.

If all student's are to be tutors, they must be well prepared to perform this task. Thus, in-depth and continuous training for tutors is essential. This allows tutors to learn and refine their tutoring, communication, and problem-solving skills, and understand different learning strategies and how to be role models. Through meetings with other tutors, and in written reflections in journals, they share their feelings about the tutoring process and expand their understanding of learning through teaching.

For this approach to work, the support of the teachers is essential, particularly because of the shift in their roles to facilitators of the learning process. For this, they need preparation and support to put the tutoring programs in place. Moreover, in cross-age tutoring programs within the school day, they need to develop a working relationship and the necessary logistic arrangements with their teaching partners. Teacher support groups that meet regularly not only help to break down teacher isolation, but also lead to the development of innovative partnerships and cross-fertilization of ideas and techniques among teachers involved in similar work (Gartner & Riessman, 1994).

At a time when education is under attack—students are not sufficiently prepared to enter the workplace, too many students are dropping out of school, graduates cannot write a decent letter, and resources are shrinking—it is apparent that schools need help. A thematic and powerful peer approach may be one way to answer the question: "What unutilized resources already exist within the educational system that can help schools help themselves?"

Tutor-centered learning has been demonstrated to be highly beneficial in studies, with positive effects on cognitive outcomes as well as student self-esteem and attitudes. The peer participatory approach is valuable for students for this reason, but also in terms of a larger effort to restructure schools as learning communities and in promoting heightened respect for all students. The active involvement of students, as the most important constituency in the learning process, is essential to change the culture and ethos of the schools and the nature of the educational endeavor.

REFERENCES

Benard, B. (1990). *The case for peers.* Portland, OR: Northwest Regional Educational Laboratory.

Bloom, B. (1984). The search for methods as effective as one-to-one tutoring. *Educational Leadership, 41,* 4–17.

Cloward, R. (1976). Teenagers as tutors of academically low-achieving children: Impact on tutors and tutees. In V. L. Allen (Ed.), *Children as teachers* (pp. 219–229). New York: Academic Press.

Damon, W. (1984). Peer education: The untapped potential. *Journal of Applied Developmental Psychology, 5,* 331–343.

Gartner, A., & Riessman, F. (1994). Tutoring helps those who give, those who receive. *Educational Leadership, 52,* 58–60.

Gartner, A., & Riessman, F. (1995). *A new peer tutoring design.* New York: Peer Research Laboratory.

Goodlad, S., & Hirst, B. (1989). *Peer tutoring: A guide to learning by teaching.* New York: Nicholson Publishing.

Greenwood, C. R., Delquadri, J. C., & Hall, R. V. (1989). Longitudinal effects of classwide peer tutoring. *Journal of Educational Psychology, 81,* 371–383.

Harvard Graduate School of Education. (1987). Big kids teach little kids: What we know about cross-age tutoring. *Education Letter, 3,* 1–4.

Hedin, D. (1987). Students as teachers: A tool for improving school climate and productivity. *Social Policy, 17,* 42–47.

Levin, H. M., Glass, G. V., & Meister, G. R. (1984). *Cost-effectiveness of four educational interventions.* Stanford, CA: Institute for Research on Educational Finance and Governance.

Riessman, F., & Gartner, A. (1995). Toward a new education paradigm. In F. Riessman & D. Carroll (Eds.), *Redefining self-help* (pp.141–156). San Francisco: Jossey Bass.

Schaps, E., Lewis, S., & Watson, M. (1995). Schools as caring communities. *Resources for Restructuring, 1–2,* 4–6.

Swengel, M. (1991). Peer tutoring: Back to the roots of peer helping. *The Peer Facilitator Quarterly, 8,* 28–32.

U.S. Department of Education. (1986). *What works: Research about teaching and learning (1986).* Washington, DC: Author.

16

Peer-Assisted Learning
Beyond School

Shirley Hill
University of Dundee
Brian Gay
University of the West of England
Keith Topping
University of Dundee

Peer-assisted learning (PAL) is an effective and flexible approach to teaching and learning that can be used in a host of different settings, both during the school years and beyond. Indeed, the experience of PAL within school can provide a valuable apprenticeship for these later activities, which are often embedded within an orientation toward lifelong learning.

PAL beyond school offers multiple developmental opportunities, so that the experience in various forms can become a normal lifelong expectation. Additionally, everyone can expect to participate at different stages as tutor and tutee, leader and follower. None of us is as smart as all of us, and no one is so smart they do not need help with something, and no one is incapable of helping somebody with something. This chapter considers the opportunities and benefits of three main forms of PAL that operate beyond the school years. It is divided into three parts.

The first part describes college and university students tutoring in schools—a natural progression from cross-age tutoring within the high school. Next, peer tutoring between students within colleges and universities—both between and within different years of study—is discussed. Finally, we consider the much broader approach of mentoring—both within the workplace and between the workplace and the community. References are divided by part at the end of the chapter.

291

Each part seeks to give a very compact overview of its target area. The main purpose is to persuade the reader that PAL goes far beyond schools and permeates all of life. The overviews given here are inevitably brief, superficial, and lacking detail of implementation, but many relevant practical resources can be found in the resources and contacts section later in this book.

COLLEGE AND UNIVERSITY STUDENTS TUTORING IN SCHOOLS

In this part, we consider college and university students acting as tutors for children and young people who are in primary (elementary) and secondary (high) schools. Beginning with a definition and rationale, we summarize international research on effectiveness, offer a synopsis of two recent U.K. studies on outcomes for student tutors, and conclude with implications for onward action.

Definition and Rationale

Arrangements whereby college and university students tutor children and young people who are in primary (elementary) and secondary (high) schools can be regarded as a specific form of cross-institutional, cross-age, cross-ability, fixed-role peer tutoring (see chap. 1, this volume). In the United Kingdom, the term *student* is used only for those studying in college or university, not for those in school. Accordingly, such arrangements are often referred to as *student tutoring*. This is potentially confusing for readers in other countries, and this term will therefore used in italic throughout this chapter.

One aim of *student tutoring* is to raise the tutees' aspirations and motivation to continue their education at a higher level, through the positive role model provided by the student tutors. Learning gains for the tutees are also anticipated, from interaction with university or college students whose knowledge of particular curricular areas may be more specialized and up-to-date than that of the class teacher. The schools involved can benefit from the presence of an additional adult in the classroom, who can support the class teacher by providing individual attention and stimulus to children of all ages and abilities.

The student tutors have the opportunity to develop deeper understanding of the tutored subject, by applying their knowledge in practical contexts. They may also develop some of the transferable skills that are increasingly required in the employment market (e.g., communication, interpersonal, and organizational skills). This rationale reflects the consistent message from employers that graduates lack the skills required to meet the needs of industry and society (Colling, 1988; National Advisory Body for Public Sector Higher Education, 1986; Standing Conference of Employers of Graduates, 1985).

In the United Kingdom, *student tutoring* almost always occurs in the classroom in the presence of the classroom teacher. The vast majority of student tutors in the United Kingdom are unpaid volunteers and typically tutor for one morning or afternoon a week for 10 or more consecutive weeks. This model of *student tutoring* is both nationally idiosyncratic and unusually internally consistent. It contrasts markedly with models found elsewhere.

In North America and Israel, for instance, schemes differ from the U.K. model in place and time of occurrence of tutoring, and in the nature of the reward for tutors, most receiving some extrinsic reward for participation (e.g., course credit or payment). Whatever the format of the tutoring, various benefits for the student tutor, the tutored children, and the class teacher have been hypothesized, assumed, claimed, and anecdotally reported. Research outside the United Kingdom has tended to focus on outcomes for tutees. There are far fewer studies in the international literature that report outcomes for tutors.

Summary of International Research

Outcomes for Tutors. A great deal of subjective questionnaire feedback from tutors has been gathered in the United Kingdom (e.g., Beardon, 1990; Gadsby, 1993; Goodlad, 1985; MacDougall, 1993; Wilson, 1995). Response rates have varied, with some not known. Many studies document a consistently high rate of reporting by responding tutors of improved communication skills and self-confidence, but cognitive gains for tutors in the curriculum area of tutoring are generally reported less frequently and much more variably. Typically, one quarter of tutors report that tutoring interferes with their mainstream studies. Demographic information has rarely been provided and this, together with differences in scheme organization, has made it difficult to compare outcomes from *student tutoring* schemes in the United Kingdom with those elsewhere.

In North America, large-scale surveys (e.g., Cahalan & Farris, 1990; Reisner, Petry, & Armitage, 1990) report the typical student tutor to be

White, female, socioeconomically advantaged, receiving payment or course credit, and equally likely to tutor in primary or secondary schools. Tutees are mostly ethnic minority, male, and socioeconomically disadvantaged. Tutoring is more likely to occur on the university campus than in school (the tutor transporting the tutee) and on a one-on-one rather than group basis. Tutoring is often focused on basic skill acquisition. The objective of raising tutee aspirations is rarely mentioned in tutoring programs (although often mentioned in mentoring programs). These surveys indicated that the majority of tutoring program managers believed that most of their program goals were being met, although supportive evidence was rarely accessible.

Other studies suggest that articulating clear and achievable goals for tutors raises their satisfaction levels (e.g., Fresko & Chen, 1989) and that tutors involved in reading and writing programs can show gains in their own skills and motivation (e.g., Juel, 1991). Finally, a great deal of positive subjective feedback similar to that in the United Kingdom has also been reported (e.g., Fischetti, Maloy, & Heffley, 1989; Raupp & Cohen, 1992; Stewart & Palcic, 1992).

Outcomes for Tutees. In the United Kingdom, subjective questionnaire feedback from tutees (Beardon, 1990; Community Service Volunteers, 1994; Gadsby, 1993; Goodlad, 1985) is based on known response rates in some studies, although these are not clear in other cases. Typically, a little more than half the tutees feel that, with tutors in the classroom, they learn more and lessons are easier to follow, but there is considerable variation in tutee perceptions of whether lessons are more interesting or enjoyable. There is limited and conflicting subjective evidence on the extent to which tutors manage to be role models, and recent research provides no conclusive evidence for aspirational gains in tutees resulting from *student tutoring* (Campbell, 1995; Ellsbury, Wood, & Fitz-Gibbon, 1995; Hughes, 1993b).

In Israel, the *Perach* program deploys student tutors on a one-on-one basis with disadvantaged schoolchildren, meeting twice a week for 1 year out of school hours, on campus or in school or elsewhere for academic, cultural, or leisure activities. Subjective feedback has been very positive, but significant academic, self-concept, or aspirational gains for tutees have not been found in comparison to control groups in the short term (Eisenberg, Fresko, & Carmeli, 1980, 1981). However, at the 2-year follow-up, there was some evidence of lower tutee school drop-out and improved aspirations, together with some cognitive gain in mathematics (Eisenberg, Fresko, & Carmeli, 1983a, 1983b).

In Australia, students acting as remedial reading tutors using structured materials generated some significant gains for tutees on some reading tests, but not on others (Butler, 1991). In New Zealand, *student tutoring* operates in a somewhat similar way to the U.K. model, but with four or five tutors in each class. Little difference has been found between pretutoring and posttutoring tutee self-report measures, with much variation between classes. Although some effect on the vocational intentions of tutors was evident, there was no apparent impact on the aspirations of tutees (Jones, 1989, 1990, 1993; Jones & Bates, 1987).

In North America, a number of studies have evaluated tutee gains. Five of these have demonstrated unequivocally a significant positive effect on academic achievement, usually with a structured program of relatively frequent tutoring designed to impact reading and/or math skills with outcomes measured by norm-referenced tests (Bacon, 1992; Flippo, 1993; Juel, 1991; Ross, 1989; Schwartz, 1977). Significant self-concept gains, improved grades, and reduced drop-out rates have also been recorded, and two studies showed improvements in teacher ratings of classroom behavior (Sandler, Reich, & Doctolero, 1979; Valenzuela-Smith, 1983).

However, a similar number of studies failed to show significant gains on reading tests or other academic performance indicators (e.g., Lee, Bryant, Noonan, & Plionis, 1987; Turkel & Abramson, 1986), and some have not shown significant gains on measures of self-concept (e.g., Valenzuela-Smith, 1983). In general, there is little evidence of increased tutee aspirations, although two studies have demonstrated some improvement in the tutees' attitude to further and higher education (Rhodes & Garibaldi, 1990; Sandler et al., 1979). One study (Fischetti et al., 1989) reported an increase in the number of minority students continuing on to postsecondary school education following participation as tutees in a *student tutoring* scheme.

Outcomes for Class Teachers.   Research on outcomes for class teachers has so far only been conducted in the United Kingdom, where most tutoring occurs in the classroom. Subjective questionnaire feedback (Beardon, 1990; Community Service Volunteers, 1994; Gadsby, 1993; Goodlad, 1985; Hughes, 1993a) has involved various response rates, with some not reported. The majority of teachers responding generally report that lessons are easier to handle and more enjoyable with student tutors, and that they feel the children learn more.

However, great variability is evident. Beardon (1995) suggested that the extent of positive impact is dependent on the teacher's classroom management strategies, attitude to learning, and interpersonal skills. She argued that the most successful collaboration between student tutor and class teacher occurs when the teacher makes explicit their own aims and objectives for the lesson and engages the student tutor as a partner in achieving those objectives.

Outcomes for Tutors: Two Recent Studies

Two recent independent, but complementary, studies of student tutors throughout the United Kingdom were conducted to investigate student tutors' perceptions of the outcomes from *student tutoring* for themselves (Hill, 1996; Hill & Topping, 1995a, 1995b, 1995c).

The first study was a large-scale pretutoring and posttutoring questionnaire survey of more than 1,400 further and higher education students involved in Community Service Volunteers *student tutoring* programs throughout England and Northern Ireland. Both the prequestionnaire and the postquestionnaire asked the student tutors to rate the extent to which they believed they had developed a range of cognitive abilities (in relation to the tutored subject) and a range of transferable skills. The postquestionnaire also asked whether they believed they had enhanced each ability and skill as a result of tutoring. Data on the demographic characteristics of the tutors and details of the organizational structure of their school tutoring placements were also collected.

Demographic data showed that the typical student tutor in this study was a female, White, middle-class, second-year university student, aged 18 to 23, studying an arts and social science subject, who tutored an arts and social science subject for 2 to 3 hours, once a week, for 5 to 12 weeks. This tutoring was equally likely to have taken place in a primary or a secondary school, and only 57% likely to have been in the subject the tutor was currently studying. After tutoring, a substantial majority of students became more interested in teaching as a possible future career.

Analysis revealed several significant differences between the student tutors' preratings and postratings, and several cognitive abilities and transferable skills that the majority of students believed had been enhanced: understanding how others learn the subject; communication of subject facts; practical demonstration of subject skills; application of subject knowledge in new situations; oral communication; and listening, questioning, and clarifying. The type of school in which the students tutored, the nature of the tutoring content, and the length of their tutoring experience all seemed to influence the extent and nature of perceived tutor gains.

The second study used a reflective diary technique to investigate the tutoring process and subsequent outcomes in greater detail for a sample of 12 student tutors from one higher education institution in Scotland. The student tutors were asked to complete a reflective diary after every tutoring session for at least eight sessions. Each diary asked students to give detailed information on the tutoring process and their reflections on each tutoring session. Once tutoring was completed, the students were asked to reflect further in a structured interview. Students also completed the pretutoring and posttutoring questionnaires used in the first study.

The results from the second study were numerous and complex. Many different subjects were tutored to the entire range of primary and secondary school age tutees. The tutees were generally of average ability or were in a mixed ability group. Various numbers of children were tutored in both group and one-on-one situations. Group sizes tended to be fairly small, between two and six children, and whole class tutoring activities were rare. On average, each tutoring activity lasted 41 minutes— activities were significantly longer in secondary schools than primary schools. Students were *off task* (i.e., not tutoring) for an average 21% of each tutoring session. This was higher for primary than secondary school tutors.

Several significant differences were found between primary and secondary school tutors' reflections on the tutoring process. Tutors in secondary schools perceived the extent of tutor cognitive demand to be higher, and perceived a greater requirement for the use of cognitive abilities and transferable skills. The tutoring enhancement results were identical to those obtained in the first study, with the addition of recall of subject, confidence in knowledge of subject and collaboration with others in a group situation (which the majority of students in this study perceived to be also enhanced).

It was clear from both studies that *student tutoring* can result in gains in perceived cognitive and transferable skills for tutors. However, it was also clear that the experiences of tutors were very variable. It was concluded that automatic and wide-ranging gains should not be expected for all tutors, and that tutoring placements need to be carefully selected, structured, and supported if targeted gains are to be maximized.

Summary and Conclusions

Student tutoring programs around the world have generated a substantial body of evaluation research of very various quality.

Positive outcomes for tutors have mostly been demonstrated within the social and affective domains. Relatively few studies have explored cognitive or transferable skill gains for tutors in a rigorous manner. Subjective post-only feedback suggests tutors very often perceive gains in their communication skills and self-confidence, but from other measures there is little corroborative evidence for the former, and measures of self-concept change in tutors have yielded mixed results. Self-reported tutor cognitive gains are much less frequent, and some studies report an adverse effect on the tutor's studies. Two recent studies suggest that student tutors perceive both cognitive and transferable skill gains following tutoring, but the nature and extent of such gains are variable and dependent on individual tutoring experiences.

Cognitive and attainment gains are more frequently reported for tutees, especially in basic literacy and numeric skills. However, this finding does not relate to the U.K. model of *student tutoring*, which does not tend to focus on basic skill remediation. Subjective post-only feedback suggests tutees perceive learning benefits in the classroom, with no adverse effects reported, but self-concept gains are delayed and slight. Academic and other gains for tutees have been demonstrated, usually where the tutoring was frequent, focused on basic skills and used structured methods. Generally, evidence for increased tutee aspirations is slight and inconclusive.

Post hoc subjective feedback from class teachers has only been reported in the United Kingdom. Although the results are very variable, they suggest that the majority of teachers involved usually perceive benefits in the classroom with the presence of a student tutor. Although many studies have been conducted internationally on the outcomes for participants in *student tutoring* programs, it should be remembered that the types and models of *student tutoring* encompassed by these studies are many. Two studies exploring the same gain factor may have investigated very different models of operation with very different populations for very different purposes. Thus, *like* is rarely adjacent to or compared with *like*. Therefore, the overall patterns of outcomes certainly cannot be assumed to apply in their entirety to any single specific model.

Different formats of *student tutoring* should be actively designed, structured, contracted, and operated to maximize the likelihood that the stated objectives will be achieved. This, together with adequate monitoring and quality control of the process of tutoring, should help to avoid what sometimes appears to occur at the moment—serendipitous gains for some, coupled with considerable inequality of opportunity. Certainly, if raising tutee aspirations is to be an objective, then structuring and quality control of the tutoring experience would appear to need further thought by all concerned. Although *student tutoring* can benefit all participants, the gains offered are not automatically achieved.

It is clear that *student tutoring* programs, in whatever format, should specify clear, realistic and achievable goals. If these are measurable, enabling improved quality of evaluation research, so much the better. Further thought about evaluation methodologies is necessary. Meanwhile, *student tutoring* programs should not be marketed in a context of unrealistically raised expectations, because subsequent disappointment will damage dissemination, replication, and embedding of the initiative.

PEER TUTORING WITHIN COLLEGES AND UNIVERSITIES

This part comprises a summary review of the literature on the effectiveness of various forms of peer tutoring between students within colleges and universities.

The Current Context

The quality and cost effectiveness of teaching and learning in the sector is increasingly coming under the microscope. There has long been concern that traditional curricula, delivered and assessed in traditional ways, promote a surface approach to learning rather than a deep or even a strategic approach (Entwistle, 1992). Teaching quality assessment exercises consistently result in criticism of departments for failing to promote the development of transferable skills in their students (Barnett, 1992; Ellis, 1993). At the same time, increased student numbers coupled with reduced resources have often resulted in larger class sizes, thus encouraging a reversion to a traditional lecturing style of delivery and a reduction in small group and tutorial contact—in short, less interactive teaching and learning.

The dual requirement to improve teaching quality and also do more with less has recently increased interest in peer tutoring in higher education. However, it would be unwise to seize upon peer tutoring as a universal, undifferentiated, and instant panacea.

The Effectiveness Research

There is very substantial evidence in the literature that peer tutoring is effective and cost-effective in schools (see chaps. 5–9, this volume). However, it cannot be automatically assumed that the same is therefore true of peer tutoring in colleges and universities.

Previous Reviews.   Previous reviews and surveys of peer tutoring in higher education include those of Goldschmid and Goldschmid (1976), Cornwall (1979), Whitman (1988), Lee (1988), Lawson (1989), and Moore-West, Hennessy, Meilman, and O'Donnell (1990). All of these are well worth reading, but tend to be discursive rather than conclusive.

Nevertheless, a considerable amount is already known about the effectiveness of peer tutoring in higher education. It is already widely used, in further and higher education, in a variety of different forms. Surveys suggest several hundred institutions deploy this interactive method of teaching and learning. Of course, the existence of one small pilot project at one time in an institution does not constitute peer tutoring on a large scale across the curriculum which is quality controlled and embedded within the organizational culture. Of the different formats and methods, the Personalized System of Instruction (PSI) and Supplemental Instruction (SI) have most nearly approached the latter scenario. The findings of a more recent review of the research on this topic (Topping, 1996) are presented next. Readers should consult this reference for greater detail.

Effectiveness of Different Types of Tutoring

Cross-year, small-group tutoring, usually with one upper year tutor to a small group of lower year tutees, is the format least disparate from traditional methods. The evidence suggests it can work well. Studies of achievement gains almost all indicate outcomes as good as or better than similar size group tutoring by faculty, and student subjective feedback is generally very positive.

The Personalized System of Instruction (PSI) has been widely used and evaluated in the United States (Kulik, Kulik, & Cohen, 1979). It involves students working through programmed texts individually, then having their knowledge and understanding checked out by student "proctors." Two thirds of studies found PSI involvement associated with higher class marks and 93% of studies found PSI associated with higher final examination performance, compared to control groups. PSI also improved longer term retention of the material learned.

Supplemental Instruction (Martin & Arendale, 1992) adopts a very different model of operation and has become more popular outside the United States than PSI. It involves upper year students acting as guides to the processes and procedures of learning rather than curriculum content, often in small groups. There is very substantial and persuasive evidence of impact on dropout rates, course grades, and graduation outcomes. Research in the United Kingdom is improving in quality and also demonstrating positive outcomes. Graduation outcomes tend not to be increased to the same extent as by PSI, but SI targets difficult courses so the two cannot be directly compared.

Same-year dyadic (paired) fixed-role tutoring has been the subject of several studies over the years, research of mixed quality yielding mixed results. However, two good quality studies found improved achievement from this format, whereas three others found achievement the same as with faculty teaching. Same-year dyadic (paired) reciprocal tutoring has been the focus of fewer studies, but these were of high quality. Increased attainment was demonstrated by all four studies. There was also evidence of reduced student stress. The degree of structure in the program was also related to outcomes.

Dyadic, cross-year, fixed-role tutoring has been the subject of three studies of poor quality. Same-year group tutoring has yielded positive subjective feedback in four studies, but produced no harder evidence on achievement outcomes. Nine studies of peer-assisted writing showed generally favorable outcomes in terms of subjective feedback. Gains in writing competence were shown in two or three of the four relevant studies, despite the inherent difficulty of this kind of research.

There is as yet little substantial evidence that peer assistance in distance learning improves achievement outcomes, but this area is even more difficult to research.

Summary

In summary, three methods of peer tutoring in higher education have already been widely used, have been demonstrated to be effective, and merit wider use in practice. These are cross-year small-group tutoring, the PSI, and SI. Same-year, dyadic reciprocal tutoring has been demonstrated to be effective, but has been relatively little used as yet, and merits much wider deployment. Same-year, dyadic fixed-role tutoring and peer-assisted writing have shown considerable, but not necessarily consistent, promise and should be the focus of continuing experimentation and more research of better quality. In three areas there are just the beginnings of a satisfactory body of evaluation research: dyadic cross-year fixed-role tutoring, same-year group tutoring, and peer-assisted distance learning.

The Future

It is essential that subsequent research strives to achieve adequate quality in design and execution, and addresses issues of achievement gain and parameters of successful course completion as well as subjective participant feedback. If achievement gains can be demonstrated that go beyond the narrow confines of the institutional assessment system and endure in the longer term, so much the better. This implies that impact on wider cognitive abilities and transferable skills should also be measured. However, peer tutoring is always likely to be a relatively small component of the whole higher education experience, so the extent to which it is realistic to expect associated gains to be widespread, maintained, generalized, and measurable is debatable.

MENTORING IN AND BETWEEN THE WORKPLACE AND THE COMMUNITY

The application of mentoring as a contribution to organizational effectiveness is becoming more accepted internationally. It has been widely embraced within the private sector and is now increasing in terms of acceptability within the public sector. Although significant investment is being made in the practice, there is little solid research that is able to indicate the impact of mentoring in increasing individual effectiveness within organizations. Not withstanding that, there is significant anecdotal evidence of a positive relationship between the development process of mentoring and an individual's contribution to their employing organization. Mentoring activity is visible at a number of strategic points within the individual's working life (Zey, 1996).

Mentoring and Induction

The range of mentor–protege activity offers organizations a wide range of possible engagement. It encompasses a spectrum from exploring and reviewing to training and directing. The cost of employing and retraining individuals can be very high, and mentoring is frequently associated with the induction process. Increasingly, individuals in the initial phases of employment within an organization are linked with established members of staff, who can help them socialize more effectively into the new host organization (Boags, Scales, Brandt, & Graham, 1996).

The capability of the mentor to intravenously inject appropriate values and behaviors into individuals is one that has great appeal to managers.

Providing a context within which new appointees can discuss their hopes and aspirations and indeed their emerging understanding of the organization in a risk-free way helps create a positive climate for the development of confidence and acquisition of skills (Montgomery, 1993).

Mentoring and Staff Development

For some organizations, mentoring is the cornerstone of staff development strategy (Conway, 1994). It underpins professional, personal, and continuing professional development. Provision of trained mentors to provide support and guidance to individuals who are undertaking in-house professional development programs or sponsored external qualifications linked to professional practice is now well established (Borredon, 1995).

Many professions seek increasingly to provide mentors for newly qualifying practitioners internally rather than externally (Topping, McCowan, & McCrae, 1998). Within these activities the role of the mentor can move from the role of joint explorer through to that of coach or trainer. In the latter case the objectives of the interaction between the protege and the mentor include clarifying, summarizing, and demonstrating the necessary knowledge and skills (Murray & Owen, 1991). In the former case, the nature of the relationship between the mentor and protege can be much looser—the participants discuss and explore their own ongoing interaction within the organization, and learn the ways in which the organization's structure can function and the roles they are to play over time within it (Gay & Stephenson, 1996).

Mentoring and Personal Development

This type of mentoring exploration with an individual in a risk-free, nonthreatening environment can be important in the development of aspiration, potential, confidence, awareness, social skills, business acumen, and competence in future senior professionals. However, there are many different mentoring skills associated with each area of application of the mentoring process, and the need for the training of mentors has become increasingly recognized (Gay, 1994). This training and the subsequently enriched mentoring process embody personal development opportunities for the mentors themselves.

Additionally, some major organizations view participation in mentoring within the community increasingly as a dimension of the personal and professional development of the individual employees. This is far more than organizations merely seeking to increase their public profiles within the communities from which they draw their employees and consumers. It is seen as putting something back into the community, and also as an opportunity for employees to gain insight into the social structures and processes that exist in the community around the organization.

There is an expectation that such community-based mentoring activities involve elements of gain in transferable skill for the mentors within them. Individuals involved in such processes can gain an increased awareness of the importance of interpersonal skills, empathy, and compassion. In industry, as anywhere else, emotional intelligence pays dividends (Goleman, 1996).

Mentoring and Lifelong Learning

The increasing awareness of the need for lifelong learning and continual professional development would suggest that the place of mentoring within the strategic considerations of organizations for the development of their staff will become more established. Once mentoring is embedded within organizations, participation as mentor or protege in succeeding iterative cycles will be viewed as normal—a routine expectation (Levinson, Darrow, Klein, Levinson, & McKee, 1978).

This will become a necessity for effective organizations as they seek to remain competitively effective, but it will also become a requirement of professional bodies that individuals continuously update their professional skill and practice. Joint pressure from these two sources emphasizing the need for lifelong learning must enhance the status, frequency, depth, and range of application of mentoring—colleague assisted learning. This particular form of peer-assisted learning (PAL) will be seen as a prime source of professional development leading to organizational effectiveness (Robertson, 1992).

Mentoring and the Learning Organization

Increased interest in the development of learning, understanding of how we learn, and awareness of preferred learning styles within the organizational context lead to the development of the *learning organization*. The organization itself becomes the hub for interaction of interconnecting assistive learning networks. The cumulative effect of this process is a focus on the organization as a legitimate source of lifelong learning, and as a natural context for learning and work-based learning (Engestrom, 1994).

An interesting example of this is a project that evolved into a learning organization model (Robertson & Priest, 1995). The project started by working with corporate organizations to evaluate work-based learning for academic credit. This evolved into an ongoing activity where support staff used their existing job functions for negotiated learning contracts. These contracts included the resource of a mentor, in addition to an academic advisor, to increase the potential for work-based learning and promote increased organizational effectiveness as well as evaluation for academic credit.

Organizations as Mentors

Organizations can become mentors of other organizations. For example, in the United States corporations seeking major government contracts have to be prepared to help develop emerging small- to medium-sized enterprises in geographical zones of the United States which are deemed to be disadvantaged, at their own cost. This is slowly creating a culture whereby large organizations see it as part of their corporate responsibility to develop small organizations to the point where they can become recognized and well-established commercially in their own right, and achieve the required quality assurance standard.

This is normally undertaken through the placement of staff from the sponsoring organization into the developing organization, making accessible knowledge and skills training. Such mentoring organizations can also assist in providing and maintaining a market for the products of their partner firms by appropriate outsourcing. Gansior and Garcia (1996) indicated how one mentoring organization (Stewart & Stevens) worked with the Electro-National Corporation in Mississippi to achieve ISO 9002. In addition, technology transfer and engineering development aid was provided. (See Part 19 of the "Small Business and Small Disadvantaged Business Concerns" of Subchapter D of U.S. Government Contracts.)

Summary

Clearly, what we are seeing here is a whole range of mentoring processes, each of which is tailored to suit specific needs at appropriate stages in the development of both the individual and the organization. Skills required of a mentor to help individuals with exploration and discovery of new ways of defining and managing the reality around them vary considerably from those that are required for the training and directing of individuals on highly focused areas of skills acquisition. Organizations are increasingly prepared to develop a deep understanding of the dynamics of the mentoring process, the skills and knowledge associated with its effective delivery, and the range of possible outcomes. Mentoring is being welcomed and embedded within organizational practice.

REFERENCES: STUDENT TUTORING

Bacon, C. S. (1992). *Pre-service teachers and at-risk students.* Unpublished paper, Indiana. (ED 351 308)

Beardon, L. A. (1990). Cambridge STIMULUS. In S. Goodlad & B. Hirst (Eds.), *Explorations in peer tutoring* (pp. 82–97). London: Kogan Page; New York: Nichols.

Beardon, L. A. (1995). How can tutors be most effective in the classroom? In A. Daniel (Ed.), *Learning together: Student tutoring research and evaluation papers on pupil aspirations and student tutor skills* (pp. 151–162). London: Community Service Volunteers.

Butler, S. R. (1991). Reading program—Remedial, integrated and innovative. *Annals of Dyslexia, 41,* 119–127.

Cahalan, M., & Farris, E. (1990). *College sponsored tutoring and mentoring programs for disadvantaged elementary and secondary students. Higher education surveys – report number 12.* Washington, DC: U.S. Department of Education Office of Planning, Budget and Evaluation. (ED 323 884)

Campbell, I. (1995). Student tutoring and pupil aspirations towards further and higher education. In A. Daniel (Ed.), *Learning together: Student tutoring research and evaluation papers on pupil aspirations and student tutor skills* (pp. 31–66). London: Community Service Volunteers.

Colling, C. (1988). The graduate citizen: Competent employee or ineffective illiterate? *Bulletin of Teaching and Learning, 1,* 6–8.

Community Service Volunteers (1994). *CSV Learning Together annual review 1993–1994.* London: Author.

Eisenberg, T., Fresko, B., & Carmeli, M. (1980). *A tutorial project for disadvantaged children: An evaluation of the PERACH project.* Rehovot, Israel: Perach, Weizmann Institute of Science.

Eisenberg, T., Fresko, B., & Carmeli, M. (1981). An assessment of cognitive change in socially disadvantaged children as a result of a one to one tutoring program. *Journal Of Educational Research, 74*(5), 311–314.

Eisenberg, T., Fresko, B., & Carmeli, M. (1983a). A follow-up study of disadvantaged children two years after being tutored. *Journal Of Educational Research, 76*(5), 302–306.

Eisenberg, T., Fresko, B., & Carmeli, M. (1983b). *The effect at different grade levels of one and two years of tutoring.* Rehovot, Israel: Perach, Weizmann Institute of Science.

Ellsbury, J., Wood, J., & Fitz-Gibbon, C. (1995). The impact of student tutoring on pupils' educational aspirations: Evidence from Tyneside. In A. Daniel (Ed.), *Learning together: Student tutoring research and evaluation papers on pupil aspirations and student tutor skills* (pp. 67–84). London: Community Service Volunteers.

Fischetti, J., Maloy, R., & Heffley, J. (1989). Undergraduates tutoring in secondary schools: Collaborative opportunities for teacher education. *Action In Teacher Education, 10*(4), 9–14.

Flippo, R. F. (1993, April). *Literacy, multicultural and sociocultural considerations: Student literacy corps and the community.* Paper presented at the Annual Meeting of the International Reading Association, San Antonio, Texas. (ED 356 466).

Fresko, B., & Chen, M. (1989). Ethnic similarity, tutor expertise and tutor satisfaction in cross-age tutoring. *American Educational Research Journal, 26*(1), 122–140.

Gadsby, M. (1993). *The Birmingham connection: Student tutoring scheme.* London: Community Service Volunteers.

Goodlad, S. (1985). Putting science into context. *Educational Research, 27*(1), 61–67.

Hill, S. (1996). *Student tutoring: An analysis of the tutoring process and outcomes for tutors.* Unpublished masters thesis, University of Dundee.

Hill, S., & Topping, K. J. (1995a). Cognitive and transferable skill gains for student tutors. In S. Goodlad (Ed.), *Students as tutors and mentors* (pp. 135–154). London: Kogan Page.

Hill, S., & Topping, K. J. (1995b). Participant outcome evaluation of student tutoring: A national United Kingdom survey. In A. Daniel (Ed.), *Learning Together: Student tutoring research and evaluation papers on pupil aspirations and student tutor skills* (pp. 97–120). London: Community Service Volunteers.

Hill, S., & Topping, K. J. (1995c). Reflecting on student tutoring: An analysis of the tutoring process and outcomes for tutors. In A. Daniel (Ed.), *Learning together: Student tutoring research and evaluation papers on pupil aspirations and student tutor skills* (pp. 121–150). London: Community Service Volunteers.

Hughes, J. (1993a). *The Pimlico connection: Students tutoring in schools.* 18th Annual Report 1992–93. London: Imperial College of Science and Technology, University of London.

Hughes, J. (1993b, April). *The effectiveness of student tutoring to raise pupils' aspirations.* Paper presented at The Second Scottish Conference on Student Tutoring, Glasgow.

Jones, J. (1989). *Effect of university student tutors on school student's attitudes and aspirations. Report to the Department of Education.* Auckland: University of Auckland.

Jones, J. (1990). Tutoring as field-based learning: Some New Zealand developments. In S. Goodlad & B. Hirst (Eds.), *Explorations in peer tutoring* (pp. 98–109). Oxford: Blackwell.

Jones, J. (1993, August). University students as tutors in secondary schools. In *Proceedings of a Conference on Peer Tutoring at the University of Auckland, New Zealand.* Auckland: Higher Education Research Office and University of Auckland.

Jones, J., & Bates, J. (1987). *University students as tutors in secondary schools.* Auckland: Higher Education Research Office, University of Auckland.

Juel, C. (1991). Cross-age tutoring between student athletes and at-risk children. *The Reading Teacher, 45*(3), 178–186.

Lee, S., Bryant, S., Noonan, N., & Plionis, E. (1987). Keeping youth in school: A public-private collaboration. *Children Today, 4,* 15–21.

MacDougall, G. (1993). *Student tutoring in Tayside: A report on the student tutoring programme 1992/3.* Dundee: Tayside Regional Council.

National Advisory Body for Public Sector Higher Education (NAB) (1986) *Transferable personal skills in employment: The contribution of higher education.* London: Author.

Raupp, C. D., & Cohen, D. C. (1992). "A thousand points of light" illuminate the psychology curriculum: Volunteering as a learning experience. *Teaching Of Psychology, 19*(1), 25–30.

Reisner, E. R., Petry, C. A., & Armitage, M. (1990). *A review of programs involving college students as tutors or mentors in grades K–12 (volumes I and II).* Washington, DC: Policy Studies Institute, U.S. Department of Education.

Rhodes, E. M., & Garibaldi, A. M. (1990). Teacher cadets answer the call. *Momentum, 21*(4), 36–38.

Ross, S. M. (1989, February). *The Apple Classroom of Tomorrow Program with at-risk students.* In Proceedings of Selected Research Papers Presented at the annual meeting of the Association For Educational Communicators and Technology, Dallas TX. (ED 308 837)

Sandler, I. N., Reich, J. W., & Doctolero, J. (1979). Utilization of college students to improve inner-city school children's academic behavior. *Journal of School Psychology, 17*(3), 283–290.

Schwartz, G. (1977). College students as contingency managers for adolescents in a program to develop reading skills. *Journal of Applied Behavior Analysis, 10,* 645–655.

Standing Conference of Employers of Graduates (SCOEG). (1985). *What employers look for in their graduate recruits.* London: Author.

Stewart, M. E., & Palcic, R. A. (1992). *Writing to learn mathematics: The writer–audience relationship.* Paper presented at the Annual Meeting of The Conference On College Composition and Communication, Cincinnati Ohio, March 19–21, 1989. (ED 347 549)

Turkel, S. B., & Abramson, T. (1986). Peer tutoring and mentoring as a drop-out prevention strategy. *Clearing House, 60*(2), 68–71.

Valenzuela-Smith, M. (1983). *The effectiveness of a tutoring program for junior high Latino students.* San Francisco: University of San Francisco. (ED 237 307)

Wilson, M. F. (1995). Student tutors' skills gains at Cardiff institute of higher education. In A. Daniel (Ed.), *Learning together: Student tutoring research and evaluation papers on pupil aspirations and student tutor skills* (pp. 85–96). London: Community Service Volunteers.

REFERENCES AND SUPPLEMENTAL BIBLIOGRAPHY: PEER TUTORING WITHIN HIGHER EDUCATION

American River College. (1993). *A.R.C. Beacon project: Student catalyst program—peer assisted learning, first semester summary report.* Sacramento, CA: American River College. (ED 355 995)

Amundsen, C. L., & Bernard, R. M. (1989). Institutional support for peer contact in distance education: An empirical investigation. *Distance Education, 10*(1), 7–23.

Annis, L. F. (1983). The processes and effects of peer tutoring. *Human Learning, 2*(1), 39–47.

Arneman K., & Prosser M. (1993). The development of two peer tutoring programmes in the faculty of dentistry, University of Sydney. In *Proceedings of Conference on Peer Tutoring at University of Auckland 19–21 August 1993* (pp. 7–20). Auckland: Higher Education Research Office and University of Auckland.

Bargh, J. A., & Schul, Y. (1980). On the cognitive benefits of teaching. *Journal of Educational Psychology, 72*(5), 593–604.

Barnett, R. (1992). *Improving higher education.* Buckingham: Open University Press.

Beach, L. R. (1960). Sociability and academic achievement in various types of learning situations. *Journal of Educational Psychology, 51*(4), 208–212.

Bell, E. (1983). The peer tutor: The writing center's most valuable resource. *Teaching English in the Two-Year College, 9*(2), 141–144.

Benware, C. A., & Deci, E. L. (1984). Quality of learning with an active versus passive motivational set. *American Educational Research Journal, 21*(4), 755–765.

Bidgood, P. (1994). The success of Supplemental Instruction: The statistical evidence. In C. Rust & J. Wallace (Eds.), *Helping students to learn from each other: Supplemental Instruction* (pp. 71–79). Birmingham: Staff and Educational Development Association.

Black, J. (1993). Peer tutor support in nursing and midwifery at Otago Polytechnic. In *Proceedings of Conference on Peer Tutoring at University of Auckland, 19–21 August 1993* (pp. 33–36). Auckland: Higher Education Research Office & University of Auckland.

Bobko, E. (1984). The effective use of undergraduates as tutors for college science students. *Journal of College Science Teaching, 14,* 60–62.

Bridgham, R. G., & Scarborough, S. (1992). Effects of Supplemental Instruction in selected medical school science courses. *Academic Medicine, 67*(10), 569–571.

Button, B. L., Sims, R., & White, L. (1990). Experience of proctoring over three years at Nottingham Polytechnic. In S. Goodlad & B. Hirst (Eds.), *Explorations in peer tutoring* (pp. 110–119). Oxford: Blackwell.

Cone, A. L. (1988). Low tech/high touch criterion-based learning. *Psychological Reports, 63*(1), 203–207.

Cornwall, M. G. (1979). *Students as teachers: Peer teaching in higher education.* Amsterdam: C.O.W.O., University of Amsterdam.

Davis, C. S. (1978). Peer tutors: Their utility and training in the Personalised System of Instruction. *Educational Technology, 18,* 23–26.

Ellis, R. (1993). *Quality assurance for university teaching.* Buckingham: Open University Press.

Entwistle, N. (1992). *The impact of teaching and learning outcomes in higher education: A literature review.* Sheffield: Universities and Colleges Staff Development Unit, CVCP.

Falchikov, N. (1990). An experiment in same-age peer tutoring in higher education: Some observations concerning the repeated experience of tutoring or being tutored. In S. Goodlad & B. Hirst (Eds.), *Explorations in peer tutoring* (pp. 120–142). Oxford: Blackwell.

Fantuzzo, J. W., Dimeff, L. A., & Fox, S. L. (1989). Reciprocal peer tutoring: A multimodal assessment of effectiveness with college students. *Teaching of Psychology, 16*(3), 133–135.

Fantuzzo, J. W., Riggio, R. W., Connelly, S., & Dimeff, L. (1989). Effects of reciprocal peer tutoring on academic achievement and psychological adjustment: A component analysis. *Journal of Educational Psychology, 81*(2), 173–177.

Fineman, S. (1981). Reflections on peer teaching and peer assessment: An undergraduate experience. *Assessment and Evaluation in Higher Education, 6*(1), 82–93.

Freemouw, W. J., & Feindler, E. L. (1978). Peer versus professional models for study skills training. *Journal of Counseling Psychology, 25*(6), 576–580.

Gere, A. R. (1987). *Writing groups: History, theory and implications.* Carbondale IL: Southern Illinois University Press.

Goldschmid, B., & Goldschmid, M. L. (1976). Peer teaching in higher education: A review. *Higher Education, 5,* 9–33.

Hart, G. (1990). Peer learning and support via audio-teleconferencing in continuing education for nurses. *Distance Education, 11*(2), 308–319.

Hartman, H. J. (1990). Factors affecting the tutoring process. *Journal of Educational Development, 14*(2), 2–6.

Hay, I. (1993, August). Writing groups in geography. In *Proceedings of Conference on Peer Tutoring at University of Auckland,* (pp. 101–122). Auckland: Higher Education Research Office & University of Auckland.

Healy, C. E. (1994). Supplemental Instruction: A model for supporting student learning. In H. C. Foot, C. J. Howe, A. Anderson, A. K. Tolmie, & D. A. Warden (Eds.), *Group and interactive learning* (pp. 171–176). Southampton & Boston: Computational Mechanics.

Hendelman, W. J., & Boss, M. (1986). Reciprocal peer teaching by medical students in the gross anatomy laboratory. *Journal of Medical Education, 61*(8), 674–680.

Holladay, J. (1989). *Monroe County Community College writing across the Curriculum: Annual report 1988–89.* Michigan: Monroe County Community College. (ED 310 820)

Holladay, J. M. (1990). *Writing across the curriculum: Annual report 1989–90.* Michigan: Monroe County Community College (ED 326 260).

House, J. D., & Wohlt, V. (1990). The effect of tutoring program participation on the performance of academically underprepared college freshmen. *Journal of College Student Development, 31,* 365–370.

Johansen, M. L., Martenson, D. F., & Bircher, J. (1992). Students as tutors in problem-based learning: Does it work? *Medical Education, 26*(2), 163–165.

Johnston, C. (1993, August). The integration of trainee teachers in an undergraduate peer tutoring project at the University of Melbourne. In *Proceedings of Conference on Peer Tutoring at University of Auckland, (pp. 145–157).* Auckland : Higher Education Research Office & University of Auckland.

Keller, F. S. (1968). "Goodbye, teacher...". *Journal of Applied Behavior Analysis, 1*(1), 79–89.

Kenney, P. A., & Kallison, J. M. (1994). Research studies on the effectiveness of Supplemental Instruction in mathematics. *New Directions for Teaching and Learning, 60*(4) (Special issue on Supplemental Instruction), 75–82.

Kulik, J. A., Kulik, C. C., & Cohen, P. A. (1979). A meta analysis of outcome studies of Keller's Personalised System of Instruction. *American Psychologist, 34*(4), 307–318.

Lawson, D. (1989). Peer helping programs in the colleges and universities of Quebec and Ontario. *Canadian Journal of Counselling, 23*(1), 41–56.

Lee, R. E. (1988). Assessing retention program holding power effectiveness across smaller community colleges. *Journal of College Student Development, 29*(3), 255–262.

Levine, J. R. (1990). Using a peer tutor to improve writing in a psychology class: One instructor's experience. *Teaching of Psychology, 17*(1), 57–58.

Lidren, D. M., Meier, S. E., & Brigham, T. A. (1991). The effects of minimal and maximal peer tutoring systems on the academic performance of college students. *Psychological Record, 41*(1), 69–77.

Loh, H. (1993, August). Peer assisted study sessions in anatomy for nursing students. In *Proceedings of Conference on Peer Tutoring at University of Auckland* (pp. 193–202). Auckland: Higher Education Research Office and University of Auckland.

Longuevan, C., & Shoemaker, J. (1991, November). *Using multiple regression to evaluate a peer tutoring program for undergraduates.* Paper presented at the Annual Meeting of the California Educational Research Association, San Diego, CA. (ED 341 717)

Louth, R., McAllister, C., & McAllister, H. A. (1993). The effects of collaborative writing techniques on freshman writing and attitudes. *Journal of Experimental Education, 61*(3), 215–224.

McDonnell, J. T. (1994). Peer tutoring: A pilot scheme among computer science undergraduates. *Mentoring and Tutoring, 2*(2), 3–10.

McKellar, N. A. (1986). Behaviors used in peer tutoring. *Journal of Experimental Education, 54*(3), 163–167.

Magin, D., & Churches, A. (1993, August). Student proctoring: Who learns what? In *Proceedings of Conference on Peer Tutoring at University of Auckland* (pp. 215–226). Auckland: Higher Education Research Office and University of Auckland.

Mallatrat, J. (1994). Learning about the learners—The impact of a peer tutoring scheme. In H. C. Foot, C. J. Howe, A. Anderson, A. K. Tolmie, & D. A. Warden (Eds.), *Group and interactive learning* (pp. 189–194). Southampton & Boston: Computational Mechanics.

Martin, D. C., & Arendale, D. R. (1990). *Supplemental Instruction: Improving student performance, increasing student persistence.* Kansas City, MO: University of Missouri.

Martin, D. C., & Arendale, D. R. (1992). Supplemental Instruction: Improving first-year student success in high-risk courses. *The Freshman Year Experience: Monograph Series No. 7.* Columbia, SC: South Carolina University. (ED 354 839)

Martin, D. C., Blanc, R. A., & DeBuhr, L. (1983). Breaking the attrition cycle: The effects of Supplemental Instruction on undergraduate performance and attrition. *Journal of Higher Education, 54*(1), 80–89.

Maxwell, M. (1990). Does tutoring help? A look at the literature. *Review of Research in Developmental Education, 7*(4), 3–7.

Meredith, G. M., & Schmitz, E. D. (1986). Student-taught and faculty-taught seminars in undergraduate education: Another look. *Perceptual and Motor Skills, 62*(2), 593–594.

Moody, S., & McCrae, J. (1994). Cross year peer tutoring with law undergraduates. In H. C. Foot, C. J. Howe, A. Anderson, A. K. Tolmie, & D. A. Warden (Eds.), *Group and interactive learning* (pp. 201–210). Southampton & Boston: Computational Mechanics.

Moore-West, M., Hennessy, A., Meilman, P. W., & O'Donnell, J. F. (1990). The presence of student-based peer advising, peer tutoring & performance evaluation programs among U.S. medical schools. *Academic Medicine, 65*(10), 660–661.

Moust, J. H. C., De Volder, M. L., & Nuy, H. J. P. (1989). Peer teaching and higher level cognitive learning outcomes in problem-based learning. *Higher Education, 18*(6), 737–742.

Moust, J. C., & Schmidt, H. G. (1992, April). *Undergraduate students as tutors: Are they as effective as faculty in conducting small-group tutorials?* Paper presented at the American Educational Research Association Symposium on Rewarding Teaching at Research Universities, San Francisco, CA. (ED 346 774)

Moust, J. H. C., & Schmidt, H. G. (1994a). Facilitating small-group learning: A comparison of student and staff tutors' behavior. *Instructional Science, 22,* 287–301.

Moust, J. H. C., & Schmidt, H. G. (1994b). Effects of staff and student tutors on student achievement. *Higher Education, 28,* 471–482.

National Center for Supplemental Instruction. (1994). Review of research concerning the effectiveness of SI. Kansas City, MO: NCSI, University of Missouri at Kansas City.

O'Donnell, A. M., Dansereau, D. F., Rocklin, T., Lambiotte, J. G., Hythecker, V. I., & Larson, C. O. (1985). Co-operative writing: Direct effects and transfer. *Written Communication, 2*(3), 307–315.

Oley, N. (1992). Extra credit and peer tutoring: Impact on the quality of writing in introductory psychology in an O. A. college. *Teaching of Psychology, 19*(2), 78–81.

Olson, G. A. (Ed.) (1984). *Writing centers: Theory and administration.* Urbana, Il: National Council of Teachers of English.

Quintrell, N., & Westwood, M. (1994). The influence of a peer-pairing program on international students' first year experience and use of student services. *Higher Education Research and Development, 13*(1), 49–57.

Riggio, R. E., Fantuzzo, J. W., Connelly, S., & Dimeff, L. A. (1991). Reciprocal peer tutoring: A classroom strategy for promoting academic and social integration in undergraduate students. *Journal of Social Behavior and Personality, 6*(2), 387–396.

Rizzolo, P. (1982). Peer tutors make good teachers: A successful writing program. *Improving College and University Teaching, 30*(3), 115–119.

Robin, A. L., & Heselton, P. (1977). Proctor training: The effects of a manual versus direct training. *Journal of Personalised Instruction, 2,* 19–24.

Rosen, S., Powell, E. R., & Schubot, D. B. (1977). Peer-tutoring outcomes as influenced by the equity and type of role assignment. *Journal of Educational Psychology, 69*(3), 244–252.

Rust, C. (1993, June). *Supplemental instruction at Oxford Brookes university.* Paper given at Peer Tutoring Consortium Conference, University of Glamorgan.

Rust, C., & Wallace, J. (Eds.). (1994). *Helping students to learn from each other: Supplemental Instruction.* Birmingham: Staff and Educational Development Association.

Rye, P. D., Wallace, J., & Bidgood, P. (1993). Instruction in learning skills: An integrated approach. *Medical Education, 27,* 470–473.

Schaffer, J. L., Wile, M. Z., & Griggs, R. C. (1990). Students teaching students: A medical school peer tutorial programme. *Medical Education, 24*(4), 336–343.

Schmidt, H., Arend, A. V. D., Kokx, I., & Boon, L. (1994). Peer versus staff tutoring in problem-based learning. *Instructional Science, 22,* 279–285.

Sherman, J. G. (1992). Reflections on PSI: Good news and bad. *Journal of Applied Behavior Analysis, 25*(1), 59–64.

Topping, K. J. (1996). The effectiveness of peer tutoring in further and higher education: A typology and review of the literature. *Higher Education, 32*(3), 321–345.

Topping, K. J., Hill, S., McKaig, A., Rogers, C., Rushi, N., & Young, D. (1997). Paired reciprocal peer tutoring in undergraduate economics. *Innovations in Education and Training International, 34*(2), 96–113.

Topping, K. J., Simpson, G., Thompson, L., & Hill, S. (1997). Faculty-wide accredited cross-year student supported learning. *Higher Education Review, 29*(3), 41–64.

Topping, K. J., Watson, G. A., Jarvis, R. J., & Hill, S. (1996). Same-year paired peer tutoring with first year undergraduates. *Teaching in Higher Education, 1*(3), 341–356.

Wallace, J. (1993, June 23). *Supplemental Instruction at Kingston University.* Paper given at Peer Tutoring Consortium Conference, University of Glamorgan.

Whitman, N. A. (1988). *Peer teaching: To teach is to learn twice* (ASHE-ERIC Higher Education Report). Washington, DC: ERIC Clearinghouse on Higher Education.

REFERENCES: MENTORING

Boags, R., Scales, B., Brandt, R., & Graham, J. (1996). *Expanding Du Pont's best practice mentoring program.* Proceedings of Ninth Diversity in Mentoring Conference, April, 1996. Kalamazoo, MI: International Mentoring Association, Western Michigan University.

Borredon, E. (1995). *How does mentoring contribute to management education?* Unpublished master's thesis, University of Lancaster.

Conway, C. (1994). *Mentoring managers in organisations.* Berkhamstead U.K.: Ashridge Management Research Group, Ashridge Management College.

Engestrom, Y. (1994). *Training for change: New approaches to instruction and learning in working life.* Geneva: International Labour Office.

Gannior, R. M., & Garcia, R. (1996). Fortune 500 mentors Fortune 500 K. In *Proceedings of ninth diversity in mentoring conference,* (pp. 294–317) April 1996. Kalamazoo, MI: International Mentoring Association, Western Michigan University.

Gay, B. (1994). What is mentoring? *Education and Training, 36*(5), 4–7.

Gay, B., & Stephenson, J. (1996, April). A coat of many colours. In *Proceedings of Ninth Diversity in Mentoring Conference,* (pp. 128–142). Kalamazoo, MI: International Mentoring Association, Western Michigan University.

Goleman, D. (1996). *Emotional intelligence.* London: Bloomsbury.

Levinson, D. J., Darrow, C., Klein, E., Levinson, M., & McKee, B. (1978). *The seasons of a man's life.* New York: Ballantine.

Montgomery, D. L. (1993). *Critical success factors in matching formal mentoring pairs in organisations.* Unpublished doctoral thesis, The California School of Professional Psychology, Berkeley, CA.

Murray, M., & Owen, M. A. (1991). *Beyond the myths and magic of mentoring.* San Francisco, CA: Jossey-Bass.

Robertson, C. (1992). *Work-based learning contracts.* (Oxford Polytechnic/Employment Department). London: Her Majesty's Stationery Office.

Robertson, C., & Priest, J. (1995). *A place of learning—A place for learning.* (Oxford Brookes University/Employment Department). London: Her Majesty's Stationery Office.

Topping, K. J., McCowan, P., & McCrae, J. (1998). Peer mentoring of students in social work training. *Social Work in Education, 17*(1), 45–56.

Zey, M. G. (1996). *The mentor connection: Strategic alliances in corporate life.* (3rd ed.). New Brunswick & London: Transaction Publishers.

17

Summary and Conclusions

Stewart W. Ehly
University of Iowa
Keith Topping
University of Dundee

This text has covered the broad territory of peer-assisted learning (PAL), probing into the factors that account for the success of the interventions that fall under the PAL label. In this final chapter, we summarize key evidence supporting the utility of PAL interventions, highlight the main issues raised by the contributors, and present a strong case for the adoption and evaluation of such strategies.

As noted in the preface, the authors view PAL as

1. a group of learning strategies complementary to professional teaching but definitely not surrogate professional teaching;
2. structured to ensure gains for all participants in one or more domains,
3. available to all on an equal opportunity basis, since all have something to give,
4. carefully organized and monitored by professional teachers with an extended conception of their role (p. xxx).

Within the five parts of the text, the contributors have offered details on PAL activities, and provided the reader with the opportunity to:

1. Introduce recent developments in PAL.
2. Review options for interventions.
3. Reflect on relevant theory and research refining understanding of options consider evidence for effectiveness.

4. Develop an integrated and reflective view of PAL.

5. Give the reader sufficient organizational detail to pursue innovation in their own practice.

To assist the reader, we have highlighted key conclusions and future directions from the five thematic sections. The notion of embedding PAL into the ongoing life of the classroom is addressed in depth and serves as a bridge to our closing argument.

The Basis and Benefits of PAL

Part I, "The Basis and Benefits of Peer-Assisted Learning," was designed to enable improvement in the application of known procedures and the design of new procedures, as well as enabling better prediction of outcomes. The chapter by Foot and Howe considered relevant theory and fundamental research in educational, developmental, and social psychology that illuminates the impact of PAL. Exploring the factors that might account for the success of peer tutoring, these authors discussed the means by which a shared experience can produce benefits for both participants. In particular, Vygotsky's focus on the child's experiences during peer interactions provided not only a vocabulary for considering the dynamics of PAL, but a set of lenses through which to view events in the classroom.

The learning that occurs during PAL also reflects, as Foot and Howe expressed, the "very process of generating dialogue, of having one's beliefs and ideas challenged." Anyone who has worked with peer tutorials and other forms of PAL has experienced the excitement of children as they respond to the challenges of a common task. Whether preschoolers or adolescents, students become involved with a kind of cognitive and social engagement possible only with peers, free of the barriers of status and power that can affect adult–child relations.

Foot and Howe set the tone for the remaining chapters by acknowledging the limits to our knowledge of PAL. Much more rigorous evaluation of programs and research under controlled conditions is needed before we can speak with complete confidence on optimal arrangements for peer learning. The authors' emphasis on training, structure, and monitoring is echoed across all other discussions of PAL strategies.

In chap. 3, Maheady reviewed the advantages and disadvantages that PAL can have in relation to teacher-mediated instruction. Maheady examined the impact of children on their peers. Of special merit in the literature on peer tutoring is the strong evidence on mutual benefits for participants. Maheady promoted the use of multiple opportunities for PAL, so that children can experience both leader and follower (e.g., tutor and tutee) roles (Chapman, Fantuzzo, Ginsburg-Block, and Gartner echoed his argument in their chapters).

Maheady succeeded in linking PAL techniques to broader agendas for school reform. Clear evidence of student gains on outcomes considered important by parents and educators provided a compelling case to build a school reform program around a core set of PAL activities. Teachers benefited not only through improvements in student learning, but in having the opportunity to devote more time to interventions with individual children. Maheady also identified the potential of PAL approaches for school professionals themselves.

We especially appreciated Maheady's consideration of the disadvantages or challenges to PAL techniques. The literature has generated few discussions of the ethical dilemmas facing adults as they seek to implement PAL. Strict attention to informed consent, for both parents and students, is only the beginning of the educator's responsibility to ensure acceptable outcomes. Maheady provided guideposts for planners so that full accountability exists and activities are monitored and evaluated. Much thought and discussion are needed before many parents and educators will be satisfied that any ethical dilemmas involved in PAL interventions are resolved.

In chap. 4, Chapman considered key organizational components and mechanisms in PAL that are associated with successful outcomes. Her discussion reinforced the importance of attending to selection, training, monitoring, and evaluation throughout all forms of PAL.

Chapman's chapter was also valuable in providing an overview of the commonalities in the literature on peer tutoring, peer modeling, peer education, peer counseling, peer monitoring, and peer assessment. Chapman highlighted how a child's skills and engagement in both tutor and learner roles adds to the learning that is experienced and applauded the efforts of educators who have an explicit plan for the recruitment, selection, and training of tutors. We argue that similar benefits are likely to be achieved when teachers prepare students who will be on the receiving end of any PAL intervention. The recipient's perspective of PAL activities remain an almost invisible part of the discussion of such educational offerings.

Chapman also acknowledged the limits of our knowledge as to the optimal implementation of PAL strategies. Her recommendations on how to proceed in the absence of clear signposts were not only sound, but encouraging. Chapman was convinced we have sufficient confidence in the value of peer influence that practitioners are justified in pursuing any of the PAL options.

Methods to Enhance the Effectiveness of Peer Tutoring

Part II focused on peer tutoring, considering methods to enhance effectiveness with a diverse collection of learners. The five chapters in this part demonstrated that peer tutoring is a robust method that can be used to good effect with all students, including those experiencing difficulty in traditional teacher-directed learning activities. Chapter 5 by Topping reviewed specific methods, which have been extensively implemented and evaluated, for paired peer tutoring in reading, spelling, and writing. Topping is best known internationally for his programs and research for educators on paired learning. His work on Paired Reading, Cued Spelling, and Paired Writing were presented in the chapter, with special attention to the organization of peers in activities with classmates. Each option in paired learning was discussed, with details on how to train students, monitor their interactions, and assess results. The research evidence on the approaches, built on a foundation of peer tutorials, was encouraging: Children experience increased mastery as well as boosts to self-confidence and greater enjoyment of learning. Given the importance of literacy in every school's program and the ever-present need for materials and activities that complement teacher-led instruction, paired learning provides a viable direction to expand PAL activities within schools.

In chap. 6, Arreaga-Mayer, Terry, and Greenwood from the Juniper Gardens Children's Project discussed how whole classes can be involved in peer tutoring, with organizational and ecological advantages. The work of Greenwood and his colleagues stimulated a broad array of research and implementation projects, with results applauded by many of the authors of the current text. The classwide peer tutoring (CWPT) methodology has more than 15 years' of data to verify the important impact of peers on learning experienced with classmates. Now that its developers have implemented the program with passage reading, reading comprehension, sight-word reading, mathematics, spelling, science, and social studies instruction, a wider range of educators have even stronger motivation to use the strategy.

The idea of engaging entire groups of children in peer tutorials has existed for more than a century. The CWPT method provides a structure to group arrangements that allows every student to experience a lead role with peers over time. The authors offered a typical daily format to give readers a vision of the process by which CWPT engages children in learning. Classroom teachers play an important role in training students for peer tutoring activities, and thus require training to guarantee that procedures for implementation, monitoring, and evaluation are reliably and validly delivered. Of special note within the description of CWPT was the reference to the continuing development of assessment materials that will reflect accurately children's growing mastery of the instructional requirements within the classroom.

Fantuzzo and Ginsburg-Block considered reciprocal peer tutoring (RPT) in chap. 7. The approach is methodologically important in that it focuses attention on the structure and quality of interaction between peers as the main vehicle for improved learning, and affectively and ethically important in that everyone gets to be a tutor. The RPT program was developed to target low-achieving students in urban elementary schools within the United States. Although many of the approaches considered in this text have been used with students considered high risk (by any definitional standard), the RPT approach seeks directly to combine peer teaching activities and peer-managed group reward contingencies with a population labeled *high risk*.

The intervention requires a familiar agenda of training, monitoring, and evaluation. The authors identified the work of Vygotsky, Piaget, and others as theoretical influences for the structure of the RPT approach. The social elements of tutoring reinforce the cognitive engagement of participants, producing retention of information and consolidation of skills so important to children's academic success.

A feature of special interest within the chapter was the role of parents in support of tutoring activities. Given the possible hesitation of some parents regarding peer tutoring, questioning reliance on peer-directed rather than teacher-directed instruction, the emphasis on parent partnerships was noteworthy. Parents have a major impact on all facets of children's growth and development; any means by which educators can recruit parents to support educational strategies known to benefit children will strengthen relations between home and school as well as children's opportunities for learning.

In chap. 8, developing the theme that all students have something to give and can themselves benefit by giving, C. Maher, B. Maher, and C. Thurston considered programs that deploy disruptive students as tutors. Maher and his students considered the growing numbers of students receiving special services for their behavioral and emotional difficulties. Peer tutoring has been implemented in a wide array of settings with students identified as disruptive. Can such students engage in tutoring, as tutor or learner? C. Maher affirmed "yes", and offered evidence that benefits can take the form of increased learning and social competence.

The authors considered programs in both elementary and secondary school settings, focusing on the merits of A VICTORY factors that accounted for success. Maher's recommendations for structuring tutorials reflected attention to systemic variables that can be manipulated to support a broad agenda for program implementation. Procedural guidelines were offered, providing clear directions for selecting, training, implementing, and evaluating successful tutorials. For several years, C. Maher's research has provided educators with abundant testimony to the power of peers as partners in learning. To provide disruptive students with the opportunity to experience PAL requires educators and support professionals to prepare themselves and their students for the behavioral, as well as cognitive, expectations of peer tutoring.

In the final chapter of Part II, Scruggs and Mastropieri reviewed the deployment of students with other kinds of special educational needs as both tutees and tutors. The authors summarized more than 25 years of evidence attesting to the benefits and limitations of peer tutoring, and pointed toward promising developments in the literature. From the meta-analytic studies in the early 1980s, the research literature had come to the consensus that tutoring in pursuit of academic gains is a positive venture for both the tutor and tutee (learner). Less compelling evidence had been produced to support affective benefits for participants, although abundant support is available, within this text, that select benefits can be achieved under specific conditions. The mainstreaming and inclusion movements, within the United States and elsewhere, have been implemented so that classmates can benefit from their involvement, both academic and social, with each other. Peer tutoring can thus satisfy a sociopolitical as well as academic agenda for many observers and consumers of school programs. Tutoring has been shown to result in learning for children of all ages, regardless of educational classification or placement.

Scruggs and Mastropieri, from their own work as well as from their analysis of the literature, concluded that children in special education programs can derive social benefits via involvement in peer tutoring. Particular attention is necessary to the selection and training of students with special needs, as well as to all aspects of the implementation procedures involved in tutorials. They were optimistic that emerging peer programs that provide adequate structure for learners (e.g., the PALS program described in Fuchs, Fuchs, Mathes, & Simmons, 1997) ensures that all children can experience the benefits of peer tutoring activities.

Peer Facilitation and Education

In Part III, "Peer Facilitation and Education," authors considered PAL interventions within three categories. Schunk, in chap. 10, discussed peer modeling in the context of motivation, self-efficacy, and self-managed and independent learning. The chapter discussed how peers can prove more effective than teachers in promoting deeper understanding of vital life issuessuch as: health, HIV and AIDS, drugs, sex, smoking, alcohol, driving, and violence prevention. In essence, Schunk confirmed the vital importance of peer models in the cognitive, social, and emotional development of children. Drawing on social cognitive theory, Schunk examined the factors through which peers have such a potent effect.

The practical consequences of Schunk's argument included the need for greater awareness in training programs of the prerequisite skills of both peers (e.g., motivation, level of development). Peer programs seem especially powerful in developing the student's sense of self-efficacy. Of interest to researchers is Schunk's attention to individual characteristics and behaviors that can be studied further to clarify the consequences of peer interventions for participants. The reader leaves Schunk's chapter more firmly convinced than ever in the advantages of PAL, for interventions that target both mastery and coping. Schunk's comments on self-regulation are an area of great potential for future research on PAL strategies.

The goal of self-regulation is embedded in many of the peer health education programs considered by Mathie and Ford in chap. 11. Formal and informal activities with peer leaders have become a key element within programs addressing smoking, sexual activity (and associated sexually transmitted diseases), and drug use/abuse by children and adolescents. As the authors attested, traditional (i.e., adult-delivered) health education programs have attracted bad press, due to their less than optimal impact on populations considered to be at risk. The idea of using peers in teaching roles has appealed to some health educators and has been a focal point of several intervention programs.

The consequences rather than the antecedents to peer strategies were an important element within Mathie and Ford's analysis. When social inoculation is the goal, whether translated as abstinence or as limits to high-risk behaviors, students could benefit on a long-term basis from participation in peer education programs. Our understanding of the ultimate merits of activities that involve peer educators delivering an anti-high-risk message remains limited; these authors were quite correct in arguing that much more needs to be done to establish greater confidence in the likelihood of immediate and long-term benefits from programs. The highly controversial nature of the behaviors being targeted by peer health programs provides immediate, and at times unwelcome, publicity on PAL strategies being implemented by schools and other community agencies. The need to address concerns of parents and other community members prior to peer health interventions may not be unique among PAL activities, but can produce an intense debate between advocates of peer-directed and adult-directed strategies.

In chap. 12, Ehly and Vazquez considered peer counseling interventions. Reliance on peers to provide an emotional support system within the school and community has been studied since the 1970s, but have been much more effectively documented within historical studies of family life (see, e.g., the five-volume *History of Private Life*, or the more recent two-volume *History of the Family* by Burguière, Klapisch-Zuber, Segalen, & Zonabend, 1996a, 1996b). The first studies of peer counseling activities concentrated on extending the reach of traditional school counseling programs; more recent efforts have been directed at many of the behaviors mentioned previously as the focus of peer health education.

Peer counseling programs appear most successful when adult leaders attend to providing understandable structure to the actions of participants, provide training that alerts peer counselors to key behaviors to observe as well as to emit, and monitor process and evaluate outcomes. The range of helping behaviors that can be expected of peer counselors will increase with age, although age is no guarantee of the student's ability to listen and respond to affective signals from a peer. Ehly and Vazquez focused on some cultural factors that can influence the development of a peer counseling program. We have much more to learn about the impact of culture not only on behavior but on the effectiveness of educational and mental health strategies sensitive to the needs of individual children.

Structured Peer Feedback

Part IV explored the yet more innovative area of structured peer feedback. In chap. 13, Henington and Skinner discussed peer monitoring, and the impact of process checking of study behaviors on learning outcomes. Peer monitoring interventions include a cluster of strategies that contribute to the development of children's self-management. Peers as trained monitors of academic behaviors have not been widely discussed in the literature, yet the potential for their use is well-established throughout this entire text. Henington and Skinner provided valuable guidelines that educators can enact to involve students in data gathering and feedback on the progress of classmates and other peers.

As yet, peer monitoring seems novel to many teachers. Reliance on peers as trained monitors may be viewed as difficult (e.g., too hard to train peers) or ethically complex (e.g., given confidentiality issues, can teachers rely on peers to gather certain data?), producing a host of difficult questions from students, parents, other educators, and administrators. As with most novelties, frequent and successful use of peer monitoring will resolve much of the hesitation of observers and participants. The final judgment on the merits of the strategy may rest on the success of peers in assisting teachers and each other to enhance opportunities for positive learning outcomes. Henington and Skinner were convincing in their discussion of the benefits, for both students and their teachers, that can be derived from same-age and cross-age applications of peer monitoring techniques.

In chap. 14, O'Donnell considered how peer assessment of the quality of the final products of learning can concentrate the mind of assessor and assessed, while permitting more immediate feedback than an overworked teacher could offer. As O'Donnell noted, the process of peer assessment can assist children to develop techniques for self regulation, thus producing additional long-term benefits.

Peer assessment concentrates on the summative evaluation of the products of learning as generated by a peer. Although the current literature has reported on only a narrow range of studies promoting the relevant techniques (e.g., peer evaluation of writing), this PAL intervention choice is very promising. O'Donnell, although recognizing the limits of peers in offering feedback on academic products, did view peer assessment as consistent with many schools' adoption of portfolios to evaluate student progress. Rather than relying exclusively on a teacher's assessment of progress, she promoted opportunities to involve peers in the evaluation process.

Peers can be allies of the teacher in directing a learner's attention to the requirements of assigned tasks, providing interim feedback on the impact a piece of writing might have on an intended audience, and suggesting editing ideas. The quality of peer assessment information will depend, O'Donnell argued, on the cognitive and social demands of the task. Training peers for the responsibilities of the feedback process will be a high priority in schools that decide to implement the activity. The author cited a number of studies that will attract attention to the potential value of this PAL option.

Embedding and Extending PAL

Part V considered necessary the embedding and extending of PAL, because too many approaches in education come and go according to changes in fashion rather than in their effectiveness. The success of embedding any educational technique will reflect not only the merits of the particular intervention, but the willingness of students, teachers, administrators, and parents to support the implementation and evaluation of innovative methods. Many PAL strategies have been perceived as worth the initial effort due to the wide success of peer tutoring.

Gartner's publications on peer tutoring have received broad attention for more than 25 years. Gartner's seminal work in the United States with Riessman on peer tutoring is familiar to many readers. Her chapter focused on developmental and chronological progression in tutoring experience and systemic expansion and embedding across the school. In chap. 15, Gartner raised the dilemma facing all those who care about public schools: Broad public criticism of current schooling practices has produced recommendations that would drastically change the funding of public education, while school reform efforts in response to such criticism have produced few lasting improvements. Rather than despair, Gartner endorsed the concept of students as *prosumers*, "education consumers who produce learning." The prosumer would be engaged in any and all of the PAL strategies considered in this text, as well as other strategies yet to be developed.

The proposal to build on what we know to enhance student growth and development parallels other proposals in education that place students in a more academically empowered position in relation to the adults who supervise and instruct them. An educational ethic in which every learner attends not only to personal growth but the growth of others is an exciting affirmation of PAL.

Chapter 16 summarized the use of PAL beyond the elementary and secondary school. PAL programs for tutoring, counseling, and health education represent only a small selection of potential applications with adult learners. Hill, Gay, and Topping considered evidence on college students tutoring regular school students, peer tutoring within further and higher education establishments, and mentoring within and between universities and the professional and industrial workplace. Given multiple developmental opportunities, tutoring can become a normal lifelong expectation, and the experience of being a tutee is the best preparation for becoming a tutor. Positive results in achieving academic and social or affective outcomes were reported by the authors.

Perhaps the most exciting development noted by Hill, Gay, and Topping involved mentoring in and between the workplace and community. In many parts of the world, increasing attention of parents, educators, and community groups has been devoted to the transition that students make from their educational or preparation programs to adult work sites. Within the abundant literature on school reform is the argument that students arrive at work sites with prerequisite academic preparation (for the most part), but lacking in the social and emotional skills necessary to work with others and to accept feedback. PAL strategies are tools that can be used collaboratively by schools, community agencies, and work sites to increase the likelihood of on-the-job adjustment as well as long-term satisfaction with the cognitive and affective demands of adult labor. Benefits to individuals, of course, are not limited to their place of employment but extend to all facets of their personal life. Imagine a lifelong commitment to understanding oneself in relation to peers, whether on a local, national, or global scale. Gergen's (1991) book on dilemmas of identity in contemporary society provided another form of testimony as to how our connections with peers are an invaluable resource to meeting the challenges of a world that appears to become ever more complex.

EMBEDDING PAL

How, then, to ensure the longer term success of the strategies considered within this text? Embedding PAL within an organization or larger community requires careful attention to the needs of the learner, educator, and system. In order for a PAL initiative to last and/or grow, there are some considerations that should be met.

Cost–Benefit Balance for All

The benefits must outweigh the costs *for all concerned* if the initiative is to endure. For the initiating teacher, costs will be in terms of time devoted, materials and other resources, and the general harassment and stress involved in doing anything new. All of these must be kept as low as possible.

On the benefit side, the teacher will need both subjective and objective evidence of impact in relation to the objectives set.

More than that, the initiative also has to *feel good*. It should have a warm and satisfying social and emotional tone that might benefit from a little deliberate cultivation. However, no teacher is an island, and the initiative also needs to be compatible with the current local philosophy, political correctness, and mood of the professional peer group and senior policy dictators. Fortunately, PAL has largely escaped adverse politicization; it is right up there with motherhood and apple pie in terms of acceptability.

A similar analysis can be applied to the other participants—the tutors, the tutees, and the head of the institution. They also need minimization of time wasted and harassment, to feel good about the project, to be clear what they are getting out of it and the other participants are getting out of it, and to be able to confidently assert their support for it in the face of incredulity from their peer group.

Objectives and Applications

Be clear about the different objectives for different types of PAL. Your objectives for a specific project might be in the cognitive, affective, or social domain, or some combination. Do not let someone else evaluate your project against a different set of objectives.

Use a mixture of cross-age and same-age, cross-ability and same-ability, fixed role and reciprocal role methods. Choose your format as discriminately as you can to suit your objectives and possibilities. Consider which formats will suit which subjects, topics, activities, classes, rooms, and so on.

Plan for flexibility. With effort, you can devise a format or method that will fit into any local exigencies: complex organizations, highly structured timetables, lack of physical space, lack of appropriate furniture, poor acoustics, rigid attitudes in adults in positions of power, rigid attitudes in children who have learned to prefer passive inertia, and so on. Do not be overly ambitious initially—many small steps get you there quickest in the end.

Materials, Methods, and Monitoring

Materials should preferably be low cost, already on hand, differentiated for different needs, attractive and durable. A simple system for tracking current possession might be necessary, but bureaucracy that makes more work should be avoided.

A clear and simple method for interaction should be prescribed at the outset. The participants should always receive good quality training. Methods need to be truly and consistently interactive, or one partner will go to sleep. The method must involve modeling as well as much discussion, questioning, and explaining. There must be clear procedures for the identification, diagnosis, and correction of errors.

The method must build in and capitalize on intrinsic satisfaction for all participants. Once the participants are experiencing success, they should not become dependent on a routine method, and the times and boundaries within which they are encouraged to be creative and take the initiative should be clarified.

Close monitoring of participant behavior is especially necessary at the beginning, where deviation can lead to failure that will be attributed to the teacher. After an initial period of getting it right, creative and reflective deviance might be encouraged, but will need close monitoring. In the longer run, some drift is almost inevitable—a constant check should be made to ensure that it is productive.

Evaluation, Iteration, and Rejuvenation

Projects must target gains for all participants (particularly the tutors and tutees or whatever the partners are called). Evaluation also should seek to check whether there are long-term as well as short-term gains, and whether cooperative helping generalizes outside the specifically nominated PAL sessions.

Teachers might consider the extent to which they can give away some of the organization and management to the children. Obviously, they would need to repeatedly check on this, especially with younger children. Of course, teachers would wish positives to be accentuated and negatives to be eliminated. Keeping the *feel good* factor going is important. However, a degree of self-management (which can include self-monitoring) can heighten self-esteem and responsibility and help make initiatives self-sustaining.

Initiating a project (especially in an inert environment) is very demanding in terms of time and energy, although that capital investment is almost always later considered worthwhile. Once things are up and running smoothly, it is tempting to either relax, or rush on and start another project with a different group. The latter is more dangerous than the former—teachers should be careful not to spread themselves too thin. After a few weeks or months, most initiatives need some rejuvenation—not necessarily an organizational improvement, just a change to inject some novelty.

Fortunately, PAL is very flexible and offers many ways for injecting novelty—change of partners, subject topics or activities, format of operation, and so on. However, PAL should not be used for everything, or learners will overdose. Productivity can be enhanced by giving students time to rest and then returning to a modified format soon afterward.

Once PAL is accepted and deployed by more staff, some coordination will be necessary. Working together can help build iterative cycles of involvement in different kinds of PAL in different formats with all children in roles as tutees and tutors at different times, in a developmental progressive sequence. If, for example, all tutees in a cross-age, cross-ability project know that in the following year they will all be the tutors, being the tutee is likely to be more readily accepted. Being a tutee is the best apprenticeship for being a tutor.

Beyond this, however, are the systemic implications of frequent and various but equal opportunities for all to be both tutee and tutor. These lead to a positive ethos in which PAL is accepted as something normal permeating everyday life—a learning tool as natural as opening a book or turning on a computer. When class members can explain to a newcomer from another district what PAL is all about, and shows amazement when they discover that PAL is not used globally, the technique has been successfully embedded.

Creating the Future

Finally, we would like to encourage readers to talk over these successful methods with colleagues, try out some of the ideas presented here, and contribute to the expansion and improvement of practice and knowledge and even the literature on PAL. We hope that this book will inspire and encourage practitioners to successfully use and develop an increasing number of types of PAL methods, with bigger and more challenging target populations. As attention to PAL increases, we envision ever higher quality and sophistication of implementation in schools around the world.

The research literature on education provides testimony to the very real challenges facing schools and the educational process. Children and adolescents may be cast as passive recipients of educators' instructional efforts, but readers of this text know otherwise. Students are active participants with adults and each other in responding to the academic, social, and emotional challenges of school and community life. PAL represents a collection of strategies that view students as catalysts in their own growth and development, as well as contributors to the lives of their classmates. We urge readers to provide, monitor, and evaluate PAL programs in their schools.

To readers involved in research within schools, we similarly encourage attention to PAL in its myriad forms. Interventions under the PAL rubric have attracted widely varying degrees of rigorous research and evaluation. As several contributors have noted, peer tutoring research has evolved sufficiently to encourage firm confidence in the merits of implementation. A growing number of PAL strategies have experienced the benefits of strong research programs. Given our emphasis in this text on the classroom practitioner, we endorse action research programs that view teachers as collaborators with university faculty. Out of such collaborative efforts will emerge a more sophisticated awareness of the conditions under which PAL options work best.

Researchers with university connections have access to resources not readily available to practitioners in elementary and secondary schools. We appeal to academicians to focus PAL research programs on issues of greatest importance to practitioners, enter into school-university partnerships to reinforce the relevance of research efforts, and to disseminate findings quickly and in accessible forms to all interested teachers, administrators, support professionals, parents, and students. PAL can benefit every learner; we should not and cannot fail to promote the implementation of current programs and to encourage ongoing innovations in methods and materials.

REFERENCES

Burguière, A., Klapisch-Zuber, C., Segalen, M., & Zonabend, F. (Eds.). (1996a). *A history of the family: Volume I: The impact of modernity.* Cambridge, MA: Harvard University Press.

Burguière, A., Klapisch-Zuber, C., Segalen, M., & Zonabend, F. (Eds.). (1996b). *A history of the family: Volume II: Distant worlds, ancient worlds.* Cambridge, MA: Harvard University Press.

Fuchs, D., Fuchs, L. S., Mathes, P. G., & Simmons, D. C. (1997). Peer-assisted learning strategies: Making classrooms more responsive to diversity. *American Educational Research Journal, 34,* 174–206.

Gergen, K. J. (1991). *The saturated self: Dilemmas of identity in contemporary life.* New York: Basic Books.

Afterword[*]

Gita L. Vygotskaya
Moscow Academy of Education

This volume on peer-assisted learning is an important one, because it is in the work of the people who read it and act on it that I see the realization of my father's ideas and plans.

Lev Semenovich Vygotsky was very familiar with the works of Western psychologists. You only need to open any of his texts to be sure of this, and I am very pleased that the psychologists of the West also increasingly know his work.

In his article "The Historical Meaning of Crisis in Psychology," he criticized the old academic psychology, and pointed out that one of the causes of the crisis in psychology was its distancing from actual practice. For a long time, this thought of Vygotsky did not receive the attention it deserved. The way out of the crisis, Vygotsky saw, was in having theory developed in parallel with changes and advances in practice. In this sense, the psychologist is not just a researcher, but also a constructor.

In his short life, Lev Vygotsky worked a lot. First, he started as a school teacher. According to memoirs of his students, he was a talented and lively teacher. Suffice it to say that 60 years later, his students remembered the themes of his lessons. He created teaching–learning processes as a mutual activity with his students, and in conjunction with their interests, leaning heavily on those interests and developing them.

Second, Vygotsky worked in school with teachers as a psychologist–consultant. In collaboration with them, he studied individual differences in the development of children. He created new methods of instruction specific to each age group. He introduced into psychology such notions as *sensitive periods of development*, *empirical* and *scientific concept formation*, and of

---

*Dr. Boris Gindis, who is associated with Touro College, New York, kindly translated this from the Russian language.

course the *zone of proximal development.*

Third, in the late 1920s and early 1930s he sparked much interest with his medico-pedagogical conferences. These conferences were related to consultations he offered for children with special needs. The conferences allowed him to study variants of psychological and personal development. These conferences were attended by teachers, doctors, psychologists, special educators, and students from all of Moscow. It was impossible to seat all those attending, and many had to stand by open windows. They followed attentively how Vygotsky examined each child, talked to him or her, and the parents and teachers, indicating what further work was required, and what conditions would boost the child's development.

Vygotsky's first major work was published in 1926—a book titled *Pedagogical Psychology.* In publishing this book, his goal was to produce a work of a mainly practical character. He wrote in the preface that the book was intended "to come to the aid of the school and teachers, in working out a scientific understanding of the educational process resulting from advances in psychological thought." How similar to the aim of this book on peer-assisted learning.

However, the fate of Vygotsky's first book was sad: Soon after his death, the book was prohibited. The reason was rooted in the fact that in the pages of the book there were several mentions of certain individuals deemed to be *enemies of the people* in the light of the (then) ruling ideology. For a long time (more than 50 years) the book was hidden in the darkest corners of libraries, and one could not even see it, much less borrow it. The book was returned to public readership only in 1991, when it was republished, although it is still unknown in the West.

In this book and several articles (all published after his death), Vygotsky laid out many interesting and important thoughts that hold scientific and practical value for education today. Pedagogical psychology, he noted, should become a hands-on science. It should not be limited by purely theoretical problems, such as describing the nature of development; rather, it should teach us how to lead development. "Good education is ahead of development," he wrote; "thus it creates the zone of proximal development."

Vygotsky loved children, both his own and others, and worked splendidly with them. Who better to say this than me, his constant guinea pig. My teacher, Professor Zaporozetz jokingly told me: "half of child psychology in Russia is built on you, so the science is obliged to you a great deal."

I remember very well sitting at the table with many blocks before me. Next to me is my father and with his small script, he is writing down everything I am doing and saying. He tested on me the procedures later called *Vygotsky's Block Test*, the *Method of Double Stimulation*, and the Sakharov–Vygotsky *Test of Concept Formation.*

Another memory recalls that on the floor of our very small room, there was a labyrinth constructed from different objects with an orange in the center. If we could lead the orange through the maze, it would be ours. We wanted it a great deal and we tried very hard. So my father conducted on me and my cousin those experiments that Keller did with apes.

Vygotsky understood children, their attitudes, and points of view. Probably because of this, children were at ease around him, and his experiments were often perceived as interesting games. Another episode from my childhood secured me a place in the history of psychological science. I relate it here.

Once, after several rainy days, my sister, my cousin, and I were taken outside for a walk. We went alongside the river; for some reason on that particular night, a bridge caught my attention and captivated my imagination. It appeared to me so monumental and everlasting, while the river beneath seemed sorrowful and helpless. I was so impressed by what I saw that I could not wait to share this with my father. I burst into the room, and very excitedly shouted out: "Daddy, I know where rivers come from!" Everybody in the room quieted down awaiting my explanation. My father hugged me and asked gently: "So, where do they come from?" Then, in a tone of great discovery, I announced: "They are dug out from beneath the bridges!" Many years later, as an adult, I found these words in one of his works. Before them I found a phrase: "One little girl once said ... " I knew well who this little girl was!

Vygotsky loved to watch children at play. He was overjoyed when my friends would come over and we would start some sort of game. We would play just two steps from his desk. Once in a while he would look at us, then go back to his work. He died at a very young age, without realizing many of his plans. One historian of psychology said that if Pavlov and Freud had passed away at the same age, the world would not have known the theory of conditioning and psychoanalysis as we know them now. Ideas presented so many years ago by a young scientist are now central to many significant innovative movements in education in Russia, and indeed throughout the world.

More than 60 years have passed, but the theory he created lives on. There have been many conferences and publications of all kinds all over the world celebrating the centenary of his birth in 1996. Nevertheless, it still seems to me that in the works of Vygotsky there is one main direction—working with children, their parents, their teachers, counselors, and psychologists—in a word, with those whose responsibility it is to bring up, educate, and develop children. His works have many ideas not yet realized.

I encourage readers to take inspiration from my father and from books like this one on peer-assisted learning, which seeks to blend science and good practice to help accelerate the development of children. Please accept my good wishes as you put into practice and further develop the scientific legacy of my father, Lev Semenovich Vygotsky.

Resources and Contacts

General

The National Peer Helpers Association (NPHA), P.O. Box 2684, Greenville, NC 27858, USA, publishes *The Peer Facilitator Quarterly*, which includes many articles on peer education and addresses issues of evaluation as well as practice. Also available is a very substantial bibliography on various aspects of peer education and helping. NPHA also supplies a newsletter, organizational checklist, standards, and a code of ethics for implementing peer helper programs. An annual NPHA conference is held in the United States.

Peer Resources, 1052 Davie Street, Victoria, British Columbia V8S 4E3, Canada produces a catalog including many practical resources for various types of peer assisted learning, counseling and helping. They also operate training institutes and provide bibliographies, as well as publishing the *Peer Counsellor Journal*. Contact the Peer Resources Network (http://www.islandnet.com/~rcarr/peer.html and via email at: rcarr@islandnet.com).

Mentoring and Tutoring is a practitioners' journal produced by Trentham Books, Ltd., Westview House, 734 London Road, Oakhill, Stoke-on-Trent ST4 5NP, U.K.

The National Tutoring Association, P.O. Box 154, Ashley, PA 18706 USA also offers annual conferences and a regular newsletter.

CHAPTER 5: PAIRED LEARNING IN LITERACY

The key resources for this chapter follow:

Topping, K. J. (1995). *Paired reading, spelling and writing: The handbook for teachers and parents*. London & New York: Cassell.

Topping, K. J. (1997). *Duolog reading: A video training pack*. Madison WI: Institute for Academic Excellence.

Additionally:

A Teacher's Manual and NTSC training video titled *Paired Reading: Positive Reading Practice* is available from the North Alberta Reading Specialists' Council, Box 9538, Edmonton, Alberta T6E 5X2, Canada.

A Cued Spelling training videotape is available from the Kirklees Psychological Service, Civic Centre 1, High Street, Huddersfield, West Yorkshire, HD1 2NF, England.

The *Paired Reading and Paired Learning Bulletins* are available on microfiche from ERIC (1985 ED 285 124, 1986 ED 285 125, 1987 ED 285 126, 1988 ED 298 429, 1989 ED 313 656, 1990 discontinued).

For paired learning in maths and science:

Topping, K. J. (1998). *The paired science handbook: Parental involvement and peer tutoring in science.* London: Fulton; Bristol PA: Taylor & Francis.

Topping, K. J., & Bamford, J. (1998). *The paired maths handbook: Parental involvement and peer tutoring in mathematics.* London: Fulton; Bristol PA: Taylor & Francis.

Topping, K.J., & Bamford, J. (1998) *Parental involvement and peer tutoring in mathematics and science: Developing paired maths into paired science.* London: Fulton; Bristol PA: Taylor & Francis.

Further information about the Centre for Paired Learning is on the web site at: <http://www.dundee.ac.uk/psychology/c_p_lear.html>.

CHAPTER 6: CLASS WIDE PEER TUTORING

Greenwood, C. R., Delquadri, J., & Carta, J. J. (1988). *ClassWide Peer Tutoring (CWPT): Teachers manual.*

Greenwood, C. R., Terry, B. J., Delquadri, J., Elliott, M., & Arreaga-Mayer, C. (1995). *ClassWide Peer Tutoring (CWPT): Effective teaching and research review.*

For training of trainers in the use of the CWPT, contact Dr. Carmen Arreaga-Mayer or Dr. Barbara Terry.

Reference: Juniper Gardens Children's Project, 650 Minnesota Avenue, Second Floor, Kansas City, KS 66101. Telephone: (913) 321-3143; Fax: (913) 371-8522 or e-mail: camayer@kuhub.cc.ukans.edu

CHAPTER 8: DISRUPTIVE STUDENTS AS TUTORS

Brophy, J. (1996). *Teaching problem students.* New York: Guilford.

Maher, C. A., & Zins, J. E. (1988). *Psychoeducational interventions in the schools.* Elmsford, NY: Pergamon.

Maher, C. A., & Bennet, R. E. (1984). *Planning and evaluating special education services.* Englewood Cliffs, NJ: Prentice-Hall.

Maher, C. A., Illback, R. I., & Zins, J. E. (1986). *Organizational school psychology: A handbook for professionals.* Springfield, IL: Charles C. Thomas.

CHAPTER 9: TUTORING AND STUDENTS
WITH SPECIAL NEEDS

Ehly, W. W., & Larsen, S. C. (1980). *Peer tutoring for individualized instruction.* Boston: Allyn & Bacon.

Fuchs, D., Mathes, P. G., & Fuchs, L. S. (1996). *Peer-Assisted learning strategies - Reading.* (Available from Douglas Fuchs, Box 328 Peabody, Vanderbilt University, Nashville, TN 37203).

Jenkins, J. R., & Jenkins, L. M. (1981). *Crossage and peer tutoring: Help for students with learning problems.* Reston, VA: Council for Exceptional Children.

Topping, K. (1988). *The peer tutoring handbook: Promoting co-operative learning.* Cambridge, MA: Brookline Books.

CHAPTER 10: PEER MODELING

Bandura, A. (1986). *Social foundations of thought and action: A social cognitive theory.* Englewood Cliffs, NJ: Prentice Hall. (See chap. 2.)

Brody, G. H., & Stoneman, Z. (1981). Selective imitation of same-age, older, and younger peer models. *Child Development, 52,* 717–720.

Brody, G. H., & Stoneman, Z. (1985). Peer imitation: An examination of status and competence hypotheses. *Journal of Genetic Psychology, 146,* 161–170.

Dowrick, P. W., & Biggs, S. J. (Eds.). (1983). *Using video: Psychological and social applications.* Chichester, England: Wiley.

Hosford, R. E. (1981). Self-as-a-model: A cognitive social learning technique. *The Counseling Psychologist, 9*(1), 45–62.

Rosenthal, T. L., & Zimmerman, B. J. (1978). *Social learning and cognition.* New York: Academic Press.

Schunk, D. H. (1987). Peer models and children's behavioral change. *Review of Educational Research, 57,* 149–174.

Schunk, D. H. (1996). *Learning theories: An educational perspective* (2nd ed.). Englewood Cliffs, NJ: Merrill. (See chap. 4).

Schunk, D. H., & Hanson, A. R. (1985). Peer models: Influence on children's self-efficacy and achievement. *Journal of Educational Psychology, 77,* 313–322.

Schunk, D. H., Hanson, A. R., & Cox, P. D. (1987). Peer model attributes and children's achievement behaviors. *Journal of Educational Psychology, 79,* 54–61.

Shaftel, F. R., & Shaftel, G. (1982). *Role playing in the curriculum* (2nd ed.). Englewood Cliffs, NJ: Prentice-Hall.

Strain, P. S. (Ed.). (1981). *The utilization of classroom peers as behavior change agents.* New York: Plenum.

Strain, P. S., & Odom, S. L. (1986). Peer social initiations: Effective intervention for social skills development of exceptional children. *Exceptional Children, 52,* 543–551.

CHAPTER 11: PEER EDUCATION FOR HEALTH

Bonati, G., & Hawes, H, (1992). The child-to-child trust. Available from TALC (Teaching Aids at Low Cost), P.O. Box 49, St. Albans, Herts. AL1 4AX, U.K.

Center for Population Options (CPO). (1990). *Guide to implementing TAP: Teens AIDS prevention peer education program.* CPO, 1025 Vermont Avenue NW Suite 210, Washington, DC 20005, USA.

Community Service Volunteers, 237 Pentonville Road, London N1 9NJ, U.K.

Flay, B.R. (1985). Psychosocial approaches to smoking prevention: A review of findings. *Health Psychology, 4,* 449–488.

Hansen, W., & Graham, J. (1991). Preventing alcohol, marijuana and cigarette use among adolescents: Peer pressure resistance training verses establishing conservative forms. *Preventive Medicine, 20,* 414–430.

May, C. (1991). Research on alcohol education for young people: A critical review of the literature. *Health Education Journal, 50*(4), 195–199.

Milburn, K. (1995). A critical review of peer education with young people with special reference to sexual health. *Health Education Research: Theory and Practice, 10*(4), 407–420.

Moskowitz, J. M. (1989). The primary prevention of alcohol problems: A critical review of the research literature. Journal of Studies on Alcohol, 50(1), 54–88.

Rickert, V. (1991). Effects of a peer counselled AIDS education program on knowledge, attitudes and satisfaction of adolescents. *Journal of Adolescent Health, 12,* 38–43.

Schaps, E., Di Bartalo, R., Palley, C., & Churgin, S. (1981). A review of 127 drug abuse prevention programs. *Journal of Drug Issues, 11*(1), 17–43.

Telch, M. J., Miller, L. M., & Killen, J. D. (1990). Social influences approach to smoking prevention: The effects of videotape delivery with and without same-age peer leader participation. *Addictive Behaviors, 15,* 21–28.

Tobler, N. (1986). Meta analysis of 43 adolescent drug prevention programs: Quantitative outcome results of program participants compared to a control or comparison group. *Journal of Drug Issues, 16*(4), 537–567.

Newitt, K., Karp, M., Totten, C., & McCoy, M. (1991) *Peer Education Handbook, HIV/AIDS.* Eastern Health and Social Services Board, 12–22 Linenhall Street, Belfast, Northern Ireland BT2 8BS.

A Peer Education Clearinghouse with a focus on health issues also including a national database of projects and other services is operated by Advocates for Youth, 1025 Vermont Avenue NW, Suite 200, Washington, DC 20005, USA. Tel (202) 347-5700, email jane@advocatesforyouth.org.

CHAPTER 12: PEER COUNSELING

Basics of Peer Counseling—Video lasting 39 minutes, US NTSC VHS, $30 from the Department of Psychology, University of Michigan, 580 Union Drive, Ann Arbor, MI 48109-1346, USA.

Bonati, G., & Hawes, H. (1992). *The child-to-child trust.* Available from TALC (Teaching Aids at Low Cost), P.O. Box 49, St Albans, Herts AL1 4AX, U.K.

Bowden, B. (1988) *Peer counseling training manual.* Birmingham, AL: Bradford Publishing.

Canfield, J., & Wells, H. C. (1976). *100 ways to enhance self-esteem in the classroom.* Englewood Cliffs, NJ: Prentice-Hall.

Carr, R. A., & Saunders, G. (1980). *Peer counselling starter kit.* Victoria, BC: Peer Resources.

Community Service Volunteers, 237 Pentonville Road, London N1 9NJ, operate a wide range of service learning projects, and provide information and contacts.

De Rosenroll, D. (1989). A practitioner's guide to peer counseling research issues and dilemmas. *Canadian Journal of Counseling, 23*(1), 75–91.

ERIC published a "Searchlight Plus" in 1981 on peer counseling, containing annotations for 128 published articles and 50 other documents.

Fast Forward Positive Lifestyles Ltd., 4 Bernard St., Edinburgh EH6 6PP, Scotland, operate projects in peer counseling and peer education.

Home-Start UK, 2 Salisbury Road, Leicester LE1 7QR, U.K., operate projects in peer counseling and peer education.

Ibis Trust, 32 Weymouth Street, London W1N 3FA, U.K., operate projects in peer counseling and peer education.

Lieberman, D. J. (1989). *Peer counseling in the elementary school: Promoting personal and academic growth through positive relationships.* Unpublished document, Nova University, Florida. (ED 323 449). Includes training materials and worksheets with evaluation instruments used.

Marsico, J., & Nelson, J. (1983). *A "do it yourself kit" for implementing a high school peer counseling program in three easy steps.* Lakewood, CO: Jefferson County School District R-1. (ERIC Document Reproduction No. ED 232 123)

Myrick, R., and colleagues have produced many manuals and handbooks for peer helping, facilitation and intervention, and also at least two videos. All of these are published by Educational Media Corporation, Box 21311, Minneapolis, MN 55421-0311, USA—a catalog is available. A manual by Painter, C.

(1989). *Friends helping friends: A manual for peer counselors,* should be available from the same source.

Peer Career Counselors: A Conceptual and Practical Guide, by Rey Carr. A detailed rationale and plan to help students help each other in career awareness and development (through Peer Resources Network bookstore).

Peer Support Networker is a newsletter edited by Prof. Helen Cowie, Dept. of Psychology & Counselling, Roehampton Institute, Whitelands College, West Hill, London SW15 3SN, U. K. The first issue (March 1995) included useful lists of "common concerns" of and guidance for peer counselors. Cowie and Sonia Sharp have also produced a video, "Time to Listen: Peer counsellors challenge school bullying," available from the same address.

Peer mediation is an interest of a number of organizations, including Quaker Peace and Service, The Friends' Meeting House, Euston Road, London NW1 2BJ and the National Peace Council, 88 Islington High Street, London N1 8EG, England.

Peer Resources, 1052 Davie Street, Victoria, British Columbia V8S 4E3, Canada produces a catalog including many practical resources for various types of peer-assisted learning, counseling, and helping. They also operate training institutes and provide bibliographies.

Peers helping kids, by Trevor Cole. A Peer Counseling Manual For Elementary and Middle Schools (through Peer Resources Network bookstore).

The Personnel & Guidance Journal (now the *Journal of Counseling and Development*) published a special issue in 1974 called "Paras, Peers & Pros." *The Elementary School Guidance Journal* had a special issue in 1976 devoted to "Peer Facilitators."

Resource Publications Inc., 160 E. Virginia St. #290, San Jose, CA 95112-5876, USA, have a catalog of resources, including a section on peer helping containing several items.

Roberts, G. (1988). *Student workbook.* Victoria, BC: Peer Resources (see address above).

Salmon-White, S. (1990). *Peers helping peers: Programs for the preadolescent.* Basingstoke: Taylor & Francis.

Samuels, D., & Samuels, M. (1975). *The complete handbook of peer counselling.* Miami, FL: Fiesta Publishing.

Sturkie, J., & Gibson, V. (1989). *The peer counselor's pocketbook.* San Jose, CA: Resource Publications.

Teenage Parenthood Network, Young Mums Educational Trust, Larkfield Centre, 39 Inglefield Street, Glasgow G42 7AY, Scotland.

Tindall, J. A. (1985). *Peer power, book one: Becoming an effective peer helper*. Muncie, IN: Accelerated Development, Inc.

Tindall, J. A. (1989). *Peer power, book two: Applying peer helper skills*. Muncie, IN: Accelerated Development, Inc.

Tindall, J. A. (1989). *Peer counseling: An in-depth look at training peer helpers*. Muncie, IN: Accelerated Development, Inc.

Tindall, J. A. (1994). *Peer programs*. Muncie, IN: Accelerated Development, Inc. (Accelerated Development, c/o Taylor & Francis, 1900 Frost Road Suite 101, Bristol, PA 19007-1598, USA)

CHAPTER 13: PEER MONITORING

Kalfus, G. R. (1984). Peer mediated intervention: A critical review. *Child and Family Behavior Therapy, 6*, 17– 43.

Saudargas, R. A., & Fellers, G. (1986). *State-event classroom observation system: Research edition*. Knoxville, TN: University of Tennessee, Department of Psychology. (Dr. Richard Saudargas, Psychology Department, University of Tennessee, Knoxville, TN 37996).

Shapiro, E. S. (1996). *Academic skills problems: Direct assessment and intervention* (2nd ed.). New York: Guilford.

School Psychology Review, 21, (1992). Special interest miniseries on self-management interventions in the schools.

CHAPTER 14: PEERS ASSESSING PEERS

Carlson, D. M., & Roellich, C. (1983, April 14–16). *Teaching writing easily and effectively to get results: The evaluation process*. Paper presented at the annual meeting of the National Council of Teachers of English, Seattle, WA. (A guide for teachers in developing student skills in analysis, evaluation, proofreading. Rating scale for Grades 6–12 included.)

Christensen, L, Haugen, N. S., & Kean, J. M. (1982). *A guide to teaching self/peer editing*. Madison WI: School of Education, University of Wisconsin-Madison. (Booklet of procedures/techniques for teachers at elementary, middle, & high school levels. Appendices with resources.)

McLane Elementary School. (1982). *Handbook for assessing composition.* Olympia, WA: Office of Public Instruction. (Product of the Oral and Written Communication Task Force; Developed by the staff of the McLane Elementary School, Olympia, WA, School District. Contains writing analysis procedures for Grades 2–6, originally intended for use by teachers.)

All these items are available from ERIC.

CHAPTER 16: PAL BEYOND SCHOOL

Student Tutoring

Hughes, J. (Ed.). (1994). *Students as tutors in schools: Resource pack – International edition* (2nd edition). Poole, U.K.: BP Educational Services. ISBN 0 86165 201. Contains overhead masters and other useful materials. An accompanying video and other booklets are also available. Contact BP Educational Service, PO Box 934, Poole, Dorset BH17 7BR, U.K.; email bpes@bp.com.uk; fax (44) (0)1202 661999.

Topping, K. J., & Hill, S. (1996). *The effectiveness of student tutoring: Staff development pack.* Dundee, Scotland: Centre for Paired Learning, University of Dundee.

Peer Tutoring Within Higher Education

Topping, K. J. (1996). *Effective peer tutoring in further and higher education* (SEDA Paper 95). Birmingham: Staff and Educational Development Association. ISBN 0 946815 29 1. This staff development pack reviews the many different types of peer tutoring possible in higher education, gives definitions and a typology, and summarizes the international effectiveness research on them to date. Forty overhead transparency masters enable persuasive staff development activities to be conducted. The pack goes on to outline how to organize peer tutoring, prompting the reader to reflect and record their own planning decisions on the structured pro forma provided. Other useful resources are included.

Donaldson, A. J. M., Topping, K. J., Aitchison, R., Campbell, J., McKenzie, J., & Wallis, D. (1996). *Promoting peer assisted learning among students in further and higher Education* (SEDA Paper 96). Birmingham: Staff and Educational Development Association. ISBN 0 946815 34 8. This is intended for staff to read and reflect on and then put directly into the hands of students. It is written as a do-it-yourself manual for those students who do not have, or do not want, PAL organized for them by their departmental academic staff, but are interested in benefiting in an informal self-managed way. It comprises several units covering different forms of PAL.

Both available from: SEDA Administrator, Gala House, 3 Raglan Road, Edgbaston, Birmingham B5 7RA, U.K., tel (44) (0)121 440 5021 ; fax (44) (0)121 440 5022, email: office@seda.demon.co.uk. <web: http:// www.seda.demon.co.uk>.

Also see:

De Silva, D., & Freund, E. (1985). *A tutor handbook for TRIO programs: Operation success.* Wichita, KS: Wichita State University. ERIC ED 269 492

Donaldson, A. J. M., & Topping, K. J. (1996). *The peer tutor training handbook for higher and further education.* Dundee, Scotland: Centre for Paired Learning, University of Dundee.

Griffiths, S., Houston, K., & Lazenblatt, A. (Eds.) (1995). *Peer tutoring: Enhancing student learning through peer tutoring in higher education.* Coleraine, Northern Ireland: University of Ulster. ISBN 1 85923 066 9. Available from: Educational Development Unit, University of Ulster at Jordanstown, Shore Road, Newtownabbey BT37 0QB, Northern Ireland.

Martin, D. C., & Arendale, D. R. (1993). *Supplemental Instruction: Improving first-year student success in high-risk courses* (2nd ed.). Monograph No. 7. Columbia, SC: University of South Carolina.

Martin, D. C., & Arendale, D. R. (Eds.). (1994). *Supplemental Instruction: Increasing achievement and retention.* New Directions for Teaching and Learning No. 60. San Francisco: Jossey-Bass.

Rust, C., & Wallace, J. (1994). *Helping students to learn from each other: Supplemental Instruction* (SEDA Paper 86). Birmingham: Staff and Educational Development Association. ISBN 0 946815 83 6. (See SEDA contact details.)

Topping, K. J., McCrae, J., & Moody, S. (1994). *Peer tutoring in higher and further Education: A video training pack.* Dundee, Scotland: Centre for Paired Learning, University of Dundee.

Topping, K. J. (1996). *Same-year paired peer tutoring in further and higher education* [video]. Dundee, Scotland: Centre for Paired Learning, University of Dundee.

Mentoring

Caldwell, B., & Carter, E. (Eds.). (1993). *The return of the mentor: Strategies for workplace learning.* London & New York: Falmer.

Crockett, L., & Smink, J. (1991). *The mentoring guidebook.* Clemson, SC: National Dropout Prevention Center.

De Rosenroll, D., Saunders, G., & Carr, R. *The mentor program development kit.* Theory, practical tips and training workshop activities for mentor programmes. Also available in French. From the Peer Resources Network bookstore.

Fullerton, H. (Ed.). (1996). *Facets of mentoring in higher education* (SEDA Paper 94). Birmingham: Staff and Educational Development Association. ISBN 0 946815 19 4. (See SEDA contact details.)

Jacobi, M. (1991). Mentoring and undergraduate academic success: A literature review. *Review of Educational Research, 61* (4), 505–532.

Jeffrey, H., & Ferguson, S. (1992). *The mentoring guidebook.* London: North London College Mentor Programme.

Kwalick, B., et. al., (1988). *CUNY/BOE student mentor programme: Mentor handbook.* New York: City University of New York.

The Mentoring Institute. (1990). *Annotated bibliography on mentoring, vol. 2.* Vancouver, B.C.: Author.

The Mentoring Institute (TMI), 675 Inglewood Avenue, West Vancouver, British Columbia V7T 1X4, Canada also has a catalog of resources, bibliographies, and training opportunities.

Mentoring and Tutoring is a practitioners' journal produced by Trentham Books, Ltd., Westview House, 734 London Road, Oakhill, Stoke-on-Trent ST4 5NP, U.K.

Merriam, S. (1983). Mentors and proteges: A critical review of the literature. *Adult Education Quarterly, 33,* 161–173.

Tierney, J., et al., (1995). *Making a difference: An impact study of Big Brothers/Big Sisters.* Philadelphia, PA: Public/Private Ventures. (Available in microfiche from ERIC ED 390 973.)

Mentoring Contacts

The National Mentoring Network, Business & Technology Centre, Green Lane, Particroft, Eccles, Salford M30 0RJ, U.K.

Roots & Wings (BITC), 8 Stratton Street, London W1X 5FD, U.K.

European Mentoring Centre, Burnham House, High Street, Burnham, Bucks SL1 7JZ, U.K.

European Consortium for Learning Organisation, Vanelle de Lauriers 8, 1300 Wavre, Belgium

International Mentoring Association, Office of Conferences and Institutes, Western Michigan University, Kalamazoo, Michigan 49008-5161, USA.

<http://www.indiana.edu/~rugsdev/ima.html >

email: cedu_ima@wmich.edu.

Private/ Public Ventures, 399 Market Street, Philadelphia, PA 19106, USA.

About the Contributors

The Editors

Keith Topping is director of the postgraduate training program for school psychologists and director of the Centre for Paired Learning in the Department of Psychology, University of Dundee, Scotland. He has authored or co-authored 13 books (including the *Peer Tutoring Handbook*) and more than 150 other publications.

Stewart Ehly is professor and director of training for the School Psychology Program in the Division of Psychological and Quantitative Foundations at The University of Iowa. He has authored three books (including *Peer Tutoring For Individualized Instruction* and *Individual and Group Counseling in Schools*) and more than 90 other publications.

The Contributors

Carmen Arreaga-Mayer, PhD, is project director of a Language Minority Interventions Grant at the Juniper Gardens Children's Project, assistant scientist, Schiefelbusch Institute for Life Span Studies, and courtesy professor, Department of Special Education, University of Kansas. Her research work emphasizes the use of ecobehavioral approaches to the observational assessment of student behaviors in natural settings and the use of the ClassWide Peer Tutoring procedures to increase the academic and oral engagement levels of culturally and linguistically diverse students with and without disabilities in inclusive settings. Dr. Arreaga-Mayer serves as consultant to a number of school districts in designing effective district and classroom options for the inclusion of special needs students.

Elaine Chapman BA Hons., PhD, has broad interests in the areas of educational and social psychology, and has been conducting research into peer-mediated learning procedures for the past 6 years. Her work has focused mainly on the use of cooperative learning to improve cognitive, attitudinal, and social outcomes for both disabled and regular school children. She is currently a lecturer in the School of Educational Psychology, Measurement and Technology, University of Sydney, Australia.

John W. Fantuzzo is the Diana Riklis professor of education in the Graduate School of Education at the University of Pennsylvania. He received his doctoral training in clinical child psychology. His research and grant experience have focused primarily on the design, implementation, and evaluation of school- and community-based prevention strategies for vulnerable, low-income children and families in high-risk urban environments.

Hugh Foot is professor of Psychology at the University of Strathclyde, Glasgow, Scotland. He has published about 100 items including 10 books on areas such as humor and laughter, children's friendships and social relationships, group and interactive learning, children helping children, road safety, children's pedestrian behavior, and social psychology.

Nicholas Ford is senior lecturer in the Department of Geography, University of Exeter, England. He has researched widely on population, reproductive, and sexual health with particular reference to young people's lifestyles and HIV prevention in the United Kingdom and Thailand. Following one of the first sets of sexual behavior surveys in the late 1980s, his research findings have been used to develop a number of peer educational strategies in collaboration with health authorities in the Southwest of England. He has published more than 100 chapters, articles, and other publications in this area of research.

Enedina García-Vázquez teaches in the Counseling and Educational Psychology Department in the College of Education at New Mexico State University. She is the training coordinator of the school psychology program. Dr. García-Vázquez has published manuscripts on peer tutoring, effects of language use, acculturation and psychological factors, skin color and community interest, and mentoring. Dr. García-Vázquez is co-author of a chapter titled "Facilitating Peer Tutoring Programs," published in *Best Practices in School Psychology—III.* Her current research focuses on the development of an acculturation instrument for adolescents and the effects of acculturation on psychological factors and academic success.

Audrey Gartner is co-director of the Peer Research Laboratory, at the Center for Advanced Study in Education, Graduate School and University Center, of the City University of New York. She has been responsible for the development, implementation, and study of a number of peer and cross-age tutoring programs at the elementary, intermediate, and high school levels.

Her main research interests are on the impact of tutoring activities on a broad range of student tutors. She has written articles and contributed book chapters on peer tutoring, presented at national and international conferences, and has consulted with schools across the USA.

Brian Gay is a private consultant working in the fields of mentoring and coaching within personal, professional, and organizational development. He was previously head of the Educational Initiatives Section at the University of the West of England, Bristol.

Marika Ginsburg-Block is a doctoral graduate of the School, Community, and Clinical Child Psychology Program at the University of Pennsylvania. She is the coordinator of Project P.L.U.S. (Peer Learning in Urban Schools), has published two major evaluations of Reciprocal Peer Tutoring with John Fantuzzo, and is joining the faculty at the University of Minnesota.

Charles R. Greenwood, PhD, is director, Juniper Gardens Children's Project, senior scientist, Schiefelbusch Institute for Life Span Studies, and courtesy professor, Department of Special Education and Human Development and Family Life, University of Kansas. Dr. Greenwood heads the program of research at the Juniper Gardens Children's Project (JGCP), a community-based center located in a poverty community in northeast Kansas City, Kansas. In 1996, the JGCP received the CEC's annual research award for its 30-year contribution to the knowledge and practice of special education. He is an investigator with the Early Research Institute on Substance Abuse and a leader of the Risk, Intervention and Prevention Theme of the Kansas Mental Retardation Research Center. His research has focused on teaching, parenting, and caregiving strategies that impact the development of persons living in poverty and with disabilities.

Carlen Henington, PhD, is an assistant professor in the Counselor Education/Educational Psychology Department at Mississippi State University. She received her doctorate in school psychology from Texas A&M University. Her research interests include behavioral pediatrics, disruptive behavior disorders in children (conduct disorder, oppositional defiance, ADHD, aggression) and their impact on children's peer interactions, and interventions for children with developmental disabilities.

Shirley Hill is currently manager of the Access Centre for students with disabilities at Dundee university, serving the universities of Dundee, Saint Andrew's, Abertay, and Northern College, where she specializes in assistive technology for learning support. She was previously a research psychologist in the Higher Education Effective Learning Project, based in the Centre for Paired Learning in the department of psychology at the University of Dundee.

Christine Howe is a reader in psychology at Strathclyde University and director of the Centre for Research into Interactive Learning. Her research interests are peer collaboration, computer-assisted learning, science education, conceptual development, first- and second-language acquisition, and gender issues in social interaction. She has produced more than 80 books, chapters, and articles, the former including "Acquiring Language in a Conversational Context", "Language: A Special Case for Developmental Psychology", "Group and Interactive Learning", "Conceptual Structure in Childhood and Adolescence: The Case of Everyday Physics", and "Social Interaction in Classrooms: The Gender Dimension."

Larry Maheady is on the faculty in the School of Education at the State University of New York, College at Fredonia, where his primary responsibilities include teaching preservice and inservice teachers, conducting research on classroom-based interventions, and providing service to the college, local school districts, and professional organizations. Dr. Maheady has authored or co-authored more than 60 articles in refereed journals, 4 book chapters, and 1 text, *Educating Students with Behavior Disorders.* He has presented at more than 100 international, national, or state-level conferences and has conducted more than 75 inservice workshops in 25 different states. In addition, he serves as associate editor for two special education journals *Teacher Education and Special Education* and *Education and Treatment of Children.*

Brian C. Maher is an advanced student in school psychology in the applied department of the Graduate School of Applied and Professional Psychology (GSAPP), Rutgers University, and is a candidate for the degree of doctor of psychology. He holds a bachelor's degree with majors in psychology and English, as well as a master's degree in psychology from Rutgers University. He is certified as a school psychologist and is currently assistant to the editor for *Special Services in the Schools.* His professional interests include the planning and evaluation of school-based programs targeted to students and staff.

Charles A. Maher is full professor of psychology, Graduate School of Applied and Professional Psychology, Rutgers University and former chair of its Department of Applied Psychology. At Rutgers, Dr. Maher directs applied research projects having to do with measurement and evaluation of education training programs, professional self-management, team development, sports psychology, and executive achievement. Relatedly, he supervises the education of doctoral students in school psychology, organizational psychology, and clinical psychology. Dr. Maher has authored more than 300 journal articles and 16 books in areas of program planning, program evaluation, organizational behavior management, team development, executive achievement, workplace literacy, professional self-management, sports psychology, and individual education of adolescents and adults. He is a licensed practicing psychologist and also credentialed as a school superintendent, principal, social worker, reading teacher, teacher of the handicapped, and international management consultant.

Margo A. Mastropieri is professor of special education at Purdue University. She has experience with students with special needs in a variety of clinical and educational settings, and received her PhD in special education from Arizona State University in 1983. She has directed several federal grants, most recently in mnemonic (memory-enhancing) instruction and science education for students with special needs. Mastropieri is the author or editor of 13 books, and has authored or co-authored more than 150 book chapters and journal articles in the field of special education. She is the co-editor of *Learning Disabilities Research & Practice* and *Advances in Learning and Behavioral Disabilities*

Elspeth Mathie is research fellow in the Institute of Population Studies, University of Exeter, England. Her main research interests have been young people and sexual health and she has worked with colleges and health authorities to design and evaluate peer education projects. Publications include evaluation reports of local peer education projects. Elspeth has a particular focus on qualitative research methods and her current work involves examining the acceptability of new contraceptive methods, including the female condom and the new fertility awareness monitor.

Angela O'Donnell is an associate professor of educational psychology at Rutgers University. She received her PhD in experimental psychology from Texas Christian University. She received an MS in experimental psychology, an MEd in special education, and a BEd in education and English literature. Her research interests include cooperative and collaborative learning, text processing, and learning strategies. She teaches courses in educational psychology, learning strategies, cooperative learning, and cognition and memory.

Dale H. Schunk is professor and head of the Department of Educational Studies at Purdue University. He holds a PhD in educational psychology from Stanford University. His teaching and research interests include learning, motivation, modeling, and self-regulation. He has published more than 60 journal articles and chapters and has written and edited books on learning, motivation, and self-regulation. Currently, he is conducting research on self-regulation strategies used by college students learning computer skills. He has received the Early Contributions Award in educational psychology from the American Psychological Association and the Albert J. Harris Research Award from the International Reading Association.

Thomas E. Scruggs is professor of special education at Purdue University. After working for several years as a special education teacher in a variety of settings, he received his PhD in special education in 1982. He is the co-editor of *Learning Disabilities Research and Practice,* the journal of the Division for Learning Disabilities of the Council for Exceptional Children. He is also the co-editor of the research annual, *Advances in Learning and Behavioral Disabilities.* Scruggs is the author or editor of 14 books, and has authored or co-authored more than 170 book chapters and journal articles in the field of special education.

Christopher H. Skinner, PhD, is a professor in the Counselor Education/Educational Psychology Department at Mississippi State University, where he is the program coordinator of the school psychology programs. He received his doctorate in school psychology from Lehigh University. Dr. Skinner's research has focused on applying behavioral analysis and assessment procedure to improve students' academic skills.

Barbara J. Terry, PhD, is assistant research scientist at the Juniper Gardens Children's Project and the Schiefelbusch Institute for Life Span Studies, University of Kansas. Dr. Terry has worked as a teacher, consultant and trainer at the elementary and secondary levels. She has a wide range of professional interests including the use and validation of ClassWide Peer Tutoring procedures, classroom behavior management strategies, and risk intervention and prevention.

Cynthia J. Thurston is an advanced student in school psychology in the applied department of the Graduate School of Applied and Professional Psychology (GSAPP), Rutgers University, and is a candidate for the degree of doctor of psychology. She holds a bachelor's degree with majors in psychology and English from Syracuse University, as well as a master's degree in psychology from Rutgers University. She is certified as a school psychologist, and is currently assistant to the editor for *Peace and Conflict: Journal of Peace Psychology*. Her professional endeavors include extensive experience in behavior management training to parents and caregivers of developmentally disabled family members.

Gita L. Vygodskya, the daughter of Lev Vygotsky, received her doctorate in psychology from Moscow State University in 1963. She has worked for many years as a research associate at the Institute of Defectology (special education) of the Academy of Education in Moscow. Dr. Vygodskya is the author of many articles published in Russia and the West. She is now retired, but continues to be involved in research on the theory and history of psychology. Her latest book is a scientific biography of her father: *Lev Vygotsky: Life and Work, Brush Strokes to the Portrait.*

Herbert J. Walberg was awarded a PhD degree in educational psychology by the University of Chicago. After teaching at Harvard, he was appointed research professor of education at the University of Illinois at Chicago. He has written or edited 50 books and authored more than 300 articles on such subjects as educational productivity, teaching effectiveness, home influences on learning, and the development of talent. Frequent advisor to the U.S. Department of Education, other federal and national agencies, and foreign ministries of education, he has also testified before the U.S. Congress and federal courts on educational policy. He is a fellow of four academic societies, permanent secretary and member of the International Academy of Education, and chairman of the board of the Heartland Institute, a think tank that provides policy perspectives to 8,000 legislators and news people in North America and elsewhere by fax, the Internet, a magazine, and books.

Author Index

Subject Index